Amer. Finland, 1939

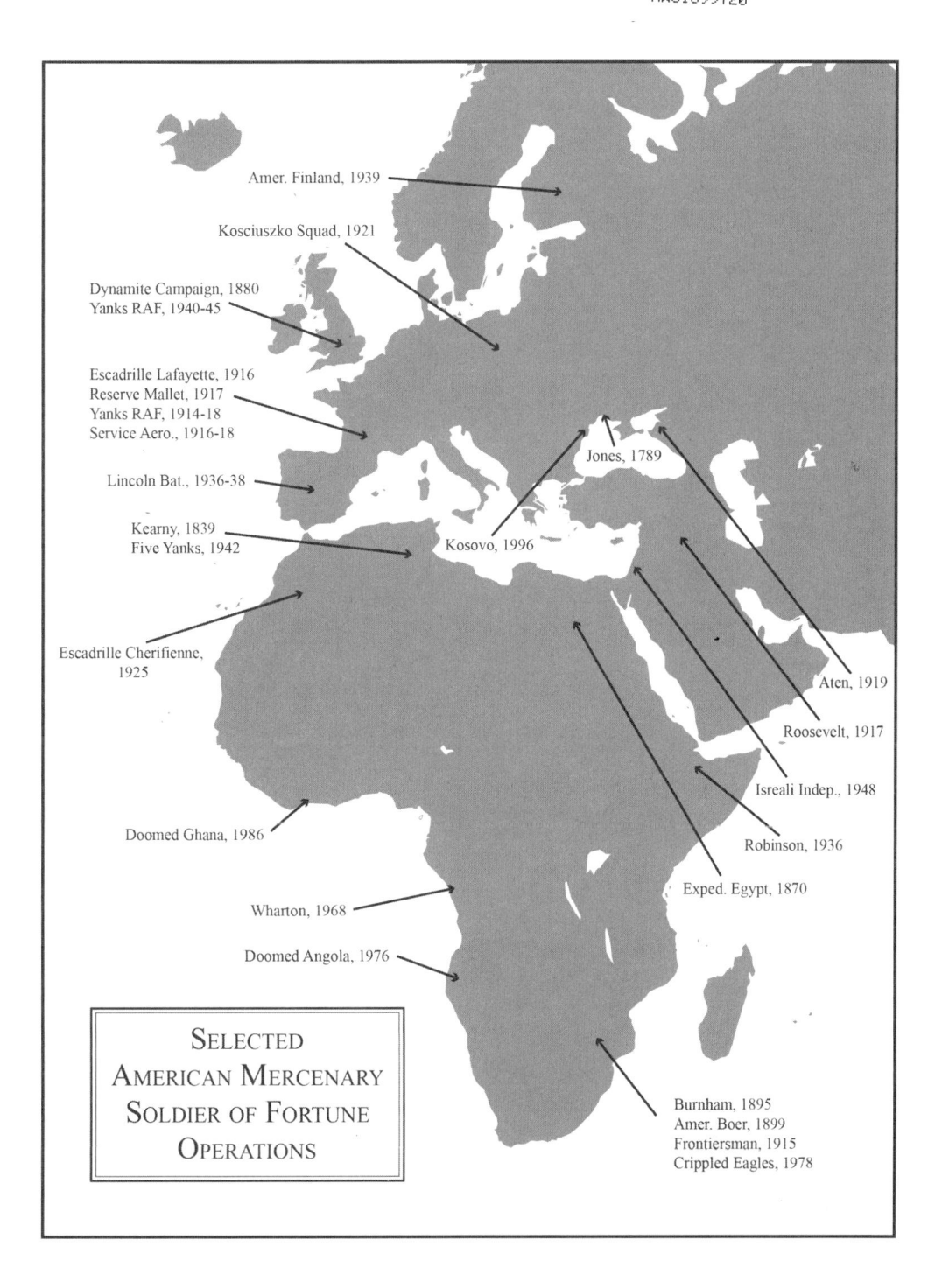

Kosciuszko Squad, 1921

Dynamite Campaign, 1880
Yanks RAF, 1940-45

Escadrille Lafayette, 1916
Reserve Mallet, 1917
Yanks RAF, 1914-18
Service Aero., 1916-18

Jones, 1789

Lincoln Bat., 1936-38

Kearny, 1839
Five Yanks, 1942

Kosovo, 1996

Escadrille Cherifienne, 1925

Aten, 1919

Roosevelt, 1917

Isreali Indep., 1948

Doomed Ghana, 1986

Robinson, 1936

Exped. Egypt, 1870

Wharton, 1968

Doomed Angola, 1976

SELECTED
AMERICAN MERCENARY
SOLDIER OF FORTUNE
OPERATIONS

Burnham, 1895
Amer. Boer, 1899
Frontiersman, 1915
Crippled Eagles, 1978

FAME-FORTUNE-FRUSTRATION

Books by Jay Mallin Sr.

Caribbean Crisis : Subversion Fails in the Dominican Republic (1965)
Fortress Cuba: Russia's American Base (1965)
Terror in Viet Nam (1966)
"Che" Guevara on Revolution: A Documentary Overview (1969)
Strategy for Conquest; Communist Documents on Guerrilla Warfare (1970)
Terror and Urban Guerrillas: A Study of Tactics and Documents (1971)
Ernesto "Che" Guevara, Modern Revolutionary, Guerilla Theorist (1973)
General Vo Nguyen Giap, North Vietnamese Military Leader (1973)
Fulgencio Batista, Ousted Cuban Dictator (1974)
Merc: American Soldiers of Fortune (1979)
(with Robert K. Brown)
Covering Castro: Rise and Decline of Cuba's Communist Dictator (1994)
Adventures in Journalism: A Memoir (1998)
The Taking of Miami (1998)
Cuba's Armed Forces: From Colony to Castro (2000)
Betrayal in April : A Novel (2000)
(with Bob Smith)

Books by Robert L. Scheina

American Battleships, 1886-1923: Pre-dreadnought Design and Construction (1980)
(with John C. Reilly)
U.S. Coast Guard Cutters & Craft of World War II (1982)
Latin America : A Naval History, 1810-1987 (1987)
U.S. Coast Guard Cutters and Craft, 1946-1990 (1990)
Low Intensity Conflict in Latin America: Does Mahan Have a Place? (1990)
Iberoamerica: Una Historia Naval 1810-1987 (1991)
Santa Anna : A Curse Upon Mexico (2002)
Latin America's Wars (2003)
Villa : Soldier of the Mexican Revolution (2004)
Struggle Against America's Dark Side: Arson, Assassination, Bribery, etc. (2013)

FAME-FORTUNE-FRUSTRATION
AMERICAN MERCENARIES
AND SOLDIERS OF FORTUNE
1788 to 2014

by

Jay Mallin Sr.

and

Robert L. Scheina

DBM Press LC
Springfield, VA
2014

© 2014 by Jay Mallin Sr. and Robert L. Scheina

All Rights Reserved. No part of this publication may be reproduced or transmitted in any form or by any means, electronic or mechanical, including photocopying, recording, or any information storage and retrieval system now known or to be invented, without permission in writing from the publisher, except by a reviewer who wishes to quote brief passages in connection with a review written for inclusion in a magazine, newspaper or broadcast. Inquiries on reproducing sections of this book should be addressed to the publisher.

First published in 2014 by:
DBM Press, LC
6412 Brandon Ave, #123
Springfield, VA 22150
dbmpress@yahoo.com

See our catalogue at http://www.dbmpress.com

For quality used and rare books, go to: http://www.UsedMilitaryBooks.com

Library of Congress Control Number: 2013958413

ISBN-10: 0-9816102-8-5 ISBN-13: 978-0-9816102-8-3

First Edition

1st Printing
10 9 8 7 6 5 4 3 2 1

Cover design by Jay Mallin (www.JayMallinPhotos.com)
1948 Air Battle art on back cover by Phyllis Saroff (www.saroffillustration.com)
Map illustrations by Jon Peterson

Interior design and layout by AuthorSupport.com

Printed in the United States of America by Bang Printing

This book is dedicated to our grandchildren who made the tumult of having children worthwhile.

Kelsey Carollyn Frydl
Brennan Michael Frydl
Jacob Richard Brown
Joshua Robert Brown
Jacob Samuel Mallin
Jeremy William Mallin

Contents

Foreword . . . . *ix*
Acknowledgments. . . . . *xi*
Introduction. . . . . *xiii*

Odyssey of John Paul Jones in Russia, 1788-89. 1
Aaron Burr Conspiracy, 1804. 6
Long Expeditions into Texas, 1819-21. 13
Porter Clan in the Service of Mexico, 1826-29. 17
Americans in Argentine-Brazilian Naval War, 1825-28. 22
Remember the Alamo, 1836. 27
Remembering the Alamo at Sea, 1837-44. 38
Odyssey of Phillip Kearny, 1839-40 and 1859 43
Odyssey of B.S. Osbon, 1840s-50s 48
López Round Island Expedition to Cuba, 1848-49 51
López Cardenas Expedition, 1850 55
López Bahia Honda Expedition, 1851. 60
Coe and the Blockade of Buenos Aires (1852-53) 64
Walker Expedition against Mexico, 1853-54. 67
Walker Expedition against Nicaragua, 1855-58 71
Crabb's Expedition into Mexico, 1857. 78
Walker Expedition against Honduras, 1860 81
Ward and the Taiping Rebellion, 1860-64 84
Benito Juárez' American Brigade of Honor, 1865-67 91
Ex-Confederates fighting for Maximilian, 1865-67 96
Odyssey of John Tucker in the Pacific War, 1865-67 100
Union Balloonists during War of the Triple Alliance, 1867-68 . . . 106
American Fenians Expedition into Canada, 1866-70 110
Virginius Affair, 1870-73 118
Expeditionaries in Egypt, 1869-78 125
Odyssey of George Boynton Stone, 1866-1906 136
Odyssey of Charles Read, War of the Pacific, 1880 146
Six Americans Fighting for Chile, 1879-91 150
Dynamite Campaign against Great Britain, 1881-85 154
Dynamite Fleet to Brazil, 1893-94 162
Frederick Burnham and the Matabele Wars, 1893-96. 166
Odyssey of Philo McGiffin in China, 1885-94 172
Americans in Boer Wars, 1899-1900. 177
Odyssey of Lee Christmas in Central America, 1897-1920 184

Odyssey of Homer Lea in China, 1900-12	189
Gringo Airmen in the Mexican Revolution, 1910-15	196
Gringo Cowboys in the Mexican Revolution, 1910-17	202
Expeditions against Northern Mexico, 1911	210
Yanks in the RFC, RNAS and RAF, 1914-18	217
Legion of Frontiersmen, 1915-18	226
Odyssey of Kermit Roosevelt, 1917, 1939-41	231
Americans in the French Réserve Mallet, 1917	238
Americans in the French Foreign Legion, 1831-present	245
L' Escadrille Lafayette, 1916-18	253
Americans in the French Service Aeronautique, 1916-18	261
Cooper's Kosciuszko Squadron, 1918-21	265
Odyssey of Marion Aten in Russians, 1919	269
Escadrille de la Guarde Cherifienne in Morocco, 1925	273
Four Americans Flying for China, 1932-45	277
Odyssey of the Brown Condor in Ethiopia, 1935-36	282
Odyssey of the Flying Barber, 1933-36	288
Abraham Lincoln Battalion in the Spanish Civil War, 1936-38	292
American Flyers for Republicans in the Spanish Civil War, 1936-38	301
Americans in Russo--Finish War, 1939-40	307
Yanks in the RCAF & RAF, 1940-45	312
Five Yanks in North Africa, 1941-43	323
Claire Chennault and Flying Tigers, 1941-42	327
Yanks in the CNAC, 1942-45	338
Claire Chennault and Civil Air Transport (CAT), 1946-50	343
Two Yanks Fighting for Israel, 1948	347
Odyssey of William Morgan in the Cuban Revolution, 1958-60	353
Odyssey of Hank Wharton in Biafra, 1965-68	356
Crippled Eagles in Rhodesia, 1966-80	361
Angola Fiasco, 1976	368
Odyssey of Mike Echanis in Nicaragua, 1978-79	372
Doomed Expedition to Dominica, 1981	375
Doomed Expedition to Haiti, 1982	378
Doomed Expedition to Ghana, 1986	381
Doomed Expedition to Suriname, 1986	386
American Sons of Kosovo, 1996-99	388
UAE's Mercenary Army, 2010-Present	395
Concluding Observations	399
Index	403

Foreword

More than 10,000 - not possible - really! That is how many Americans these authors have identified as being mercenaries and soldiers of fortune.

Where did they fight - everywhere! Not a continent escaped these American adventurers. They fought in jungles, mountains, and deserts. They fought on and under the sea.

Who did they fight for - scores of well-known national flags and some of would-be nations that most of us cannot identify.

Who are these fellows - the authors of this book - one an academician, the other a journalist - delved into old and new books and historical records. They here describe well-known mercenaries and soldiers of fortune, and also combatants lost in the mist of history.

What is unique about this book - it throws open the door and reveals the breadth of the activities of these American mercenaries and soldiers of fortune!

Lt. Col. Robert K. Brown, USA Ret.
Editor/Publisher of *Soldier of Fortune* Magazine
Author of *I Am Soldier of Fortune: Dancing With Devils*
Co-Author *MERC: American Soldiers of Fortune*

Acknowledgments

Authors are very needy people, and we are no exception. Remembering who saved us from our own shortcomings is easy, but finding the words to express adequately our gratitude is difficult. Each contributor gave us something unique. These were our helpers:

- London Orcurto, our computer guru, like Sherlock Homes solved mystery after mystery for us working from the smallest of clues. Among her important finds were discovering the surname of George Boynton Stone and which Baker commanded the Dynamite Fleet of 1893-94.
- Jay Mallin, photographer and son of the author, designed the covers and spine. He also converted our collection of historical photographs and original drawings onto digital formats.
- Jon Peterson, a talented artist, working from photographs, drew original sketches of Rudy Augarten, Michael Echanis, David Marcus, and Kermit Roosevelt. Mr. Peterson also prepared the maps of the Western Hemisphere, Europe/Africa, and Asia. petejkjz@version.net
- Phyllis Saroff, a talented artist, working from photographs, created the scene of the air battle on 16 October 1948 between the Israeli Avia S-199 and the Egyptian Spitfire which is featured on the back cover. Ms. Saroff also drew the original sketch of Florin Krasnigi. www.saroffillustration.com
- Dan Burkhard, a talented artist, working from photographs, drew original sketches of Eugene Bullard, James McGovern, Jr., William Morgan and John Robinson. dkburkhard@gmail.com
- Robert Browning, Coast Guard historian, provided important leads to Civil War

veterans who took up arms for causes other than those of the United States.
- Chris Havern, historian provided valuable leads to those American Irishmen who fought against the British for control of Ireland.
- Frank Cooling, Civil War scholar, gave sage advice and encouragement that helped us stay the course.
- Robert Jones, an eminent officer who served in the 7th Special Forces, was the former Deputy Assistant Secretary of Defense and is a professor of homeland security, helped us work through the modern era.
- Jerry and Michelle Dorris of AuthorSupport.com who accomplished the difficult task of taking a manuscript with many parts and numerous embedded illustrations with captions and making it all look excellent.
- Finally, we give our sincerest thanks to our publisher, Bill Boik at DBM Press, LC for championing our work.

Introduction

An American mercenary is an individual who courts danger for profit, adventure, pleasure or ideology while acting for other than the United States government. This definition excludes the following:

> American arms' merchants, such as Charles Flint who sold weapons to revolutionaries during the 1890s, but did not put themselves in danger to deliver their goods; the Rough Riders of 1898 who were paid by the U.S. government; numerous American military instructors, such as Colonel William C. Brooks who was employed as the Commander of the Honduran Air Force and Aviation Military School in the late 1930s but flew no combat missions; the American B-25 pilots who were paid by the CIA to fly protection for those landing at the Bay of Pigs.

We do not consider as mercenaries (or soldiers of fortune) Americans who either fought against the United States or whose actions could have led to fighting with American armed forces. We do consider the Burr Conspiracy as a grey area since it is arguable as to where his motivation was filibustering or treason. We have excluded the following:

- Benedict Arnold the American Revolution and the War of 1812
- The Irish San Patricio Battalion in Mexico, 1846-48
- American slave runners, 1808-63
- Unionists blockade runners, 1861-65
- Lt. Maritn J. Monti (USAAF) World War II
- Bobby Garfield Vietnam War

Fame–Fortune–Frustration

What is the difference between a soldier of fortune and a mercenary? Mostly, your attitude toward the righteousness of the cause because the term soldier of fortune has a positive connotation and the term mercenary has a negative one. Those who are pro-Israel would see David "Mickey" Marcus as a soldier of fortune and those who are pro-Palestine would see him as a mercenary.

When is a mercenary not a mercenary? A mercenary, according to the dictionary, is "a soldier hired to serve in a foreign army."[1] A mercenary fights - alone or in a group - in a foreign country for pay, adventure or a cause, or a combination of these. But what if the group is covertly funded by the home country, with individual members knowing this or not? Are they still mercenaries or simply soldiers acting for their own countries? Unfortunately it is usually futile to attempt to determine whether any particular mercenary group is being secretly funded. In recent decades the Central Intelligence Agency has spread its funds everywhere. For the purpose of this book, groups have been included if, despite covert funding, their members did not know where the money came from, and if the group is historically recognized as a mercenary organization. Case in point, fifty years after American Volunteer Group made aviation history, it was finally revealed that the Flying Tigers were a U.S. government sponsored covert operation, financed through Lend-Lease.

Defining American citizenship during the nation's early decades is difficult. For example, at what point do Irish immigrants who fought for the Union during the Civil War become citizens? Following the war, a number of these individuals were involved in mercenary activities against the British Empire. If we have erred, it is on the side of inclusion.

Concerning American citizenship, a particularly perplexing challenge is that of Henry Ronald Douglas MacIver. He was born three miles off the coast of Virginia to a Scottish father and an American mother. Henry was reared in Virginia and educated in Scotland. He served in armies on every continent. In 1884 MacIver wrote a book titled *Under Fourteen Flags*. A correspondent for the New York *Herald* wrote than when arrested at the close of the U.S. Civil War: "He [MacIver] claims British protection as a subject of her British Majesty...."[2] A war correspondent in Serbia during the 1870s described MacIver as: "A Scotch soldier of fortune...."[3] In the early 1900s biographer Richard Davis wrote, "With the exception of the United States, of which he [MacIver] is now a naturalized citizen, the general has fought in nearly every country in the world...."[4] We believe that during his "fighting years" MacIver was a British subject and not an American. His more important expeditions were assembled in London and targeted primarily against European countries. True he did raise expeditions in New York and targeted the Americas. But he claimed to be a British citizen while involved in mercenary activities in the Americas.

On the other hand we have the Irish activist Jeremiah O'Donovan Rossa (frequently his surname is cited as O'Donovan). Born in Ireland in 1831, he came to the United States in 1863 and returned to Ireland within two years although his wife remained behind. In 1869 Rossa was elected to the House of Commons from Tipperary (although not seated because of a conviction for treason-felony), and in 1871 he was an unsuccessful candidate for the New York state senate. Rossa explained in a book he wrote: "I also asserted that we Irish of New York are American politicians before we are Irish, or anything else."[5] American Judge, Richard L. Larremore, granted Rossa American citizenship in 1871 even though he had not met the five- year residency requirement.

A perplexing group is those prominent American officers who retire to fight for another entity. For us a determining factor for inclusion is where the individual courted danger. Therefore, we have included Philip Kearny who fought for the French in the 1850s after resigning from the U.S. Army. We have excluded Douglas MacArthur who served as a field marshal for the soon-to-be independent Philippines after resigning from the U.S. Army. In that capacity MacArthur never courted danger.

Another group we have excluded from the book, because they were noncombatants, were the 3,500 American volunteers who served in various ambulance corps in France and Italy during World War I. Many of these individuals were pacifists and would be appalled to be included between these covers. Among their numbers were Ernest Hemingway[6], John Dos Passos and e.e. cummings. On the other hand, we have included those individuals who went to France to serve as ambulance drivers but delivered munitions to the front as members of the *Reserve Mellet* (an element of the French army). And we have also included those American humanitarians who, after they served in one of the ambulance corps, joined the French Foreign Legion or the *Lafayette Escadrille*.

Yet another perplexing group is Executive Outcomes. This organization recruited and trained significant numerous of mercenaries to fight in Africa during the 1990s. We have not been able to identify any Americans in their employment.

This book is organized into expeditions (when multiple Americans are involved) and odysseys (when a single American is involved). Organizing the book by biographies proved impractical since too many mercenaries lived in the shadows and important details of their lives remained hidden.

At least one American participated in each entry listed and in most entries, many more. Frequently, knowing their exact number is impossible. In the British-Chinese patrol against pirates during the 1840s, American B.S. Osbon identified the nationalities of his fellow warriors, mentioning British and other Europeans in detail but never talking about another American. A decade later, however, while serving in the Argentine Navy, he does cite other Americans there. Since he had had knowledge of the overall operation against the pirates, it is logical to conclude that at least while Osbon was there, he was the only American.

Verifying claims concerning mercenaries can be difficult. One of those individuals whose military career was embellished by Hollywood was the silver-screen cowboy Tom Mix. Mix did serve in Cuba (1898), the Philippines (1901-02) and China (1901-02) for Uncle Sam, making him a soldier. He did not fight in the Boer War (1900) and the Mexican Revolution (1910) as claimed by some biographers, thus, he was not a mercenary.

Albert Bigelow Paine, who wrote the personal memoirs of B.S. Osbon, cites few facts which can be verified concerning Osbon's days serving in the British-Chinese patrol against pirates. And yet, a later chapter dealing with Osbon's service in the Argentine Navy is specific enough to be easily verified. Therefore, we are inclined to believe both to be credible.

[1] *Webster's New World Dictionary*. (New York: Simon & Schuster, Inc., 1990. p. 369.
[2] Richard Harding Davis, "Major-General Henry Ronald Douglas MacIver," pp. 3-32, *Real Soldiers of Fortune.* New York: Charles Scribner's Sons, 1911, p. 15.
[3] Davis, "Major-General Henry Ronald Douglas MacIver," p. 26.
[4] Davis, "Major-General Henry Ronald Douglas MacIver," p. 31.
[5] Jereniah O'Donovan Rossa, *O'Donovan Rossa's Prison Life; Six Years in Six English Prisons.* New York: Published by P.J. Kennedy, 1874, p. 431.
[6] Ernest Hemingway (1899-1961), served in World War I as a volunteer in an American ambulance unit serving with the French army. Afterward he served with the Italian Arditi. The Arditi was an Italian military unit but according to "Hemingway in the 90s" by Michael Reynolds this was a "fictional experience - it didn't happen." By the time of the Spanish Civil War Hemingway was already an accomplished writer and not a warrior. Nevertheless, he has become the most famous American connected to the Spanish Civil War.

Odyssey of John Paul Jones

1788-89

Goal:

To seek employment in a command position which led to fighting for the Russians against the Turks.

Background:

Russia and Turkey fought to control the confluence of the Dnieper and Bug Rivers into the Black Sea. The fighting centered on the Liman estuary. This estuary on the north side of the Black Sea is about 30 miles long east to west and between two and eight miles wide north to south. The average depth is 18 feet and many shallows bedevil maritime traffic. The Dnieper River enters the estuary from the east, the Bug River from the north, and together they flow to the west emptying into the Black Sea. The Turkish fort Ochakov on the north shore dominated the entrance into the Black Sea and it was protected by the Turkish fleet which took up station in the Liman to the east of the fort. To counter this, the Russians built fort Kinburn on the south shore opposite the Turkish fort.

Leadership:

John Paul Jones was hired by Catherine the Great, the czarina of Russia, to command her naval forces fighting against the Turks because of his reputation as a bold, fearless fighter. He soon discovered that his leadership was challenged by those around him. German-French Prince Nassau-Siegen, commander of the Russian small craft (known as the flotilla), was

Fame–Fortune–Frustration

John Paul Jones (1747-92) became America's first admiral - although his appointment came from Russia and not the United States. Jones embarked on a career path that would be followed by other U.S. naval officers. Following U.S. wars the navy typically downsized and ambitious officers, like Jones, sought employment in foreign navies - those of China, Egypt, Mexico, Peru, Texas and Russia.

Harper's Encyclopedia of United States History (New York, 1902)

a confidant of Russian Prince Grigory Alexandrovich Potemkin, who rivaled Jones for the attention of the czarina. In addition, Jones was envied by Russian Rear Admiral Count Nicholas Mordvinov who commanded the naval base at Kherson which was to supply Jones' command. To make matters worse, the commander of Jones' flagship, Greek Captain Brigadier Panaiotti Alexiano, was angry that he did not receive the appointment given to Jones and threatened to resign and take the ship's crew with him. Temporarily, Jones was able to placate these rivals.

Volunteers:

The historian Samuel Eliot Morison described those fighting under Jones as "a scratch collection of vessels manned by impressed serfs, Cossacks, Volga boatmen and Levantine pirates, officered in part by adventurers of six or seven nations."[1]

Compensation:

The pay scale for a captain in the Continental Navy was $32.00 a month. As a Russian rear admiral Jones was paid about $145 a month.

Opposition:

The warships on both sides were given grandiose classifications - ship-of-the-line, frigate, sloop. None of them measured up to their designations. Typical of this, Jones' flagship, the *Vladimir*, was classified as a ship-of-the-line and pierced for 66 guns. It mounted, however, a mere 24 guns, the armament of a minor frigate at best. Both fleets could be divided into two categories, deep-draft, sailing ships and shallow-draft, oar-propelled craft. Apparently the Turks had more sailing ships (perhaps 12 to Russia's nine) and the Russians possessed more oar-propelled craft (no accurate numbers are available).

Like that of Russia, the Turkish navy was manned by an eclectic gathering of men, many of whom were forced to be there either as serfs or slaves. The Turkish fleet was commanded by an able admiral, Hassan el Ghazi, known as "the Capudan Pasha" (lord captain).

Strategy

Jones knew that first he had to subject to his will the members of the Russian fleet, both officers and men, and then had to take advantage of his superior firepower over the Turks and not let the fighting devolve into a hand-to-hand melee.

OPERATIONS:

Jones deployed his fleet four miles east of fort Ochakov where the Liman narrowed, choosing to fight from anchor. Jones convinced Prince Nassau-Siegen to deploy his flotilla in support of Jones' sailing ships. Opening the first Battle of Liman, Nassau-Siegen attacked, without adequately notifying Jones, in the early hours of 17 June 1788 and the Russian flotilla was beaten back. On the morning of the 18th the Turks attacked the Russian right flank. Boarding a cutter, Jones directed the repositioning of his sailing ships. As the consequence of a fortuitous wind change, he moved five ships of his left wing, bringing the Turks under crossfire. They pulled back after losing several vessels.

The second Battle of Liman began on 27 June. Hassan el Ghazi attacked. The Russian fleet had remained in its defensive anchorage. At about 2 p.m. the Turkish 64-gun flagship ran aground about a mile from the Russian fleet. The other vessels anchored in disorder. Jones reconnoitered in a small boat. The wind, however, did not favor an attack by the Russian sailing ships. At 2 a.m. on the 28th the Turkish lord captain was able to refloat his flagship and attacked. A general melee followed until once again the Turkish flagship grounded along with the warship carrying his second-in-command. The Russian flotilla attacked and burned the stranded warships. Nassau-Siegen actions, however, had left the Russian sailing ships exposed to an attack by the Turkish flotilla and it sank a Russian frigate. Jones was able to restore his authority over at least part of the Russian flotilla and together with the Russian sailing ships drove the Turkish fleet back toward the mouth of the Liman. There the Russians had placed gun batteries which along with their fleet drove many of the Turkish ships aground. In two days of fighting the Turks had lost ten large ships and five small vessels, 1,673 prisoners, and some 3,000 seamen killed. Russian losses were one frigate, 18 men killed and 67 wounded.

Jones continued to take part in the fighting, including assisting Potemkin capture fort Ochakov on 12 July. In spite of his successes Jones was relieved of his command on 31 October 1789.

IMPACT:

Jones had won for the Russians control of the Liman estuary and with it the entrance into the Black Sea and a sea route to Constantinople. Jones had conquered on the sea but was defeated in the czarina's court. The court dandies, particularly Prince Grigory Alexandrovich Potemkin and Prince Nassau-Siegen, who Jones had forced to support him, were more skilled at political intrigue and were able to convince the czarina that in fact they had orchestrated the victory at Liman and not Jones. Rear Admiral Joseph F. Callo concluded, "The political process was complete; the innocent had been punished and the guilty rewarded."[2]

Jones is best remembered for his role in the American Revolution. The inscription on his black marble sarcophagus below the Naval Academy's chapel reads, "He gave to our navy its earliest traditions of heroism and victory."[3]

BIOGRAPHIES:

John Paul (1747-92) was born in Scotland and added the name Jones later. He became a mariner at the age of 13, sailing on the merchant brig *Friendship* as an unpaid apprentice. For several years he sailed on board different British merchant ships and slavers. He became disgusted by the cruelty in the slave trade and in 1768 he abandoned his position as first mate on the *Two Friends* and returned to Scotland. During his next voyage on board the brig *John*, both the captain and first mate died of yellow fever. Jones safely navigated the ship back to port. The grateful owner gave Jones ten per cent of the cargo profits and made him master of the ship. On his second trip to the West Indies, the short-tempered Jones flogged a seaman, who died a few weeks later. Shortly afterward, Jones killed a crewman with a sword in Tobago; Jones claimed self defense. Jones fled the island and made his way to Fredericksburg, Virginia, where his brother had lived and died, leaving a plantation but no local relatives.

Jones chose to fight for his new, young country and went to seek a commission in the new Continental Navy. With support from influential friends, on 7 December 1775 he was appointed a first lieutenant and commander of the newly-converted 24-gun *Alfred*. Throughout 1776 and most of 1777 Jones commanded various Continental warships but not without controversy. He feuded with the Navy chief, Commodore Esek Hopkins, who Jones believed was holding up his advancement. Next Jones was sent to France, carrying the news of General John Burgoyne's surrender at Saratoga, New York. Jones was befriended by the U.S. commissioner to France, Benjamin Franklin. Commanding a number of warships, Jones had mixed results in European waters until 23 September 1779. There off Flamborough Head in Yorkshire, while in command of the 40-gun old East Indiaman the *Bonhomme Richard* (the name chosen by Jones to honor Ben Franklin's *Poor Richard's Almanack*) Jones captured the superior 50-gun frigate *Serapis*. During this battle Jones was challenged by his adversary who asked whether Jones had "struck" his colors. Jones shouted his to-be-famous response, "I have not yet begun to fight."[4] After a furious fight the *Serapis* surrendered to the *Bonhomme Richard,* which shortly sank from her damages. This was Jones' most glorious moment, hailed in both France and the United States. Jones held additional commands both in European and American waters, but the war soon ended. The young republic, desperately short of money, disbanded its navy.

Without a navy, Jones sought employment elsewhere. Catherine II invited him to Russia to command her Black Sea fleet in a war against the Turks. Jones arrived in Russia on 4 May 1788 and took command of the flagship *Vladimir,* lying in the Liman estuary, on 9 June. Following his service in the Russian navy Jones returned to Paris and, in declining health, lived there until his death 18 July 1792. In 1905 President Theodore Roosevelt ordered that Jones' remains be brought back to the United States. John Paul Jones was interred in a crypt at the Naval Academy in Annapolis, Maryland.

QUOTATIONS:

[1] Samuel Eliot Morison, *John Paul Jones - A Sailor's Biography*. Boston: Little, Brown, and Co., 1959. p. 361.

[2] Joseph F. Callo, "John Paul Jones Makes Admiral," *Naval History* pp. 35-37 (April 2006) p. 35.

[3] James C. Bradford, "An American Hero's Relevance," *Naval History* pp. 38-44 (April 2006) p. 44.

[4] Fletcher Pratt, *The Navy - A History*. Garden City, NY: Garden City Publishing Co., Inc., 1941. p. 58.

SOURCES:

Stephen Howarth, *To Shining Sea - A History of the U.S. Navy 1775-1991*. New York: Random House, 1991.

Jay Mallin and Robert K. Brown, *Merc: American Soldiers of Fortune*. New York: Macmillan Publishing Company, 1979.

Webster's American Military Biographies. Springfield, Mass.: G. & C. Merriam Co., 1978.

AARON BURR CONSPIRACY

1805-06

GOAL:

This remains an enigma - at the least, this was a filibustering expedition to conquer lands belonging to Spain, and at the most, a conspiracy to create a new nation out of the United States west of the Appalachian Mountains and Spanish lands beyond the Sabine River.

BACKGROUND:

The purchase of the Louisiana Territory from the French by President Thomas Jefferson forever changed the map and the character of the United States. This redefined the West from the land between the Appalachian Mountains and the Mississippi River to the lands of the Louisiana Purchase. In 1803 there was an uneasiness in the air. In the old West there was a feeling of misgiving toward the Spaniard. For years the Spanish Empire stifled American western commerce coming down the Mississippi River. Some Americans believed that the Spanish inhabitants of the Louisiana Territory would not peacefully submit to their new sovereign, the United States.

Enter Aaron Burr - in 1804 he was nearing the end of his term as vice president while fearing a possible indictment for killing Alexander Hamilton in a duel. Burr confided in the British minister to the United States, Anthony Merry, that with naval and financial backing he would "effect the separation of the western part of the United States."[1] Burr stated that within two weeks of the end of his term he would establish a new government in New Orleans if Merry would provide a loan of 100,000 pounds and the support of a British naval squadron.

Unaware of the full extent of Burr's ambition, many western Americans saw Aaron Burr as the new champion of their dreams - punishing the Spanish Empire for the economic pain it had inflicted and pushing it out of the path of expansion.

In March 1805 Aaron Burr's term as vice president expired. Almost immediately he began a five-month trek through the "old" West of the United States to evaluate the mood of the population. During his trip he was the off-and-on traveling partner of General James Wilkinson who was heading to St. Louis in the Louisiana Territory to take charge of his new post as the governor of that territory. Among the influential individuals that Burr shared wine and food with were the renowned Indian fighter Andrew Jackson and the flamboyant Irishman and owner of an island in the Ohio River Harman Blennerhassett. He was a rich immigrant with more money than common sense. In June Burr met with Wilkinson for four days at Fort Massac and speculated over the conquest of the Spanish Southwest. With the aid of Wilkinson, Burr traveled to New Orleans, now in the hands of the United States. Burr judged New Orleans as being ripe for change. He again eagerly met with Jackson and Wilkinson on his way back East. He reported to Wilkinson that Jackson was ready to fight the Spanish, and Burr and Wilkinson went so far as draw up lists of officers for their army. In the late fall Burr returned to Washington, D.C.

Burr called on British Minister Merry, who had no response from the Foreign Office to Burr's earlier proposal. Persistent Burr increased his demands. He now wanted 110,000 pounds and a larger naval force to include three ships-of-the-line. Burr stated that he was set to act in March 1806 and tantalized the British minister with what he wanted to hear. Burr told the minister that once he had established his western federation, "the Eastern States will separate themselves immediately from the Southern. He continued, "[T]hus the immense power which has risen up with such rapidity in the Western Hemisphere will, by such a division, be rendered at once informidable."[2] A few days later Burr dined with President Jefferson, and the president told him that prospects looked good for the purchase of the Floridas from Spain; the president had no plans for war. Unfortunately for Burr, Wilkinson was not a discreet man while intoxicated, and rumors abounded. On 1 December 1805 Jefferson received an anonymous letter warning him of Burr's conspiracy.

Aaron Burr (1756-1836) was an enigma. Two villainous acts turned his image from that of a "founding father" into a shady opportunist. His first dark deed was the killing of Alexander Hamilton in a duel on 11 July 1804. Although a means to solving serious social disputes, dueling was already beginning to lose its acceptability, particularly in the North. Burr's second devious deed was his military excursion into the Mississippi River Valley, the purpose of which is still argued. Whether Burr was a traitor - attempting to split the United States - or a filibuster - attempting to wrestle Spanish territory from that crown, is still disputed.

James D. McCabe, *Pictorial History of the United States* (Philadelphia, 1877)

LEADERSHIP:

Aaron Burr, although possessing a small frame, was surprisingly robust and had a graceful manner. Additionally he was highly intelligent and a skilled orator. These qualities gave him a commanding presence.

VOLUNTEERS:

At least 30 and perhaps as many as 100 men volunteered for an enterprise - vague as it was.

COMPENSATION:

The volunteers were motivated by anti-Spanish diatribe. They were told that they were to establish an armed settlement on some land that Burr had acquired. Each man was to be rewarded with 100 acres. Harman and Margaret Blennerhassett, who had become infatuated with Burr, funded much of the endeavor.

OPPOSITION:

A few thousand American soldiers garrisoned the millions of square miles of the Louisiana Territory and the old West. And a few thousand Spanish troops garrisoned the millions of square miles west of the United States. Both militaries were like a few fleas traveling across the back of an elephant. Without intelligence the odds of being at the right place and right time to break up or oppose an invasion force were astronomical.

STRATEGY:

There were many clues to Burr's projected strategies - in fact, too many. These clues depended upon to whom he was talking or writing and what he was trying to get from them. Assuming Burr's real objective was to separate the old West from the United States, this would have depended more on political intrigue than military might. Assuming Burr's real goal was the conquest of Spanish lands, a likely strategy would have been to seize an important political center and declare the entire territory as conquered.

OPERATIONS:

After dining with President Jefferson, Burr knew he must act at once. Two confederates, Sam Swartwout and Peter Ogden, led a small band of men across country to join General Wilkinson. Each man carried a copy of a coded letter:

> "The Eastern detachments, from different points and under different pretenses, will rendezvous on the Ohio 1st November .... Naval protection of England is secured.... It will meet us at

the Mississippi.... Wilkinson shall be second to Burr only.... Burr will proceed westward 1st August.... Burr's plan of operation is to move down rapidly from the Falls [of the Ohio] on the 15th of November, with the first five hundred or a thousand men ... to be at Natchez between the 5th and 15th of December ... there to be determined whether it will be expedient to seize or pass by Baton Rouge..."[3]

Wilkinson received the coded letter at Natchitoches on the Red River in early October 1806. After decoding it, he must have appreciated the recklessness of the scheme. He "read" the American westerners very differently than Burr and perceived no popular groundswell for separation from the Union or a military adventure. Wilkinson immediately wrote to President Jefferson expressing his loyalty to the Union and began arresting suspected conspirators.

Burr, not guessing Wilkinson's future duplicity, began his second trip to the West in August 1806. Blennerhassett now started to assemble men, boats and munitions at his island near Mariette, Ohio. As Burr traveled southwestward he told each successive crowd what they wanted to hear - the Union forever and down with Spain. After receiving Wilkinson's warning, Jefferson issued a presidential proclamation on 27 November warning citizens against persons conspiring against Spain and ordered the arrest of persons involved in military expeditions. Governor Edward Tiffin of Ohio sent the state militia to seize the boats and supplies at Blennerhassett's Island. Blennerhassett escaped down the river with at least part of the expedition and was met by Burr near the mouth of the Cumberland River.

Burr's flotilla, now composed of 13 boats and some 60 men, drifted down to Fort Massac on the Ohio River. The lieutenant in charge, ignorant of the president's proclamation, provided a guide to the former vice president's expedition. As the flotilla drifted downriver, the muskets were unpacked and the men began to drill. Now Burr rushed ahead of the flotilla to Judge Peter Bruin's plantation 30 miles above Natchez expecting news from General Wilkinson. Here he learned that the general had betrayed him and that Acting Governor Cowles Mead of Mississippi had issued an arrest warrant for Burr's arrest. On 17 January 1807 Burr surrendered to civil authorities professing his innocence. A grand jury in Natchez refused to indict Burr and issued a presentment against General Wilkinson accusing him of making illegal arrests in New Orleans. However, the presiding judge, Thomas Rodney, refused to lift Burr's bond. Burr learned that General Wilkinson had offered $5,000 for Burr's capture, alive or dead. There could be little doubt which the general would prefer. Burr decided to make a run for it.

Acting Governor Mead encircled Burr's camp and arrested his supporters. On 19 February 1807 Burr was arrested by Lieutenant Edmund Gaines near Fort Stoddert, Alabama, while trying to reach Spanish territory. Burr was rushed across the United States under military guard to Richmond, Virginia, where he was brought before U.S. Supreme Court Chief Justice John Marshall and tried for treason.

Impact:

This enterprise collapsed in its embryonic stage. It would hardly be worth more than a footnote in history books except for the fact that Aaron Burr, former vice president of the United States, was its instigator. Attached to that name was the potential to reshape history. We will probably never know if Aaron Burr planned to be a filibuster, a traitor, or just an adventurer.

Biographies:

Aaron Burr (1756-1836) was descended from New England clergy on both sides of his family. This was as close as one could get to being a New England aristocrat. He graduated from Princeton in 1772 at the age of 16 with honors. Burr served in the Revolutionary army from 1775 until 1779. His path crossed that of General George Washington, and neither man liked the other. Leaving the army he practiced law in New York City and was a member of the New York state legislature. In 1789 he married Theodosia Prevost, ten years his senior; they had a daughter. Also in that year he was appointed attorney general of New York and in 1791 commissioner of revolutionary claims. Burr served in the U.S. Senate (D-NY) between 1791 and 1797. In the 1800 presidential election Burr and Thomas Jefferson both received 73 electoral votes. On the 36th ballot the House of Representatives chose Jefferson over Burr to be president; Burr became vice president (1801-05). Seeing his national political ambition blocked by Jefferson, Burr ran for the governorship of New York. He was defeated in large measure due to the influence of his local rival, Alexander Hamilton. As a consequence, Burr provoked a duel with Hamilton and on 11 July 1804 mortally wounded him. Both Federalists and Democrats were outraged.

During Burr's second trek west he was arrested on 19 February 1807 and taken to Richmond under guard to be tried for treason. Ultimately his acquittal was heavily dependent upon four factors. Foremost, on 31 August Chief Justice John Marshall declared that only an overt act sustained by the testimony of two witnesses could prove the charge of treason. Second, the prosecution's chief witness, General

James Wilkinson, had much to hide and could not reveal full details of Burr's activities without implicating himself. Third, the British minister to the United States, Anthony Merry, who was privy to Burr's plans, was not a witness nor would he consent to being a witness. And fourth, Burr's team of lawyers was superior to that of the prosecution. On 1 September Burr was acquitted by a jury. After his acquittal Burr traveled to England and France, partially to escape his creditors and partly to win support from Great Britain and France for an expedition against Spain's colonies in the Americas. In 1812 he gave up his ambition for conquest and returned to the United States financially ruined. Burr practiced law in New York City until his death in 1836.

James Wilkinson (1757-1825) was born in Calvert County, Maryland, and served in the Continental Army from 1776 until 1778 when he was forced to resign due to his involvement in the Conway Cabal (a letter questioning George Washington's leadership skills). He entered the mercantile world and move West. In 1787 he traveled to New Orleans and entered into a business arrangement with the Spanish governor, Esteban Mir. To culminate the arrangement, Wilkinson signed a loyalty oath to the Spanish king and agreed to provide information in exchange for 2,000 silver dollars a year (although payments were irregular). In 1790, nearly bankrupt, Wilkinson reentered the U.S. army and fought against the Indians. Through the deaths of senior officers in 1796, Wilkinson became the ranking officer in the U.S. Army. He represented the United States in taking possession of the Louisiana Territory from the French in 1803. He served as the governor of the Louisiana Territory between 1805 and 1806. He became the government's chief witness against Burr. Wilkinson's testimony proved to be a double edged sword for the prosecution. Although he denounced Burr, Wilkinson was limited as to what he would testify to since much of what he knew would incriminate himself as well. Wilkinson was acquitted by a court of inquiry and later by a court-martial in 1811. His poor performance along the Canadian frontier during the War of 1812 was investigated, but he was acquitted of misdoings. Wilkinson was honorably discharged from the army in 1815. Traveling to Mexico in 1821, he acquired a land grant in Texas but died before he could take possession.

QUOTATIONS:

[1] John Dos Passos, "The Conspiracy and Trial of Aaron Burr," *American Heritage* vol. 17, no. 2, pp. 4-9, 69-84 (February 1966) p. 70.

[2] Dos Passos, "The Conspiracy," p. 73.

[3] Dos Passos, "The Conspiracy," p.74.

Sources:

Dictionary of American Biography. 10 vols. plus sup. 1 thru 8. New York: Charles Scribner's Sons, 1936 & 1990.

Benson John Lossing, ed. *Harper's Encyclopedia of United States History.* 10 vols. New York: Harper & Brothers, 1902.

David O. Stewart, "Burr in the Saddle," *The Quarterly Journal of American History.* Vol. 25, no. 2 (Winter 2013) pp. 56-59.

James Long's Expeditions

1819-21

Goal:

To seize Texas, which in 1819 was still part of the Spanish empire.

Background:

In 1819 the United States and Spain signed the Transcontinental Treaty (also known as the Adams-Onís Treaty), which transferred Florida to the United States in exchange for U.S. recognition of the Sabine River as the boundary between the Spanish empire and the United States. Thus, the government in Washington was relinquishing any claim to Texas. American merchants in places like Natchez, Tennessee, believed that this was a poor deal since it excluded their commercial activities west of the Sabine River. Prominent citizens of the region promoted a public meeting in Natchez in May 1819 that inspired filibustering expeditions into Spanish Texas. Historian Harris Gaylord Warren wrote, "American citizens have been noted for their assumption that they are endowed with an inalienable right to go wherever their inclinations might lead them."[1]

Leadership:

Militia General John Adair was offered command of the expedition but he refused. Next, the instigators turned to merchant James Long, who accepted. What role his uncle-in-law, General James Wilkinson, played is unclear.

Volunteers:

Typically, filibusters were recklessly brave, accustomed to hardships, and unscrupulous. In all probability, these filibusters, who purchased their own weapons were well armed since the prospect of capture could lead to execution.

Compensation:

The expedition was financed through some $500,000 in subscriptions by the merchants of Natchez, Tennessee, who hoped to profit from the enterprise. The volunteers were promised adventure and a league of land.

Opposition:

Long's filibusters initially could expect to be opposed by Mexican militia who were poorly trained and poorly armed. Mexican revolutionaries and royalists had been fighting a life-death struggle in central Mexico since 1810 and neither could spare seasoned troops to protect the far-away provinces.

Strategy:

Grab, hold and boldly declare that possession determined ownership.

Operations:

Beginning in the spring of 1819, Eli Harris led an advance force from Natchez, Tennessee, to Nacogdoches, then in the Spanish province of Texas. Some 120 filibusters crossed into Texas on 8 June. Long left Natchez on 17 June leading 70 more men. By the time the expedition reached Nacogdoches, its numbers swelled to some 300 men. Long established a provincial government and on 23 June 1819 Texas was declared an independent republic. Long then dispersed small groups to find provisions in the surrounding country. Supplies coming from the United States had been intercepted by government authorities. Long sought an alliance with the pirate Jean Lafitte, who controlled Galveston Island. The pirate responded cautiously.

The Mexican royalists reacted and dispatched some 550 men under Colonel Ignacio Pérez to drive the invaders out. The colonel advanced cautiously from San Antonio toward Nacogdoches. While Long was negotiating with Lafitte, Pérez intercepted the small bands of filibusterers and captured them. Major Hamlin Cook and the filibusters garrisoning Nacogdoches fled across the Sabine River into the safety of the United States. Pérez had captured 26 Americans, three Mexicans and one Black slave.

In the Spring of 1821 Long led a second expedition, composed of 51 men, into Texas. Professing loyalty to the Mexican independence movement, Long's force walked into La Bahia (now Goliad) on 4 October unopposed. Within a few days Long's entire following was captured by Colonel Pérez. Long's men were sent to Monterrey, Mexico. Long, after spending a short time in prison was allowed to proceed to Mexico City. There he found friends among the Mexican republicans but fell out with the imperialists. Long decided to leave Mexico City but on 8 April he was shot and killed by a sentinel at the Los Gallos Barracks, ostensibly because of a misunderstanding.

Impact:

Historian Warren wrote, "The chief motive which animated the leaders of Long's expedition was the desire for land."[2] In spite of the titanic political struggle still raging in central Mexico between those who had recently deserted the Spanish king in favor of independence, as personified by Augustín de Iturbide, and the old revolutionaries, who had been fighting for more than a decade as personified by Guadalupe Victoria, the filibusters failed in their goal. The Mexican leaders were acutely aware of the vulnerability of Mexico's outlying provinces to filibustering expeditions but had few resources to spare from their internal feud.

Biographies:

Eli Harris (unk) was a printer whose press was in Nacogdoches, Spanish Texas.

James Long (*ca* 1793-1822), possibly born in North Carolina, migrated with his parents to Kentucky and Tennessee. He worked in his father's store and studied medicine. He joined the army as a surgeon and served at the Battle of New Orleans. Long settled in Natchez, Tennessee, and married Jane Wilkinson, the niece of General James Wilkinson. Long resigned from the army and purchased a plantation near Vicksburg, Mississippi. In 1817 he joined W.W. Walker as a merchant out of Natchez.

Quotations:

[1] Harris Gaylord Warren, *The Sword was their Passport*. Baton Rouge, Louisiana: Louisiana State University Press, 1943, p. 237.

[2] Warren, *The Sword was their Passport*, p. 237.

Sources:

Dictionary of American Biography. 10 vols. plus sup. 1 thru 8. New York: Charles Scribner's Sons, 1936 & 1990.

Nathaniel W. Stephenson, *Texas and the Mexican War*. New Haven: Yale University Press, 1921.

Lynn L. Perrigo, *Our Spanish Southwest*. Dallas: Banks Upshaw and Company, 1960.

Porter Clan in the Service of Mexico

1826-29

Goal:

To help Mexico defeat Spain in exchange for financial reward.

Background:

Many individuals marked the Plan of Iguala of 1821 as the end of the War for Mexican Independence. But Fernando VII, king of Spain, was not ready to concede. Fernando mistakenly believed that the reemergence of a conservative Europe at the Peace of Vienna in 1815 offered him the possibility of military aid to re-conquer his lost colonies. To keep his dream alive while he developed a strategy and built a land force to re-conquer his lost territory, Fernando initiated an aggressive naval war against Mexico. The commerce of this new nation was heavily dependent upon trade through the port of Vera Cruz (later Veracruz) thus making it an inviting target for a naval blockade. At the beginning of the 19th Century, Mexico did not have a particularly strong naval tradition. Not surprisingly Mexico sought out a foreign naval officer with a fighting reputation to lead its navy in the continuing war with the mother country.

Leadership:

Mexico's search for an officer to command its fleet coincided with David Porter's feud with senior officers of the U.S. Navy. His reputation was well known in Mexico due to his daring exploits as the captain of the U.S. frigate *Essex* and as commander-in-chief of the West Indies Squadron. David Porter was given the title of commander-in-chief of the Mexican navy with the rank of general of marine. He could appoint and dismiss officers at will. He also controlled Fort San Juan d'Ulloa, which protected Vera Cruz.

VOLUNTEERS:

For naval warfare, the new Mexican government was heavily dependent upon soldiers of fortune and foreign-built ships to fight the Spaniards. The Mexican War for Independence had been a land affair and few Mexicans had served in the Spanish navy prior to the conflict. Therefore, Mexico had few sailors to oppose the Spanish fleet. Also, the great shipbuilding area of colonial Spain in the New World was Cuba and not Mexico.

The Mexican navy was composed of the frigate *Libertad* (32 guns), brig *Guerrero* (20 guns), and half a dozen lesser warships.

COMPENSATION:

Porter's salary was $12,000 a year and he was awarded a significant tract of land.

OPPOSITION:

Although the Spanish navy had been significantly reduced by the Napoleonic Wars, it still possessed some significant warships.

STRATEGY:

Porter's strategy was first to organize and train the fleet. This was no easy task since many of the Mexican officers were from the upper crust of society and resented Porter's authority. The second was to cruise the Caribbean to seek out and destroy Spanish commerce and when possible attack Spanish warships. Spain's strategy was to use its Caribbean colonies, particularly Cuba, as its base of operations against Mexican commerce.

OPERATIONS:

In the spring of 1827 the Mexican squadron under Porter's command put to sea. Most of the ships were commanded by Americans - nephew David H. Porter commanded the frigate *Libertad* (32 guns), Charles Hawkins commanded the brig *Herman* (unk. guns), and [fnu] Wise commanded the brig *Bravo* (unk. guns). The *Victoria* (unk. guns) was commanded by the Mexican [fnu] Machen. The squadron captured one prize before encountering two Spanish 60-gun frigates and a brig. The two squadrons sailed parallel courses but the Spaniards dis-

---

David Porter (1780-1843) was the patriarch of a family which spawned three generations of soldiers of fortune. David won fame as a frigate captain in the War of 1812. David Dixon, his son, would win fame in the U.S. Civil War as an admiral. They both fought for Mexico in the 1820s. David Essex, his grandson, was a drunkard who served in the Egyptian army in the 1870s.

Harper's Encyclopedia of United States History (New York, 1902)

appeared at night. Ultimately, Porter established a base of operations at Key West, waters he know well from his days as commander-in-chief of the West Indies Squadron. A Spanish squadron of four frigates and three brigs halfheartedly blockaded Key West. Nevertheless, Porter's ships came and went almost at will. The Mexican squadron took more prizes and raided along the Cuban coast.

In one notable incident, David H. Porter (21 years old), now commanding the prize schooner *Esmeralda* (unk. guns) captured a number of small coastal craft. When the weapons were returned to the cabin, David D. Porter (13 years old son) noted that some were missing. Suspecting a mutiny, the two Porters armed themselves. The mutinous ringleader, an Englishman, leading some Mexicans, unsuccessfully attempted to overpower the Porters. Two of the mutineers were killed.

The money acquired by Porter through the sale of captured goods practically made his squadron self sustaining. Some local American merchants did not appreciate the competition and demanded that an American naval squadron be sent to stop the practice. When it arrived the officers were in sympathy with Porter and not much was done to curb his activities. Also, the Spanish ambassador in Washington repeatedly complained of Porter's violation of U.S. neutrality; this also went unheeded. Finally, as the winter months set in, Porter slipped past the Spanish squadron at night and returned to Vera Cruz.

Although welcomed as a hero, circumstances immediately turned bad for Porter. The Mexican government did not approve naval appropriations nor was the prize money owed to Porter and his men given to them. Porter then received a message to proceed to Mexico City on important business. This was a ploy to place him on a road where he could be assassinated. The attempt failed. A second unsuccessful attempt to assassinate Porter occurred one night in his quarters. The instigator of these plots was never uncovered but Antonio López de Santa Anna (future victor at the Alamo) was suspected.

But that was not the worst of it. The 20-gun *Guerrero*, commanded by nephew David H. Porter, was raiding along the Cuban coast when the brig was overhauled by the 64-gun *Lealtad*. In a two-hour gun battle the *Guerrero*, the only active Mexican warship, was pounded to pieces. David H. Porter, along with half the crew, was killed and David D. Porter was taken prisoner. All was bleak.

The salvation of the future arrived in a letter from Mahlon Dickerson, a close friend of President Andrew Jackson, and future secretary of the navy. He wrote:

> "The President [Jackson] expressed the highest respect for your character and services, together with his utter detestation

of the persecution that drove you into exile.... He has authorized me to say that it would give him the highest satisfaction to see you again in this country and that should you return he would provide for you in some way agreeable to yourself."[2]

Impact:

As the young Mexican government devolved into turmoil so had Porter's stay. Jealous Mexican officials plotted against Porter. Twice assassination attempts were made against his life. His salary went unpaid and the grandiose land-grants amounted to nothing. His successes at sea had little impact. All of this cost him his nephew David H. and his son Thomas (to yellow fever). Historian Archibald Turnbull attributed to David Porter the following statement: "Better a subordinate berth under those [American] colors, than the highest honors in a doubtful service."[1] Porter returned to Washington a financially strapped and unemployed naval officer.

Biographies:

David Porter (1780-1843) was born in Boston, Massachusetts. He went to sea in 1796 with his father, a merchant ship captain, during which time the younger Porter saw his first action off Jérémie, Haiti, against a British warship. He joined the U.S. Navy in 1798 as a midshipman and was on board the *Constellation* (36 guns) when it captured the French frigate *Insurgente* (36 guns). Porter was advanced to lieutenant in 1799 and soon commanded the *Enterprise* (12 guns) during the war with Tripoli. He led a landing party and was twice wounded. A little later he was captured by North African pirates and imprisoned. In 1806 Porter was promoted to master commandant. He married Evelina Anderson, from a prominent family of Chester, Pennsylvania, and they had ten children. Porter commanded the naval station in New Orleans for two years.

Early in the War of 1812, while commanding the frigate *Essex* (32 guns), Porter captured the British warship *Alert* (20 guns) and eight merchant prizes. In 1813 he sailed the *Essex* into the Pacific hunting for British whale ships. Making his base of operations the Galapagos Islands, he captured a dozen whalers. On 28 March 1813, the *Essex* was captured by two British warships. The *Essex* lost 155 men of a 225-man crew in the fight before striking its colors. Porter was paroled, returned home, and participated in the defense of Washington, D.C., in September 1814.

In 1815 Porter was appointed to the Navy Board and purchased land near the White House. In 1823 he became the commander-in-chief of the West Indies Squadron, which hunted pirates. Porter landed a force on the Spanish colony of Puerto Rico to redress what he believed was an insult to an American officer. He was recalled to Washington and court-martialed. Porter was suspended from duty for six months. He believed the punishment was unjustified and thus began a long-standing feud with senior naval officers. He resigned from the navy in 1826. At this point Porter entered the service of the Mexican navy.

In 1830, following service in the Mexican navy, Porter was appointed the U.S. consul-general to Algiers. Next, he served as the U.S. chargé d'affaires to Turkey and was made minister in 1839 when that rank was created. He served in that post for 12 years.

David Dixon Porter (1813-91) was born in Chester, Pennsylvania, and was the third of ten children of David and Evelina Porter. He possessed a limited formal education and at the age of 10 sailed with his father in the West Indies Squadron. Then David D. traveled with his father to Mexico and became a midshipman in the Mexican navy. He served under his cousin, David H. Porter, on board the *Esmeralda* (32 guns) during a cruise off Key West and the coast of Cuba. David D. was on board the Mexican brig *Guerrero* (22 guns) when it was captured by the Spanish frigate *Lealtad* (64 guns). He was confined in Havana, Cuba. When released he returned to the United States. In 1829 David D. was appointed midshipman in the U.S. Navy. He led a long and distinguished career, ultimately becoming the U.S. Navy's second admiral at the time of the U.S. Civil War (1861-65).

Quotations:

[1] Archibald Douglas Turnbull, *Commodore David Porter 1780-1843*. New York, The Century Co., 1929, pp. 291-92.

[2] Turnbull, *Commodore David Porter*, p. 300.

Sources:

Dictionary of American Biography. 10 vols. plus sup. 1 thru 8. New York: Charles Scribner's Sons, 1936 & 1990.

William R. Manning, *Diplomatic Correspondence of the United States concerning the Independence of the Latin-American Nations*. 3 vols. New York: Oxford University Press, 1925.

Americans in the Argentine-Brazilian Naval War

1825-28

Goal:
The Americans who fought in this war were motivated by adventure, money, and for some, a dislike for the English.

Background:
The United Provinces of la Plata (the future Argentina) and the Empire of Brazil fought over the control of *Banda Oriental* (the future Uruguay) while many of the people in *Banda Oriental* did not want to be subjugated by either of their neighbors. The fighting which had been going on primarily on land since 1811 took on a naval character in 1825.

Leadership:
The Argentine navy was led by the bold Irishman William Brown. Although the most accomplished American officers fought as privateers, they had to be inspired by Brown and to some degree, were subject to his wishes.

Volunteers:
Apparently Americans fought on both sides during the conflict. Many more, however,

Americans in the Argentine-Brazilian Naval War, 1825-28

In one respect, the Argentine-Brazilian naval war of 1825-28 was a replay of the War of 1812. A significant number of British officers and seamen fought for the Brazilians and more than a few Americans fought for the Argentines. In this illustration the Argentine brig General Brandzen (8 guns) commanded by American Captain George Coleman DeKay, captures the Brazilian brig Cacique (18 guns) commanded by British Captain George Manson, on 9 September 1827.

Courtesy U.S. Naval Historical Center

fought for the Argentines than for the Brazilians. This was both a naval war - navy against navy - and also a war on commerce, privateers attacking trade. Brazil's seaborne trade was much larger than that of Argentina making it more vulnerable. Argentina and its ally Uruguay (which perceived Argentina to be the lesser of two evils) commissioned 57 privateers.

The Argentine navy was decidedly inferior to the Brazilian fleet. Over half of the 56 officers were American, British or Irish. In 1825 the Argentine navy possessed two brigs and a few gunboats. Numerous warships were soon purchased.

Compensation:

Prize money was the primary attraction for the crews of privateers. When a merchant ship trading with the Brazilians was captured, it was brought into a friendly port, typically Buenos Aires, and a prize court determined whether it was a legitimate prize. If so, the ship and its cargo were sold at auction, the Argentine government took a significant share and the remainder was divided among the crew of the privateer.

Opposition:

The Brazilian navy, created by the English soldier of fortune Admiral Thomas Cochrane, emerged from the Brazilian War for Independence (1822-23) fairly intact. One-third of its officers were English and many of its 1, 200 sailors were English, Irish and American soldiers of fortune. The navy possessed one ship-of-the-line, 29 medium-sized warships, and some 35 lesser war craft.

Strategy:

The Brazilian strategy was to blockade the Argentine warships in Buenos Aires. The Argentine strategy was to draw the larger, deeper-draft Brazilian warships into the shallow waters off Buenos Aires and capturing them by boarding. When neither side was able to get the other to play into its hands, Brown led raids against the Brazilians. Although these typically failed, the aggressiveness of Brown's strategy enhanced his reputation.

Operations:

An aggressive naval war took place between the Argentine and Brazilians, primarily in the Rio de la Plata estuary. Both sides sustained numerous casualties but neither was able ever to win a significant advantage.

Privateering was another matter. Prior to the fighting at sea, the Brazilian trade had been booming. Privateers, warships-for-hire, captured 405 prizes, of which 139 reached Argentine ports to be condemned as prizes.

The American George DeKay, commanding the brig *General Brandzen* (eight guns), was one of the more aggressive privateers. On 26 June 1827 he attacked the Brazilian naval lugger *Príncipe Imperial* (14 guns) and the naval schooner *Isabella* (five guns). The *Príncipe Imperial* fled and the *Isabella* surrendered. On 9 September DeKay boarded and captured the naval brig *Cacique* (18 guns) off the coast of Pernambuco. The *Cacique* sustained six dead and 17 wounded and the *General Brandzen* lost one dead and 14 wounded. Finally on 16 June 1828 a Brazilian squadron commanded by the Englishman James Norton ran down the *General Brandzen*. Rather than see his ship fall into enemy hands DeKay burned it.

On 25 January 1828 another American privateer, John H. Coe, commanding the *Niger* (11 guns), attacked the Brazilian naval corvette *Maria Isabel* (28 guns). Coe attempted to board the much more powerful Brazilian warship three times before quitting the fight. On 28 March the *Niger*, still commanded by Coe, was captured by the Brazilian brig *Caboclo* (unk. guns) commanded by the Englishman James Inglis.

Impact:

The naval war was a bloody stalemate. However, the attack on Brazilian commerce by privateers, including those commanded and manned by Americans, was another matter. In May 1827 the English commercial newspaper *The British Packet* wrote:

"The damage inflicted is immense. Many of the corsairs [privateers], and probably all, have made successful voyages to the coast of Brazil and, if the war continues, the commerce of that country will be shaken to its foundation."[1]

Biographies:

George Colman DeKay (1802-49) was born in New York. He went to sea at an early age and by 20 years of age he commanded his own ship. DeKay served in the Chilean navy in 1824 and took part in the siege of Callao, Peru. DeKay offered to serve in the Brazilian navy but was rejected, so he turned to privateering for Argentina. He died in Washington,, D.C.

Quotations:

[1] Jan Read, *The New Conquistatores*. London: Evans Brothers Limited, 1980. p. 134.

SOURCES:

Botto, *Campanhas navais Sul-Americanas*. Rio de Janeiro: Impresa Naval, 1940.

Teodoro Caillet-Bois, *Historia naval Argentina*. Buenos Aires: Emecé Editores, 1944.

Robert L. Scheina, *Latin America's Wars*. 2 vols. Washington, D.C.: Brassey's, Inc., 2003.

Phillis Wheelock, "An American Commodore in the Argentine Navy," *The American Neptune*. Vol. 6; no. 1 (Jan 1946) pp. 5-18.

"Remember the Alamo!"

1836

Goal:

To defend a strongpoint, the Alamo, against a numerically superior Mexican army.

Background:

Mexicans began a revolt against Spain in September 1810. They did not achieve independence until 24 August 1821. This did not bring peace to Mexico. To the contrary the country was plunged into political and military turbulence as conservatives and liberals fought for control of the country. Politically the most agile of these men was Antonio Padua María Severino López de Santa Anna y Pérez de Lebrón (1794-1876). He possessed the knack of continually changing sides and always landing on top. During a 22-year period he served as president 11 times, twice as a liberal and nine times as a conservative. A historian described him: "A corrupt and ruthless politician, thief, compulsive gambler, opium addict and liar, he was known to his countrymen as *Don Demonio* ("Sir Devil") ...."[1]

In 1727 a Spanish colony in northern New Spain (the future Mexico) was formed into the province of Tejas. Bordering on the United States, it inevitably became of increasing interest to Americans. A number of filibustering expeditions against Tejas were launched but failed. Although there was official resistance to American settlers, this eventually ended. Beginning in 1824, in 12 years almost 28,000 settlers came in. And also inevitably, there was talk of annexing Texas - as it was known - to the United States. In a letter dated 13 February 1833 to U.S. President Andrew Jackson a Texan leader, Samuel P. Houston, a veteran (wounded twice) of the 1812 war, said of annexation, "That such a measure is desired by nineteen-twentieths of the population I cannot doubt."[2]

James Bowie (1796-1836) was one of those individuals to whom history has been very kind (thanks to Hollywood). His name lives on because of the wide-blade knife which bears his name and to his death at the Alamo. Many of his other deeds - slave trading and questionable land deals - have been overshadowed.

Courtesy wikimedia.org

The desire for annexation morphed into calls for Texan independence. Another Texan leader, Stephen F. Austin, declared: "War is our only recourse. No halfway measures, but war in full."[3] A sub-issue was the matter of slavery: Americans favored it; Mexico had declared it to be illegal. A convention of Texans proclaimed independence on 2 March 1836. Sam Houston was appointed military commander. A small Texan army came into being, sometimes numbering only 300 or so soldiers. There were battles with the poorly trained Mexican army. The Texans usually won. The Texans, however, had different views of what they were doing. A volunteer later commented that "some were for independence, some were for the [liberal Mexican] Constitution of 1824, and some were for anything, just as long as it was a row."[4]

In October and November the Texans laid siege to San Antonio de Béxar (now San Antonio). On 9 December 1835 the town was captured. Just to the north were the buildings of a former mission, San Antonio de Valero, better known as El Alamo, probably named for nearby *Alamo* (cottonwood) trees.

LEADERSHIP:

The Mexicans were led by the notorious Santa Anna. The overall military leader of the Texans was Sam Houston. The men of the Alamo were commanded by William B. Travis, who shared the command briefly with James Bowie. Bowie had been ill, probably with typhoid; his condition worsened and he was confined to his bed throughout the siege.

VOLUNTEERS:

All the defenders at the Alamo were volunteers. Americans were the most numerous, many from Tennessee. Texans were the next largest group although it was hard to distinguish who was an American and who was a Texan. There were also a few from other countries including Great Britain. Even the reported number of men defending the Alamo varies between 183 and 260.

Compensation:

The men of the Alamo received no pay. But many had come in hopes of obtaining some of the huge tracks of land that were up for grabs.

Opposition:

Sources do not agree on the size of the Mexican army and figures range between 2,000 and 6,000 men. It is unknown how many Santa Anna lost on the harsh march north to San Antonio and he also dispatched some of his troops on secondary tasks. The force he retained for the siege of the Alamo probably exceeded 2,000 men. The quality of the Mexican army was a mixed bag. Most of the men were poorly trained and poorly armed conscripts. There were a few elite troops on whom Santa Anna lavished money.

Strategy:

The strategy of the defenders was to hold out against an overwhelming force until help arrived, although they were not sure from where. Santa Anna planned to surprise the defenders by sending mounted troops in advance of his main army but this was mishandled by subordinates. Regardless, the Mexican army arrived a month earlier than the defenders expected.

Operations:

Sam Houston wanted the Alamo destroyed. With previously-installed cannon and thick adobe walls (but no roof) it might become an enemy stronghold. Houston sent James Bowie, a former slave smuggler and land speculator, to do the destruction. Bowie took 30 men but decided to hold the potential fort.

Mexican President and Generalissimo Santa Anna became determined to recapture San Antonio - and the Alamo. Word spread far that a battle was shaping up. Volunteers came to assist the Alamo defenders, who had concentrated in the main building. William Travis, lawyer and colonel in the Texas cavalry, arrived with 30 men on 3 February. On 8 February David "Davy" Crockett, famed frontiersman, came with 12 Tennessee volunteers. During the forthcoming siege he would entertain the defenders with his fiddle-playing. Travis would become commander of the garrison.

Santa Anna arrived at San Antonio on 23 February 1836 with an army. The defenders numbered about 250 men. Travis attempted to negotiate but the Mexican chief refused to do so, saying there could be "no guarantees for traitors."[5] A Mexican bombardment began on 25 February and an artillery duel ensued. When Santa Anna pushed his smaller guns closer to the makeshift fortress walls, the gunners were fired on by the defenders, some of whom had four and five loaded rifles apiece. Travis sent out a message asking for assistance and declaring; "... [O]ur flag still waves proudly from the walls - I shall never surrender or retreat."[6]

Santa Anna decided on an all-out assault on the Alamo. At five in the morning on 6 March a bugle sounded in the Mexican lines and shouts of "Viva Santa Anna!" Four columns advanced on the Alamo from different directions. Scaling ladders were used to attack the walls. Travis was shot in the head and died. Mexican bands struck up their blood-curdling "*Deguello*" ("Beheading"). A Mexican lieutenant colonel later described the fighting:

"... [T]he courage of our soldiers was not diminished as they saw the comrades failing dead or wounded, and they hurried to occupy their places and to avenge them, climbing over their bleeding bodies. The sharp reports of the rifles, the whistling of bullets, the groans of the wounded, the cursing of the men, the sighs and anguished cries of the dying, the arrogant harangues of the officers, the noise of the instruments of war and the inordinate shouts of the attackers, who climbed vigorously, bewildered all and made of this moment a tremendous and critical one. The shouting of those being attacked was no less loud and from the beginning had pierced our ears with desperate, terrible cries of alarm in a language we did not understand."[7]

The Mexicans swarmed over the walls. The fierce combat moved to the rooms of the edifices. Mexican officer de la Peña wrote:

> "... [T]hey [the Mexicans] turned the enemy's own cannon to bring down the doors to the rooms or the rooms themselves; a horrible carnage took place .... The tumult was great, the disorder frightful; it seemed as if the furies had descended upon us; different groups of soldiers were firing in all directions ... so that one was as likely to die by a friendly hand as by an enemy's."[8]

The outcome of the Battle of the Alamo could not be doubted. It was over by around eight in the morning of 6 March, Santa Anna came in about an hour later to inspect his trophy. He ordered that the few prisoners be executed. Children and wives of the defenders who were in the buildings were spared. (Some men evidently had managed to escape during the night before the battle.)

The Alamo defenders lost 187 men. The Mexicans lost 521. The dead defenders were cremated on funeral pyres. Many of the Mexican dead were buried; some bodies were thrown into the San Antonio River.

The above is the classically accepted account of what happened at the Alamo. A scholar, Dr. Philip Thomas Tucker who delved deeply into the Mexican and "Tejano" sources, recently developed a different account of what happened.[9]

The Alamo leaders, in Tucker's view, suffered from "collective inexperience and lack of military training.... Combined with little tactical insight, and aggravated by personal ambitions and priorities, the failure of command judgment doomed the Alamo garrison to a tragic fate."[10] The result was a "fatal decision to maintain a remote garrison in an indefensible place, in a distant land that belonged to another republic ...."[11] Less than 200 men were defending a perimeter of nearly 540 yards. There were other factors working against Alamo men: they were overconfident, overlooking the fact that Mexican cavalry were quality troops. There was illness among the defenders - an outbreak of small pox. They had failed to prepare for a siege, such as clearing the brush from around to buildings where a clean line of fire was essential.

Messages asking for assistance for the Alamo sent to the Texan military chief, Sam Houston, were futile. "Houston remained drunk much of the time in Washington-on-the-Brazos," according to Tucker.[12] Santa Anna sent out a probe on 25 February 1836; it was repelled. The last week of that month, nearly a fortnight before the actual assault, Santa Anna's artillery began a bombardment. The guns, however, were of poor quality; none of the defenders was killed. Santa Anna planned to launch 1,400 of his best soldiers against the garrison in four columns, one on each side of the fort. Artillery was also set up on each side. The bombardment, however, would cease hours before the attack to reduce the alertness of the defenders.

According to Tucker the actual attack took only about 20 minutes, from around 5:30 to about 5:50 in the morning of 6 March. The Alamo men, or most of them, were asleep when Mexican troops poured over the walls and through a gate. Some 120 of the defenders tried to flee in three groups. They were massacred outside the walls. A Mexican officer wrote in his journal, "The enemy attempted in vain to fly [from the Alamo], but they were overtaken and put to the sword."[13] Travis, to avoid being captured, killed himself with a knife. Crockett, too, remained inside the fort. Barely 300 Mexicans were killed or wounded, many by "friendly fire." Santa Anna later stated of the battle, "It was but a small affair."[14]

Impact:

The siege bolstered Santa Anna's prestige among the Mexicans, but at the same time it provided Sam Houston with time to build up his Texan forces. The Alamo would become a psychological factor in the months which followed. On 21 April 1836 the Texan troop charged against the Santa Anna-led army at the Battle of San Jacinto with yells of "Remember the Alamo!"

It is impossible to say how many of the Alamo defenders were American soldiers of fortune. Some were fighting for the thrill and others against what they perceived to be Mexican tyranny. Among these individuals there had to be those who considered themselves Americans and not Texans regardless of the outcome.

Biographies:

William Charles M. Baker (unk.-1836), born in Missouri, held the rank of captain. He probably commanded the volunteers who accompanied James Bowie to the Alamo. He was killed during the final assault.

John Joseph Baugh (*ca*.1803-36), a gentleman planter, was from Virginia and held the rank of captain. Dependable, he was Travis' executive officer with whom he did not get along. Baugh was killed during the final assault.

John Walker Baylor, Jr. (*ca*.1814-unk.) was from Fort Gibson, Arkansas. A medical doctor, he was a rifleman in Captain Dimmit's company. Apparently Baylor left the Alamo as a courier on 25 February 1836.

James Butler Bonham (1807-36) was from a wealthy family in Montgomery, Alabama. He was expelled from South Carolina College for being too vocal in support of states' rights. Practicing law in South Carolina, he answered a call for volunteers to aid Texas. He held a rally in Mobile, Alabama, in October 1835 to support the Texans. He organized the Mobile Grey Volunteers, and the group arrived in San Antonio in December. At the Alamo Bonham served as a courier. Twice he carried messages out of the Alamo and returned each time. He was killed during the assault.

James "Jim" Bowie (1796-1836) is remembered for the knife he devised, which bears his name: it has a crossguard, wide blade and curved it. Born in Kentucky, he moved to Missouri and then to Louisiana, where he and his brothers farmed, logged, roped and rode alligators. Bowie became wealthy smuggling slaves and making questionable land deals. Hearing of land and silver opportunities in Texas, he moved there. He married the daughter of a vice-governor, befriended the elite class, became a Mexican citizen and gained control of some 750,000 acres. He sympathized with the Texan cause, joined the rebels and fought in several battles, including the one at San Antonio de Béjar. He arrived at the Alamo on 19 January 1836, convinced that it was an important outpost that had to be defended. With the help of an engineer he set about fortifying it. He wrote in a letter ... [W]e will rather die in these ditches than give it up to the enemy."[10] Ill and bedridden, Bowie is believed to have killed himself rather than be captured.

Daniel W. Cloud (*ca.*1812-36), an unsuccessful lawyer, was from Kentucky and served as a private. Cloud was killed in the final assault.

Lemuel Crawford (*ca.*1814-36) was from South Carolina and served as an artilleryman. Crawford was killed in the final assault.

David "Davy" Crockett (1786-1836) was a frontiersman well known to Americans. He would disappear into the woods for long periods of time and write accounts of his adventures. He claimed to have killed 108 bears in an eight-month period. Crockett was born in rural Tennessee, the son of a Revolutionary War veteran. He took up farming. He fought in the Creek War (1813-14). He married and had three children. When his wife died, he remarried. Crockett was also a politician. He was elected to a magistracy and to the state legislature (1821-25). He served three terms in Congress but was defeated when he ran for a fourth term. He reportedly told his former constituents, "You may all go to hell and I will go to Texas."[11] He left Tennessee in October 1835, went to Texas, organized a company of Tennessee mounted volunteers. He and his men arrived at the Alamo in February. In a speech he declared, "I have come to aid you all that I can in your noble cause."[12] It is believed that Crockett fled the Alamo with fellow Tennesseans but was captured and executed.

Robert Crossman (*ca.*1810-36) was from Pennsylvania and served as a private. Crossman was killed in the final assault.

Charles Despallier (*ca.*1818-36) was from Louisiana and served as an aide to Travis. In late February 1836, serving as a courier, he left the Alamo and returned with the Gonzales Ranging Company on 1 March. Despallier was killed in the final assault.

Robert Evans (*ca.*1800-36), born in Ireland, was from New York. He was a major and served in the artillery. He torched powder magazines during in the final assault and he was killed.

James L. Ewing (*ca.*1812-36) was from Tennessee. He was a private and served as an artilleryman. Ewing was killed during the final assault.

William Keener Fauntleroy (*ca.*1814-36) was from Kentucky and served as a private. Fauntleroy was killed during the final assault.

John Hubbard Forsyth (*ca.*1798-1836) was from Kentucky. He was a captain commanding a cavalry company. He worked in the infirmary at the Alamo. Forsyth was killed during the final assault.

James W. Garrand (*ca.*1813-36) was from Louisiana and served as a private. Garrand was killed during the final assault.

James Girard Garrett (*ca.*1806-36) was from Louisiana and served as a private. Garrett was killed during the final assault.

James C. Gwynne (*ca.*1804-36) was from Mississippi and served as a private. Gwynne was assigned to the artillery and was killed in the final assault.

William B. Harrison (*ca.*1811-36) was born in Ohio. As a captain, he was the commander of the Tennessee Mounted Volunteers. Harrison was killed in the final assault.

Joseph Mark Hawkins (*ca.*1799-1836) born in Ireland, was from Louisiana and served as a private. Hawkins was killed in the final assault.

John M. Hays (*ca.*1814-36) was from Tennessee and served as a private. Hays was killed during the final assault.

William Daniel Hersee (*ca.*1805-36), born in Great Britain, was from New York and served as a sergeant. He served in the artillery. Hersee was killed during the final assault.

Samuel P. "Sam" Houston (1793-1886) had the distinction of being the only American to be governor of two states: Tennessee and Texas after it became a state in 1845. After his father died and his mother moved the family from Virginia to Tennessee, Houston went off to join the Cherokee Indians. Called "The Raven," he lived with the Indians for three years. The War of 1812 broke out between the United States and Great Britain. Houston joined the army and was wounded twice. He served for five years, achieving a lieutenancy. Back in civilian life he studied law, was an Indian agent with the Cherokees and became a lawyer. He launched a political campaign, was elected to Congress in 1823 and 1825 and governor in 1827. He was also a major general in the state militia. After a breakup with his wife, Houston resigned from the governorship and returned to the Cherokees. Because of heavy drinking, he was now known as "Big Drunk." In 1832 he was in or en route to Texas. He joined the revolutionary cause and by 1835 was leading the rebels. He held the rank of major general. On 21 April 1836, in command on 743 raw troops, he met on the banks of the San Jacinto River about 1,600 Mexicans led by Santa Anna and defeated them. The next day Santa Anna was taken prisoner. Texas' independence became reality. Houston served two terms as president of the Republic of Texas. When Texas became a state in the Union, he served as a senator.

Following this he was elected (1859) to the governorship. Houston opposed Texas joining the Confederacy and as a result was forced to leave office in March 1861.

William D. Howell (*ca.*1791-1836) was from New York and was a doctor. He served as a rifleman. Howell was killed during the final assault.

Joseph Kerr (*ca.*1814-36) was from Louisiana and served as a private. Kerr was killed during the final assault.

Nathaniel Kerr (unk.-1836) - Joseph's brother - died from a disease at the Alamo on 19 February 1836.

William Irving Lewis (*ca.*1807-36) was born in Virginia and raised in Philadelphia, Pennsylvania. He was the son of a prominent physician. Private Lewis was killed during the final assault.

William Linn (unk.-1836) was from Boston, Massachusetts, and was a member of the New Orleans Greys. Private Linn was killed during the final assault.

William T. Malone (*ca.*1818-36) was probably born in Ireland and was from Alabama. An artilleryman, private Malone was killed during the final assault.

William Marshall (*ca.*1808-36) was from Arkansas. Private Marshall was killed during the final assault.

William McDowell (*ca.*1793-1836) was from Tennessee. Private McDowell was killed during the final assault.

Willis A. Moore (*ca.*1808-36) was from Mississippi. Private Moore was killed during the final assault.

Robert Musselman (*ca.*1798-1836) was born in Ohio and was from Pennsylvania. He served in the U.S. Army and campaigned against the Seminole Indians. Sergeant Musselman was killed during the final assault.

James Clinton Neill (1790-1845) was veteran U.S. Ranger (Battle of Nerw Orleans) who joined the "Tejano" cavalry as a lieutenant colonel. On 21 December 1835 Houston asked him to take command of the Alamo. His tenure was short. He left 11 February to care of his ailment-stricken family. He returned to the Alamo three days later to settle a command dispute between Travis and Bowie. It was decided they would share command.

Edward Nelson (*ca.*1816-36) was from South Carolina. Private Nelson was killed during the final assault.

George Nelson (*ca.*1805-36) was from South Carolina. Private Nelson was killed during the final assault.

John Purdy Reynolds (*ca.*1807-36) was from Lewiston, Pennsylvania, and was a doctor by profession. He worked in the infirmary. Private Reynolds was killed during the final assault.

James Madison Rose (*ca.*1805-36), a nephew of former President James Madison, was from Arkansas. Private Rose was killed in the final assault.

Isaac Ryan (*ca.*1805-36) was from Louisiana. Private Ryan was killed in the final assault.

Cleveland Kinloch Simmons (*ca.*1806-36) was from South Carolina. Lieutenant Simmons served in the cavalry company and was killed in the final assault.

John William Smith (1792-1845), a Missourian, was one man who carried messages for Travis who survived. Early in March 1836 he was ordered to take a message to the independence convention that was meeting in Washington-on-the-Brazos. Smith slipped through enemy lines and rode over 200 miles in less than 57 hours. He thus escaped death at the Alamo. He went on to a political career, being elected the first mayor of San Antonio and later a member of the Texas Senate.

Burke Trammel (*ca.*1810-36), born in Ireland, was from Tennessee. Serving as an artilleryman, Trammel was killed in the final assault.

William Barret Travis (1809-36) was born in South Carolina but moved to Alabama. He received a good education and taught school, read law and was admitted to the bar before he was 20. He married, practiced law and published a little newspaper, the *Claiborne Herald*. He joined the state militia. In 1831 Travis left his child and pregnant wife and headed for Texas. The reason for his doing so is not known; one version has it that he killed a man who had made advances to his wife. In San Felipe, Texas, Travis worked as a lawyer. Wearing a white hat and riding a black mare, he became known as a gentleman gambler and womanizer. He joined the revolutionists and in June 1835 led a march on an army garrison. Commissioned a lieutenant colonel in the rebel cavalry, he and a group of men were sent to San Antonio to reinforce the Alamo. Travis wrote in a letter, "It [the Alamo] is the key to Texas."[9] According to Tucker, Travis committed suicide by stabbing or shooting himself.

Asa Walker (*ca.*1813-36) was born in New York. Private Walker was killed during the final assault.

QUOTATIONS:

[1] Philip Haythorthwaite, *The Alamo and the War of Texas Independence 1835-36*. London: Osprey Publishing, 1986, p. 5.

[2] Terry D. Hooker, *The Revolt in Texas Leading to It's Independence from Mexico, 1835-36*. Cottingham, England: El Dorado Books, 1993, p. 5.

[3] Haythorthwaite, *The Alamo*, p. 6.

[4] Robert L. Scheina, *Latin America's Wars*. 2 vols. Washington, D.C.: Brassey's, Inc., 2003, vol. 1, p. 159.

[5] Albert A. Nofi, *The Alamo and the Texas War for Independence*. New York: Da Capo Press, 1994, p. 113.

[6] Haythorthwaite, *The Alamo*, p. 12.

[7] José Enrique de la Peña, "Recuerda el Alamo!" *American Heritage* pp. 57-97 (October 1975) p. 94.
[8] De la Peña, "Recuerda el Alamo!" p. 95.
[9] Phillip Thomas Tucker, *Exodus from the Alamo*. Philadelphia: Casemate Publishers, 2011.
[10] Tucker, *Exodus from the Alamo*, p. 78.
[11] Tucker, *Exodus from the Alamo*, p. 80.
[12] Tucker, *Exodus from the Alamo*, p. 167.
[13] Tucker, *Exodus from the Alamo*, 4.
[14] Tucker, *Exodus from the Alamo*, p.4.
[15] Mary Deborah Petite, *1836 Facts About the Alamo*. Mason City, Iowa: Savas Publishing Company, 1999, p. 41.
[16] Petite, *1836 Facts About the Alamo*, p. 42.
[17] Petite, *1836 Facts About the Alamo*, p. 43.
[18] Petite, *1836 Facts About the Alamo*, p. 52.

Sources:

Bill Groneman, *Battlefields of Texas*. Plano, Texas: Wordware Publishing, Inc., 1998.

Richard Bruce Winders, *Crisis in the Southwest*. Wilmington, Delaware: Scholarly Resources Inc., 2002.

Robert L. Scheina, *Santa Anna A Curse upon Mexico*. Washington, D.C. Brassey's, Inc, 2002.

http:en.wikipedia.org/wiki/Antonio_L%o%pez_de-Santa_Anna.com

Remembering the Alamo at Sea

1838-44

Goal:

To help Texas maintain its independence from Mexico.

Background:

The Texas navy came into existence in early 1836. Four small warships flying the lone star flag disrupted Mexican commerce as fighting evolved on land. The Battle of San Jacinto (21 April 1836) was credited with winning Texas its independence from Mexico. That conclusion was not so evident in the late 1830s. The fighting continued on land and at sea.

At sea the results were mixed. On 17 April 1837 the Mexican brigs *Vencedor del Alamo* and *Libertador* captured the Texas navy warship *Independence*. In reprisal, the secretary of the navy, S. Rhodes Fisher, ordered the Texas warships *Brutus* and *Invincible* to attack Mexican commerce in spite of orders from Texas' new president, Sam Houston, to the contrary. With Fisher on board, the Texas warships sailed off the coast of Mexico causing mayhem. As they were returning to Galveston harbor the *Brutus* and *Invincible* were intercepted by the more powerful Mexican brigs *Iturbide* and *Libertador* and were run aground on 29 August. The Texas navy ceased to exist.

Leadership:

Who was in charge of the Texas navy? That was a contentious question. The elected president was constantly confounded by difficult appointees. First, the secretary of the navy,

Rhodes Fisher, refused to obey orders, and then the Texas navy commodore and fleet commander, Edwin Moore, was just as contentious.

Volunteers:

How many Americans served in the Texas navy is not known because it was almost impossible to distinguish between an American and a Texan - mostly, it was whatever a person claimed to be. On 23 January 1840 U.S. Secretary of State John Forsyth wrote to the Texan minister to the United States, Richard G. Dunlop, "It is not necessary for the undersigned [John Forsyth] to remind General Dunlop that extreme care is made necessary on the part of this government by the extraordinary facility with which the citizens of Texas are confound [confused] with citizens of the United States ...."[1]

Texas Commodore Edwin Moore, commanding the brig *Wharton*, took advantage of this confusion. In late 1839 he was in New York harbor openly buying weapons and recruiting by subterfuge. Historian Tom Henderson Wells wrote, "Many sailors enlisted, signing statements that they were 'sailormen hailing from Texas and calling themselves Texians' ...."[2]

Throughout much of the fighting between Texas and Mexico, New Orleans was virtually being used by the Texas navy as its home port and this is where the navy recruited many of its sailors. This port attracted freebooters from all over the world and few questions were asked as to a man's identity. Although the officers of the Texas navy were in the full-time employment of Texas, the crews were signed on for the lengths of the cruises, which typically were for a few months each.

Edwin Moore (1810-65), a U.S. Navy veteran, commanded the Texas navy in Texas' post-independence, on-and-off war with Mexico. His relations with President Sam Houston were so bad that Houston declared Moore a pirate and had him court-martialed. Acquitted, Moore unsuccessfully campaigned for money he had loaned to Texas to keep its fleet at sea and unsuccessfully tried to rejoin the U.S. Navy.

Courtesy wikimedia.org

Compensation:

Almost no one in the service of Texas was regularly paid - the navy was no exception. The lure of prize money did attract adventurers into the navy.

Opposition:

The Mexican navy led a chaotic existence. The country had been plagued by revolution after revolution since independence in 1821. It was impossible to create and sustain a navy under these conditions. The naval force that existed in 1837 was under the leadership of a few British officers on extended leave from the Royal Navy. The backbone of the fleet was two British-built side-wheel steamers, the *Guadalupe* and the *Moctezuma*.

STRATEGY:

Commodore Edwin Moore seized control of Texas' strategic decision-making and rented the financially strapped Texas fleet to the rebellious would-be nation of Yucatan in spite of opposition by the president of Texas.

OPERATIONS:

The Texas navy was re-born in 1838 when six warships were ordered constructed in the United States and others were purchased. These ships arrived in 1838 and 1839. While diplomatic missions to Mexico City failed, the Texas warships in league with rebellious Yucatecans attacked coastal cities south of Vera Cruz. These operations could not be sustained due to wear and tear and costs.

In 1842 Mexico struck back. It seized by stealth the three-ship Yucatecan navy and it purchased the two side-wheel steamers *Guadalupe* and *Moctezuma*. Each was armed with a 68-pound Paixhan pivot gun that outranged any cannon in the Texas fleet. Texas Commodore Moore sailed looking for the Mexican fleet in spite of orders from newly-elected President Sam Houston not to do so. Moore's foray was funded by the Yucatan rebels ($8,000 a month stipend) and by contributions from American and Texas businessmen. On 13 May 1843 Moore's two war sloops, the *Austin* and the *Wharton*, caught a six-ship Mexican squadron somewhat scattered along the Campeche coast north of the Yucatan. Moore unsuccessfully endeavored to prevent the steamer *Moctezuma* from rejoining the other Mexican warships. A general battle ensued. The Texans were handicapped by a lack of steam and the Mexicans were handicapped by yellow fever which ravaged their crews. The battle was inconclusive.

Both sides prepared to renew the fight. The Mexicans laid up one of their warships and distributed the men among their yellow fever-infected crews. Complicating the Mexican problem, British mercenaries fighting in their fleet quit and the Mexicans had to replace them with inexperienced soldiers. Moore borrowed a few long-range guns from his Yucatecan allies. The battle was renewed on 16 May. At first the lack of wind favored the Mexican steamers, and then the wind sprang up and the Texans held the advantage briefly. The wind then vanished. The result was another inconclusive battle.

By early June Moore learned that President Houston had declared Moore's actions to be illegal and piratical acts. The Texas warships returned to Galveston on 14 June. Moore was subjected to a protracted court-martial and exonerated. Texas and Mexico signed a truce accord on 15 February 1844.

Impact:

The Texas navy was a sad affair - almost always desperately broke. On 23 October 1842 Lieutenant D.H. Crisp wrote to Commodore Moore, "The navy appears to be *hard up*, and I think we are finished."[3] Its one saving grace was that the financial and political support for the Mexican navy was just as bad.

It is a guess as to how many Americans served in the Texas navy. The crews of the warships were small and the entire fleet was never at sea at one time. Many nationalities were represented by the sailors seeking employment in the wide-open port of New Orleans. But the number of Americans serving in the Texas navy had to be at least a few hundred.

Commodore Moore may have been a competent naval officer but he was a horrible politician. He could not accept that, right or wrong, the elected president was in charge. Texas' forays at sea between 1837 and 1844 were inconclusive but they did help to keep a weak Mexico off balance.

Biographies:

Samuel Edgerton (unk.-1840) served under Edwin Moore on board the U.S. warship *Boston*. Edgerton joined the Texas navy as Moore's steward. He died from yellow fever on board the Texan *Austin* near Tabasco.

Charles E. Hawkins (1801-37) entered the U.S. Navy. He was a midshipman in 1818 and resigned from the Navy in 1826. He accompanied David Porter to Mexico and joined its navy. Hawkins took part in the capture of Spanish merchant shipping off the coast of Cuba. By 1834 Hawkins was working on the Chattahoochee River. In the fall of 1835 he was Mexican General José Antonio Mejía's *aide-de-camp* in Mejia's unsuccessful rebellion against Antonio López de Santa Anna, then President of Mexico. Hawkins joined the Texas navy in 1836 and was given command of the *Independence*. He was promoted to commodore. Hawkins died of yellow fever in January 1837 in New Orleans while the *Independence* was being refitted.

A.C. Hinton (unk.) entered the U.S. Navy as a midshipman in 1827 and resigned from the Navy in 1833. Between April 1839 and February 1840 he was the commanding officer of the Texas war steamship *Zavala*.

Edwin Ward Moore (1810-65) was born in Alexandria, Virginia, to a well-to-do family and entered the U.S. Navy in 1825 as a midshipman. He became a passed midshipman in 1831 and a lieutenant in 1835. In April 1836 while serving in the West Indies Squadron Moore was offered the position of commander of the Texas navy by President Mirabeau Lamar. Moore attempted to recruit Americans into the Texas navy, which U.S. Secretary of State John Forsyth saw as a violation of the Neutrality Act of 1818. Moore resigned from the U.S. Navy in July 1839 before a court-martial could be convened. He joined the Texas navy with the rank of post-captain (but was addressed as commodore).

Following Moore's discharge from the Texas navy he settled in New York and unsuccessfully tried to re-enter the U.S. Navy. He married in 1849 and in 1860 went to Galveston, Texas, and was involved in the construction of a federal building. Moore did not participate in the U.S. Civil War. He died in Virginia.

James O'Shaunssey (unk.) entered the U.S. Navy as a midshipman in 1833 and resigned from the Navy in 1839. Between September and November 1840 Lieutenant O'Shaunssey commanded the Texas schooner *San Jacinto* and between January and March 1841 he commanded the Texas schooner *San Bennard*.

Quotations:

[1] William Manning, ed. *Diplomatic Correspondence of the United States. Inter-American Affairs 1831-1860*. 12 vols. Washington: Carnegie Endowment for Peace, 1939, vol. 12, p. 22.

[2] Tom Henderson Wells, *Commodore Moore and the Texas Navy*. Austin: University of Texas Press, 1960, p.21.

[3] Alex Dienst, *The Navy of the Texas Republic, 1835-1845*. Temple, Texas: n.p., 1909. http://www.archive.org/details/navyofrepublicof00dienich.

Sources:

Enríque Cardenas de la Peña, *Semblanza maritima de Mexico Independiente y revolucionario*. Dos tomos. Mexico: Secretaría de Marina, 1970.

Jim Dan Hill, *The Texas Navy*. Chicago: University of Chicago Press, 1937.

Johnathan W. Jordan, "Commodore Edwin Ward Moore." Texas Association, 2000-01.

Robert L. Scheina, *Latin America's Wars*. Two vols. Washington, D.C.: Brassey's, Inc., 2003.

Odyssey of Phil Kearny

1839-40 and 1859

Goal:

Kearny was driven to be the premiere soldier of his day.

Background:

The U.S. Army could not be pleased with its performance during the War of 1812. Although the war ended on a victory, the Battle of New Orleans, this fight was one of the few high points for the Army. It became clear that fighting European troops was clearly different than fighting Native Americans. A few American officers traveled to Europe to study and learn European tactics. Some went on their own initiative and others were sent by the U.S. government. Most prominent among these were Winfield Scott and Philip Kearny. Although of different generations, they shared many characteristics. Both possessed the safety net of family wealth, were extremely competent, and some would say extremely arrogant.

Leadership:

Phil Kearny inspired his men with his courage. He led by example. He demanded strict discipline, sometimes rewarding particularly good soldiers with cash from his own pocket. Kearny made sure his men had good food, weapons and horses. Kearny was well liked by the rank and file.

Volunteers:

Once while retaining his status in the U.S. Army, Kearny volunteered for temporary ser-

Fame—Fortune—Frustration

Phil Kearny (1814-62) was rich, educated and smart - perhaps too smart. He could not help but point out errors to his superiors when he thought they were wrong. This was not a winning trait for a junior military officer, particularly one who served as an aide to General Winfield Scott. Scott was endowed with the same attributes as Kearny. Kearny sought an outlet for his quest for military fame during brief furloughs in the French army. His battlefield successes were never enough to satisfy his ego.

Harper's Encyclopedia of United States History (New York, 1902)

vice in the French army and on a second occasion, he served in the French army after retiring from the U.S. Army. This second odyssey qualified him as a soldier of fortune if the first did not.

Compensation:

Kearny, who was personally wealthy, never fought for money. He did receive the pay of an officer in the U.S. Army but it mattered little.

Opposition:

As an American soldier Kearny fought the enemies of the United States, Mexico, Native Americans and the Confederacy. As an American soldier of fortune, Kearny fought Arabs and Austrians. The Arabs in particular were fierce opponents.

Strategy:

Kearny's specialty was the cavalry. He co-wrote the book on cavalry tactics and choose to be at the point of attack when the opportunity presented itself. He mastered his trade.

Operations:

In 1839 the secretary of war sent three promising dragoon officers to study French cavalry tactics and then write a manual about them. The French cavalry, living off its Napoleonic reputation, was perceived to be the best in the world; the U.S. Army lacked a manual on cavalry tactics. Kearny was one of the three officers selected. They sailed for France, where the U.S. ambassador greeted them, and later they met and were guests of the French king. On 8 October they arrived at the cavalry school at Saumur, about 170 miles southwest of Paris. Kearny's wealth permitted him to entertain lavishly and he made a favorable impression on his hosts.

Toward the end of 1839 an insurrection flared in the colony of Algeria against French rule. It was led by an Arab sheik, Abd el-Kader. Kearny heard that troops were to be sent to Algeria and he asked the War Department for permission to accompany them. His offer was not objected to (which Kearny interpreted as permission) and the American ambassador gave his blessing. Kearny wangled an appointment to the staff of the French commander, the duc d'Oréans, eldest son of the king. He also obtained an assignment to the *First Chasseurs d' Afrique*, probably the best cavalry regiment.

Kearny's joining the French forces was delayed by illness but on 1

May 1840 he reported to the duc in Algeria. He joined the *chasseurs* at the base of Mount Mozia on 8 May. Within a few hours after arriving, Kearny received his first combat experience. He was in the saddle, helping beat off a band of raiders. In the following days Kearny participated in a succession of fights with the Arabs. On one occasion he organized a bayonet charge by dismounted troops which dislodged a pocket of Arab resistance. A former *chasseur* recalled: "How many times I have seen him far in the advance, pursuing *les Arabes* ... sword and pistol ready ... the reins in his strong teeth .... He was *magnifique*, that Kearny ...."[1] For his service to France he was awarded the *Légion d'Honneur*. On 15 July Kearny bade farewell to his comrades and returned to the United States.

Kearny's U.S. military career had many valleys and a few peaks between 1840 and 1851 when he retired from the U.S. Army for a second time. In April 1859 war broke out between Sardinia and Austria. France was treaty-bound to Sardinia. Kearny told his second wife: "I am a soldier ... my second country - France - is in peril. What course can I pursue other than to fight for her ....?"[2] By 12 May Kearny had joined the *chasseurs* gathered with the French army in Genoa. Wearing his U.S. Dragoons uniform, Kearny participated in one of three major battles of the short conflict. He was in a successful cavalry charge to capture a fortified Austrian hill. An infantry officer who witnessed the battle recalled "... [The *chasseurs*] raced at the enemy ... but not even the fleetest could keep up with Phil Kearny, bridle in his teeth, saber flourished overhead ...."[3] Kearny was in the saddle some 17 hours, with short breaks. The French emperor personally awarded him a second *Légion d'Honneur,* the only foreigner so honored. When the U.S. Civil War began in April 1861 Kearny returned home to fight for the Union.

IMPACT:

Philip Kearny had the fortune to be born rich and the misfortune to have a dream of becoming a great military hero. This dream went unfulfilled. He was brave, inspiring, gifted at tactics and skilled as a strategist. Perhaps his greatest shortcoming was that he would not hide these attributes from less gifted military superiors.

BIOGRAPHIES:

Philip Kearny (1814-62) was born in New York City to a wealthy and prestigious family. He went to the "best" schools. His father wanted him to become a well rounded gentleman. Kearny loved to ride, so he had his own thoroughbred horses. He had a French riding instructor who was a former cavalry captain. An Italian fencing master taught him the art of dueling. A professional boxer taught him how to use his fists. He had tutors for dancing and for etiquette.

Kearny wanted a military life. His uncle was a major in the army. But Kearny's father would hear none of this. He warned his son that he would cut off his financial support if he insisted on joining the military. So Kearney studied law for four years at Columbia University, graduating with honors in June 1834. He traveled in Europe and afterward, for two years, clerked in a law office. In September 1836 Kearny's grandfather, John Watts, died. He left his grandson over $1,000,000. Kearny was now free to do with his life whatever he pleased. He joined the First U.S. Dragoons as a second lieutenant and served under his uncle. He took part in an uneventful expedition into Pawnee and Comanche territory before being sent to France to study cavalry tactics. At this time he joined French forces and fought in North Africa.

Back in the United States, Kearny became aide-de-camp of the army commander in chief, Major General Alexander Macomb. Then, after a paper-shuffling War Department job, he was appointed aide-de-camp to Macomb's successor, Major General Winfield Scott. With the two officers who had accompanied him to France, Kearny wrote a cavalry manual. He married and the Kearny home became one of Washington's top party places, and the couple was among the top party-goers.

Kearny's career in the U.S. Army never lived up to his dreams. Frustrated by the lack of fighting, he took an extended leave of absence and on 2 April 1846 retired from the Army. In less than a month the United States was at war with Mexico and Kearny was reinstated. He again found combat, fought bravely, lost his left arm, and in his opinion, was poorly rewarded for his service. He separated from his wife in September 1851 and retired again from the Army in October 1851. Kearny returned to Paris and fell in love with American Agnes Mitchell. They lived together both in the New York and Paris for a number of years before marrying. The in 1859 he again temporarily served in the French cavalry.

With the outbreak of the Civil War Kearny returned to the United States. He unsuccessfully endeavored to find an appointment in the Union Army. Instead he was accepted into the New Jersey State Militia as a brigadier general. He was shot dead by a sniper at the close of the Second Battle of Bull Run while reconnoitering the enemy.

QUOTATIONS:

[1] Irving Werstein, *Kearny the Magnificent*. New York: The John Day Company, 1962. p. 78.

[2] Werstein, *Kearny*. p. 142.

[3] Werstein, *Kearny*. p. 147.

SOURCES:

Harper's Encyclopaedia of United States History. New York: Harper & Brothers Publishers, 1902.

Stewart Sifakis, *Who Was Who in the Civil War*. New York: Facts on File, 1988.

Ezra J. Warner, *Generals in Blue*. Baton Rouge. Louisiana: Louisiana State University Press, 1964.

Webster's American Military Biographies. Springfield, Massachusetts: G. & C. Merriam Company, 1978.

Odyssey of B.S. Osbon

late 1840s or early 1850s

Goal:

B.S. Osbon explained: "I was attracted [to fight pirates] chiefly by the desire for adventure."[1]

Background:

Historian Grace Fox wrote: "Piracy was an evil well rooted in the habits of the life along the South China coast when the China trade was thrown open to the British public in 1834. Throughout the centuries the petty fishermen frequenting these waters had been alternately traders and pirates in accordance with the extent of their catch."[2]

In 1858 merchant T. Robinson Warren added: "The lion and the lamb lie down together. Under the very shadows of the fleet of men-of-war stationed here [China] for no other purpose in the world other than to exterminate the pirates, lay scores of junks, whose sole and only business in the world is to rob the weaker, though ostensibly engaged in fishing."[3]

In the late 1840s or early 1850s, Osbon joined a flotilla in Hong Kong which was funded by the British and Chinese governments to hunt down pirates. He was assigned to boat *Number 23*. The crew was composed of 20 Europeans, 12 Chinese and officered by two Englishmen.

Leadership:

Osbon's rapid rise in the anti-pirate flotilla spoke highly of his seamanship and bravery.

Volunteers:

Approximately 35 volunteers (mostly Europeans) manned a forty-foot sail- and oar-powered boat. Each craft was armed with a small howitzer and outfitted with an abundance of boarding weapons.

COMPENSATION:

For this dangerous job, the volunteers were well paid and shared in prize money. Prize money was calculated by the number of prisoners and "pig-tails" (proof of death) sent back to Hong Kong.

OPPOSITION:

Chinese pirate junks were heavily manned - typically 180 to 200 men. Osbon wrote, "The pirates were like devils, but we were all good swordsmen, and we cut them down almost as fast as we could get at them."[4]

STRATEGY:

The anti-pirate flotilla was divided into divisions; each division was made up of six boats. Each division sailed independently and was assigned a number of small junks to be used as scouts and pickets. Most fighting was done at close quarters, the objective being to capture the pirate junks by boarding.

OPERATIONS:

Osbon wrote: "My boat, *Number 23*, belonged to the 'lucky division,' and in the six months I remained with her we engaged eleven junks, which we destroyed, and five with which we had running fights but lost them, owing chiefly to fogs."[5]

While serving in the anti-pirate service Osbon rose through the ranks. The Englishman commanding *Number 23* was severely wounded and his number 2 had resigned. Osbon was given command. The *Number 23* boat soon led the attack and capture of the junk commanded by the chief pirate in those waters. In its cargo was $60,000 in specie. Osbon was ordered to Hong Kong to testify at the prize court. When he returned to the flotilla, Osbon was promoted to a division commander. The work increasingly became routine, Osbon had accumulated a significant amount of prize money and he resigned.

IMPACT:

Osbon summed up the fighting: "Such battles were short but very fierce, for the Chinaman is a good fighter and has no fear of death."[6]

As Osbon rose through the ranks he became familiar with the operations of these pirate hunters. He identified the nationalities of many of his colleagues but never once mentioned another American. Apparently he was the only one present among the pirate hunters.

Biographies:

B.S. Osbon (1827 - unk.) born in Wye, New York, was the son of an itinerant Methodist minister. Befriended by the Indians who lived in that region, he developed a love for the outdoors and a wanderlust. Not a particularly good student, Osbon began running away from home at the age of 11 years. He loved the water and found jobs on canal barges, tugboats and pilot boats. He would be caught and returned home, only to run away again. At the age of 13 years his father found him a job on packet that carried immigrants from Europe. Osbon spent a short time in the U.S. Navy, apparently most of it in New York Harbor on board the receiving ship *North Carolina*. Navy life was dull and he "resigned" and left. (His father did succeed in getting him a discharge.) In 1847 Osbon signed on the whale ship *Junior* and sailed to the Pacific and Antarctic. In the Pacific he signed on to a succession of ships, entering Hong Kong on board the U.S. merchantman *Oneco*, which a few days earlier had fought a gun battle with a Chinese pirate junk.

Following his service in the flotilla employed to hunt down pirates, Osbon remained in Hong Kong briefly and then continued his trck, arriving in Argentina in 1853. (*See* John Coe and the Blockade of Buenos Aires, 1852-53).

Quotations:

[1] Albert Bigelow Paine, *A Sailor of Fortune*. New York: McClure, Phillips & Co., 1906, p. 44.

[2] Grace Fox, *British Admirals and Chinese Pirates 1832-1869*. Westport, CT: Hyperion Press, Inc., 1973, p. 77.

[3] T. Robinson Warren. *Dust and Foam on Three Oceans and Two Continents*. New York: Charles Scribner, 1858, p. 289.

[4] Paine, *A Sailor of Fortune*, p. 47.

[5] Paine, *A Sailor of Fortune*, p. 45.

[6] Paine, *A Sailor of Fortune*, p. 46.

Sources:

A.G. Course, *Pirates of the Eastern Seas*. London: Frederick Muller Ltd., 1966.

Narciso López' Round Island Expedition

1848-49

Goal:

To separate Cuba from Spanish control.

Background:

Three competing factions vied for control of Cuba - those who sought continued Spanish control; those who wanted independence; and those who want annexation to the United States. The issue was complicated by the fact that Cuba's economy was largely based on sugar which was harvested by slave labor.

Leadership:

Narciso López, by default, became the leader of the expedition. Wealthy Cubans, who backed the expedition, courted American General William Worth, who delayed in his decision and then unexpectedly died. Next, the wealthy Cubans had hoped to entice a prominent southern American to lead it. They offered the command to Jefferson Davis and then Robert E. Lee; both declined. This left Narciso López, who had adopted Cuba as his homeland.

Volunteers:

The men who joined the expedition were mostly very recent immigrants to the United States; some cut-throats; and some veterans of the recent war with Mexico. An observer de-

Fame–Fortune–Frustration

scribed the recruits as the "most desperate looking creatures as ever were seen would murder a man for ten dollars."[1]

In addition to the volunteers, the Cuban separatists believed they could fill out their ranks with field hands. They would have little if any military training, and almost no weapons.

COMPENSATION:

Probably land-grants were offered to those in the expedition to be given upon the successful completion of the expedition.

OPPOSITION:

The pro-Spanish forces were composed of some 25,000 Spanish soldiers, mostly concentrated around Havana, and a larger number of poorly trained and poorly equipped militia. They were principally controlled by the wealthy, pro-monarchy land-owners.

STRATEGY:

The expedition would land on Cuba and rally hundreds if not thousands of Cubans, and march on Havana.

OPERATIONS:

Those wishing to separate Cuban from Spain recruited perhaps 1,300 filibusterers in New York City and they sailed in the streamers *New Orleans* and *Sea Gull* to Cat and Round Islands near Pass Christian in the Mississippi River. These men were joined on 31 July 1849 by 200 recruits from New Orleans who were carried to the islands by the steamer *Fanny*. Some sources place the total size of the force at no more than 800 men. Under orders from President Zachery Taylor, Commander Victor Randolph, USN, blockaded the islands with six warships. Early in September the isolated filibusterers surrendered to the navy. The filibusterers were transported to the mainland and freed; they were allowed to retain their weapons and after a brief time the steamers *New Orleans* and *Sea Gull* were returned to their owners.

IMPACT:

The expedition was still-born, having never sailed from the United States. Spanish authorities were pleased that the Zachery Taylor Administration aggressively enforced the 1818 Neutrality laws.

Narciso López (1798-1851) was not an American but all his filibustering schemes against Cuba were instigated in the United States and the majority of his followers were Americans. The attraction for these fighters was not López but Cuba. Southerners wanted Cuba as a slave state. Expansionists wanted Cuba because it lay on a critical trade route between the United States and South America. Businessmen wanted Cuba because it was a major producer of valuable crops of sugar.

Carlos Villanueva, *Resúmen de la historia general de América* (Paris: 1913)

Narciso López' Round Island Expedition, 1848-49

BIOGRAPHIES:

Narciso López (1798-1851) was born in Spanish Venezuela into a family of moderate wealth. During the early years of the War for Independence (1810-24), he fought for the revolutionaries and was captured. To avoid execution, he changed sides; it was common for the victor of a battle to fill out his ranks by offering amnesty to enemy soldiers. By the age of 21 years, López had become a colonel and when the royalist cause collapse in Spanish South America, he fled to Cuba and then to Spain. López fought in the first Carlist War (1834-39) for Queen Isabella rising to the rank of major general. In 1839 he was appointed governor of Valencia, Spain. López returned to Cuba in 1843 and married into a wealthy Creole family. In June 1848 Secretary of State James Buchanan warned the Spanish Minister in Washington, Angel Calderón de la Baca, that López was planning a revolt against Spanish rule. López fled the island for New Orleans.

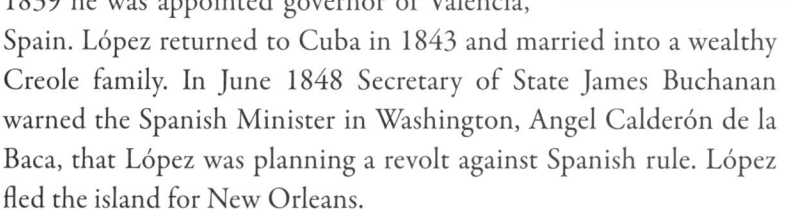

John Thomas Pickett (1823-84), born in Kentucky, was descended from a long line of military men going back to his great-grandfather, an officer in the American Revolutionary War. Pickett studied law and then was appointed a cadet at the U.S. Military Academy. He resigned from the Academy before finishing his studies and was named U.S. consul to the West Indies. He served until 1848 when he became involved with Lopez, participating in his expeditions as a lead officer with the rank of lieutenant colonel. After these adventures he resumed his diplomatic career, becoming U.S. consul in Vera Cruz, Mexico. He held this post from 1853 to 1861. With the outbreak of the U.S. Civil War he sided with the South. Initially Pickett was appointed Secretary of the American Peace Commission. Next, he became the Confederate commissioner to Mexico. In 1862 Pickett was appointed a colonel and then served as the Assistant Adjutant-General on the staff of General John C. Breckinridge. After the war he settled in Washington, D.C., and practiced law there. An attack of paralysis led to his death.

John Pickett (1823-84) was one of the many future Confederate officers who joined filibustering expeditions to Latin America during the 1850s. He came from a prominent family whose members had served in the Revolutionary War (1776-1781). Pickett briefly attended the West Point military academy but did not graduate. He held a diplomatic post in the West Indies prior to joining one of the López expeditions against Cuba.

Anderson C. Quisenberry, *Lopez's Expeditions to Cuba, 1850-1851*. (Louisville, Kentucky, 1906)

QUOTATIONS:

[1] Basil Rauch, *American Interests in Cuba 1848-1855*. New York: Columbia University Press, 1948. 114.

Sources:

Anderson C. Quisenberry, *Lopez's Expedition to Cuba - 1850-51.* Louisville, Kentucky: John P. Morton & Company, 1906.

David F. Long, *Gold Braid and Foreign Relations: Diplomatic Activities of U.S. Naval Officers 1798-1883.* Annapolis: U.S. Naval Institute Press, 1988.

Josef Opatrny, *U.S. Expansionism and Cuban Annexation in the 1850s.* Prague: Charles University, 1990.

Narciso López' Cárdenas Expedition to Cuba

1850

Goal:

Once again, to separate Cuba from Spain. Colonel Roberdeau Wheat addressed the American filibusters on board the brig *Susan Loud*, "Liberators! Behold your flag! Three cheers for the Cuban flag!"[1]

Background:

Narciso López was not a quitter. Even though his first attempt to lead a filibustering expedition to Cuba had failed, he still believed in the undertaking. He broke off relations with those who wanted to annex Cuba to the United States and placed his faith in a plan to create an independent Cuba.

In order to get past the U.S. law against filibustering, López employed the ruse that his new effort was an expedition of emigrants to California via Panama. In order not to call attention to themselves, the men would sail without their weapons. They would then land on an uninhabited island, recover their weapons, which were to be shipped separately, and train.

Leadership:

López offered command of the expedition to a southern hero of the war with Mexico (1846-48), General John Quitman, but he declined. Once again, by default, López was to head the expedition.

Thomas Hawkins (1820-79) was from a prominent family which settled in Virginia and moved on to Kentucky. He was wounded during Lopez' Cardenas expedition of 1850 when a pistol accidently discharged during a council of war on board the steamer Creole as it was being chased by the Spanish warship Pizarro. Hawkins served in the Union army during the Civil War (1861-65).

Anderson C. Quisenberry, Lopez's Expeditions to Cuba, 1850-1851. (Louisville, Kentucky, 1906)

VOLUNTEERS:

This time, many of López' 600 volunteers were veterans of the Mexican War (1846-48) and they were organized into "regiments" that bore the names of states. All were Americans except for a dozen Cubans. Some of the weapons bore the markings of the Mississippi state arsenals. The filibusters were issued red shirts, the uniform of revolution.

COMPENSATION:

The filibusters were to be paid the same as those persons serving in the U.S. Army. At the end of the first year or on the successful completion of the expedition (whichever came first), the officers were to receive a $10,000 bonus and each soldier was to receive a $4,000 bonus or its equivalent in land.

OPPOSITION:

The pro-Spanish forces on land remained numerous (see López' Round Island Expedition, 1848-49). Additionally, the Spanish navy had sent some of its new steamers to Cuban waters.

STRATEGY:

López' plan was to land his force within a few days' march to the west of Havana. Gathering Cuban volunteers along the way, he would then destroy a key bridge connecting Havana to the east, thus cutting off reinforcements. López believed that within a few weeks he would raise thousands of Cubans with which to attack and capture Havana.

OPERATIONS:

The expedition got off to a rocky start when the Kentucky regiment arrived in New Orleans on 11 April 1850 prior to its transport being ready. The leaders feared this might cause the intervention of federal authorities. Finally on 25 April the Kentucky regiment sailed on board the *Georgiana* which was soon followed by two other sail craft. The force was taken to the Island of Contoy off the coast of Yucatan. There the men were armed and trained. The force, reduced to 521 men through desertion, sailed for Cuba in the steamer *Creole*. The Spaniards had gotten word of the expedition and the warships steamer *Pizarro* (6 guns) and brigantine *Habanero* (20 guns) were on the search. They did captured two of the sail craft which were returning to New Orleans to get supplies but narrowly missed the overloaded *Creole*.

López wanted to land at Matanzas, Cuba, but he had no artillery to deal with the town's seaward defenses. So he chose to land at Cárdenas, capture the town by surprise, and then take the railroad to Matanzas. López anticipated that Cubans would flock to his banner. During the evening of 18 May the invaders disembarked at Cárdenas, about 85 miles east of Havana. A few yards from the wharf the *Creole* ran aground. The following morning Colonel John T. Pickett leading 25 men of the "Kentucky Regiment" captured the railway station. Once aroused, the town's garrison put up a stout fight for three hours. López implored the townspeople to rise up and drive the Spaniards from the island; not one Cuban volunteered! In the meantime Spanish reinforcements could be seen gathering outside of town. The filibusters beat off attacks and fled to the *Creole*. While steaming out of the harbor the steamer grounded again and lay dangerously exposed for five hours. Items, including some weapons, were thrown overboard and finally the steamer re-floated.

López wanted to try another landing but his men were dispirited and demanded the steamer sail for Key West, Florida, 90 miles to the north. The *Creole*, straining to make ten knots speed, entered the American port with the 13-knot *Pizarro* in hot pursuit. The filibusters abandoned the *Creole* and the *Pizarro* had to be satisfied with capturing the *Creole* without crew or filibusters.

IMPACT:

The filibusters sustained 14 killed and thirty wounded. López surrendered to the U.S. attorney in Savannah, Georgia, knowing he would not be indicted in that city. He was released on the grounds that there was insufficient proof that he conspired to violate the Neutrality Act of 1818. The federal government did not give up easily. In New Orleans U.S. attorney charged sixteen of the leaders of the expedition, including López, with violating the Neutrality Act of 1818. After three hung juries the government gave up.

Spain unsuccessfully endeavored to revive a proposal for a tripartite pact among France, Great Britain and the United States which would guarantee Spain's sovereignty over Cuba.

BIOGRAPHIES:

Thomas T. Hawkins' (1820-79) family was prominent in Virginia and Kentucky, dating back almost to the Jamestown Settlement. The

Colonel Theodore O'Hara, Kentucky Regiment (1820-67) fought in the Mexican War (1846-48). He was brevetted to major for gallantry at the battles of Contreras and Churubusco. During a filibustering expedition to Cuba O'Hara led the Kentucky Regiment during an attack on Cardenas. He was shot in both legs and had to be carried back to the steamer Creole. O'Hara served in the Confederate army during the U.S. Civil War (1861-65).

Anderson C. Quisenberry, Lopez's Expeditions to Cuba, 1850-1851. (Louisville, Kentucky, 1906)

family numbered several warriors. Hawkins, Pickett and O'Hara commanded the "Kentucky Regiment" which was part of Lopez's force. Hawkins received a leg wound from an accidental shot at the end of the Cardenas adventure. He served the Union during the Civil War. Holding the rank of lieutenant, he was aide-de-camp to then-Brigadier General John C. Breckinridge. When Breckinridge was promoted to major general Hawkins became a colonel. Hawkins was an expert in duelling and was consulted on this in several cases, including one in which Breckinridge was involved.

John A. Logan (unk.), a scion of a historic Kentucky family, was a captain and veteran of the Mexican War. He was wounded and died of his wounds.

John McFarland McCann (unk.) was the Episcopal chaplain of the expedition. He was killed in battle.

Theodore O'Hara (1820-67) was born in Danville, Kentucky. He graduated from St. Joseph's College, Bardstown, Kentucky, in 1839 and practiced law. He worked as a clerk in the Treasury Department in Washington, D.C. O'Hara fought in the Mexican War (1846-48) and was brevetted to major on 20 August 1847 for gallantry at the battles of Contreras and Churubusco. Before and after the war he worked on the staff of the Frankfort, Kentucky, newspaper *Yeoman*. O'Hara joined the López expedition in the winter of 1849-50 with the rank of colonel and recruited and commanded the 240-man Kentucky Regiment. He was shot in both legs while attacking the Spanish barracks at Cárdenas. He was carried back on board the *Creole* and escaped back to the United States.

After returning from the expedition O'Hara met with fellow soldier of fortune William Walker. He cooperated with him in organizing Walker's ill-fated expedition to Nicaragua. O'Hara helped found and became an editor of the Louisville, Kentucky, newspaper *Louisville Times*. Upon the outbreak of the U.S. Civil War O'Hara joined the Confederate forces. On the staff of General Albert Sidney Johnston, he held his dying chief in his arms at the Battle of Shiloh. He later joined the staff of General John C. Breckinridge and accompanied him on a long retreat to the Florida coast. O'Hara died of malaria.

William Redding (unk.), who was color sergeant, carried the "Free Flag of Cuba" in the battle and brought it back to the U.S. in tatters.

Chatham Roberdeau Wheat (1826-62), born in Maryland, his father was an Episcopal minister who changed parishes fairly frequently. Wheat, called Rob, had seven brothers and sisters. His father moved the family to New Orleans, Louisiana, and then to Nashville, Tennessee. Wheat graduated from the University of Nashville in 1845, a classmate of James Walker, the brother of William Walker. Wheat served in the Mexican War (1846-48) and fought in General Winfield Scott's campaign in the Valley of Mexico.

When Wheat attempted to join the second López expedition he was told there was no more space. So Wheat offered to charter the brig *Susan Loud* and raise his own company. He recruited heavily from the rogues of New Orleans. One hundred and thirty men joined. During the attack on Cárdenas, Wheat was wounded in the shoulder and returned to the steamer *Creole*. (*See* entry Narciso López' Bahia Honda Expedition to Cuba, 1851 for later career)

Quotations:

[1] Charles L. Dufour, *Gentle Tiger The Gallant Life of Roberdeau Wheat*. Baton Rouge: Louisiana State University Press, 1957. p. 41.

Sources:

Anderson C. Quisenberry, *López's Expeditions to Cuba 1850 and 1851*. Louisville: John P. Morton, 1906.

Basil Rauch, *American Interests in Cuba 1848-1855*. New York: Columbia University Press, 1948.

Dictionary of American Biography. 10 vols. plus sup. 1 thru 8. New York: Charles Scribner's Sons, 1936 & 1990.

Los primeros movimientos revolucionarios del general Narciso López 1848-50. Havana: Oficina del Historiador de la Ciudad de La Habana, Cuba, 1950.

Narciso López' Bahia Honda Expedition to Cuba

1851

Goal:

A third attempt to separate Cuba from Spain

Background:

With the death of Zachary Taylor on 9 July 1850 and the ascendency of Millard Fillmore to the presidency, Washington once again vigorously enforced the anti-filibustering laws. This event coincided with a third and final attempt by Narciso López to evict the Spanish from Cuba.

U.S. law enforcement stepped up its vigilance of López' activities. In April 1851 U.S. marshals seized two ships belonging to López in New York Harbor and arrested some Hungarian and Polish recruits who were on board. They were soon released after a mistrial but the seizure delayed López' plans. He was aware that revolutionaries on Cuba planned to declare independence on 4 July and he wanted to take advantage of that event.

Leadership:

The leadership of the anti-Spanish movement was fragmented. In Cuba a band of revolutionaries declared independence on 4 July and sought to place the island under the protection of the United States. In the United States, López had been elevated in the minds of most including himself as the inevitable leader of any expedition to Cuba. The famed Hungarian soldier of fortune "Major" Louis Schlesinger was his *aide-de-camp.*

Volunteers:

López rushed the assembly of his 450-man "army," most of whom were ruffians. There was a "German Regiment" and a "Hungarian Regiment," byproducts of the ill-fated European revolutions of 1848. López was forced to leave behind a "regiment" raised in Kentucky which had not arrived in time for the hurried sailing from New Orleans. Many of the filibusters were armed with condemned muskets although some carried personal side arms.

Compensation:

Since this endeavor was not as well financed as López' previous expeditions, in all probability the participants were given promises about future payment.

Opposition:

Spanish forces had not changed since López' failed earlier expedition to Cuba (see López' Cárdenas Expedition, 1850).

Strategy:

López' strategy was to join forces with the revolutionaries in Cuba and then attack the Spaniards.

Operations:

On 3 August 1851 López sailed in the overly crowded steamer *Pampero* from New Orleans. He expected to be followed by a second wave which would include the Kentucky regiment. López was unaware that the revolutionaries in Cuba had already been eliminated. He landed at Bahia Honda, fifty miles west of Havana. The choice of the site was based on misleading information planted by the Spanish Captain General that the Cubans in that region were ready to join the revolution. After landing, López sent the *Pampero* back to Key West for supplies. The Spanish warship *Pizarro* spotted the steamer and rushed to Havana to spread the alarm. Eight hundred Spanish soldiers embarked on the *Pizarro* and sailed to Bahia Honda.

At Bahia Honda López split his force. He led 323 men to Los Pozos

William Crittenden (1823-51) was one of many soldiers of fortune who came from politically elite families. He was the nephew of a Kentucky governor and of an U.S. attorney general. Crittenden was captured by Spanish authorities during López' Bahia Honda expedition of 1851 and executed.

Anderson C. Quisenberry, Lopez's Expeditions to Cuba, 1850-1851. (Louisville, Kentucky, 1906)

while "Colonel" William Crittenden assembled a baggage train and followed. The Spanish troops who had landed at Bahia Honda defeated the filibusters piecemeal. López tried to escape into the mountains but was captured on 31 August. All the filibusters were either killed or captured.

Impact:

Fifty of the filibusters, including Crittenden, were shot on 16 August following a court martial. López was garroted on 1 September. The remainder of the filibusters were imprisoned in Spain. American Southerners clamored for U.S. intervention. Some 2,000 would-be rescuers gathered at New Orleans. Historian Charles Dufour wrote, "But the police, acting quickly and effectively, dispersed the filibusters, cleared their camp, and brought to an end the fanastic Lopez adventure."[1] This excitement was drown out by the approaching Civil War. Spain again sought international help to maintain its sovereignty over Cuba but could find no nation willing to help.

Biographies:

William Logan Crittenden (1823-51), was appointed to the U.S. Military Academy from Kentucky and graduated in 1845 the "goat" (last in class) of the class. He served in the Mexican War (1846-48) and fought at the Battle of Palo Alto (8 May 1846) and the Battle of Resaca de la Palma the following day. Crittenden believed his service went unrewarded. William was the nephew of Kentucky Governor John Crittenden (1848-60). On 1 March 1849 Crittenden resigned his commission and soon joined the third López expedition. (At this time his uncle John J. Crittenden was the U.S. attorney general.) López gave William Logan Crittenden the rank of "colonel" and he commanded the Kentucky Regiment, perhaps 50 men. The entire expedition was captured in Cuba. Crittenden and some of his men were captured in four small boats while trying to escape. They were taken to Castle *Atares* in Havana. Crittenden was executed first, alone, on 16 August 1851. According to legend, when he was ordered to turn his back and kneel, he replied: "A Kentuckian kneels to none except his God, and always dies facing his enemy."[2] (numerous variations of this quotation are recorded).

Louis Schlesinger (unk.) was a veteran of Lajos Kossuth's failed 1848-49 revolutionin Hungary. With the rank of major, in April 1851 he recruited several hundred Hungarians and Poles in New York for López. They were, however, stopped by U.S. authorities and Schlesinger was arrested. While awaiting trial her went to New Orleans and sailed on the August expedition with several Hungarians. He was captured by the Spanish but escaped.

John Pragay (unk.) was another Hungarian who joined López. A general, he was a veteran of the Hungarian revolution. He was wounded and died of his wounds.

Chatham Roberdeau Wheat (1826-62) - (*see* entry Narciso López' Cárdenas Expedition to Cuba, 1850 for earlier career and William Walker's Expedition against Nicaragua, 1855-57 for later career) - was to be a member of the second wave which never sailed.

QUOTATIONS:

[1] Charles L. Dufour, *Gentle Tiger The Gallant Life of Roberdeau Wheat*. Baton Rouge: Louisiana State University Press, 1957. p. 60.

[2] John E. Kleber, *The Kentucky Encyclopedia*. Frankfort: University of Kentucky Press, 1992, p. 571.

SOURCES:

George W. Cullum, ed., *Biographical Register of the Officers and Graduates of the U.S. Military Academy*. New York: various publishers through Supplement 8, 1879-1940.

Philip S. Foner, *A History of Cuba and its Relations with the United States*. 2 vols. New York: International Publishers, 1962-63.

Anderson C. Quisenberry, *López's Expeditions to Cuba 1850 and 1851*. Louisville: John P. Morton, 1906.

Basil Rauch, *American Interests in Cuba 1848-1855*. New York: Columbia University Press, 1948.

James S. Robbins, *Custer, Pickett and the Goats of West Point*. http://lastintheirclass.com/Crittenden.html.

John Coe and the Blockade of Buenos Aires

1852-53

Goal:

To prevent the port of Buenos Aires from dominating the interior provinces by prohibiting it to collect the tariffs on all imports and exports.

Background:

Following the United Provinces' (the future Argentina) declaration of independence from Spain in 1810, the region remained in almost constant turmoil. One of many disputes was the relationship between the port Buenos Aires and the interior provinces. On 11 September 1852 the port declared its independence from the interior. As a consequence, strongman Hilario Lagos led the *gauchos* (cowboys) of the Province of Buenos Aires against the citizens in the city (the *Porteños*). Supporting Lagos was the strongman of the northwest, José Urquiza, who sent a provincial squadron to blockade Buenos Aires.

Leadership:

American Commodore John Coe was hired to command the provincial squadron and blockade the port. Cole had demonstrated leadership and bravery as a privateer during a naval war with Brazil (1825-28).

VOLUNTEERS:

Soldiers of fortune, including Americans, abounded in the region due to the decades long fighting that plagued the Río de la Plata. The ships they manned were small coastal merchantmen which had been armed with whatever could be scrounged together.

COMPENSATION:

Most of the adventurers were drawn to the fight to get rich. How much they received is unclear. A few were there for the thrill.

OPPOSITION:

Like those fighting for the provinces, the sailors fighting for the port were mostly mercenaries. Both fleets were a mismatch of converted merchant brigs and schooners.

STRATEGY:

Most of the fighting in the estuary evolved around the blockade of Buenos Aires.

OPERATIONS:

Challenges to fight were issued and accepted. On more than one occasion when the fleets met the fighting devolved into hand-to-hand combat. In one engagement nine of the 11 officers on the flagship of the provincial fleet, *El Correo* (unk. guns), were killed or seriously wounded. On 17 April 1853 Coe defeated the *Porteño* fleet and blockaded the port.

IMPACT:

The naval fighting came to an abrupt end on 20 June when Coe sold out to the *Porteños* for 26,000 ounces of gold. B.S. Osbon, who had briefly fought under Coe's leadership remembered:

> "Commodore Coe had sold out the Argentine Navy for half a million dollars, one-half of which went with him to London, while the other half I brought to New York and delivered to his wife. I got nothing but glory. The revolution was over."[1]

On 8 January 1855 the port and the interior provinces signed a peace treaty. But neither side observed the terms for very long and the trade war was renewed between the two sides.

Biographies:

John Halstead Coe (1806-64) was born in Springfield, Massachusetts. During the South American Wars for Independence, Coe served in the Chilean navy in 1824 on board the warship *Protector* (unk. guns) and took part in the siege of Callao, Peru. During the naval war between Argentine and Brazil (1825-28) he fought as a volunteer for Argentina during the Battle of Quilmes (29 July 1826). In late 1826 Coe served on board the Argentine corvette *Chacabuco* (20 guns) during its raid along the Brazilian coast. Late in the war he commanded the privateer *Niger* (11 guns). In 1841 Coe commanded the Uruguayan navy and clashed with the Argentine fleet led by Admiral William Brown on a number of occasions.

Quotations:

[1] Albert Bigelow Paine, *A Sailor of Fortune: Personal Memoirs of Captain B.S. Osbon*. New York: McClure, Phillips & Co., 1906, p. 75.

Sources:

Atlas Historico-Militar Argentino. n.p.: Colegio Militar de la Nacíon, 1970.

David F. Marley, *Wars of the Americas*. Santa Barbara, Calif.: ABC-CLIO, 1998.

William Walker's Expedition against Mexico

1853-54

Goal:
To conquer territory in northern Mexico and turn it into a U.S. protectorate at the least and U.S. territory, which permitted slavery, at the most.

Background:
Once the United States had taken Alta California from Mexico as a result of the 1846-48 war, American filibusters focused on conquering Baja California. The capital of the territory, Ensenada, lay only 80 miles from San Diego and 1,400 miles from Mexico City. And, the Mexican government was in chaos following a recent defeat.

The first filibustering attempt against Baja California and Sonora was led by John C. Morehead in 1851 but once it had crossed into Mexico the men deserted. Next came William Walker. He traveled to Guaymas in northern Mexico in an unsuccessful attempt to secure a mining concession. This was a ploy to gain entry into Mexico. Returning to San Francisco, Walker recruited a band of filibusters, raised money, and purchased arms and munitions.

Leadership:
William Walker was the unquestioned chief of the expeditions in which he participated.

William Walker (1824–60) was undoubtedly the most notorious filibuster of the 19th Century. This may be attributed to the impact he had on the national scene. He seized and controlled, for a brief period of time, the all-important Nicaragua transit route across the Isthmus of Panama. Perhaps more important, slave-holders in the South saw in his exploits a means of adding new slave territory - northern Mexico for example - to offset the growing strength of the North.

James Roche, *The Story of the Filibusterers* (New York, 1891)

VOLUNTEERS:

Walker's band was drawn from the brawling streets of San Francisco, and was undoubtedly international in composition. T. Robinson Warren described them as: "... every ruined gambler, outlaw, and used-up person in California flocking to his [Walker's] standard."[1]

COMPENSATION:

Walker was very charismatic and undoubtedly promised his followers fame and fortune.

OPPOSITION:

The struggle between Mexican Conservatives and Liberals was renewed following Mexico's defeat by the United States a few years earlier. In the remote states, at the best, the Mexicans could field only poorly trained and poorly equipped militia who on occasion formed temporary alliances with bandits and Indians.

STRATEGY:

Typical of filibuster expeditions, the strategy was to grab, hold, and declare that possession determined ownership.

OPERATIONS:

After one failed start, Walker and 45 followers sailed on board the bark *Caroline* on 16 October 1853. Flying the Mexican flag, the *Caroline* entered La Paz, on the northeast coast of the Baja California peninsula. Walker captured the port and the territorial governor. After looting the port, the filibusters made Walker "President of the Republic of Lower California." Walker declared the civil code of Louisiana (which permitted slavery) to be the law of the land. He learned that Mexican troops were on their way, and as he was withdrawing Walker was attacked by the town's people. Both sides sustained casualties.

On 29 November Walker landed at Ensenada on the west coast of Baja California. While there, the first mate of the *Caroline* seized control of the ship and sailed off, taking with him many of their weapons and much of their supplies. The intrepid Walker seized horses from local ranches and sent a little force against a small settlement at Santo

Tomás, 30 miles south of Ensenada. Forewarned, the Mexican garrison beat off the filibusters and followed them back to their camp. On 14 December Walker drove off the attacking Mexicans.

Back in California, Walker's friends recruited reinforcements. Local law enforcement was unable or unwilling to enforce the anti-filibustering laws. Some 250 more men landed at Ensenada, joining Walker, but they brought few supplies. Walker confiscated from the Mexicans what his men required, paying for it with worthless script from the "new" republic.

On 18 January 1854 Walker annexed the state of Sonora (without even having set foot in the state). Now he declared the new name for his country the "Republic of Sonora." Walker then suppressed a serious mutiny among his new recruits. A court-martial ordered two of the newcomers shot and two others publicly whipped. Walker then gave the company a choice - follow him or be sent back to the United States. Some 130 (including the original 45) chose to remain with Walker.

Walker's "army" marched south and captured Santo Tomás without a fight in mid-February. Next he captured the town of San Vicente but his army suffered from desertions. Walker reversed his line of march and headed north. His army crossed the Colorado River (then a dangerous undertaking) on rafts. Sick and starving, and harassed by Indians and Mexican bandits, the "army" shrank to a few dozen men. After holding a council of war, Walker decided to return to San Vicente in Baja California.

While re-crossing the Colorado River, Walker's "army" was attacked by Indians, whom they beat off. The Indians now kept their distance, preferring to rob the graves of the filibusters who died from their wounds. Walker arrived back at San Vicente on 17 April. The 18-man garrison he had left behind was nowhere to be found. Discouraged, Walker and his weary "army" marched toward California. Three miles short of the border, Mexican irregulars blocked the "army's" path northward but the Mexicans had no stomach for a fight with these desperate men.

On 8 May 1854 Walker and 33 followers surrendered to Major Justus McKinstry of the U.S. Army at San Diego, California. All were paroled on the pledge that they present themselves for trial in San Francisco. After eight minutes of deliberation, the jury acquitted Walker.

Impact:

Walker became an instant hero among Southern expansionists. He had demonstrated that he was brave and would act decisively. Mexico remained impotent to deal with the likes of William Walker.

Biographies:

William Walker (1824-60), born in Nashville, Tennessee, was only 5'2" tall and weighed about 120 pounds. A contemporary wrote, "To have looked at William Walker, one could scarcely have credited him to be the originator and prime mover of so desperate an enterprise as the invasion of the state of Sonora. His appearance was that of anything else than a military chieftain."[2] He became the most infamous American filibuster of the 19th Century. A child prodigy, Walker graduated at the top of his University of Nashville class at the age of about 14 years. Restless, in 1845 he traveled to Europe and moved from city to city. Returning home, Walker received a medical degree from the University of Pennsylvania. He practiced medicine briefly and then moved to New Orleans, Louisiana, to study law and work for a newspaper. Following the death of his fiancée in 1849 from cholera, Walker moved to San Francisco in mid 1854. Following his excursion into Mexico, Walker became the editor of the *Commercial Advertiser* newspaper in San Francisco.

Quotations:

[1] T. Robinson Warren, *Dust and Foam, or three Oceans and Two Continents*. New York: Charles Scribner, 1858. p. 213.

[2] Warren, *Dust and Foam*, p. 211.

Sources:

Jay Mallin and Robert K. Brown, *Merc: American Soldiers of Fortune*. New York: Macmillan Publishing Company, 1979.

Lynn I. Perrigo, *Our Spanish Southwest*. Dallas: Banks Upshaw and Company, 1960.

J. Fred Rippy, "Anglo-American Filibusterings and the Gadsden Treaty," *The Hispanic American Historical Review* 5: 2 (May 1922) 155-80.

Ron Soodalter, "A Man of Destiny," *Military History* (May 2010) pp. 42-49.

Rufus Kay, Wyllys, "The Republic of Lower California," *Pacific Historical Review* 2: 2 (1933) 194-213.

WILLIAM WALKER'S EXPEDITION AGAINST NICARAGUA

1855-57

GOAL:

To take control of Nicaragua and the transit route across Central America.

BACKGROUND:

Given mid-19th century technology, Nicaragua was the best location for a trans-isthmus crossing. Traveling up the San Juan River from the Gulf of Mexico by canoe, then across Lake Nicaragua in a shallow-draft, paddle-wheel steamer one would come within 30 miles of the Pacific Ocean. The last leg of the trek was by a stagecoach over a macadamized road from La Virgin to San Juan del Sur on the Pacific coast. The 1848 discovery of gold in California would make those who controlled this route very rich.

In 1851 Cornelius Vanderbilt formed the Accessory Transit Company which was awarded the concession for transit privileges by the Nicaraguan government. But during these decades, Nicaragua never had a stable government, so the contract was always in jeopardy. The Liberals and the Conservatives (labels with no ideological meaning) were constantly at war with one another. In 1854 the Liberals were already employing an American soldier of fortune, C.W. Doubleday, who led some 30 adventurers. The superiority of the weapons of these men - rifles - made such an impression on the Liberals that they decided to recruit 300 more adventurers armed with rifles. Byron Cole, a previous owner of the San Francisco newspaper *Commercial*

Fame–Fortune–Frustration

Like much pre-photography news art, this depiction of the 1855 Battle of Rivas between William Walker's filibusters and the Nicaraguan Liberals is based more on the imagination of the artist than historical fact. Walker's followers had no uniforms. Each man wore a red ribbon around his black "slouch" hat so that he could be distinguished from the enemy. Walker's men were typically heavily armed - a rifle, musket or shotgun - at least one pistol, and a Bowie knife. Most often they supplied their own weapons.

Frank Leslie's Illustrated Newspaper (17 May 1856)

Adventurer, convinced the Liberals that William Walker was just the man they needed.

Leadership:

Once again William Walker dominated the military operations but more subtle and influential were the financial giants who vied for the control of the isthmus. Cornelius Vanderbilt wrote to his rivals J.P. Morgan and Cornelius Garrison, "Gentlemen: You have undertaken to cheat me. I won't sue you, for the law is too slow. I'll ruin you."[1]

Volunteers:

Initially Walker was able to recruit 58 followers. But he knew that success would bring more. These filibusters armed themselves and bought all the weapons they could afford. Most carried a rifle, at least a pistol and a "Bowie" knife. They wore no uniforms in spite of contemporary illustrations depicting otherwise. They did have red ribbons around their hats; this was all that distinguished them from other well-armed travelers. Soon many more adventurers joined them.

Compensation:

Walker demanded that the Nicaraguan Liberals award him with 52,000 acres of land and that the contract should refer to his men as "colonists." This was to circumvent the provisions of the 1818 U.S. Neutrality Act. As the fighting continued, Walker demanded more.

Opposition:

Both the Nicaraguan Liberals and Conservatives could field a few hundred veteran soldiers. They were armed with worn-out muskets and not rifles; muskets that possessed inferior accuracy and range compared to the rifle. The remainder of the opposing armies were poorly trained and poorly armed militia (many forced conscripts), possessing a few ancient firearms.

Strategy:

Walker's strategy was to take control of the transit route by rapidly defeating the Conservatives. He counted on his better armed, highly motivated men. Then he would turn on the Liberals.

Operations:

On 4 May 1855 Walker's expedition sailed from San Francisco on board the leaky brig *Vesta*. Landing in Nicaragua, Walker met with the Liberal president at Leon, Nicaragua, in mid June. Walker's men were designated the *American Phalanx*. Supported by 100 Liberals, they were ordered to capture the city of Rivas (defended by 600 Conservatives) strategically located on Lake Nicaragua. Walker attacked on 28 June only to find that his Liberal allies had deserted him. Suffering six dead and 12 wounded, Walker retreated to Realejo and boarded the *Vesta*.

Following more fighting between the Liberals and Conservatives, the Liberals pleaded for Walker's return. Byron Cole, who had returned to Nicaragua, negotiated a new contract between the Liberals and Walker which gave Walker more concessions. Walker's force, which had been augmented with local volunteers, landed at San Juan del Sur, the Pacific terminus of the Accessory Transit Company's route across the isthmus. On 29 August the Conservatives fled without fighting. But on 3 September they fell upon Walker's force as it was advancing against Rivas. The fighting lasted two hours before the Conservatives fell back. Both Walker and Doubleday were wounded; the Conservatives sustained 160 casualties.

On 3 October the Accessory Transit steamer *Cortes* landed 35 volunteers and C.J. McDonald, the confidential agent of Cornelius Garrison, the San Francisco manager of the Accessory Transit Company. Walker was given possession of the company's steamer *La Virgin* on

Chatham Wheat (1826-62) was a well traveled soldier of fortune. As a "colonel" he commanded the Louisiana Regiment in López' expedition to Cardenas, Cuba, in 1850. He fought with William Walker in Nicaragua in the mid 1850s. Wheat briefly served with the Italian national hero Giuseppe Garibaldi in late 1860. Fighting for the Confederacy, he was killed during the Seven Days Battle.

Courtesy wikimedia.org

Fame–Fortune–Frustration

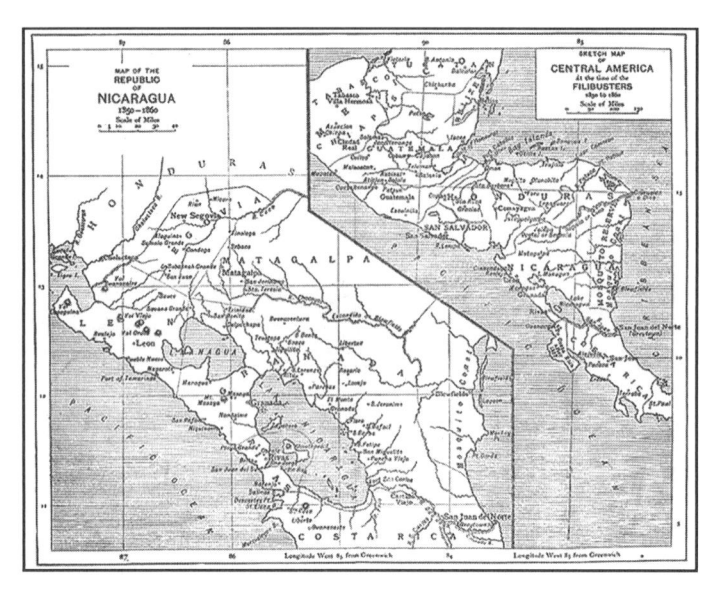

Map: Nicaragua and Central America 1850s-1860s Courtesy wikimedia.org

Lake Nicaragua. Using the steamer, Walker surprised and captured the Conservative stronghold Granada. He then orchestrated the formation of a new national government, holding the title of *Generalissimo*. McDonald immediately advanced Walker $20,000 in gold. By early 1856 Walker's filibuster force had grown to 1,200 men. Many of these men had fought in the failed European revolutions of 1848. The Accessory Transit Company carried volunteers from New York and California without charge.

Walker became entangled in a power struggle for control of the transit route across the isthmus. J.P. Morgan and Cornelius Garrison, who had backed Walker, wanted to wrestle control of the company from Cornelius Vanderbilt. They persuaded Walker to revoke the Accessory Transit Company's charter. Vanderbilt was furious.

Those opposed to Walker began to unite. On 26 February 1856 Costa Rica declared war on Nicaragua, expressly to drive out the filibusters, and Walker's Nicaragua reciprocated. Louis Schlesinger led 200 recently arrived filibusters into Costa Rica and they were defeated at *Hacienda de Santa Rosa*. Fifty filibusters were killed and those captured were executed. The Costa Ricans overran southern Nicaragua, catching Walker by surprise. He retreated to Granada. Cholera, however, broke out among the Costa Rican soldiers and they were forced to abandon the invasion. Rebounding, Walker declared himself president of Nicaragua and re-established slavery, thus winning political support among the pro-slavery element in the United States.

In the north the nations of El Salvador, Guatemala, and Honduras, together with Nicaraguan émigrés joined forces in late 1856 and attacked Granada, Walker's capital, which he successfully defended. In the south Costa Rica reentered the fight and succeeded in cutting the transit route. Walker successfully counterattacked, driving them back into Costa Rica. At this point Cornelius Vanderbilt took his revenge. He hired his own soldiers of fortune, headed by the Englishmen R.C. Webster, and sent modern Minié muskets to the Costa Ricans. In December 1856 this force captured the Fort Castillo which guarded the southeast entrance to Lake Nicaragua, thus cutting the transit line. In the north, the anti-Walker forces reassembled and drove Walker into Rivas.

In January 1857 more filibusters arrived on the Caribbean side of the isthmus. These filibusters began fighting their way through the forts along the San Juan River held by the mercenaries commanded by Webster and Costa Rican soldiers. The American filibusters advancing up the river were joined by 100 men under Colonel H.T. Titus who had bypassed the forts coming from the lake. The united filibusters attacked the major fortification, Fort Castillo, but failed to take it. Captain Marcellus French, leading 135 filibusters from Texas, traveled up the river and joined those below the fort. In spite of their increased numbers the leaders decided that without artillery it was impossible to take Fort Castillo. The officers decided, taking those who were willing, to go back down the river, cross the isthmus of Panama, and join Walker from the Pacific side. On the way down the river the boiler in their ship exploded, killing 20 men. The dejected party arrived back at Greytown and learned that they had missed the steamer to Panama. They abandoned their efforts to join Walker and sailed for New York, arriving on 29 April.

By early 1857 a stalemate had settled in. Walker controlled the Pacific terminus and Vanderbilt and his Costa Rican allies the Caribbean one. No traffic could move across the continent. Walker's force had been reduced to 500 men, half of whom were sick or wounded. On 1 May 1857 Walker surrendered to Captain Charles H. Davis, commander of the U.S. sloop *St. Marys* (20 guns). He was returned to the United States for trial.

But Walker's assault on Nicaragua was not yet over. Walker, supported by pro-slavery southerners, sailed from New Orleans on 14 November 1857. Ten days later he landed at Greytown, the Caribbean terminus of the trade route and surprised the defenders. However, the U.S. steam frigate *Wabash* (40 guns) arrived in port and its commanding officer, Commodore Hiram Paulding, arrested Walker and returned him to the United States.

Impact:

Walker's invasion fleetingly united the nations of Central America to fight this external threat. Even far-away Peru contributed money.

Walker's activities demonstrated the unlimited power of wealthy American industrialists such as Cornelius Vanderbilt and the immaturity of the political systems within Central American nations. Both realities would continue to shape the history of the isthmus for the next one hundred years.

BIOGRAPHIES:

Frank Anderson (unk.) joined Walker in January 1857 with the rank of colonel.

Timothy Crocker (unk.-1855) served with Walker during his expedition in Mexico. Crocker was one of the initial 58 filibusters to go to Nicaragua and Walker's third-in-command at the Battle of Rivas. He was killed during the attack.

George R. Davidson (unk.) served with Walker during his expedition in Mexico. Davidson joined Walker's Nicaraguan expedition in October 1855.

C.W. Doubleday (unk.) joined Walker in January 1857 with the rank of colonel.

Parker French (unk.) was a Californian apparently employed by the Nicaraguan Conservatives. He was captured in August 1855 by Walker and changed sides. Walker sent French back to California to raise money and recruits.

Charles Gilman (unk.) served with Walker during his expedition in Mexico, where he lost a leg. Gilman joined Walker's Nicaraguan expedition in October 1855.

Charles Frederick Henningsen (1815-77) was probably born in Belgium and became a British citizen in 1830 when his parents immigrated to England. He fought in the Spanish First Carlist War (1834-39) where he was knighted. In 1845 Henningsen fought against the Russians in the Caucus Mountains. Next, he distinguished himself fighting the Austrians for the Hungarians at Comorn. He married the niece of Georgia Senator John Berrien. In October 1856 Henningsen joined Walker's expedition. He brought with him $30,000 worth of stores, arms, and munitions. Walker appointed him brigadier general and Henningsen served until the collapse of the expedition. Following his fighting in Nicaragua, he served in the Confederate army between 1861 and 1862 without distinction. Henningsen was an accomplished author writing history, poetry, and military strategy.

Achilles Kewen (unk.-1855) served in at least one of Narciso López' expeditions during his failed attempts to conquer Cuba. Kewen was one of the initial 58 filibusters to go to Nicaragua and was Walker's second-in-command at the Battle of Rivas. He was killed during the attack.

S.A. Lockridge (unk.), awarded the rank of colonel, in late 1856 he was sent to New Orleans where he recruited some 200 men. They were intercepted at Puntas Arenas at the mouth of the San Juan River by the British gunboat *Cossack* and 20 British subjects were persuaded to give up the adventure.

Peter Alexander Selkirk McGlashan (1831-1908), born in Edinburgh, Scotland, came to California at the time of the gold rush. He served in Walker's expedition to Nicaragua. McGlashan entered the Confederate army in 1862. He claimed to have risen to the rank of brigadier general. Since Confederate records are incomplete this can not be confirmed.

Thomas Alfred Smyth (1832-65), born in Ireland, immigrated with his family and settled in Philadelphia, Pennsylvania. He served in Walker's expedition to Nicaragua. Smyth served in the Union army during the Civil War and fought in the Irish brigade, attaining the rank of brigadier general. He holds the distinction of being the last Union general killed in the war.

H.T. Titus (unk.), from Kansas, earned the rank of coronel.

Robert Tyler (ca. 1833-65), apparently born in Baltimore, Maryland, he served in Walker's expedition to Nicaragua, possibly as a first lieutenant. During the Civil War he served in the Confederate army. Tyler was wounded at Shiloh and again at Chickamauga. He was promoted to brigadier general in 1863 and killed at Fort Tyler on 16 April 1865.

Chatham Roberdeau Wheat (1826-62) had served in a Narciso López' expeditions to Cuba. Wheat sailed to join Walker in late 1856 bringing 40 recruits. He and those with him were unable to fight their way through and abandoned the effort. Wheat fought briefly for Giuseppe Garibaldi between October and November 1860. During the U.S. Civil War Wheat fought for the Confederacy and took part in the Shenandoah Valley campaign. He was killed during the Seven Days Battle.

QUOTATIONS:

[1] David F. Long, *Gold Braid and Foreign Relations*. Annapolis: U.S. Naval Institute Press, 1988, p. 129.

SOURCES:

Dictionary of American Biography. 10 vols. plus sup. 1 thru 8. New York: Charles Scribner's Sons, 1936 & 1990.

Ricardo Fernández Guardia, *Cartilla Histórica de Costa Rica*. 6th ed. San José: Librería é Imprenta Lehmann, 1933.

William Oscar Scroggs, "William Walker and the Steamship Corporation of Nicaragua," *The American Historical Review* 10: 4 (July 1905) 792-811.

Stewart Sifakis. *Who was Who in the Civil War*. New York: Facts on File Publications, 1988.

William Walker, *The War in Nicaragua*. Tucson: The University of Arizona Press, 1985.

Henry Crabb's Expedition against Mexico

1857

Goal:
To conquer the state of Sonora, Mexico, and declare it independent.

Background:
The Mexican government remained in chaos. Although the longtime opportunist Antonio López de Santa Anna had served his eleventh and last term as Mexico's president, the bitter struggle between the Liberals and Conservatives continued as did the vulnerability of Mexico's northern frontier to exploitation by American adventurers.

Apparently Henry Crabb was asked by the prominent Ainza family of Sonora, Mexico, into which he had married, to recruit a force in California and come to the family's aid. The family was engaged in a local feud and was losing.

Leadership:
Henry Crabb was a brash, self-confident individual but lacked innate military skills and training.

Volunteers:
Crabb had promised his in-laws that he would raise 1,000 men and come to their rescue. He succeeded, however, in convincing only 55 adventurers to sail with him from California.

COMPENSATION:

Exactly what was promised to the volunteers is not known. Surely, the adventurers had to be inspired by the tales circulating in San Francisco of William Walker's successes in Nicaragua.

OPPOSITION:

Although the Mexican army was only marginally better than the one that existed when William Walker invaded in 1854, the nation's cleansing itself of Antonio López de Santa Anna provided a new spirit of nationalism which could be summed up by saying, Mexican territory is no longer for sale.

STRATEGY:

In order to circumvent the 1818 U.S. Anti-Filibustering Act, Crabb called his expedition the Gadsden Colonization Company. Beyond that, Crabb's strategy was the classic grab, hold, and declare that possession determined ownership.

OPERATIONS:

On 22 January 1857 Crabb and 55 followers sailed from San Francisco, California, on board the steamer *Sea Bird* and landed a short distance from San Pedro. As it marched southeast the party was joined by other adventurers but also suffered from desertions. Crabb crossed the U.S.-Mexico border near the town of Sonoyta, Sonora. In order to speed his march he ordered his wagons containing most of his ammunition and protected by 20 men to follow as best they could and he proceeded ahead with 68 followers. Crabb and nine others entered Sonoyta on 21 March and purchased food; he also learned that a Mexican force was being assembled to challenge him.

Crabb proceeded south to the village of Caborca. On 1 April his force was strung-out as it entered the village. Two hundred Mexicans attacked from ambush; they were soon reinforced by 600 more. The filibusters fought their way into the village and held out for six days, surrendering on 6 April. The Mexicans had lost 35 killed and 18 wounded and Crabb's casualties were ten dead and seriously wounded. The next day 59 Americans were executed. The only individual spared was a fourteen-year-old boy. A Mexican patrol captured Crabb's supply train and another patrol crossed into Arizona, where it killed four individuals.

IMPACT:

Both the United States and Mexico accused the other of violating its sovereignty. In 1857, however, both had more serious domestic issues to deal with in spite of the advice offered by the U.S. Minister to Mexico, John Forsyth, to President James Buchanan in April 1857:

> "You want Sonora? The American blood spilled near its line would justify you seizing it.... Say to Mexico ... give us what we ask for in return for the manifest benefits we propose to confer upon you for it, or we will take it."[1]

Biographies:

Henry A. Crabb (1827-57) began practicing law in 1845 in Vicksburg, Mississippi. He killed a man in a duel during the election campaign of 1848. Crabb traveled to California and worked as a lawyer, holding a state political office. He was a defense witness during the 1854 filibustering trial of William Walker. In 1855 he unsuccessfully ran for a U.S. Senate seat as a member of the "Know-Nothing" Party.

Quotations:

[1] Philip S. Klein, *President James Buchanan - A Biography*. University Park: The Pennsylvania University Press, 1962, p. 322.

Sources:

Hubert Howe Bancroft, *History of the Northern Mexican States and Texas*. 2 vols. San Francisco: The History Company, 1889.

David F. Marley, *Wars of the Americas*. Santa Barbara, California: ABC-CLIO, 1998.

Rufus Kay Wyllys, "Henry A. Crabb - A Tragedy of the Sonora Frontier," *Pacific Historical Review* vol. 9; no. 2 (Jun 1940) 183-94.

William Walker's Expedition against Honduras

1860

Goal:

To take control of the transit route across the isthmus.

Background:

A turf dispute between Honduras and Great Britain provided Walker with an excuse to return to Central America. In May 1860 Great Britain agreed to restore the Bay Islands to Honduras. An inhabitant of the islands, which lay just off the coast of Honduras, wrote to Walker asking him to prevent their transfer from Great Britain to Honduras.

Leadership:

Although Walker had been run out of Nicaragua, his reputation as a leader among extreme southern expansionists had been enhanced.

Volunteers:

Walker was supported by perhaps one hundred or so adventurers but these did not include many of his intrepid "officers" from the forays into Mexico and Nicaragua.

Compensation:

These filibusters undoubtedly succumbed to Walker's usual promises of fame and fortune.

Opposition:

Although the Honduran army was a rag-tag affair, it had been one of the mainstays against Walker during his Nicaraguan escapades.

Strategy:

Walker had no real interest in the Bay Islands but saw this as an opportunity to re-insert himself in the struggle for control the transit across the isthmus.

Operations:

Walker's "army" sailed from New Orleans throughout April and May 1860 on board coastal sail craft. One ship, the *Clifton,* was turned back after a British inspection at Belize. It contained most of the supplies and munitions. Walker arrived off the Bay Islands on board the *Taylor* but hesitated to act since his scattered force had not yet reassembled. His force waited on the uninhabited island of Ruatan, enduring the worst of the rainy season. Finally he turned his attention to the Honduran mainland and seized fortress Trujillo, losing six men killed and a dozen wounded. Walker, however, took the funds in the custom house. These had been pledged by the Honduran government to the British to pay debts to their citizens. Within a few days Commander Norvell Salmon of the British steam war sloop *Icarus* (11 guns) arrived and told Walker he must withdraw. He did so, fleeing along the east coast, all the while being harassed by the Hondurans. Walker was twice wounded. Finally, on 5 September Walker surrendered to Salmon. When he discovered that Salmon was going to surrender him to the Hondurans, Walker wrote, "I hereby protest before the civilized world that when I surrendered … [it] was expressly made in so many words to him, as a representative of Her Britannic Majesty."[1] But Walker's fate was sealed. He was executed by firing squad on 12 September 1860. The surviving fifty filibusters were turned over to the U.S. Navy and returned to the United States.

Impact:

Walker's adventure in Honduras was anti-climatic. By 1860 the United States was no longer focused on the isthmus and Walker's legacy had already been established.

Biographies

Thomas Henry (unk.-1860) served under Walker in Nicaragua. He was wounded numerous times and was constantly involved in brawls and dueling. He served as Walker's aide during the Honduras campaign. Henry was severely wounded while intoxicated after the capture of Trujillo and died.

Quotations:

[1] Laurence Greene, *The Filibuster*. New York: The Bobbs-Merrill Company, 1937. p. 325

Sources:

Hubert Howe Bancroft, *History of Central America*. 3 vols. San Francisco: The History Company Publishers, 1887.

David F. Long, *Gold Braid and Foreign Relations: Diplomatic Activities of U.S. Naval Officers 1798-1883*. Annapolis: U.S. Naval Institute Press, 1988.

Frederick T. Ward and the Taiping Rebellion

1860-64

Goal:

There were three important interests. For the Taiping rebels the goal was to oust China's well-entrenched imperial regime. The goal of the Qing Dynasty was to remain in power in the face of a rebellion which spread across the southern parts of the country. The goal of the wealthy merchants of Shanghai was to preserve the flow of silks, satins, and teas from the interior. This could best be accomplished by supporting the Qing Dynasty.

Background:

Hong Hsiu-ch'uan (1814-64) was a Christian convert, who, having had visions, maintained that he was the younger brother of Jesus Christ. Hong established a sect which followed his beliefs. By 1850 he had between 10,000 and 30,000 followers. The authorities were alarmed at the growth in the size of the sect and ordered the members to disperse. A local force was sent to attack them when they refused. The imperial troops were routed and a deputy magistrate killed. A full-scale attack was launched by government forces in January 1851. Hong's followers emerged victorious and beheaded the Manchu commander of the government army. On 11 January 1851 Hong declared the founding of the "Heavenly Kingdom of Transcendent Peace" with its capital at Nanjing. Hong launched a rebellion against the ruling Manchu-led Qing Dynasty which grew into widespread civil war in southern China. It became known as the Taiping Rebellion.

Frederick T. Ward and the Taiping Rebellion, 1860-64

LEADERSHIP:

Frederick Townsend Ward's previous military experience plus an ability to empathize with the Chinese led to his selection by Shanghai merchants in the spring of 1960 to head a force of foreign nationals that was organized to defend the city against encroaching rebel Taiping forces. The generals of the Chinese army were directly accountable to the imperial court and Emperor Xianfeng (1838-61), a Mongolian. The Taiping rebels were led in spirit and sometimes in person by Hong Hsiu-ch'uan, although an amateur, he exhibited innate military skills.

VOLUNTEERS:

Ward scoured the wharves of Shanghai for every Westerner, sober or otherwise, capable of firing a weapon. Among them were drifters, deserters and discharged seamen. With this, the "Shanghai Foreign Arms Corps" was born. By June 1860 Ward had a contingent of 100 Westerners, trained in the use of rifles and Colt revolvers.

COMPENSATION:

Historian Robert Douglas wrote, "It was arranged by the wealthy Chinese merchants of the [patriotic] association that this auxiliary force [of foreign mercenaries] should under any circumstance receive a certain fixed rate of pay, and that their stipends should be liberally supplement by rewards in return for every city or stronghold they might take."[1] This attracted a small but steady stream of Western volunteers. In addition to motivation, good pay helped prevent looting, which Ward saw as an occurrence that turned people against the soldiers.

OPPOSITION:

One to three million Taiping rebels were arrayed against three to five million imperial troops. The rebels had one advantage: many of them were volunteers fighting for a cause. On the government's side the soldiers were partially, possibly entirely, made up of conscripts. Some of the officers were not military but rather Confucian scholars.

STRATEGY:

Ward endeavored to offset the numerical inferiority of his force by giving it superior firepower and Western training. All sides employed traditional land warfare tactics.

Frederick Ward (1831-62) was born in Salem, Massachusetts, into a seafaring family. A rebellious youth, his father secured him a position as a second mate on board the clipper ship Hamilton. Ward served in one of William Walker's expeditions and was in the French army during the Crimean War where he was dismissed for insubordination. Ward found his niche in China. There he commanded mostly foreign mercenaries whose numbers probably included other Americans. Their names have been lost in history.

Courtesy of: wikimedia.org

Operations:

In June 1860 the Foreign Arms Corps went into action alongside Imperial forces probing Taiping advances. They recaptured two towns the rebels had taken. They were then forced by circumstance (and the urging of their Shanghai backers) to assault the Taiping-occupied and fortified city of Sung-Chiang without artillery - a near-impossible task. The attack failed, sending the defeated force back to Shanghai. By mid-July, however, Ward had recruited additional Westerners and over 80 Filipino "Manilamen," and he had purchased several artillery pieces. Once again his forces assaulted Sung-Chiang. They were successful, but at a heavy cost. Out of a force of roughly 250 men, 62 were killed and 100 were wounded, including Ward himself.

On 2 August Ward led the Foreign Arms Corps against Chingpu, next town from Sung-Chiang on the approaches to Shanghai. As the Corps stormed the garrison walls, Taiping forces lying in ambush delivered a withering barrage of close-range musket fire. Within ten minutes Ward's men had suffered 50% casualties, and Ward himself was shot in the left jaw, with an exit wound in the right cheek, scarring him and leaving him with a speech impediment. The injury would plague him the rest of his life. Ward also lost his artillery and stores at the battle. The force retreated and Ward returned to Shanghai for medical treatment and to recruit more forces and buy additional artillery. Within several days he and the remnants of the Foreign Arms Corps again laid siege to Chingpu and bombarded it with artillery. This time, however, the Taiping dispatched a large force to break the siege, sending the Foreign Arms Corps fleeing back to the Sung-Chiang area. With Ward absent, receiving medical treatment, his second-in-command, Henry Andres Burgevine, held the Corps together. Ward left Shanghai (apparently secretly) in late 1860 for further treatment of his facial wound. The remnants of the Corps remained under the command of Burgevine.

Initially the British supported Ward. They feared that a Taiping victory would end their profitable opium and other trade with China. Ward now set about organizing a new military unit. A big difference, however, was that this force would be composed mainly not of foreigners but of local Chinese. At first, the British opposed to the creation of a Western-style Chinese-manned army and they arrested Ward in May 1861. Claiming to be a naturalized Chinese citizen, Ward avoided a trial and escaped from the British warship on which he was being detained. The British changed their minds and Ward continued with his plan. He used the more reliable elements of the Corps as a nucleus. While Ward recuperated, training of the new force was in the hands of Burgevine, who probably helped develop the concept of a Chinese-composed contingent. At some point Ward returned to command.

The recruits were trained in Western small arms, gunnery, tactics, customs, drill and ceremonies. Care was taken to instruct the Chinese to hold their fire until the targets were within effective range. Chinese had faith in the intimidating power of noise. The men were outfitted in Western-style utility uniforms, color-coded for branch of arms (infantry or artillery), with Indian Sepoy-style turbans. This garb earned them the nickname "Imitation Foreign Devils." In January 1862 Ward felt that his unit was ready, with about 1,000 trained Chinese soldiers. This was just in time to help repulse a massive rebel attack on the city. A week later Ward's forces struck at the city of Guangfulin, occupied by 20,000 Taiping troops. Ward, at the head of 500 men, attacked the city without artillery support. The defenders, seeing the strange attire and military skill of their own countrymen, wavered and fled.

Other victories followed, often against entrenched, numerically superior rebel forces. Ward, always leading his troops, suffered more wounds, including the loss of a finger to a musket ball. By March 1862 the contingent would be officially named by the Qing government, "Ever Victorious Army." Ward himself would be made first a fourth-rank, and then a third-rank, mandarin, high honors from a Manchu court. He was also given the rank of brigadier general. By September the Ever Victorious Army numbered more than 5,000 men, organized in four battalions and an artillery corps, with several riverboats used to transport and mobile artillery.

Ward's army won 11 victories in a four-month period, clearing a 30-mile zone around Shanghai. On 21 September 1862 Ward was mortally wounded at the Battle of Tzeki. He lived for a day, expiring the next morning.

Impact:

The conflict would continue for another two years. The dynasty won and was preserved - for less than 50 years. Before the war was over about 20 million people had died, mainly civilians. An estimated 50,000 imperial and 75,000 rebel soldiers had died. The Taiping Rebellion was one of the deadliest military conflicts in history.

During the rebellion, Karl Marx predicted it would "throw the spark into the overloaded mine of the present industrial system."[2] In the 20th Century, Sun Yat-sen, founder of the Chinese Nationalist Party, looked on the rebellion as an inspiration. The Chinese Communist leader Mao Zedong glorified the Taiping rebels as early heroic revolutionaries who fought against a corrupt feudal system.

In the military sphere, having a well-trained, well-armed contingent within the ranks undoubtedly was a factor in the eventual victory of the Qing regime, both through the unit's success and its serving as an example to other army units.

BIOGRAPHIES:

Henry Andrea Burgevine (1836-65) was the child of a French officer who had served under Napoleon Bonaparte and who eventually moved to Chapel Hill, North Carolina, where he became an instructor in French at the University of North Carolina at Chapel Hill. It is possible that Henry was born there. His father died in a brawl in South Carolina. Burgevine then lived with his grandparents and sister in Ashford, North Carolina. At the age of seven he moved to Washington, D.C., with his mother and became a congressional and later a senatorial page until 1853.

After traveling in India, Hawaii and Australia, Burgevine returned to Washington. He then traveled to Europe and enlisted in the French army for the duration of the Crimean War, where he was decorated for bravery. It was probably during this period that Burgevine became acquainted with Frederick Ward. At some point Burgevine sailed to China and in the early stages of the Taiping Rebellion he sided with the Qing army. Later, he became deputy commander of the contingents set up by Ward.

Burgevine succeeded to command of the Ever Victorious Army after Ward's death. Burgevine's elevation to command was apparently against Ward's wishes, who wanted his loyal Filipino subordinate Macanaya to succeed him. The imperial Chinese court selected Burgevine instead but he showed little initiative. In January 1863 the payment for the Foreign Arms Corps became overdue. Burgevine led an armed guard to the house of the paymaster in Shanghai and took 40,000 *taels* by force. The governor of the province immediately dismissed Burgevine.

As a consequence, Burgevine enlisted 100 disaffected followers and joined the rebels at Soochow. He became dissatisfied there as well and offered to change sides again, which he did in the middle of a battle. The imperial troops delivered Burgevine to the U.S. consul in Shanghai where he was charged with treason. He was released on the condition that he leave China. Breaking his promise, he again attempted to join the rebels. He was again arrested by imperial forces. In 1865 he drowned along with ten Qing police at Xiamen Sea. Some historians believe Burgevine was murdered on orders from vengeful officials angered at his shifting loyalties.

Frederick Townsend Ward (1831-62) was born in Salem, Massachusetts, a sailor's town. As a youth he was home-schooled. Between 1846 and 1848 he attended Norwich University in Norwich, Vermont, where he received some military training. Ward was a rebellious youth, so his seafaring father found him a position as second mate on the *Hamilton*, a clipper ship commanded by a family friend. He was overly officious and was thrown overboard by angry crewmen who complained that he gave too many orders for a youth. For the next few years he trod the decks as a sailor or first mate of several vessels, including a trader barque and a clipper ship. His sea days were interrupted by stints as a mercenary with one of William Walker's expeditions, as a soldier in the French army during the Crimean War (1854 - dismissed for insubordination), and possibly as a mercenary with rebel chieftain Benito Juárez in Mexico (1858). During his filibustering and Crimean periods Ward gained military skills. He learned about weapons, tactics, siege techniques and how to use riflemen in mobile platoons rather than fixed firing lines.

Ward also had a business side. In 1854 he went into the scrap metal business in Mexico, The venture failed and Ward returned to the United States. In 1859 he worked as a clerk in his father's shipping agency in New York City. Ward had sailed off to China previously, and now his father sent him and his brother Harry on a trade trip to Shanghai. Ward's interests were not solely business-related. He became executive officer on board the *Confucius*, an armed pirate-suppression river steamer. Ward married the daughter of a leading Shanghai Chinese merchant, Chang Mei; they had no children. Whether Ward came up with the idea of a military unit composed of volunteer foreigners, he was the ideal person to lead such a unit. He was selected by merchants and government officials to organize and command a foreign contingent to help defend Shanghai against advancing Taiping rebel forces.

In the years ahead Ward successively set up two military contingents, led his troops in battle, won victories, and survived 14 battlefield injuries. He typically went into battle armed only with a riding crop or cane - a leadership-style later adopted by his successor as the leader of the Ever Victorious Army once removed, British soldier Charles George "Chinese" Gordon. On 21 September 1862 Ward was mortally wounded while attacking the walled city of Tzeki. He was shot in the abdomen. One version was that he was wounded when at the base of the city wall. Ward lingered for a day expiring on the morning of 22 September. He died at the height of his fame as an officer and leader. Ward was honored with a magnificent state funeral at Sung-Chiang. Prior to his death Ward offered 10,000 *taels* to the Union government to help finance the U.S. Civil War. He left behind $75,000 after two years of soldiering.

Quotations:

[1] Robert K. Douglas, *China*, vol. 6 of *The History of Nations*, edited by Henry Cabot Lodge. New York: P.F. Collier & Son Company, 1928, p. 195.

[2] John Pomfret, "A Chinese uprising that rattled the world," *The Washington Post* (29 April 2012), p. B7.

Sources:

Dictionary of American Biography. 10 vols. plus sup. 1 thru 8. New York: Charles Scribner's Sons, 1936 & 1990.

Wikipedia, The Free Encyclopedia. *Frederick Townsend Ward*. 12 July 2013. Electronic Encyclopedia. 18 July 2013. <http://en.wikipedia.org/wiki/Frederick_Townsend_Ward>.

R. Ernest Dupuy and Trevor N. Dupuy. *The Harper Encyclopedia of Military History*. 4th edition. New York: HarperCollins Publishers, 1993.

Benito Juárez' American Legion of Honor

1865-67

Goal:

To evict Maximilian from Mexico.

Background:

In 1864 Austrian Archduke Maximilian seized control of Mexico with the help of the French Army. With the ending of the U.S. Civil War, the United States told Napoleon III, the Emperor of France, it was time for his army to leave. On 28 December 1865 E. George Squier, a former American diplomat to Central America and head of the citizens' Monroe Doctrine Committee, threatened, "If the old-world minions on our continent remain, We'll take up the old familiar guns, and go with Grant again."[1] The French departure left Maximilian to his own resources, but against mounting odds, he chose to remain and fight.

Leadership:

Benito Juárez, President of Mexico, sent Colonel George M. Green, an American in his employment, to California to recruit veteran field officers and purchase munitions. In June 1865 he recruited twenty-seven former Union officers in Los Angeles. This group of Civil War veterans formed the nucleus of what became known as the American Legion of Honor. Green commanded the group.

Fame–Fortune–Frustration

Lew Wallace (1827-1905) is best remembered as the author of Ben Hur; A Tale of the Christ. Serving in the Union army, in 1864 General Wallace delayed Confederate General Jubal Early's advance on Washington, probably saving the capital from capture. Wallace was the president of the court-martial that convicted Henry Wirz, commandant of the Confederate prison at Andersonville, Georgia. Following the Civil War, apparently Wallace was secretly a major general in the Mexican army and purchased arms and equipment for Benito Juarez.

James D. McCabe, Pictorial History of the United States (Philadelphia, 1877)

Volunteers:

Even before the U.S. Civil War had ended, American adventurers were clamoring to throw Maximilian and his French supporters out of Mexico. In June 1864 members a citizens' group called the Defenders of the Monroe Doctrine tried to sail from New Orleans, Louisiana, to Mexico but were stopped by troops commanded by Union General N.P. Banks. He seized three ships, $15,000 in green backs, and detained a dozen U.S. citizens. A year later, in June 1865 Union Colonel John Sobieski did organize a group of veterans at New Orleans which joined the Mexican army. American enthusiasm to join the fight continued. In California four hundred American volunteers aboard two ships were stopped by U.S. customs officers in May 1865.

Union General Philip Sheridan estimated that 2,000 former Confederates joined the Mexican Imperialists and Matías Romero, the Mexican minister to the United States, reported that approximately 3,000 former Union soldiers fought for the Mexican republicans. Most of these soldiers were scattered throughout the respective armies. An exception was the American Legion of Honor. The legion was armed with Henry repeating rifles, colt pistols, and was well mounted.

In addition to the American volunteers, the Mexican republicans loyal to Benito Juárez possessed an army of regulars and a large militia. Many of these individuals had been hardened by years of fighting. The republican army that besieged Querétaro in 1867 was 25,000 men strong. Following the conclusion of the American Civil War (1861-1865) large quantities of weapons and munitions were stacked on the U.S. side of the border and the Mexican republicans invited to take them.

Compensation:

The former American soldiers fighting for Juárez were to receive regular military pay, which was commensurate with their pay in the Union Army, plus between $1,000 and $2,000 worth of land depending on their rank. Since the republican government planned to confiscate the land belonging to the imperialists, the republicans, if victorious, should be in possession of much valuable land. Also land awarded to the republican soldiers and any improvements was to be exempt from taxes for five years. Those who distinguished themselves were promised more.

Opposition:

By the time the former American soldiers entered the fight, the French Army was withdrawing from Mexico; for the most part, it was permitted to go in peace. This left Maximilian with well-armed foreign mercenaries, mostly Austrians, Belgiums, some former Confederates, and Mexican imperialists. The imperialists besieged at Querétaro numbered about 10,000 men.

Strategy:

The Mexican authorities employed the American Legion as shock troops and sent it to the place of greatest need.

Operations:

On 15 June 1866 the original twenty-seven members of the legion traveled from San Francisco, California, to San Pedro by sea then overland to El Paso del Norte (today Ciudad Juárez, Mexico) by horseback, losing two men en route. They arrived on 15 September a few days too late to catch President Benito Juárez. Riding on to Chihuahua, they caught up with Juárez and were joined by Major George William McNulty and thirteen more discharged American soldiers.

Also in June 1866 Mexican General Placido Vega, who had been sent to California to raise American volunteers, sailed with forty Americans and thirty Mexican officers from San Francisco on board the bark *Keoka* and the brig *Josephine* to Baja California. Among the volunteers was Colonel Daniel E. Hungerford. En route ten Americans, including Colonel John B. Urmy and Lieutenant Colonel Albert Hahn, deserted. Finally arriving in Chihuahua, the Americans were organized into a single unit and Juárez called them the American Legion of Honor. A few weeks before Vega arrived in Chihuahua with his contingent of Americans, former Union General Lewis (a.k.a.Lew) Wallace arrived to meet with Juárez. Wallace was secretly a major general in the Mexican army who purchase arms and equipment for Juárez. The legion rode to Parral where they joined the central division of the Mexican army commanded by General Anastasio Arranda.

In January 1867 the American Legion commanded by Green fought at the Battle of Zacatecas where they took part in a fierce counter-attack. As the republican army retreated Colonel George Earl Church, a correspondent for the New York *Herald*, gave his fleet horse to President Juárez expediting his escape. The legion held the defile of Bufa permitting the republican army to escape destruction.

The American Legion, which grew to more than one hundred members, fought in numerous engagements leading up to the siege of

Querétaro. There, an incident occurred that undermined the Mexican confidence in the loyalty of the Legion. The American wife of Prince Felix Salm-Salm of Prussia requested permission to pass through the Mexican lines to join her husband, a supporter of Maximilian. A Mexican general refused the request but it was granted by the American commander of the Legion. After an unsuccessful attempt to break the siege, Maximilian surrendered on 17 May 1867.

The American Legion learned that the U. S. government had requested that Mexico spare the life of Maximilian; the Mexican government refused. Apparently, some in the legion then plotted to abduct Maximilian at night and spirit him by horseback to Matamoras and then across the Rio Grande into Texas. However, the morning of the planned abduction and without previous notice, the Legion was ordered to Mexico City, which was still in the hands of the imperialists. Apparently, General Mariano Escobedo was suspicious of the Legion's intention. The Legion was compelled to abandon the rescue plan. In June 1867 the legion joined the republican army besieging Mexico City which fell after a brief fight.

Legion members became increasingly frustrated by the constant delay in compensation and finally accepted $300 in silver as total payment.

Impact:

It is difficult to measure how important the American Legion was to the Mexican republicans' victory over the imperialists. The Legion was few in number - never more than a hundred or so fighting on battlefields where tens of thousands were engaged. On the other hand, one can point to the Legion's critical role at the Battle of Zacatecas. Considering that less than twenty years before the Legion's formation, Mexico had lost more than one-third of its territory to the United States, it is understandable that Mexican historians would be reluctant to "give the devil his due."

Biographies:

George M. Green (1836-unk.) was born in New Brunswick, New Jersey. He migrated to California in 1852 apparently with six of his brothers who became influential in California and Mexico. Green worked as a photographer in Mexico, and joined the Mexican Army in 1858. A relative, Francis L. Green, was an early member of the Legion of Honor.

Daniel E. Hungerford (unk.) fought in the U.S. War against Mexico (1846-48) and was a regimental commander in the Army of the Potomac.

Harvey Lake (unk.) served as a colonel in the California militia and a captain in the U.S. Army. He was teaching tactics at the San Francisco Armory when he joined the legion.

George William McNulty (unk.) was born in Madison County, New York, he was commissioned a captain in the Union army. He was brevetted to major in the Mexican auxiliary army.

Lewis (a.k.a.Lew) Wallace (1827-1905) was born in Brookville, Indiana. He was self-educated, adventurous, and highly motivated. He served in the War with Mexico (1846-48) as a second lieutenant in the 1st Indiana Infantry but was not involved in any serious fighting. Wallace served in the Union army with distinction during the Civil War (1861-65). Wallace had a falling out with General Henry Halleck and was twice removed from command. The first time he was restored by President Lincoln and the second by General Grant. In 1863 he saved Cincinnati, Ohio, from capture by General Edmund Kirby Smith. On 9 July 1864 he delayed General Jubal Early's advance on Washington, D.C., probably saving the capital from capture. Wallace served on the court that tried the Lincoln assassins and was the president of the court that convicted Henry Wirz, commandant of the Confederate prison at Andersonville, Georgia.

Following his adventure in Mexico, Wallace served by appointment as governor of New Mexico (1878-81) and then as minister to Turkey (1881-85). He was an accomplished author, his best-known work being *Ben Hur; A Tale of the Christ*.

QUOTATIONS:

[1] Fred Harvey Harrington, *Fighting Politician, Major General N.P. Banks.* (Philadelphia: University of Pennsylvania Press, 1948, p.193.

SOURCES:

W.A. Cornwell, "Maximilian and the American Legion," *Overland Monthly,* vol. 7 (November 1871) pp. 445-48.

Dictionary of American Biography. 10 vols. plus sup. 1 thru 8. New York: Charles Scribner's Sons, 1936 & 1990.

Robert Ryal Miller, "The American Legion of Honor in Mexcio," *Pacific Historical Review,* vol. 30, No. 3 (August 1961) pp. 229-41.

Ex-Confederates Fighting for Maximilian

1865-66

Goal:

To escape from the United States and to help Maximilian retain his throne in Mexico.

Background:

Ex-Confederates were running away from one disaster into another. Maximilian was a pathetic figure. He had convinced himself that those conservative Mexicans who supported his regime represented the desires of the Mexican people. The United States had taken no action against this clear violation of its self-proclaimed Monroe Doctrine during its Civil War. This doctrine stated Europe should not meddle in the Americas (and the United States would not meddle in Europe). With the defeat of the Confederacy, the United States made it clear to Maximilian's benefactor, Napoleon III, that it was time for France to get out of Mexico. Maximilian lived under the delusion that he and his conservative Mexicans could militarily defeat the republican Mexicans led by Benito Juárez.

Leadership:

Napoleon III of France and Mexican republican Benito Juárez made the critical political decisions for their respective sides. Each possessed competent generals who orchestrated their respective military strategies. Mercenaries did their bidding. Maximilian von Hapsburg was a helpless pawn in the game.

One unique player was General Joseph Shelby. He was elected by members of his former

Ex-Confederates Fighting for Maximilian, 1865-66

Confederate command to guide them and others who attached themselves to his party to Mexico City. Shelby was more like Moses (seeking the promised land) than like Gustavus Adolphus of Sweden, who led a mercenary army).

VOLUNTEERS:

Mexico was flooded by mercenaries during this conservative-liberal struggle. Few, however, were Americans. Over 5,000 had come from Austria (Emperor Maximilian's homeland) and some 2,000 from Belgium (Empress Carlota's homeland). Near the close of the U.S. Civil War Benito Juárez had recruited his American Legion of Honor (*see separate entry*), perhaps a few hundred Americans, mostly Unionists. With the defeat of the South thousands of ex-Confederates crossed into Mexico to escape a Yankee-dominated United States. With the exception of 600 Missourians led by General Shelby, they did not come in an orchestrated movement but more like every man for himself. Some were escaping to elsewhere, some were would-be colonists, a few sought employment in the conservative army and even fewer offered to fight with the republicans. Maximilian was afraid of angering the United States by providing a haven for large-numbers of ex-Confederates. He did, however, employ a few ex-Confederates who possessed special skills.

COMPENSATION:

Those ex-Confederates who fought probably received promises and little else.

OPPOSITION:

For the few ex-Confederates who fought for Maximilian the enemy was the republican army and the large number of sometime-irregulars and sometime-bandits, the later being the more ruthless.

STRATEGY:

Apparently none of the ex-Confederates fighting for Maximilian held significant commands. Their task was to follow orders.

OPERATIONS:

The military contributions by ex-Confederates in Mexico were mostly individual affairs lost to history. The exception to this was General Shelby's following, some 600 individuals, which trekked from the Texas border to Mexico City. Miracously, this band made the

Joseph Shelby (1830-97) led some 600 ex-Confederates in crossing the Rio Grande into Mexico in 1865. He offered their military services to the would-be emperor of Mexico, Maximilian. Maximilian turned down the offer perceiving political problems with the United States if he accepted. Apparently, as his military situation became more desperate, Maximilian changed his mind. By then, however, Shelby saw Maximilian's struggle as a lost cause and returned to the United States.

Courtesy of: wikimedia.org

1,200- mile trip without fighting a major engagement with either the imperialists or the republicans even though Shelby told the republicans that he intended to offer his services to Maximilian. Most of his following remained attached to Shelby by the time he reached Mexico City. Author George Creel wrote concerning an interview with Maximilian and Carlota, "Shelby laid down a plan to recruit forty thousand Americans against the time when the French soldiers would be withdrawn."[1] Not interested, the emperor made it clear to Shelby that he and his men were welcome as colonists but not as a military unit. Many of the senior officers with Shelby were offered civil positions but not military ones. So Shelby disbanded his following. Shelby's men scattered to the winds and a few fought for the imperial army. About 50 of Shelby's followers joined a French regiment, the Third Zouaves.

Maximilian's struggle to retain control of Mexico started to fall apart. By January 1867 the French army, and most of the European mercenaries, began to retreat to Vera Cruz for maritime evacuation, which was completed in March. According to author Creel, Maximilian sent for Shelby and asked "if it was possible to rally his countrymen." Shelby replied it was, "too late.... It was no longer a throne to be saved ...."[2] Maximilian retreated to Querétaro, some 170 miles north northwest of Mexico City. On 14 May his forces planned a desperate attempt to break the siege of Querétaro but this effort was postponed. That night Maximilian was betrayed by Colonel Miguel López who allowed the republican army through the trenches he commanded. Maximilian was captured on 15 May. He was executed by firing squad on 19 June 1867.

Impact:

Historian René Chartrand's conclusion: "They [ex-Confederates] did not form distinct units and their influence on the Imperial army was negligible."[3]

It seems highly unlikely that General Shelby could have made a difference in the outcome. If as author George Creel concluded that in 1866 Shelby tried to tantalize the emperor by suggesting he could raise 40,000 men to fight in Mexico, there is little doubt the U. S. government would have prevented this from happening. By 1867 even Shelby knew this was no more than a pipe dream.

Many prominent ex-Confederates either worked for or with the Maximilian government. These included Congressman A.H. Conrow, Major General John Bankhead Magruder, Commodore Matthew Fountaine Maury, Major General Mosby Monroe Parsons, Missouri

Governor Thomas Reynolds, Brigadier General Walter Husted Stevens, and Brigadier General Alexander Watkins Terrell. But they were not soldiers of fortune - they did not put their lives at risk on the battlefield. Their activity has left the mistaken impression that militarily ex-Confederates played a major role in the struggle between Mexican republicans and imperialists between 1865 and 1867.

BIOGRAPHIES:

Joseph Orville Shelby (1830-97), born in Lexington, Kentucky, educated at Transylvania University. A businessman, Shelby made a fortune manufacturing rope. He led a band of pro-slavery Kentuckians during the Missouri-Kansas border war of the 1850s. Joining the Confederacy, Shelby spent most of the war years west of the Mississippi River. He attained the rank of brigadier general. Without being paroled, Shelby and some 600 followers crossed the Rio Grande and trekked from the border to Mexico City only to have their services turned down by Maximilian. Shelby returned to Missouri following the death of Maximilian. Initially turning down political appointments, Shelby accepted the position of U.S. marshal for the Western District in 1893.

QUOTATIONS:

[1] George Creel, *Rebel at Large Recollections of Fifty Crowded Years* (New York: G.P. Putnam's Sons, 1947), 31.

[2] Creel, *Rebel at Large,* p. 34.

[3] René Chartrand, *The Mexican Adventure 1861-67.* Men-at Arms Series. London: Osprey, 1994, p. 38.

SOURCES:

Andrew Rolle, *The Lost Cause.* Norman, OK: University of Oklahoma Press, 1965.

Seaton Schroeder, *The Fall of Maximilian's Empire.* New York: G.P. Putnam's Sons, 1887.

Stewart Sifakis, *Who Was Who in the Civil War.* New York: Facts on File Publications, 1988.

Ezra J. Warner, *Generals in Grey.* Baton Rouge, LA: Louisiana State University Press, 1959.

Odyssey of John Tucker

1865-67

Goal:

To modernize the Peruvian navy so that it could face its foes.

Background:

Beginning in the early 1860s Spain was displaying aggressiveness in deep South America which indicated it was hoping to restore the empire that had been nearly destroyed by the Latin American independence wars. Among other actions Spain seized guano-rich (the world's primary source of agricultural fertilizer) Peruvian islands, and in another incident a Spanish warship caused a row in a Chilean port.

Leadership:

Faced with national rivalries, Chile and Peru decided to seek a foreign commander for their combined fleet. Civilian representatives of the Peruvian government talked with U.S. officials and ex-Confederates in Washington. John Randolph Tucker, a former Confederate officer who was in Virginia at the time, was brought to Washington. He was interviewed and offered the job which he accepted. As part of the deal, he named three former Confederate naval officers to be his staff. One was unable to go; the other two - Walter Randolph Butt and David Porter McCorkle - accompanied Tucker to Peru.

Volunteers:

Tucker had little with which to work. Chile had started to evolve a naval tradition during its

War for Independence (1810-24), but by the 1860s its navy had gone to pot. Chile's "fleet" was composed of a corvette and an armed transport. The Peruvian navy was only marginally better. Peru possessed two ageing frigates. Peru's naval officer corps was bloated (it included two rear admirals and 26 captains). All four of these warships were in bad condition and had poorly trained crews. Also there were squabbles in the fleet. The Chileans complained that their Peruvian allies ate and drank too much.

COMPENSATION:

In the Peruvian navy Tucker was paid the equivalent of the U.S. Navy compensation for an officer of his rank: $5,000 annually. The three naval officers were given enlistment bonuses: $1,250 for Tucker, $700 for McCorkle and $468.655 for Butt.

OPPOSITION:

Spain remained a significant naval power in spite of crushing defeats in the Napoleonic War (1800-15). In the 1860s Spain had dispatched a sizable "scientific" expedition to the west coast of South America. The squadron was built around a new, large ironclad, the *Numancia*. Also typically present were five frigates and smaller warships. The squadron, however, was at a disadvantage due to the great distance to a friendly port. Should the Chilean-Peruvian squadron ever get to sea, Spain was aware of the vulnerability of its commerce between the homeland and the Antilles.

STRATEGY:

Peru planned an offensive against Spain. The newly independent nations of Latin America had talked about the need to drive the Spanish out of Cuba since 1826.

OPERATIONS:

Chile declared war on Spain in September 1865 but Peru delayed until January 1866. This was to permit the two new ironclads building in Europe - the *Húascar* and the *Independencia* - to sail from England and France respectively and not be embargoed because Peru was at war. Bolivia and Ecuador were also part of the alliance against Spain but militarily could contribute little. Complicating the alliance were historical antagonisms. Peru was Chile's and Ecuador's chief political protagonist and Bolivia, Chile and Peru all coveted the nitrate-rich

John Tucker (1812-83) was born in Alexandria, Virginia. His father, a merchantship captain, got him a naval appointment. Once the Civil War broke out, Tucker resigned from the U.S. Navy and joined the Virginia state navy and later the Confederate navy. Following the defeat of the South, Tucker was hired by Peru, which at the time was at war with Spain. Tucker's assignment - to command the Peruvian navy in the fight against Spain - proved impossible due to his confrontations with resentful Peruvian naval officers.

Courtesy of: wikimedia.org

Atacama Desert. All these nations had serious border disputes. Chile was more stable politically than any of its three allies.

Tucker and his two-man staff arrived in Callao, Peru, on 15 June 1866. The looming appointment of a foreigner to a top command position had caused heated dissention within the Peruvian navy's officer corps. The matter was not settled until the Peruvian president ordered 39 officers into custody. Tucker was appointed the Peruvian navy chief on 23 July with the rank of *contra almirante* (rear admiral). On 13 August he was named second chief of the combined armada. The resignation the next day of the chief made him commander of the fleet.

Tucker inspected ships and found them in poor condition (the *Húascar* and *Independencia* had not yet arrived). A program of rehabilitation began but shortages of materials and limited drydock facilities slowed progress. While repairs were under way, Tucker trained his seamen for combat; working on sails, drilling with boats, practicing with the big guns and small arms. He appointed a board to prepare a code of naval regulations, a system of signals, an ordnance manual, and a handbook of fleet tactics for steam warships. And he proposed the reestablishment of a former naval academy.

Tucker also worked to overcome the prejudices between his ex-Confederates and the Peruvians. One of his staffers said that "much diplomacy" was needed to avoid "offending their sensitivity and pride."[1] This was to no avail. Events began to work against Tucker. The plans for the offensive against Spain were cancelled. A row developed over Tucker's alleged discourtesy to a visiting U.S. Navy officer. A motion was introduced in the Peruvian congress against the appointment of Tucker (the motion was sent to committee). The officers who had been arrested when Tucker assumed command were acquitted after being court-martialed and restored to duty.

Tucker apparently resigned twice; this was not accepted. Then, however, a third resignation was formally accepted by Peru's President Mariano Ignacio Prado when, on 3 April 1867, he formally met with Tucker and his two ex-Confederate staffers. Prado thanked them for their "very important services to Peru and America."[2]

Impact:

Tucker failed to achieve his assigned goal - to go on the offensive against Spain. His task was made nearly impossible by Peruvian naval officers. They were jealous of having a foreigner named commander of the navy. Also complicating his task was the animosity between the Chileans and Peruvians.

Biographies:

Walter Raleigh Butt (1839-85) was appointed an acting midshipman on 20 September 1855, midshipman on 9 June 1859, and passed midshipman on 31 August 1861. He was dismissed from the U.S. Navy on 5 October 1861 and joined the Confederate Navy. He commanded one of the gun crews on board the ironclad *Virginia* during its historic battle with the USS *Monitor*.

James F. Clark (unk.) a "presbyter," was apparently the Protestant chaplain on the Peruvian flagship *Independencia*. Crewed by a few hundred men, this would suggest that a significant number of the crew were American ex-patriots or Europeans. The *Independencia* had recently traveled from Europe to Peru.

David Porter McCorkle (ca. 1822-unk.) entered the U.S. Navy on 21 September 1841 and after graduating from the new U.S. Naval Academy was made a passed midshipman on 10 August 1847. He became a lieutenant on 15 September 1855 and was dismissed from the service on 17 May 1861. He entered the Confederate Navy and among other duties fitted the *Patrick Henry* with her armament.

John Randolph Tucker (1812-83) was born in Alexandria, Virginia. His father was a merchant sea captain who was a successful businessman, owning ships, warehouses and a store. Young Tucker loved the sea and typical of the day, received his training on the job. On 1 June 1826 he was appointed an acting midshipman in the U.S. Navy. He encountered a contretemps when he and five other midshipmen were court-martialled in Europe for non-payment of debts. The court found that the charge against Tucker was "not proved" but found him guilty of "unbecoming conduct."[3] He was publicly rebuked. The case would damage his career for years. He returned to the United States in the spring of 1831 and was assigned to a receiving ship (used for recruitment and as a barracks) in New York. He studied at a naval school in Baltimore, and upon passing an exam he was warranted a "passed midshipman" (10 June 1833). Tucker served in the South Atlantic for three years. He was commissioned a lieutenant on 6 April 1838 and then served in the Caribbean and off the East Coast of the United States in the Home Squadron. He commanded the sloop *St. Louis* in the Far East, landing sailors at Whampoa, China, to protect U.S. property and carrying those threatened by a Maori tribal uprising in New Zealand to safety. During the War with Mexico (1846-48) Tucker served as the executive officer (and commander when the captain became ill) on board the bomb brig (ship fitted with a 10-inch bombardment mortar) *Stromboli*. From 1849 until 1855 he served onboard the flagships in the Home and Mediterranean Squadrons. He was promoted to commander on 8 October 1855. In January 1858 his wife on 20 years, Virginia, died after the birth of their ninth child. In April 1859 Tucker was appointed to a board to investigate mismanagement at the various Navy yards. In May 1860 he was named ordnance officer at Norfolk.

Tucker resigned from the U.S. Navy and joined the Virginia State Navy, which was absorbed into the Confederate Navy. With the rank of commander he supervised the conversion into a warship of a sidewheel steamer, the *Yorktown*. Rechristened the *Patrick Henry*, Tucker assumed command. On 25 August 1862 he was transferred to command the armored ram *Chicora* in Charleston Harbor. In March 1863 Tucker was appointed "flag officer, commanding afloat" of Confederate ships in Charleston. During the summer of 1864, with many Charleston troops having been sent to the Virginia battlegrounds, the army in the city asked Tucker for assistance. Tucker organized about 150 of his sailors into the Charleston Naval Battalion. The battalion performed infantry duties until the fall of the city on 18 February 1864. Tucker's ships were put to the torch. Tucker and 350 sailors and marines participated in the fighting at Drewry's Bluff in an attempt to protect Richmond, Virginia. Tucker and his men joined the Confederate retreat from Richmond and surrendered along with Lee's army.

Tucker was a prisoner until 24 July 1865 when he took an oath of loyalty to the United States and the Constitution. In the civilian world there were not many jobs available for former Confederate naval officers. In the spring of 1866 Tucker accepted a position as an agent in Raleigh, North Carolina, of the Southern Express Company. And then came the proposal from the Peruvian Navy in 1866.

After resigning from the Peruvian navy in 1867, Tucker accepted the presidency of the Comisión Hidrográfica del Amazonas, officially established in May 1867. As head of the Hydrographic Commission, Tucker received the annual equivalent of $3,200. The commission's responsibilities were to explore the Amazonian system and draw hydrographic charts. In June Tucker and a party of nine, including his two former staffers, sailed for Peru. Once there they set up a base at Iquitos, some 2,000 miles up the Amazon. Tucker surveyed the river, made astronomical observations and began the construction of a fort on the Brazilian border, all the while dealing with hostile Indians, local politicians, jealous naval officers, swarms of mosquitoes and a smallpox outbreak in his staff. By the end of April 1874 the commissioned had completed drafting most of its maps. With the permission of the Peruvian government, Tucker traveled to New York to find a printer. At the time Peru was suffering a severe financial crisis. In January 1877 the minister of war and marine informed Tucker that no further funds were available and the commission was officially terminated. Numerous efforts to obtain back pay failed. The maps, which had been deposited in the Peruvian consulate in New York, vanished; later some reappeared. Tucker unsuccessfully tried to join Turkey in a war it was having with Russia. He died in Petersburg, Virginia, on 12 June 1883.

Quotations:

[1] David P. Werlich, *Admiral of the Amazon*. Charlottesville, Virginia: University of Virginia Press, 1990). p. 108.
[2] Werlich, *Admiral of the Amazon,* p. 133.
[3] Werlich, *Admiral of the Amazon*, p. 5.

Sources:

Hermenegildo Franco Castañón, *Los Apostaderos y Estaciones Navales Españoles en Ultramar.* Bazán: E.N. Bazán C.M., S.A., 1998.

Robert L. Scheina, *Latin America's Wars*. 2 vols. Washington, D.C.: Brassey's, Inc., 2003.

Stewart Sifakis, *Who Was Who in the Civil War*. New York: Facts on File Publications, 1988.

Webster's American Military Biographies. Springfield, Massachusetts: G. & C. Merriam Company, 1978.

http://en.wikipedia.org/wikiJogn_Randolph_Tucker

Union Balloonists during the War of the Triple Alliance

1867-68

Goal:
To help the Brazilian army find a path through Paraguayan defenses.

Background:
The War of the Triple Alliance began in late 1864 without a declaration and was caused primarily by the megalomania of the Paraguayan dictator Francisco Solano López. Although the war was Argentine, Brazil and Uruguay against Paraguay, by mid-1866 Brazil was doing most of the fighting and dying for the allies.

Beginning in 1865 the allies slowly fought their way up the Paraguay River toward the capital of Paraguay, Asunción, until they reached a double bend in the river, where the Paraguayans had built a powerful fortification called Humaitá. To the west across the river lay a dense *selva* (forest). The allies tried to outflank Humaitá to the east. There, the way was blocked by an extensive system of trenches known as the "Lines of Rojas." This had been designed for López by a British engineer, George Thompson. Numerous assaults against the trenches failed and cost the attackers thousands of lives. By late 1866 the allies fell into inactivity due to a shortage of manpower and political problems at home.

In 1867 Professor Thaddeus Lowe, who had won the attention of the Brazilian emperor due to his balloon operation during the U.S. Civil War, received a letter from the imperial government of Brazil. The emperor's representative offered Lowe a commission in the Brazilian army to create a balloon corps to serve in the war with Paraguay. Lowe declined the offer. He, instead, recommended two former assistants, brothers James and Ezra Allen. Lowe offered to manufacture the balloons and necessary supporting equipment. The two brothers accepted the Brazilian offer.

Leadership:

Francisco Solano López succeeded his father as "president for life of Paraguay" in 1862. Unfortunately for his small, backward country he perceived himself to be the "Napoleon of South America." Brazil was led by Emperor Pedro II, who chose competent field commanders. The presidents of Argentina and Uruguay held their offices due to their competence on the battlefield. They were, however, frequently distracted from the war by uprisings at home.

Volunteers:

The Brazilians sought out veterans who possessed unique skills and experiences. The U.S. Civil War had fathered many innovations, one of which was observation balloons.

Compensation:

Balloonist Thaddeus Lowe, who declined the task, was offered $180 per month in gold and expenses. It is reasonable to assume that James Allen was offered this amount and his brother Ezra a lesser sum. Lowe wrote in his unpublished memoirs: "To do them [the Allen brothers] justice, I do not think the pecuniary inducement played nearly so great a part in the decision to accept, as the novelty of the expedition."[1] James, the elder, received the rank of captain of engineers, and Ezra the rank of assistant aeronaut. Apparently, each brother was advanced $500.

Opposition:

The Paraguayans fired on the balloons but only presented a threat at low altitudes during ascents and descents. The real danger came from the possible malfunction of the equipment.

Strategy:

Brazil believed that victory could only be achieved by the capture of the Paraguayan capital, Asunción, and the elimination of López. To accomplish this, Brazil needed to find a route through the Paraguayan defenses. By mid-1866 the offensive capabilities of the Paraguayan army had been largely spent. In practical terms (not necessarily in the mind of Francisco Solano López), Paraguay's only hope of success lay in defense.

Operations:

Slowly the allies regained their strength as fresh troops arrived. A major shortcoming for the allies remained the lack of knowledge of the terrain. The two balloonists arrived in Brazil in March 1867. Due to a shipping error the iron filings, zinc and sulfuric acid necessary to manufacture the propellant hydrogen gas did not arrive with the equipment. James Allen with the help of the commander of the army, Marques de Caxias, scrounged materials together and improvised solutions. As recommended by Lowe, the Allens were outfitted with two balloons - the large one could accommodate six to eight persons and the small one, two persons. The first ascent occurred on 24 June. Allen accompanied by an engineer from the Argentine army and a Paraguayan dissident ascended more than 270 feet and remained aloft for two hours. There before them stretched the Paraguayan defenses, permitting them to see a way through. A proud Ezra Allen reported back to their mentor S.C. Lowe: "We have made some ten or a dozen of the finest ascensions that we ever made, and what we cannot say of the U.S. Army, it is appreciated by all concerned. "[2] (The Union army in fact gave up on the use of balloons before the Civil War ended.)

Aided by their new intelligence, on 22 July 1867, the allies waded through swamps and cut their way through thick underbrush. They were able to work around the Lines of Rojas and surround Humaitá. The fortification held out until 2 March 1868. Its fall spelled the doom of the capital and López' regime.

Impact:

It is difficult to measure the importance of the balloonists' contribution - most soldiers of fortune are tasked to destroy or capture something, a more measurable feat. Intelligence was gathered from numerous sources concerning Lines of Rojas, including through *mangrulhos,* (observation towers), scouting forays and spies. According to author F. Stansbury Haydon: "It was stated in several contemporary newspapers the Emperor Dom Pedro was so pleased with James Allen's work that he presented the aeronaut with a bonus of $10,000 in gold at the close of his operations with the army."[3] Although frequently promised bonuses upon the successful completion of their work, rarely are soldiers of fortune ever paid. The emperor's payment attests to the success of the balloon operation.

Biographies:

Ezra S. Allen (unk.) like his brother James, resided in Providence, Rhode Island. He served with his brother during the U.S. Civil War.

James Allen (unk.) unsuccessfully attempted to introduce balloons into the Union Army in April 1861 and failed due to the inferiority of his equipment. In 1862 during the Peninsula Campaign he and his brother joined the Union balloon corps organized and headed by Thaddeus Lowe. When Lowe resigned in May 1863, Allen and Ezra remained until the corps was disbanded in April.

Quotations:

[1] F. Stansbury Haydon, "Documents Related to the First Military Balloon Corps Organized in South America: The Aeronautic Corps of the Brazilian Army, 1867-68." *Hispanic American Historical Review.* vol. 19, no. 4, pp. 504-17 (November 1939) p. 505.

[2] Haydon, "Documents," p. 515.

[3] Haydon, "Documents," p. 505.

Sources:

Thomas B. Allen and Roger MacBride Allen. *Mr. Lincoln's High-Tech War*. Washington, DC: National Geographic, 2009.

The Army in Brazilian History. 3 vols. Rio de Janeiro: Biblioteca so Exército, 1998.

Javier Romero Muñoz, "The Guerra Grande: The War of the Triple Alliance, 1865-1870." *Strategy & Tactics* no. 245 (August/September 2007) 6-15.

Robert L. Scheina, *Latin America's Wars*. 2 vols. Washington, D.C.: Brassey's, Inc., 2003.

American Fenian Expedition to Canada

1866-70

Goal:

To free Ireland from English control.

Background:

The Irish Revolutionary Brotherhood (IRB) was established on St, Patrick's Day in 1858. Its American counterpart, the Fenian Brotherhood, was organized by Michael Doheny and John O'Mahony in the early 1860s. Initially these were secret societies, but the Catholic Church was opposed to all secret societies and the Fenians gave way to ecclesiastical pressure. The Fenians went to the other extreme, holding public meetings and creating an imitation American government complete with a president, senate and house of delegates.

The deep-seated anger of the Irish-Americans toward the English boiled over during the late 1850s. In 1859 Irish-born Colonel Michael Corcoran refused to call out the Irish-dominated 69th Militia Regiment of New York for a parade honoring the visiting Prince of Wales. In 1863 a Fenian congress in Chicago, Illinois, declared that the purpose of the movement was freedom for Ireland. In 1865 John O'Mahony, speaking at the Fenian convention at Cincinnati, Ohio, proclaimed: "[t]his Brotherhood is virtually at war with the oligarchy Great Britain ...."[1] The U.S. Civil War (1861-65) raised the social, economic and political stature of Irish-Americans, many of whom fought in the Union and Confederate armies.

The United States government was sympathetic to the Fenian cause. This was fueled by three factors. The United States perceived Great Britain to be its greatest rival in the Western Hemisphere. The United States was chaffing over the clandestine help the British gave to the Confederacy. And, the Irish vote was becoming increasingly influential, particularly in New York and Boston. In October 1865 a Fenian convention in New York City called for the invasion of Canada. The Fenians were permitted to buy surplus guns and ammunition from American arsenals, drill publicly, and openly recruit men in New York, Chicago and elsewhere. The green Fenian flag - with a harp and sunburst - flew over Tammany Hall in New York, the headquarters of New York's Democrat Party. It was used by the Fenians as a recruiting center.

LEADERSHIP:

Many individuals vied for the leadership of the Fenian movement in the United States. As its military campaigns waned new leaders seized the moment.

VOLUNTEERS:

At least 5,000 men in the United States answered the Fenian call to take up arms. It is impossible to know how many of these Fenians were American citizens. First, you would need to know how many were born in the United States. The answer to this is probably only a few. Second, you would need to know how many Irish-born Fenians in the United States were immigrants as opposed to emigrants. Of these immigrants you would need to know how many believed they earned American citizenship by fighting for the Union. Those fighting for the Confederacy add yet another level of complexity as related to American citizenship.

A Canadian farmer, Thomas Newbiggin, described the Ferian army camped in his fields: "There was no uniform dress, and except for some United States Army uniforms which were worn, and some peculiar green jackets, there was nothing to distinguish them from an ordinary gathering of about one thousand men. Some were older men and several others youths not exceeding fifteen years of age."[2]

COMPENSATION:

Given the difficulties the Fenians had raising money, it is doubtful that most of the volunteers received much more than promises.

Thomas Sweeny (1820-92) was born in Ireland. While serving in the U.S. Army he fought against the Mexicans (1846-48 - losing an arm), against the Indians (1850s) and against the Confederacy (1861-65). The American-Irish Fenians appointed Sweeny their secretary of war in 1865. He was arrested by the U.S. government but soon released and returned to service in the U.S. Army - such was the political clout of the Irish in America.

Courtesy of: wikimedia.org

Opposition:

In the mid 1860s Great Britain was the most powerful nation in the world. Its naval and military units, although dispersed throughout the world, could easily crush any Irish uprising once assembled. The British had infiltrated the Fenians with informants and knew their plans well in advance of their actions.

Strategy:

Competing American Fenian factions disagreed on strategy. Some wanted to free Ireland by seizing and holding Canada hostage and others wanted to foster a revolution in Ireland. Initially, those favoring the taking of Canada had their way. The plan called for a five-pronged attack along the border from Chicago, Illinois, to Vermont.

Operations:

In April 1866 some 500 Fenians assembled in Eastport, Maine. Their objective was to seize the island of Campo Bello off the coast of New Brunswick, Canada. The ship that transported them to the island was a disaster. Historian John Rutherford wrote:

> "A target for artillery practice could not be more successfully painted - black haul and straw-colored wheel house.... Her rigging was in miserable condition, her sails in a worse.... Her machinery and steaming generating powers untested; coal bunkers and magazines empty. Seriously, is it intended to put this shell on the ocean as the representative of the Fenian Navy?"[3]

Arriving off the island the Fenians on board surrendered to the American force that had arrived ahead of them. The men disbanded. On 19 May American authorities seized 1,200 muskets at Rouse's Point, New York, and on 30 May they seized another caches of arms at St. Albans, Vermont. A British spy, "Red" Jim MacDermot, kept the British authorities well informed of the Fenians' plans.
Not to be deterred, on 22 May "Colonel" John O'Neill mobilized the 13th Tennessee Fenian Regiment and joined the 17th Kentucky Fenian Regiment at Louisville, Kentucky. These 342 Fenians arrived in Buffalo, New York, on 29 May. They were quartered in the homes of local sympathizers. At Buffalo they were joined by the 18th Ohio Fenian Regiment and the 7th New York Fenian Regiment, bringing the number of Fenians to over 1,000 men. On 1 June 800 of these men commanded by John O'Neill crossed the Niagara River into Canada and occupied the village of Fort Erie. O'Neill's objective was to seize

the Welland Canal and cut off shipping between Lake Erie and Ontario. He learned that Canadian forces were converging on him from the north and the south. He knew he had to block their union. On 2 June the Fenians routed the poorly led and poorly outfitted Canadian militia, which was approaching from the south, at Limestone Ridge. The Canadians lost 12 dead and 40 wounded; the Fenians lost eight dead and 20 wounded.

O'Neill fell back to Fort Erie hoping for reinforcements from Buffalo. As the Fenians were nearing Fort Erie a small Canadian militia unit attacked them. After a brief but intense fight the Canadians were dislodged from the Fenian line of retreat. The crossing back into the United States route, however, was now being patrolled by the USS *Michigan* (eight guns). O'Neill was forced to surrender and was arrested. The United States temporarily held the Fenians and their weapons. After a short while the U.S. government quietly paid their passage home and returned their guns.

Then on 7 June another band of Fenians commanded by Brigadier General Samuel Spear briefly occupied St. Armand, Quebec. On 8 June Spear learned that U.S. marshals had seized his ammunition and supplies at St. Albans, Vermont. Spear had no choice but to retire back into the United States. A final clash took place at Pigeon Hill where the volunteer Royal Guides, a cavalry unit, charged 200 Finians protected by breastworks. The Fenians fled back across the border.

These failures against Canada caused a change in the American Feninan leadership. T.J. Kelly displaced James Stephens. Kelly and his key lieutenants crossed the Atlantic and went to London to prepare for a rebellion in Ireland. Their plan called for guerrilla warfare to begin on 11 February 1866, but the British discovered the plan when it was only practically implemented. The rebellion had no chance of success and collapsed in March.

Not appreciating the full extent of the disaster, Fenians on board the 200-ton brig *Jacknell Packet* sailed from New York in April. The ship carried 38 officers with commissions in the army of the Irish Republic signed by Colonel Kelly. In the ship's hold were three cannon, some 5,000 modern rifles and 1,500,000 rounds of ammunition. On Easter Sunday, 21 April, the men on board the brig hoisted the green flag of Ireland and renamed the ship *Erin's Hope*. The brig arrived off Sligo, Ireland, but could find no sympathizers, so it sailed down the coast looking for a place to land its cargo. Provisions running out, those on board the *Erin's Hope* sailed to Dungaroon and landed three officers who were immediately arrested. The ship sailed back to New York.

The Irish leadership on the island tried to escape. Thomas Kelly and

Thomas Deasy were tracked down and arrested in Manchester, England, on 11 September 1867. Richard Burke attempted to rescue Kelly and Deasy. Leading a group of some 30 Fenians armed with revolvers and axes they ambushed the horse-drawn police wagon transporting the prisoners from the courthouse. The police officer in charge was shot dead. Although the rescue was a success, five of the perpetrators were caught, tried, and sentenced to death. One Edward Meagher Condon, a U.S. citizen, was granted a reprieve, following the intercession of the U.S. government. Soon Burke and other Fenians were betrayed by a spy. They were sent to the Clerkenwell House of Detention. Fenians endeavored to blow a hole through the prison wall. The explosion killed 12 and injured 100 in nearby slums but failed to win the freedom of their colleagues. This inflamed British public opinion against their cause.

Back in America, the Fenians came under new leadership. John O'Neill, hero on the 1866 invasion, emerged as the new leader. He stockpiled 15,000 weapons and 3,000,000 rounds of ammunition at Franklin, Vermont. The plan was to simultaneously invaded Canada from three points - St. Albans, Vermont, and Malone and Hogensburg, New York. O'Neill could only attract 400 followers. A smaller second group assembled at Malone, New York. O'Neill, acting prematurely, invaded Canada on 25 May 1870. Once again Fenian security was compromised and the Canadian militia was waiting for them. O'Neill was arrested in the early afternoon by U.S. marshals before the fighting began. The main body of the Fenians exchanged rifle fire with the Canadians for a few hours but then retreated. Two days later, a small Fenian force entered Canada. They were confronted by Canadian troops and the Fenians fled. Many did not have funds for passage home. The return passage for some was paid for by William "Boss" Tweed of New York City.

Impact:

The Fenian strategy was a failure in Canada and a dismal failure in Ireland. The causes were numerous. The movement lacked unity; it could not keep a secret; its goal was over-reaching; its strategy was too complex; and its enemy was too powerful. The Fenians detained by the United States government were quietly released. Those captured in Canada received lengthy prison terms.

The U.S. government initially did little to stop the Fenians. In the mid 1860s the United States was still smarting over the British support of the Confederacy. But by 1866 the Fenian activities threatened to cause a war between the United States and Great Britain and that was more than the administration in Washington had bargained for. On 5 June President Andrew Johnson declared that the U.S. Neutrality Laws of 1818 would be enforced.

Biographies:

Richard O'Sullivan Burke (1838-1922), born in Macroom County Cork, Ireland, was a corporal in the South Cork militia before emigrating to the United States in 1857. He served in the 15th New York Engineers during the U.S. Civil War. In 1866 Burke was in Birmingham, England, to clandestinely purchase weapons for the Fenians. He was among those who sailed to Ireland on 11 January 1867 on board *Erin's Hope*.

William Halpin (unk.) probably served as a colonel in the Union army. The Fenians gave him the rank of "general." He clandestinely operated in Ireland for the Fenians.

Thomas J. Kelly (unk.) served in the 10th Ohio Regiment of the Union army, earning the rank of captain. He clandestinely served as an envoy between the Fenian movements in the United States and Ireland and was awarded the rank of "colonel." He was captured in Kilclooney Wood in County Tipperary in March 1867.

Gordon Massey (unk.) was a native of County Limerick. He served in the British army and fought in the Crimea, reaching the grade of corporal before emigrating to the United States. Illegitimate, he served with the Confederacy, using his mother's surname; at that time he was known as Patrick Condon. Massey joined the Fenians in Texas and traveled to New York in late 1866, where he adopted his father's surname and became Gordon Massey again. The Fenians gave him the rank of "general." He was among the Fenians who sailed to Ireland to ignite a rebellion on 11 January 1867. In a few months he turned queen's evidence against the conspirators.

John McCafferty (unk.), born in the United States, served in the Confederate army. Prior to 1867, he was arrested in Ireland while on a clandestine mission for the Fenians but was released through the intervention of American diplomacy. McCafferty held the rank of "captain" in the Fenians and was among those who sailed to Ireland on 11 January 1867 on board *Erin's Hope*.

Michael O'Brien (unk.) was born in Cork, Ireland, served in the Union army and earned the rank of captain. He was among those who sailed to Ireland on 11 January 1867 on board *Erin's Hope*.

John O'Neill (1834-78) was born in County Monaghan, Ireland, and came to the United States in 1848. In 1857 he joined the 2nd U.S. Dragoons to fight in the "Mormon War." Apparently, O'Neill deserted, traveled to California, and joined the 1st U.S. Cavalry. He returned East with his unit to fight in the Civil War. He participated in the Peninsula campaign. Known for his daring and he rose to the rank of 1st Lieutenant. O'Neill was severely wounded at Walker's Ford 2 December 1863. Believing that he had been passed over for promotion, he resigned in early 1864. O'Neill was then appointed captain in the 17th Colored Infantry but again resigned in November. O'Neill became a claims agent in Tennessee and married. In 1866 he was appointed inspector general of the "Irish Republican Army" in the United States.

Following his invasion of Canada, O'Neill led 40 Irish-Americans and *Métis* (persons of French-Indian ancestry) in an unsuccessful endeavor to cause an uprising at Pembina on Hudson's Bay on 5 October 1871. The territory was then in dispute between Canada and the United States. He was arrested by U.S. troops but released by an American court. Later he worked as an agent for land speculators who sought Irish immigrants for a tract of land in Nebraska.

Samuel P. Spear (1815-75) was born in Massachusetts and joined the U.S. Army as a private in 1833. He fought in the Seminole wars and attended the grade of sergeant. Spear served during the War with Mexico (1846-48) and was wounded in the Battle of Cerro Gordo. Following the war he was stationed on the western frontier and fought against the Sioux in Utah. His regiment was disbanded in 1861 and the officers were ordered to report to Washington. Spear did so and was given a commission to raise a cavalry regiment in Pennsylvania. He was wounded numerous times during the Civil War and rose to the rank of brigadier general. The circumstances under which Spear left the U.S. Army in 1865 are obscure. Some sources state this was due to drunkenness and un-soldier-like conduct. Spear briefly participated in the Fenian cause. During the last decade of his life he suffered from a degenerative disease.

Thomas Sweeny (1820-92) was born in County Cork, Ireland. His family immigrated to the United States in 1832. He served as a 2nd Lieutenant in the 1st New York Volunteers during the Mexican War (1846-48). He was wounded at the Battle of Churubusco and his right arm had to be amputated. Between 1848 and 1861 Sweeny fought in the Indian Wars in the southwest and in Nebraska. During the Civil War he served in the western theatre, attaining the rank of brigadier general. He was honorably discharged from the Union army in 1865. That same year the Fenians made him Secretary of War of the "Irish Republic" and he urged the conquest of Canada as a step to forward liberating Ireland. Following the invasion of Canada in 1866 Sweeny was arrested by the U.S. government but released without being tried.

He then returned to service in the U.S. army, retiring in 1870 with the rank of brigadier general.

QUOTATIONS:

[1] Robert Kee, *The Green Flag*. 3 vols. New York: Penguin Books, 1972. vol. 2, p. 21.

[2] P.G. Smith, "Fenian Invasions of Canada." *Military History*. pp. 50-56 (Feb 2000), p. 52.

[3] John Rutherford, *The Secret History of the Fenian Conspiracy*. London: Kegan, Paul and Company, 1877. p. 28.

SOURCES:

Dictionary of American Biography. 10 vols. plus sup. 1 thru 8. New York: Charles Scribner's Sons, 1936 & 1990.

Thomas Fleming, "The Green Flag in America," *American Heritage*. vol. 30; no. 4 (June/July 1979) pp. 50-63.

Florence E. Gibson, *The Attitudes of the New York Irish toward State and National Affairs 1848-1892*. New York: Columbia University Press, 1951.

Joseph McKenna, *The Irish-American Dynamite Campaign*. Jefferson, NC: McFarland & Company, Inc., Publishers, 2012.

New York Times. "Gen. Samuel P. Spear." 5 May 1875. *Obituary- New York Times*. Electronic Obituary. 18 July 2013. <http://query.nytimes.com/mem/archive-free/pdf?_r=1&res=9F01E5DA1E39EF34BC4D53DFB366838E669FDE>.

Virginius Affair

1870-73

Goal:

To provide insurrectionists in Cuba with arms, supplies and reinforcements in their war with Spain.

Background:

Cuba has long been a major interest to the United States. Early in American history important Americans, viewing the land's rich sugar lands and strategic position in the Caribbean, favored annexing the island to the United States. In 1809, in a letter to James Madison, Thomas Jefferson wrote, "I candidly confess I have ever looked on Cuba as the most interesting addition which could ever be made to our system of States."[1] Prior to the U.S. Civil War there had been three unsuccessful attempts by American filibusters to seize control of the island (*see* three López expeditions 1848 through 1851). That interest by some Americans to seize the island from Spain was rekindled following the Civil War.

Leadership:

The operations of the *Virginius* were controlled by the exile junta in New York.

Volunteers:

Those on board the *Virginius* - various captains and crew members - were a conglomeration of nationalities including Americans, Britons and Cuban exiles.

Virginius Affair, 1870-73

"*Tornado* in Pursuit of the *Virginius*." This was not a rare scene in Cuban waters beginning in the late 1860s and continuing through the 1890s. Cuban exiles in the United States were running guns to the rebels and frequently smuggled cigars out to help pay for the revolution.

Jeanie Mort Walker, *Life of Capt. Joseph Fry, The Cuban Martyr* (Hartford, 1875)

COMPENSATION:

One skipper, Francis Bowen, earned $300 monthly, and this seems to have been about average for the captains. First mates were paid $60 monthly.

OPPOSITION:

The Spanish Cuban squadron had been significantly beefed up during the 1860s and 1870s. It numbered some 25 warships.

STRATEGY:

For the *Virginius* it was a cat-and-mouse game; it was the mouse and the Spanish warships were the cats. Flying the American flag afforded the *Virginius* some protection. The *Virginius* could safely operate out of neutral ports and hide behind the skirts of American warships when they were on the scene. The one place where the *Viriginius* was not protected by the American flag was Cuban territorial waters.

OPERATIONS:

An insurrection against Spanish rule erupted in Cuba on 10 October 1868. That year, in New York, Cuban exiles organized a junta to represent the Cuban cause and to seek funds, supplies and weapons for the rebels. The junta decided that it needed a vessel for sea trans-

Joseph Fry (ca. 1824-73) was a member of the second class to graduate from the U.S. Naval Academy, Annapolis, Maryland. Being from Florida, he chose to fight in the Confederate navy during the Civil War. Fry was the captain of the *Virginius* when the steamer was captured. He was among the second group of prisoners to be executed in Santiago de Cuba.

Jeanie Mort Walker, *Life of Capt. Joseph Fry, The Cuban Martyr* (Hartford, 1875)

portation. For a price of $9,800 a ship docked at the Washington Navy Yard was purchased. It was named the *Virgin*, later changed to the *Virginius*. It had been constructed in Scotland for the Confederate navy. A sidewheel steamer with good speed (12 knots), the ship displaced 491 tons and was over 200 feet long, ten feet from waterline to deck (speed was dependent upon constant maintainance of the hull, rigging and machinery).

The *Viriginius* left New York on 4 October 1870. Flying the American flag and commanded by a series of captains, the ship sailed the Caribbean for three years. It transported men, weapons, supplies and even, on one occasion, burros. The Spanish considered the vessel to be a pirate ship. Several times the American flag saved the *Virginuis:* in at least two cases U.S. warships protected it.

On 23 October 1873 the *Virginius* sailed from Kingston, Jamaica. At least part of the crew was composed of unemployed seamen rounded up by Captain Fry. They did not know the ship's clandestine activities. The ship docked in Haiti and Jamaica, taking on weapons - including daggers - and supplies. Early in the afternoon of 30 October the *Viriginuis* was spotted by the Spanish corvette *Tornado* and a pursuit began. It was an uneven chase. Neither the *Virginius* nor its engines were in good shape. The *Tornado* fired its cannon but the shot fell short. On board the *Virginius* the crew tossed weapons and equipment overboard to lighten the ship. Even hams from the ship's larder were thrown into the boiler to increase the temperature and hopefully the speed.

The crew's efforts were to no avail. The ship's speed dropped. The vessel was shaking badly, loosening the caulking; water was coming

"Capture of the Virginius." Mercenary George Boyton Stone had sailed on an earlier smuggling run by the *Virginius* and remarked that the ship was too large to be a blockade runner. The ship had been built for the Confederate navy and prior to its capture by Spain had made successful smuggling runs.

Jeanie Mort Walker, *Life of Capt. Joseph Fry, The Cuban Martyr* (Hartford, 1875)

"The Butchery of the Crew of the Virginius." This drawing depicts Captain Fry shaking the hands of the crew members about to be executed. It is doubtful that either the executioners or those about to be executed were so well dressed.

Henry Houghton Beck, *Cuba's Fight for Freedom and the War with Spain* (Philadelphia, 1989)

in. The *Virginius* was slowly sinking. The *Tornado* fired several times. When a shot smashed into the *Virginius'* stack, Fry ordered surrender. The ship was boarded by the Spanish and taken to Santiago de Cuba.

On the night of 2 November a court marital was convened and an American and three Cubans were brought before it. Because on a previous occasion they had been tried in absentia and sentenced to death, the sentence was now confirmed. On 4 November they were executed by a firing squad. Two days later there was another court marital, this time of 37 men, including Captain Fry. On 7 November they, too, were executed. Efforts to save the men by the American and British consuls were unsuccessful (there were at least 16 British subjects on the *Virginius*).

Twelve more men, all Cuban, were shot by a firing squad on 8 November. With that the executions ended. The British rushed the war sloop *Niobe* to Santiago, and it reached there 9 November. The British vice consul, Theodore Brooks, and the commander of the *Niobe*, Sir Lambton Lorraine, met with the Spanish military commander, and the Spaniard assured the Britons that there would be no more executions. Some accounts have it that Lorraine threatened to bombard Santiago if the executions continued.

In the United States, the London *Times* reported, there was a "pitch of righteous anger."[2] There were calls for war with Spain. The *New York Times* stated there was "nothing left for the United States government but to declare war ...."[3] Rallies were held across the country. One such in St. Louis urged President Grant to suspend neutrality laws to "give the people an opportunity to inflict summary vengeance upon the bloodthirsty Spaniards and wrest the island of Cuba from their grasp."[4] From former military around the country, even an ex-Confederate colonel, Grant received offers to raise volunteer regiments. The U.S. officially

Fame—Fortune—Frustration

"Execution of Captain Fry and his comrades." Fry and many of the Virginius crew were executed by firing squad. This and other acts inflamed the anger of the American population and they called for intervention in Cuba by the U.S. government.

Jeanie Mort Walker, *Life of Capt. Joseph Fry, The Cuban Martyr* (Hartford, 1875)

protested the executions to Spain "as barbarous and brutal, and an outrage upon this epoch of civilization."[5]

There was to be no war - not for 25 years, and then because of the sinking of the U.S. battleship in Havana harbor. Instead, in 1873 there were diplomatic negotiations. Spain released the remaining prisoners and the *Virginius* (which was in such poor shape that it sank while en route to New York) and paid $80,000 in reparations to the families of the victims. The issue of punishment of the Spanish commander who had ordered the executions became nil when he died.

There would be an armistice between the rebels and the Spanish in 1878, then the start of another war in 1895, intervention by the United States in 1898 and finally Cubans would gain their independence on 20 May 1902.

"The *Viriginius* Butchery." This drawing depicts Spanish horsemen trampling the dead and dying after the shooting of the crew of the Virginius. Illustrations like this outraged the American public.

Henry Houghton Beck, *Cuba's Fight for Freedom and the War with Spain* (Philadelphia, 1989)

Virginius Affair, 1870-73

"Spanish Atrocities." This drawing depicts Spanish soldiers bayoneting survivors of the firing squad. Illustrating gore sold many newspapers in the cities of America.

Jeanie Mort Walker, *Life of Capt. Joseph Fry, The Cuban Martyr* (Hartford, 1875)

Impact:

The travels of the *Virginius* were useful to the Cuban revolutionaries but had no impact on the course of the war.

Biographies:

William Baynard (unk.) had survived a shipwreck when he joined the *Virginius* as first mate. He thought the vessel was a merchantship. (Whether he was an American is unclear).

Francis Bowen (unk.) was the captain of the *Virginius* in 1872.

Joseph Fry (ca. 1824-73) was born in Tampa, Florida. He was a member of the second class at the Naval Academy at Annapolis, Maryland. He resigned in February 1861 to join the Confederate navy, serving there throughout the Civil War. With the end of the conflict

"After the Shooting of the Crew of the Virginius." Slaves (note chains) loading the bodies of the crew into a cart. Many Americans, particularly, recently arrived immigrants, could not read but drawings were easily understood by all.

Henry Houghton Beck, *Cuba's Fight for Freedom and the War with Spain* (Philadelphia, 1989)

123

William Ryan (1840-73) - aka George Washington Ryan - was born in Ireland and was a naturalized American. Ryan fought for the North in the Civil War and rose from the enlisted ranks to become a lieutenant because of bravery. The Cuban revolutionary junta in New York made him a colonel but he preferred the title of general.

Jeanie Mort Walker, *Life of Capt. Joseph Fry, The Cuban Martyr* (Hartford, 1875)

Fry had nowhere to go until he was signed up as captain of the *Viriginius* on the basis of his naval experience. He was in the second group to be executed, walking down the line of men to bid them farewell.

William Ryan [alias George Washington Ryan] (1840-73) was born in Ireland. His family emigrated to Canada and then to the United States. He became a naturalized American. Ryan fought in the Civil War in a new York infantry regiment, rising to a lieutenancy and winning a commendation for bravery. After the war he moved to the mining camps in Montana, then at some point returned to New York. When the Cuban junta was organized in 1868 and was looking for men with military experience, Ryan signed up. He was given the rank of colonel, although he self-promoted himself to general. Ryan was the sole American among the first four men to be executed.

Edward Scott (unk.) was a 16-year-old crewman from Salem, New Jersey.

Francis Sheppherd (unk.) was the first captain of the *Viriginius*.

Quotations:

[1] http://thirdworldtraveler.com/Caribbean/USEconomicSanctions_Cuba.html

[2] Richard H. Bradford, *The Viriginus Affair*. Boulder, Colorado: Colorado Assoicated University Press, 1980. p. 70.

[3] Bradford, *The Viriginius Affair*. p. 65.

[4] Bradford, *The Viriginius Affair*. p. 66.

[5] Bradford, *The Viriginius Affair*. p. 79.

Sources:

Hermenegildo Franco Castañón, *Los Apostaderos y Estaciones Navales Españoles en Ultramar*. Bazán: E.N. Bazán C.M., S.A., 1998.

The Virginuis, Harper's Encyclopaedia of United States History. New York: Harper & Brothers, 1902.

http://en.wikipedia.org/wiki/*Viriginius*Affair.

Expeditionaries in Egypt

1869-78

Goal:
To provide Egypt with a modern army.

Background:
The khedive (and viceroy) of Egypt, Ismail Pasha, sought to build a military force that could free Egypt from the domination of the Ottoman Empire centered in modern-day Turkey.

After the American Civil War few jobs were available for veterans of either side. When it became known that the khedive was looking for experienced military men, some 50 Union and Confederate veterans answered the call. Many - Union and Reb alike - were recommended by the commander of the U.S. Army, General of the Armies William Tecumseh Sherman. They were engineers and experts in army organization and in the conduct of war, as well as frontier exploration and the building of forts and railroads.

The Americans who kept coming enjoyed the exotic sights of the country, from the Sphinx to harems to cafes to bazaars - to innumerable beggars. Although there were no problems between the blue and the grey, the Americans were resented by local people and Egyptian military officers. They were, however, invited to lavish parties hosted by the khedive. He told the Americans that if the attitude of the Egyptian officers became unsupportable, "do not hesitate to come to me for redress."[1]

Leadership:
The Americans provided leadership in reshaping and modernizing the Egyptian army. Over the Americans was Brigadier General Charles Pomeroy Stone, a Union veteran and friend

of Sherman's. He was chief of staff of the Egyptian military and confidential advisor to the khedive. Stone and a group had arrived in Egypt in the summer of 1870. Serving as inspector general was Major General William Wing Loring, a former Confederate. The Americans trained raw Egyptian recruits and even arranged literacy learning for the many illiterate officers.

VOLUNTEERS:

All Americans in the Egyptian army were volunteers. They had enlisted seeking primarily for wages but also for adventure.

Charles Stone (1824-87) graduated from West Point in 1845. He served in the Union army during the Civil War. Stone was incarcerated for 189 days under the suspicion that he was a Southern sympathizer. He was released without explanation. After serving in the Egyptian army for more than a decade, he returned to the United States. Stone is buried at West Point.

Courtesy wikimedia.org

COMPENSATION:

The Americans were paid by the Egyptian government. The annual amount for Colonel Samuel H. Lockett was indicative of salary levels: $2,500, possibly in Austrian gold coins. The Americans had to contend with erratic payments.

OPPOSITION:

In addition to hostile Egyptian officers who undermined by subterfuge the efforts of the Americans, in 1874 Egypt went to war with Abyssinia. In this war the Americans served more as advisors than commanders, much to the detriment of the Egyptian cause.

STRATEGY:

The only strategy possible against the Abyssinians, who outnumbered the Egyptian army at least five to one, was to maximize firepower through in large measure strict discipline.

OPERATIONS:

Arriving in Egypt, the Americans supervised the construction of a string of coastal fortifications on the Mediterranean shores. They partially reorganized the army. The 40,000-conscript force had been little more than a conglomeration of tribal units. Only about one-third of the officers could read and write. The Americans instructed, drilled, instilled discipline and gave weapons training. On Stone's suggestion battalion-level literacy schools were established, followed by the creation of a non-commissioned officers' school. The non-commissioned officers brought their sons to school and this led

Stone to favor setting up schools for the boys. This, too, was done. At the staff college in Cairo the Americans gave the young officers intensive instructions in tactics, surveying and transporting.

There were difficulties. There were cultural, language and turf issues. Stone attempted to build a general staff. Because of officer resistance, he was only partially successful. Another case: Colonel Walter H. Jenifer, who had led Confederate cavalry, was in command of the Egyptian cavalry. There was, however, nothing he could teach these hard-riding Bedouins. Unable to get along with them, he returned to the United States. Despite the problems, the Americans to some extent were able to convert the Egyptian force into a semblance of an American/European-style army.

The activities of the Americans were not limited to the military field. They oversaw the building of a rail system around Alexandria. In education they introduced modern engineering. Beginning in 1873, Stone sent out exploring teams to map distant lands and waterways under the khedive's reign.

The khedive suffered a military disaster. One American, Colonel James A. Dennison, had a narrow escape. In September 1875 the khedive sent a force to invade neighboring Abyssinia. The intention was to annex caravan-rich provinces (caravans paid transit-fees). The force, led by a Danish mercenary, Colonel Soren Addendrum, was largely destroyed by the Abyssinians. Dennison managed to lead his unit to safety.

The khedive wanted revenge for the humiliating defeat and ordered a new invasion. Stone organized an expeditionary army of 11,000 men, 1,100 horses and 1,200 mules. The force was led by an Egyptian, Ratib Pasha. Second in command was Major General Loring. Ten other Americans were also in the expedition. In the command structure there was a clash of cultures: the American drive for efficiency versus traditional Egyptian ways of doing things. Exasperated, Loring on one occasion exclaimed: "Every cook, sais or whatnot is a prince, and a major general's order is but a puff against a squall. We are going to the devil sure enough."[2]

The army set out for Abyssinia in January 1876. As it progressed it built fortified depots at several places to protect its routes. The Egyptian army moved slowly. It entered Abyssinian territory and built a fort at Gura. Meanwhile, the king of Abyssinia, John (Yohannes IV), was raising an army. It came to number 50,000 soldiers. John's army repeatedly attacked the Egyptians. On 10 March 1876 the Egyptians counter-attacked but were repulsed. The Egyptian commanders were killed, artillery and large quantities of ammunition were lost. The Egyptian expedition was immobilized. The invasion had failed. An armistice was arranged and on 19 April the Egyptians abandoned Fort Gura and headed for Egypt. Ironically, King John's army was disintegrating because the soldiers had not found the loot they expected to get by fighting against the khedive and the Egyptians.

Although they were not to blame, the Americans were associated with the defeats. Another factor working against them was that they had not succeeded in forging a cohesive, disciplined, well-led, high-morale, fighting army. It had been defeated twice by spear-wielding savages. Still another problem was that the khedive's monetary resources had been depleted by war, expeditions and infrastructure improvements, including canals and railroads. The Americans did not get their pay. While there was another exploratory waterways expedition and some planning for another invasion of Abyssinia, most the Americans had nothing to do. One disillusioned officer complained that the "whole confounded thing" was a miserable humbug - all show, all bunk, all make-believe."[3]

In March 1877 two officers were discharged without warning. Americans were drifting back to the United States. A board of inquiry was set up on the demand of European banks to whom the khedive was indebted. They asked in the spring of 1878 that the Egyptian army be reduced and the Americans be dismissed. The government set 30 June 1878 as the termination date for service by the Americans. By then only a dozen remained. Six Americans had died in service, mainly from non-combat causes. Stone was the last to leave Egypt, in 1883.

Impact:

The Americans had an effect on the upgrading of the Egyptian army. Colonel Lockett declared after the Americans had worked for five years: "As far as I can see, the army, both officers and men, are pretty well up to the standards of that of our country."[4] The Americans plumbed seas (determined depths), surveyed lands, discovered lakes, measured the atmosphere, initiated schools, trained soldiers, opened routes for railroads. And, as noted by two historians, in a land of bribery and corruption in public service, the Americans "brought a spirit of personal honesty and integrity."[5]

Biographies:

Vanderbilt Allen (unk.) served as a brevet major, U.S. Volunteers, during the U.S. Civil War. He served in the Egypt army between 1870 and 1872.

James Bassel (unk.), born in Virginia, attended the U.S. Military

Academy at West Point. He graduated on 17 June 1867 and was appointed a second lieutenant. He was honorably discharged at his own request on 4 November 1870. Bassel served in the Egyptian Army during 1874.

William P.A. Campbell (unk.-1874) served in the U.S. Navy from 14 December 1847 until 19 September 1861, at which time he was dismissed. Next, he served in the Confederate Navy as a lieutenant. Campbell oversaw the Egyptian steamers running between Alexandria and Constantinople. He died at Khartoum, Sudan, on 10 October 1874 while serving under Charles "Chinese" Gordon.

Charles Chaillé-Long (1842-1917), a former Union captain from Maryland, led a number of expeditions while in Egypt. He was sent on an exploratory trek to Central Africa. Among other objectives he was to obtain the agreement of the monarch of Uganda, M'Tesa, that the Egyptian khedive was his sovereign. Riding a horse, his staff on camels, Chaillé-Long had to deal with swamps, attacks of savages, crocodiles and a fever in his body. M'Tesa acquiesced to the request. To honor Long at court, he had 30 spectators garroted (strangled). He also presented Chaillé-Long with a boy and one of his own daughters, an eight-year-old. Near M'Tesa's court, Chaillé-Long became the first white man to travel on Lake Victoria. Long also discovered a new lake, Hussein (later Kioga). For his efforts Chaillé-Long was promoted to colonel, given the title of "bey" and awarded a prestigious medal. Chaillé-Long participated in other expeditions. On one of these he caused a diplomatic row by taking his men into neighboring Zanzibar, an ally of Egypt's. On another expedition he purchased from a sheik a three-foot, nine-inch pygmy woman for the price of a yard of red cloth. Upon his return to the United States Long lectured and wrote about his adventures. He joined the foreign service and worked at posts in Egypt and Korea.

Raleigh Edward Colston (1825-96) was born in Paris, France, granted U.S. citizenship, and educated at the Virginia Military Institute. He was a brigadier general in the Confederate Army and performed poorly at the Battle of Chancellorsville. Colston was then given less important commands. Between 1873 and 1878 he served in Egypt as a colonel. His assignments included teaching at the military academy in Cairo; exploring and mapping the desert between the Nile River and the Red Sea; conducting a hydrographic survey of the bay of Berenice; and participating in an expedition to Kordofan, Sudan. He was practically paralyzed during a camel accident.

James A. Dennison (unk.) served as a Union private during the U.S. Civil War. He then attended the U.S. Military Academy and graduated as a second lieutenant. Dennison served in the U.S. Army until 1870. He served in Egypt during 1875 and 1876. Dennison took part in the expedition to Abyssinia and in the Gura campaign.

Henry C. Derrick (unk.) served as a captain in the Confederate Army. He was in Egypt between 1875 and 1878. During that time Derrick was the chief engineer during the Gura campaign and helped map various areas of Egypt.

William W. Dunlap (unk.) served as a colonel in the Confederate Army. He was in Egypt during 1871 and served at the artillery school at Damietta.

William McEntyre Dye (1831-99) was born in Pennsylvania and graduated from the U.S. Military Academy at West Point in 1853. Prior to the Civil War Dye served primarily in Texas. In the Union army he participated in numerous campaigns including Vicksburg, Red River and Mobile. He received brevet promotions up to brigadier general and at one point was in command of a brigade. He was honorably discharged at his own request on 30 September 1870. In 1873 he went to Egypt and joined the Khedive's Army. In 1876 he was on Stone's staff and was put in charge of communications during the ill-fated Gura invasion. Dye asked Stone to send him a clerk "who writes English and French" and "who stinks, or has some other repulsive quality which will protect him in my employ."[6] Wounded in the Gura campaign, Dye left Egypt in June 1878. Returning to the United States, he served as the superintendent of the Metropolitan Police of the District of Columbia between 1883 and 1886. Next, he went to Korea and was the military advisor and inspector-general for that country's king (1888-96).

Eugene Oscar Fechét (unk.), born in Michigan, attended the U.S. Military Academy at West Point. He graduated on 15 June 1868 and was appointed a second lieutenant. Between 1868 and 1875 Fechét served primarily on the West Coast. He resigned on 15 March 1875. Fechét served as *Chef d'Escadron* in the Egyptian Army between 24 October 1872 and 14 February 1874 and was primarily engaged in surveying work. Beginning in 1875 he was involved in mining in northern South America and in 1885 served as the U.S. consul at Paso del Norte, Mexico.

Charles W. Field (unk.) was born in Kentucky and graduated from the U.S. Military Academy at West Point on 1 July 1849. Appointed a second lieutenant, he primarily served in Texas until the outbreak of the U.S. Civil War. Field, a cavalry officer, fought for the Confederacy. Between 17 July 1875 and 31 March 1877 he served as a colonel of engineers in the Egyptian Army. In 1875 and 1876 Field was inspector-general during the Abyssinian campaign. Returning to the United

States, he served as the doorkeeper of the U.S. House of Representatives between 1878 and 1881.

Charles I. Graves (unk.) served in the U.S. Navy between 17 December 1853 and 24 December 1861. He attained the rank of lieutenant before being dismissed. Graves served in the Confederate Navy throughout the U.S. Civil War. He served in Egypt between 1875 and 1878. Graves' assignments included drawing maps for fortifications, participating in the Gura campaign, surveying east of Cairo, and surveying for a lighthouse at Cape Guardafui.

Wilburn B. Hall (unk.) served in the U. S. Navy between 9 June 1855 and 7 March 1861. He attained the rank of lieutenant before resigning. Hall served in the Confederate Navy throughout the U.S. Civil War. He served in Egypt between 1874 and 1877. Hall's assignments included serving on the general staff; surveying lower Egypt; and various tasks related to education.

Cornelius Hunt (unk.-1873) served as a master's mate in the Confederate Navy. He arrived in Egypt in 1870 and was killed in a riding accident on 28 February 1873. He was assigned to teach at the military school at Abourkir.

Henry Irgins (unk.-1878) served as a sergeant, U.S. Volunteers, during the U.S. Civil War. He worked in Egypt between 1876 and 1878. Discharged, Irgins died en route to the United States.

Walter H. Jenifer (unk.) was as a colonel in the Confederate Army. He worked in Egypt in 1871 and 1872, serving as inspector of cavalry in Alexandria.

Thomas D. Johnson (unk.) served as a private in the Confederate Volunteers. He worked in Egypt between 1875 and 1877. Johnson served in the Gura campaign as a staff surgeon.

Beverly Kennon (unk.) served in the U.S. Navy from 22 August 1846 until 22 April 1861. He attained the rank of lieutenant before resigning. During the U.S. Civil War Kennon served in the Confederate Navy. He worked in Egypt between 1870 and 1874. His assignments included working on coastal defenses.

Robert S. Lamson (unk.) served in Egypt in 1875 and 1876. He participated in the Gura campaign.

Samuel H. Lockett (unk.) served as a colonel in the Confederate Army. He worked in Egypt between 1875 and 1877. He participated in the Gura campaign and was involved in mapping.

Charles F. Loshe (unk.-1878) served as a lieutenant in the U.S. Volunteers during the American Civil War. Loshe worked in Egypt between 1875 and 1878. He participated in the Gura campaign and was involved in surveying. He died at Suakin.

William Wing Loring (1818-86), born in Wilmington, North Carolina, fought against the Seminoles, the Mexicans, the Mormons and the Union. He lost an arm in Mexico. Starting as a captain in the U.S. and then Confederate armies, he won ascending promotions, had a number of commands and in the Civil War participated in several campaigns. He took part in the defense of Vicksburg, Mississippi, against the assault by Major General Ulysses S. Grant. Out of work with the war over, Loring went to Egypt in 1870. After serving as inspector general of the Egyptian army, he was put in charge of coastal defenses, making him the only American in direct command of a considerable number of Egyptian troops. Later he was second in command of the second ill-fated invasion of Abyssinia. He returned to the United States in 1878.

Chancellor Martin (unk.), born in Illinois, attended the U.S. Military Academy at West Point. He graduated on 15 June 1868 and was appointed a second lieutenant. He was honorably discharged at his own request on 1 September 1870. Martin served as a major on the general staff of the Egyptian army between January 1874 and 31 March 1877.

Alexander M. Mason (unk.) served as a lieutenant in the Confederate navy during the American Civil War. He worked in Egypt between 1870 and 1878., involved in numerous mapping expeditions.

James M. Morgan (unk.) attended the Confederate naval academy. He worked in Egypt between 1870 and 1872.

Thaddeus P. Mott (unk.) served as a colonel, U.S. Volunteers, during the American Civil War. He worked in Egypt between 1869 and 1875. He had a number of assignments related to recruiting Americans for service in Egypt.

Edmund Parys (unk.-1874) served in the U.S. Navy between 1862 and 1870 with breaks in service. He worked in Egypt between 1871 and 1874. He died in Egypt on 13 April 1874.

David Essex Porter (unk.) was the grandson of a War of 1812 commodore (David Porter) and the son of a Civil War rear admiral (David D. Porter). David Essex Porter had been a captain in the Union army. He arrived in Egypt in 1875 and participated in the Gura campaign as assistant to the chief engineer. Porter had a personal problem: he was an alcoholic. The khedive compelled his resignation and he left Egypt in October 1876. According to a fellow officer, Porter had been "getting drunk, abusing Egyptian government [officials] from the khedive down in public places, ... borrowing money upon false pretenses and swindling right and left."[7]

Henry G. Prout (unk.) served in the Massachusetts Militia during the U.S. Civil War. He worked in Egypt between 1872 and 1878. In addition to serving on the general staff, Prout was involved in mapping. In 1876 he was the governor-general of Sudan during the absence of General Charles "Chinese" Gordon.

E. Sparrow Purdy (unk.-1881) served as a brevet lieutenant colonel of U.S. Volunteers during the American Civil War. He served in Egypt between 1870 and 1878. He was involved in mapping.

Horatio B. Reed (unk.) served as a brevet lieutenant colonel of U.S. Volunteers during the American Civil War. He served in Egypt in 1874 and 1875. He returned to the United States due to illness.

Alexander Welch Reynolds (1816-76), born in Clarke county, Virginia, graduated from the U.S. Military at West Point on 1 July 1838. Appointed a second lieutenant, he fought against the Seminole Indians between 1838 and 1840. During the War with Mexico (1846-48) Reynolds served on convoy duty in the southwest. He was dismissed in 1855 in a dispute over finances, but he was shortly reappointed. In 1861 he joined the Confederate Army, served in the Western Theater, and rose to the rank of brigadier general. He was seriously wounded at the Battle of New Hope Church. Following the Civil War, Reynolds served as a colonel on the staff of William W. Loring in the Egyptian Army. He died in Alexandria, Egypt, on 26 May 1876.

Frank A. Reynolds (unk.-1875) served as a lieutenant colonel in the Confederate Army. He served in Egypt between 1870 and 1873. Reynolds then returned to the United States to inspect arms purchased by the Egyptian government. He died in New York, in 1875, while still in the employment of Egypt.

Thomas G. Rhett (unk.) served in the Confederate Army, attaining the rank of major. He served in Egypt between 1870 and 1874. He established a powder plant in Cairo but was frequently on sick leave.

Robert Rogers (unk.) during the early years of the Civil War served in the U.S. Volunteers and then attended the U.S. Military Academy between 1863 and 1867. He was commissioned a second lieutenant. Rogers served in Egypt in 1874 and 1875.

Richard H. Savage (unk.), born in New York, attended the U.S. Military Academy at West Point. He graduated on 15 June 1868 and was appointed a brevet second lieutenant, Corps of Engineers. He was honorably discharged at his own request on 31 December 1870. Savage served as a major in the Egyptian Army in 1872.

Henry Hopkins Sibley (1816-86), born in Natchitoches, Louisiana, was a West Pointer who fought the Seminoles, the Mexicans, the Mormons, the Navajos and the Union. During the Civil War he commanded forces that took New Mexico, but then he was driven out. He rose to the rank of brigadier general. He went to Egypt in December 1969 and was made chief of artillery. He remained in Egypt until 1874, when he was dismissed by the khedive because of drunkenness.

Charles Pomeroy Stone (1824-87), born in Greenfield, Massachusetts, graduated from the U.S. Military Academy in West Point in 1845 and served in the Army's ordnance branch. During the War with Mexico (1846-48) he received field promotions. Later, however, after resigning to enter business, he did survey work for the Mexican government. With the start of the U.S. Civil War, Stone returned to the U.S. Army. As a colonel commanding volunteers defending the capital, he played a key role during President Lincoln's inauguration. Stone was appointed commander of a regular army brigade with the rank of colonel, and he was also a brigadier general of volunteers. He was then given command of a division of three brigades along the Potomac River. One of his subordinates, Colonel Edward D. Baker, exceeded orders and took his brigade across the river at Ball's Bluff. The Confederates destroyed the brigade. Baker was killed. Stone was made the scapegoat. Accused of disloyalty, he was questioned by the Joint Committee on the Conduct of the War. On demand of the committee chairman, Stone was taken the night of 8 February 1862 to a fort, without any charges having been made. He was held for 189 days and then released. For nine months he had no assignment but then was given a staff position and participated in several Civil War campaigns. In April 1864, however, the secretary of war rescinded Stone's officer commission. On 13 September he resigned. He went on to a career in Egypt, providing him not only with wages but also an opportunity to redeem his military reputation.

After Egypt and back in the United States (1883), Stone went into business as an engineer. He won a contract to design and build the foundation for the Statue of Liberty. This was the ultimate irony: the man who had been imprisoned on an isle in New York harbor now helped construct the nation's largest tribute to liberty - on an island in New York harbor. Stone died in New York on 24 January 1887 and is buried at the Military Academy at West Point.

Edward Warren (1828-92) had been surgeon general of North Carolina's forces during the Civil War, and he made them the best cared-for in the Confederate armies. He went to Egypt in May 1873 and was named surgeon in chief. He was permitted to maintain a private practice as well. While he did well as a doctor, Warren was an irascible person who couldn't get along with Stone or the Egyptians. Having an eye problem, he went to Paris in 1876 and set up a practice there.

Quotations:

[1] William B. Hesseltine and Hazel C. Wolf. *The Blue and Grey on the Nile*. Chicago: The University of Chicago Press, 1961. p. 50.
[2] Hesseltine and Wolf, *The Blue and Grey*. p. 192.
[3] Hesseltine and Wolf, *The Blue and Grey*. p. 230.
[4] Hesseltine and Wolf, *The Blue and Grey*. p. 89.
[5] Hesseltine and Wolf, *The Blue and Grey*. p. 236.
[6] Hesseltine and Wolf, *The Blue and Grey*. p. 189.
[7] Hesseltine and Wolf, *The Blue and Grey*. p. 219.

Sources:

George W. Cullum, ed., *Biographical Register of the Officers and Graduates of the U.S. Military Academy*. New York: various publishers through Supplement 8, 1879-1940.

"Eritrios [Eritea] - The Ethiopian-Egyptian War: 1874-1876," http://www.eritrios.net/ethiopean_egyptain_war.htm

Stewart Sifakis, *Who Was Who in the Civil War*. New York: Facts on File Publications, 1988.

Ezra J. Warner, *Generals in Blue - Lives of Union Commanders*. Baton Rouge, Louisiana:

Louisiana State University Press, 1964.

Ezra J. Warner, *Generals in Grey - Lives of Confederate Commanders*. Baton Rouge,

Louisiana: Louisiana State University Press, 1959.

Webster's American Military Biographies. Springfield Massachusetts: G. & C. Merriam

Company, 1978.

Odyssey of George Boynton Stone

1866 - 1906

Goal:

"Throughout my life I [George Boynton Stone] have sought adventure over the face of the world and its waters as other men have hunted and fought for gold or struggled for fame. The love of it, whether through the out-cropping of a strain of buccaneer blood that had been held in subjection by generations of placid propriety or as a result of some freak of prenatal suggestion, was born in me, deep-planted and long-rooted."[1]

Background:

Stone's primary training ground for his mercenary career was blockade running during the U.S. Civil War. Traveling to Bermuda, he purchased the 17 knot steamer *Letter B*. Stone made four successful runs into Charleston, South Carolina. Any more, he believed, would be pressing his luck so he sold the ship in late 1864 and prepared for his foreign adventures.

Leadership:

Stone was the master of all that he undertook. Although he had partners (who were mostly silent financiers), he had no masters.

Cuban General Calixto García's army on the march during Cuba's protracted wars for independence. These soldiers are carrying single-shot, Remington rolling-block rifles. These rifles were introduced into Cuba by numerous American gunrunners. The simplistic and rugged weapons were the late 19th century's equivalent to the 20th century's Soviet-made AK-47. These rifles were very popular among revolutionary movements throughout Latin America.

Courtesy U.S. National Archives

Volunteers:

Most men who fought for Stone were cutthroats and the scum of sociality. They were well paid and knew that rarely were their activities legal.

Compensation:

Stone spent money almost recklessly but he had plenty. He was born into wealth and married into more. His blockade-running enterprises during the U.S. Civil War were very profitable and his postwar partnership in a distillery even more so. Stone advised his biographer: "He [the risk taker] must, too, be in the business chiefly for the love of the adventure it provides as royal payment, for the financial returns, except in cases out of the ordinary, are as nothing compared with the dangers that are encountered."[2]

Opposition:

To evaluate all who fought against Stone would be an almost endless task. A few general observations held true throughout his long career. He was very bigoted and held all people of color as inferior. The one nationality that Stone held in the highest regard was the British, although he does not make any observations concerning fellow Americans.

Strategy:

Stone's writing concerning gun-smuggling capture his strategy. "Carrying contraband is dangerous under the most favorable conditions.... Therefore the commander of a filibustering expedition must regard

George Boyton Stone (1842 - ca. 1911) worked as a mercenary in North America, South America, Europe, Asia and Africa. It is hard to consider him anything but a scoundrel. Stone ran the secret police for a Venezuelan dictator, robbed Chinese pirates, was involved in the slave trade, and paid another man to serve his term in an Australian prison.

Horace Smith, *The War Maker* (Chicago, 1911)

desperate changes as a part of a daily routine, but he is unwise to add to his risks by complicating his missions."[3]

Operations:

In the summer of 1866 Stone and his partner, James "Jim Jubilee Junior" Fisk, purchased the steamer *Edgar Stuart*, a former Civil War blockade runner. They also purchased some used Sharps rifles and six mountain guns. They cut a deal with the recently established Cuban Junta in New York City. The Cubans wanted to pay Stone in discounted bonds but he would have no part of that. Finally, they agreed to pay part in cash and the remainder in fine Cuban cigars on delivery of the munitions in Cuba. The arms were delivered to Cape Maisi, at the extreme eastern point of Cuba, without incident. The cigars were packed in waterproof cases with floats attached. On the return trip these were thrown overboard in the lower bay of New York harbor and picked up by boats to avoid payment of taxes. Three or four similar trips were made to Cuba, typically without any clearance papers.

One night Stone received an urgent message from the Cuban Junta. A U.S. marshal was going to seize the *Edgar Stuart* in the morning. Partly loaded, the ship immediately sailed for Baltimore, to which the remainder of the cargo had been redirected. While at sea, the *Edgar Stuart* was repainted and given a new name and a forged British identity. Arriving in Baltimore, the deception was seen through, the ship seized by a U.S. marshal and three guards placed on board. That night Stone had the guards drugged, the ship sailed and the guards were put ashore. The contraband was successfully landed some 60 miles west of Cape Maysi. The *Edgar Stuart* sailed for Halifax, Nova Scotia, to allow Fisk time to buy Stone and the ship out of trouble through his connections in Washington. On one of his next trips Stone was lucky to escape a Spanish gunboat which had been built in New York specifically for the task of catching gunrunners. One brief diversion occurred when the *Edgar Stuart* was being repaired. Accompanying Captain [fnu] Williams, Stone made the maiden voyage of the *Virginius*, a ship which he decided was too large to be a gun-runner. He would be proven correct when she was captured on 31 October 1873 by the Spanish. By 1868 the Cuban revolutionaries in New York City were out of money and dispirited. Stone decided to look elsewhere for excitement.

Establishing himself in London under the name of George MacFarlane, Stone agreed to deliver a load of arms to Don Carlos, the pretender to the Spanish throne. Stone chartered a small steamer and outfitted her to resemble the Spanish coastal streamer *Santa Marta*. The deception worked and the arms were successfully landed. Don Carlos, however, betrayed Stone and tried to have him ambushed after reluctantly paying him for the weapons. Stone was saved from that fate by an attractive young gypsy girl. This ended his dealings with Don Carlos.

In Stone's next adventure he purchased 5,000 rifles from an old English partner who had promised the seller, Austria, that the guns would not be resold to France, which was at war with Prussia. Stone, not a party to this agreement, did not find it binding on him. He used trickery to extract the guns from the Austrian arsenal at Trieste just escaping the guns of the harbor fort. He delivered his cargo of weapons to the French Committee of Safety at Bordeaux.

Shortly after his wife died, Stone looked for adventure elsewhere, this time in Venezuela via New York. In 1870 Stone purchased the schooner yacht *Juliette* and went in search of the Venezuelan exile Antonio Guzman Blanco. Stone found Guzman in Curacao and agreed on a price to bring him 3,000 old Remington rifles and 500,000 cartridges to support Guzman's planned revolution against the Monagas family. When Stone delivered the weapons, he was betrayed by General Venancio Pulgar who had had a falling out with Guzman. Stone was kept on a short leash, but got way via a harrowing four-day, open-boat escape. Meanwhile, Guzman had come to power in Venezuela without the anticipated resistance. Stone reunited with now-President Guzman in Caracas. Guzman believed Stone's story that he had remained loyal to their agreement and Guzman made Stone a personal confidant. Stone fulfilled that role for about one year before getting wanderlust again.

Stone sailed the *Juliette* to London. He changed his name to John F. Kinnear, forged a new set of papers and British registry of his yacht, took on a load of arms, and set sail for Costa Rica where he had heard a revolution was brewing. Storm damage forced Stone to seek repairs in Kingston, Jamaica. This took a few days. Knowing by now that the British authorities were suspicious of his true intensions, "a few Bank of England notes blinded him [the harbor policeman]"[4] and the *Juliette* made her escape at night through the dangerous channel while shells rained down from the local fort. After escaping from an inspection by the British warship *Bellerephon* at sea, Stone delivered the arms to the rebels in Costa Rica. He was paid in cash and coffee. Stone now returned to Venezuela and once again served as Guzman's personal confidant.

By 1873 wanderlust struck again. Stone had received a number of letters from Santo Domingo's President Buenaventura Baez seeking to hire him. Stone sailed the *Juliette* to the island nation. He was put in charge of improving the army over the objections of the minister of war, the president's brother. Stone sailed the *Juliette* to Halifax, Nova Scotia, to pick up arms. On his return he found rebels at the gates of the capital, Santo Domingo, and the president in a near state of panic. Stone took to the field of battle commanding the left flank of an army while the president's brother commanded the center and right. The men fighting under General Baez almost immediately fled and those under Stone, after a brief fight, followed. Stone was captured but that night he was rescued by the crew of the *Juliette* and he returned to Venezuela. Stone observed: "I had not drawn a dollar from Baez .... Still, I figured the experience had furnished me enough excitement to justify its cost."[5]

After leading a legitimate exploration expedition for Venezuelan President Guzman to investigate the origins of the Orinoco River, Stone devised his most ambitious illegal enterprise yet. He traveled to England where he outfitted three ships (with a plethora of forged identification papers), the purpose of which was to steal from the pirates of the China Sea. Also, all three ships - the steam yacht *Leckwith*, the brig *Surprise* and the topsail schooner *Florence* - were outfitted with materials to allow them to change their appearances at sea. The *Surprise* and the *Florence* were to serve as "cows" carrying the spoils captured from the pirates by the *Leckwith* to various ports for sale. All three ships were heavily armed and given large crews. In keeping with the deception, Stone assumed the name Dr. Burnet, a rich English physician who was cruising for reasons of health.

The first pirate junk taken by the *Leckwith* carried a cargo worth over $100,000. The pirate crew was either killed in the gun duel or drowned abandoning the junk. Some six smaller pirate craft fell for the deception and were looted and destroyed by Stone. One night two pirate craft tried to sneak up on the *Leckwith*. One fell victim to a towed torpedo that Stone had devised and the other was sunk by the *Leckwith*. Stone took his prize cargoes to Singapore. There he heard stories which incorrectly stated he was preying on legitimate commerce.

Fearing repercussions Stone went to Hong Kong in the *Surprise* to gather information. He learned that the head of the pirate fraternity, Moy Sen, had pledged to destroy him. It wasn't long before the old pirate sprang his trap. One night a large junk lay alongside the *Leckwith*. A few hundred pirates boarded the *Leckwith* at dusk. Stone had planned for this eventuality and had reinforced the *Leckwith* with men and arms from the *Surprise* and *Florence*. Although the fighting was fierce, Stone soon had the upper hand. Then a pirate steamer fell on the *Leckwith* from the stern. The fighting lasted throughout the night and again Stone prevailed. Out of the 120 men on board the *Leckwith* 21 were killed, 40 were injured seriously, and none of the remainder escaped some injury. Hundreds of pirates were killed. Two chests filled with gold and silver were found on the pirate steamer. By now Stone had lost his taste for pirates' blood and plunder. He divided the spoils among the crew - refusing a share - and eventually sailed for England.

Stone took the long way to England. He briefly visited Korea, unsuccessfully looking for buried treasure, and then sailed off the east coast of Africa looking for adventure. This he found in the illegal slave trade. The *Leckwith* highjacked the slaves being transported on board Arab dhows (coastal boats with lateen sails) and sold them ashore. A number of dhows were seized before a close encounter with the British gunboat *Penelope*. Stone chose not to press his luck, landed most of his crew off Zanzibar, sailed to the entrance of the Red Sea and scuttled the *Leckwith* to destroy evidence of his past illegal exploits. Stone and a few close confidants booked passage from Aden to England, arriving in early 1877.

Stone's next adventure was less savory than those in the China Sea and off Africa. He ran a load of guns from Amsterdam to Montenegro to be used in a rebellion against the Turks. The Austrians turned a blind eye to the affair, making it risk free.

In 1878 Stone's interests again turned to the Americas as Chile went to war against Bolivia and Peru. He was called to the offices of Sir William Armstrong & Company and told that they had a shipment of heavy guns for Peru which needed delivery to the port of Callao, then being blockaded by Chile. Stone struck a deal with the Peruvian naval attaché in London who was responsible for arranging delivery; Stone was to be paid $50,000. He purchased the steamer *Britannia* for $75,000 and renamed her *Salome*. She was fast enough (17 knots), strong enough to carry the heavy guns, and small enough to avoid easy detection. Stone carefully planned the trip, loading both regular and smokeless coal. He loaded the guns in Amsterdam under a false manifest, loaded more coal on the east coast of South America, ran well south around Cape Horn, and stayed far out to sea as he steamed up the west coast of South America. He successfully made the dash into Callao and delivered the guns. He then returned to London selling his ship for almost as much as he had paid. Stone observed: "I received my money, which was the easiest I had ever honestly earned, but it was because I understood the game and had been careful."[6]

Stone's quest for excitement had not been satisfied by the delivery of arms to Montenegro and Peru. His next scheme was a failure. Back in England, he chartered the steamer *Ferret* and re-christened himself

James Stuart Henderson. He then pretended to sink the *Ferret* off Gibraltar and named the reincarnation the *India*. What nefarious uses he planned for the ship are unclear. The deception caught up with him in Melbourne, Australia. There, by chance a suspicious harbor pilot uncovered the deception. As fate would have it, Stone stumbled on a man who was his double. The lookalike agreed to take Stone's place for $7,000, was convicted of defrauding the owner of the *Ferret* and spent seven years in prison.

It was now the early 1880s when Stone returned to London. Hearing of opportunities in the Caribbean, he sailed to Canada and purchased the fore-and-aft schooner *George V. Richards*. Next he sailed to Bridgeport, Connecticut, purchased a cargo of Sharps and Remington rifles plus ammunition and sailed for Maracaibo, Venezuela. He sold half the guns in Venezuela and half in Costa Rica.

After an interlude of a few years, Stone again returned to Australia, but to Sidney and not Melbourne for fear of being recognized as the true James Stuart Henderson. Australia had passed a Chinese exclusion law and Stone saw the potential of great profit by smuggling Chinese into the labor-starved continent. He purchased the fore-and-aft schooner *Southern Cross* and had her outfitted to carrying 200 Chinese in her hold. Stone was paid $150 for each Chinese landed in Australia. The business was so successful that Stone purchased the small steamer *Nettie H*. After eight or nine successful landings Stone lost interest and decided, near the end of 1889, to go back to the West Indies. He dallied in Egypt for a while and became involved in a plot to rescue the national hero Arabi Pasha who was being held in captivity by the British in Ceylon. The plot failed to mature.

Stone returned to New York City in 1890. He purchased the brigantine *Alice Ada*, took on a legal cargo and sailed south looking for a revolution. He established himself in Rio de Janeiro, Brazil. For the next three years President (and general) Floriano Peixoto and Admiral Custódio José de Mello jockeyed for control of the military and the government. The outcome was predictable. Peixoto controlled the army and Mello controlled the navy with a few exceptions. The new cruiser *Republica* was the one significant warship which supported Peixoto. Mello wanted Stone to destroy the *Republica* but the two could not come to terms. Spies told President Peixoto of these negotiations, so he, in turn, offered Stone an open-ended contract, the payment amount and the dangerous deed to be undertaken would be specified at a later date. Stone, a master of intrigue and believing himself a good judge of character, accepted the offer.

On 5 September 1893 Admiral Mello openly rebelled against Peixoto. After a few weeks of ineffective bombardment - the warships firing on the harbor fortifications and visa-versa with neither side doing any real damage to the other - Peixoto tasked Stone to build a torpedo that would sink Admiral Mello's principal warship, the *Aquidaban*. If Stone succeeded he was to be paid $600,000 in gold. It took Stone only ten days to manufacture the torpedo. The plan of attack was simple. A tug flying a British flag (common in the harbor) would cross in front of the *Aquidaban* on her daily route to bombard the harbor fortifications. The tug would be towing the torpedo Stone had constructed. The line would ensnare itself on the bow of the *Aquidaban* and draw the torpedo into the warship. But Mello had his spies too. The Brazilian admiral informed the British of the misuse of their flag and they seized the tug with Stone on board. He was taken to the British warship *Sirius* and after much acrimony turned over to the captain of the U.S. cruiser *Charleston*. Held incommunicado on board American warships, ultimately Stone was transported back to the United States where he was unceremoniously released. The Brazilian revolution of 1893-94 was decided in favor of President Peixoto in part by the actions of another American mercenary. (*See the entry*, Dynamite Fleet, 1893-94)

Stone was not finished with his shady undertakings. He formed the International Export & Trading Company. He wrote:

> "Through this concern it was proposed to arm and finance any promising revolution whose leaders would guarantee ... to pay us anywhere from three to ten times the amount of money we had actually invested in the enterprise, and give us valuable concessions besides."[7]

His first stop was Port-au-Prince. An old acquaintance Dominique Hippolyte, with whom he had a poor relationship, was in power and was unwilling to let bygones be bygones so Stone had to sneak out of Haiti. Next, he stopped in Panama (then part of Colombia) and met with some would-be revolutionaries. A government spy reported this activity and once again Stone had to make a quick exit. Next, Stone went to Venezuela where initially he was harshly recieved by President Joaquín Crespo whom Stone had known 20 years earlier. Stone allayed Crespo's suspicions that he was there to assassinate him and ultimately they became friends. Crespo tasked Stone to create and head a network of spies. Stone served in this capacity for two years, potentially saving Crespo's life on a number of occasions.

Crespo rewarded Stone by informing the Orinoco Company, Limited, that he would renew their concession to develop the delta's resources if the company would made Stone the manager, which they did. On 12 June 1898 Crespo was killed (probably assassinated) after having defeated a rival in battle. After Crespo's death Stone's influenced waned. He remained in Santa Catalina, far from Caracas, for some 12 years, increasingly harassed by Venezuela's new president, Cipriano Castro, until Stone finally returned to New York in early 1906, thus ending his adventurous career.

Impact:

George Boynton Stone was the quintessential mercenary. In spite of all his skullduggery one cannot point to a single conflict where his participation altered the outcome. But in fairness to Stone, that was never his goal.

Biographies:

Francis Lay Norton (*ca.* early 1830s-unk.) was extremely strong, an excellent shot and a good swordsman. Stone described him as being "completely irreligious, cynical, and cold-blooded ... he was daring to the supreme degree but never foolishly reckless...."[8] In 1866 the Cuban Junta in New York City hired Norton as an "admiral" and gave him command of the Junta's first warship, the *Pioneer*. As he sailed out of Long Island Sound, he prematurely raised the Cuban flag. The vessel not yet in international waters, a U.S. revenue cutter seized the would-be warship and declared it a filibuster. During the 1870s Norton and Stone were partners in the enterprise to rob pirates in the China Sea. They also worked together in robbing Arab slave traders of their slaves and reselling them. Norton and Stone parted ways in 1877.

George Boynton Stone (1842-*cerca* 1911) [a.k.a. George B. Boynton; George MacFarlane; John F. Kinnear; Dr. Burnet; James Stuart Henderson] was born in New York City into a prominent family. He was a turbulent youth, always in trouble which bordered on more than mischief. His father transferred him from one Vermont boarding school to another, unsuccessfully seeking a solution. In 1861 Stone enlisted in the Union Army - the choice of which side to fight for determined more by easy of entry than sympathy for the cause. His father immediately bought him out of the enlisted ranks and shipped him off to an uncle in Illinois with instructions not to let him join the military. The uncle was no more successful than the father. Stone joined the Union cavalry, fought and was wounded at the Battle of Pittsburg Landing in early April 1862. After recovering, Stone was assigned to a detachment whose duty was to intercept contraband in the mountains of Tennessee. Being involved in the capture of a suspected female spy, he later helped her escape, beginning a pattern of favoring the fairer sex. Stone contracted malaria and was sent to Woodstock, Illinois, to recuperate. He eloped with a banker's daughter and resigned from the army - his father's influence helping to smooth the legal bumps. The newlyweds spent a short time in Chicago but legal enterprises proved boring for Stone. The couple moved to New York City and Stone's next adventures began. He went into the blockade-running business and this led to his estrangement from his family. Next, Stone entered the distillery business with James "Jim Jubilee Junior" Fisk. By manipulating the alcohol contents of their product they were very successful. They sold the business, making a $350,000 profit.

QUOTATIONS:

1 Horace Smith, *The War Maker*. Chicago: A.C. McClurg, 1911, p. 9.
2 Smith, *The War Maker*, pp. 52.
3 Smith, *The War Maker*, p. 51.
4 Smith, *The War Maker*, p. 79.
5 Smith, *The War Maker*, p. 130.
6 Smith, *The War Maker*, p. 241.
7 Smith, *The War Maker*, p. 358.
8 Smith, *The War Maker*, p. 79.

SOURCES:

Robert L. Scheina, *Latin America's Wars*. 2 vols. Washington, D.C.: Brassey's, Inc., 2003.
http://query.nytimes.com/mem/archive-   free/pdf?res=F70A10FF355A17738DDDA00A94DD405B818DF1D3

ODYSSEY OF CHARLES READ IN PERU

1880

GOAL:

To help Peru obtain at least a stalemate in its war with Chile.

BACKGROUND:

Historian Frederick Pike summed up the roots of the war: "The fundamental cause of the War of the Pacific [1879-83] was the mounting power and prestige, the economic and political stability of Chile on the one hand and the weakness, the political and economic deterioration of Bolivia and Peru on the other."[1]

    American entrepreneur W.R. Grace had invested heavily in Peru. Once war broke out Peru contacted Grace to purchase arms and transport them to Peru. Grace was confronted with a number of problems. First, Grace's business partner Charles Flint was serving as Chile's consul in New York. The second problem was how to get the war materials to Peru. Chile would surely intercept shipments sent around Cape Horn and Colombia, a neutral country, would prohibit weapons from being shipped across the Isthmus of Panama. To solve these problems Flint resigned as the Chilean consul and Grace initiated a smuggling operation. Rifles were shipped in boxes marked "agricultural machinery," and cartridges were hidden in barrels of lard.

    Being farsighted Flint and Grace believed that the automotive torpedo held great promise so they began to acquire the weapon and its means of delivery, the small, fast motor launch. They purchased boats and torpedoes from John Lay, Nat Herreshoff and the U.S. Torpedo Company. Ten Pratt and Whitney torpedoes were clandestinely wrapped in oilcloth and sent across the isthmus. Although technicians were supplied by some of the manufacturers, Flint and Grace believed they needed an experienced naval officer as well.

LEADERSHIP:

Since gaining independence in 1824 Peru was governed by competing families. Although labeled Conservatives and Liberals, there was little to distinguish between their policies except for who was rewarded from the national treasury. President Ignacio Prado was in charge between the outbreak of war on 5 April 1879 and 17 December 1879, the day he fled to Europe to "seek help" whatever that meant. Next the Peruvian presidency was seized by General Nicolas de Píerola and he governed through most of the war.

VOLUNTEERS:

The U.S. Civil War (1861-65) had been the proving ground for the automotive torpedo. The weapon was extremely temperamental and required experts to prepare it for use and to successfully employ it. Flint and Grace chose a former Confederate, Charles William Read, for the job. Not only was Read experienced with torpedoes and had demonstrated bravery during the Civil War. He had also had dealings with the Colombian navy and spoke Spanish.

COMPENSATION:

Flint had turned down one offer from a job-seeker to sink the two principal Chilean warships for the then-astronomical amount of one million dollars. Apparently, Flint and Read had no trouble coming to financial terms. In addition to whatever Flint agreed to pay, Read could anticipate a significant amount of prize money from the Peruvian government if he sank any Chilean warships.

OPPOSITION:

Chile had at least a two-to-one advantage in warships over Peru and the Chilean ships were manned by superior crews. Peru, however, had a more numerous army. The Chilean army was a modern, late 19th Century force, whereas the Peruvian army was based on a colonial social structure of forced conscription. The typical Peruvian soldier had no clue why he was fighting other than that he was forced to do so.

OPERATIONS:

Read and Flint traveled together to Bristol, Rhode Island, where Read helped test Herreshoff boats. On 20 August Read along with engineer John H. Smith sailed for Peru. Upon arrival Read was made a commander in the Peruvian navy and he devised a plan to attack the two principal Chilean warships then being overhauled in Valparaiso, Chile. Read immediately incurred the jealousy of other Peruvian naval officers and foreign individuals who represented the manufacturers of competing torpedo designs. A number of Peruvian officers volunteered to undertake the dangerous mission without expecting prize money. The problem was, they knew nothing about torpedoes.

On 8 October 1879 disaster befell the Peruvian navy. For six months Peruvian Admiral Miguel Grau's cunning and luck had bedeviled the Chileans, hitting them here and there, keeping Chile on the defensive. On that day the far superior Chilean fleet caught up with Grau and captured Peru's only ironclad, the *Huáscar*. Admiral Grau and four succeeding commanding officers died in a futile attempt to defend their ship. Perhaps the only thing that stood between a methodical series of amphibious assaults by the Chileans as they moved up the coast was the torpedo.

Read was not yet ready to quit. He offered to make seaworthy one of two dilapidated river-monitors that Peru had purchased from the United States at the close of the Civil War. He would launch his torpedoes from that platform. The idea was opposed by the chief engineer of the Peruvian navy. Read saw no further possibility of success so he returned home.

Impact:

Entrepreneur W.R. Grace wrote: "The return to this country of Read ... has so disgusted me with the management of Peruvian affairs that I have lost faith in their future."[2] Read's efforts to destroy the principal warships of the Chilean navy were aborted before they were even tried. Peru was decisively defeated by Chile, which became the dominant country on the West Coast of South America.

William Grace and Company proved to be a winner. Following the war Peru was in chaos with a $250,00,000 debt. The 1890 Grace-Donoughmore Contract with Peru assumed the national debt in exchange for enormous concessions.

Biographies:

Charles William Read (1840-90) was born in Yazoo County, Mississippi. He graduated from the U.S. Naval Academy in 1860. He served in the Confederate navy throughout the Civil War. Read was assigned to numerous posts on the Mississippi River. He was the executive officer on board the river gunboat *McRae* and took over command he the captain was mortally wounded on 24 March 1861. Next he served on board the cruiser *Florida* and was placed in command of the prize *Clarence* off the coast of Brazil. Read captured 21 prizes between Charleston, South Carolina, and Portland, Maine. He boldly sailed into Portland Harbor and captured the revenue cutter *Caleb Cushing*. A few hours later, however, he was taken prisoner and held at Fort Warren. Read was exchanged on 18 October 1864 and ultimately commanded a torpedo boat division of the James River Squadron. Prior to the fall of Richmond, Read was ordered to Shreveport, Louisiana, and given command of the sea-going ram *William H. Webb*. Disguised as a Union ship, the *William H. Webb* attempted to escape down the Mississippi River and out to sea. On 24 April 1865 Read was intercepted by the Union warship *Richmond* and he was captured. Once again he was confined in Fort Warren, being released in July 1866. After the Civil War he sailed as a merchant ship captain and was an intermediary in the purchase of a gunboat by the Colombian navy.

QUOTATIONS:

[1] Fredrick B. Pike, *The Modern History of Peru*. New York: Frederick A. Praeger, Publishers, 1967, p. 142.

[2] Marquis James, *Merchant Adventurer - The Story of W.R. Grace*. Wilmington, DE: Scholarly Resources, Inc., 1993. p. 136.

SOURCES:

Dictionary of American Biography. 10 vols. plus sup. 1 thru 8. New York: Charles Scribner's Sons, 1936 & 1990.

Lawrence A. Clayton, *Grace: W.R. Grace & Co., the Formative Years 1850-1930*. Ottawa, IL: Jameson Books, 1985.

Robert L. Scheina, *Latin America's Wars*. 2 vols. Washington, D.C.: Brassey's, Inc., 2003.

Six Americans Fighting for Chile

1879-81

Goal:

To help Chile defeat Bolivia and Peru in the War of the Pacific.

Background:

The underlying cause of this war was the rivalry between Chile and Peru over which nation would control the Atacama Desert and become the most influential on the western Coast of South America. (*See* Odyssey of Charles Read in Peru, 1880)

Leadership:

All six Americans were junior officers and played no leadership roles.

Volunteers:

The motives of the six volunteers are unclear.

Compensation:

Undoubtedly they received the same pay as their Chilean counterparts.

Six Americans Fighting for Chile, 1879-81

Opposition:

The Peruvian army was feudal in nature. The officers came from the élite of society and the soldiers from the peasants. Many of their weapons were second-hand. The one advantage the Peruvian army had was that it was larger than the Chilean army. The Peruvian navy had a significant number of mercenaries among its sailors but its warships and training were inferior to those of the Chilean navy. Bolivia's armed forces were pretty much irrelevant.

Strategy:

On land the Chilean strategy was primarily one of offense and the Peruvian strategy primarily one of defense. At sea initially, the Peruvian strategy was hit and run to win time for the army to coalesce.

Operations:

On 14 April 1879 Chilean forces seized the Bolivian port of Antofagasta and the war began. The Chilean army prepared to leapfrog up the coast of South America while the navy hunted down the Peruvian fleet. The Chilean offensive was delayed by a series of successful coastal raids by Peruvian Rear Admiral Miguel Grau. Once this threat was removed with the capture of Peru's primary ironclad, the *Huáscar*, on 8 October the Chilean army fought its way up the coast. Pisagua was captured on 2 November; Tacna was captured on 26 May 1880; and Arica was captured on 7 June. Now the Chilean army was at the gates of Lima, the Peruvian capital. The fate of Lima was decided by two Chilean victories, the Battle of Chorrillos (13 January 1881) and the Battle of Miraflores (15 January). Although the war continued until 1883, the outcome had been decided.

Aside from the information recorded on this broadside, the authors have discovered nothing else concerning these six Americans. They were too young to have served during the U.S. Civil War and none show on the rosters of the officers in the U.S. Army and the U.S. Navy. Relations between Chile and the United States during the War of the Pacific (1879-81) were cool, so the publishing of this poster is most interesting.

Authors' Collection

Impact:

All six Americans were in units actively engaged in combat. But their participation made little difference in the outcome of the war. The well-led, well-trained and well-equipped Chilean armed forces defeated the far less prepared Bolivians and Peruvians.

Fame–Fortune–Frustration

During the War of the Pacific, the Peruvian sea-going monitor Huascar fights a live-and-death struggle at the Battle of Angamos on 8 October 1879 against superior Chilean warships. Five successive commanding officers would be killed on his decks before she was successfully boarded. The six Americans who were fighting for Chile would have been acutely aware that this was the most decisive event of the war.

Courtesy Chilean Navy

Historian David Long describes U.S. involvement in the war: "In general Washington carried on a pro-Peruvian policy."[1] A broadside (a single sheet of paper suitable for posting) showing the six Americans who fought for Chile was produced in that nation. Considering the poor relations between Chile and the United States, this <u>may</u> have been an attempt to use the Americans' participation as a positive influence in the relationship between the two nations.

Biographies:

Frederick Sullivan (unk.) was a lieutenant in the Chacabuco Regiment.

Louis Wargny (unk.) held the rank of standard bearer (*abanderado*) in the Valparaíso Regiment.

Yuseff (unk.) was a lieutenant in the Concepción Regiment.

John Gillman (unk.) was a second lieutenant in the navy.

Peter MacCann (unk.) was a second lieutenant in the Lautaro Regiment.

Rafael Wormald (unk.) was a second lieutenant in the Talca Regiment.

Quotations:

[1] David F. Long, *Gold Braid and Foreign Relations*. Annapolis: Naval Institute Press, 1988, p. 359.

Sources:

Comité de História Militar del Ejército, *Historia Militar de Chile*. 3 tomos. Santiago: Estado Mayor General del Ejército, 1969.

Agustín Toro Davila, *Síntesis Histórico Militar de Chile*. 2 tomos. Santiago: Fondo Editorial Educacíon Moderna, 1969.

Dynamite Campaign against Great Britain

1881-85

Goal:

To attack Great Britain on its home turf.

Background:

Although American-Irish Fenian operations in the 1860s against the British Empire were a dismal failure (*see* American Fenian Expedition to Canada, 1866-70), the movement did not lose its dedication to freeing Ireland from English rule.

John Devoy and Jeremiah O'Donovan Rossa (frequently his surname is cited as O'Donovan) reorganized the American-Irish republican movement and renamed it the *Clan na Gael*. The leadership was divided as to whether or not to promote violence to achieve Irish independence. Initially, the more conservative Devoy favored a political solution. In June 1880 Rossa split with the *Clan na Gael*, and created the United Irishmen of America, which favored violence.

Leadership:

The leadership for the dynamite campaign was splintered between the United Irishmen of America and the *Clan na Gael*. Although the initial bombers of 1881 were from Rossa's organization, the later bombers were from both the United Irishmen of America and the *Clan na Gael*.

Dynamite Campaign against Great Britain, 1881-85

Volunteers:

Historian Joseph McKenna writes: "The senior guardians were advised not to select volunteers, and special choice was made of men without families. So great was the care taken in the selection of agents that their whole career and character was inquired into beforehand without their knowledge."[1]

Compensation:

Although the Fenian movement was active in both Ireland and America, its funds came primarily from the United States. Sir William Harcourt, the British home secretary, observed: "[T]he Irish subscriptions [donations] are coppers, but the gold and silver come from Fenianism in America."[2] In 1875 Rossa appealed for donations to the "skirmishing fund." This was a "secret" fund used to finance military adventures against Great Britain. Within a year $23,500 had been collected.

Opposition:

Even though the British empire possessed the strongest military in the world, the American-Irish had some advantages. First, due to the American-Irish's increasing political influence, the United States served as a safe haven and a base of operations. Second, the American-Irish were not constrained by international borders. Third, new, powerful explosives - nitroglycerin and dynamite - had recently been developed that provided an aggressor with new, powerful weapons. The Fenians also financed the building of a submarine.

The submarine had long been the dream of the underdog in its struggle against a superior maritime power. Fortuitously for the Irish cause, a recently arrived Irish immigrant, John P. Holland, possessed the flare for mechanical genius. In mid-1876 he asked the Fenians to fund the development of his "wrecking boat" [the term submarine not in use] to which they agreed. Although Holland was not a member of a radical Irish group, he intensely disliked the English and was not naïve as to the intended use of his boat.

First, Holland built a 30-inch working model and successfully demonstrated it at Coney Island for his benefactors. Next, he supervised the construction of a mini-boat - 14 feet, 6 inches - called *Boat No. 1*. Placed in the water on 1 February 1877 it immediately sank. The boat was raised and successfully tested by mid-summer. On 3 May 1879 Holland embarked on the construction of his second submarine, the *Fenian Ram* - 31 feet. The boat was launched in mid-1883 and was successfully tested. In November John Breslin and other Fenians, who

Jeremiah O'Donovan Rossa's (1831-unk.) American citizenship was determined by Judge Richard L. Larremore, who granted him that status. This made Rossa eligible to run for state office even though he had not met a five-year residency requirement. Although Rossa never carried out any dynamite bombings personally, he was the heart and soul of the anti-British movement in the United States.

Courtesy wikimedia.org

questioned the expenditures of money from the "Skirmishing Fund," forged Holland's signature and highjacked the *Fenian Ram*. Holland was disgusted and refused to have any more dealings with the Fenians. The boat became a curiosity piece.

Strategy:

Appreciating its inability to directly confront the powerful British military, the Feninian movement decided to target British civilians. This brought it into conflict with British civil authority.

On 28 August 1880 Patrick Ford's newspaper, the *Irish World*, laid out the American-Irish strategy,

> "England could be invaded by a small and resolute group of men - say ten or a dozen, when a force of a thousand times this number coming with ships and artillery, and banners flying could not effect a landing .... Then, tens of thousands of Irishmen, from long residence in the country, know England's cities well .... When the night for action came - the night that the wind was blowing strong - this little band would deploy ... and at the same instant 'strike with lightning' the enemy of their land and race."[3]

Operations:

Rossa's followers struck first. A dynamite explosion occurred on 14 January 1881 at the government armory in Salford, near Manchester. The armory, housing 5,000 guns, was destroyed and two passersby were seriously injured, a boy later dying of his injuries. On 18 March the bombers attempted to blow up the residence of the lord mayor of London but the bomb was discovered by a police constable before it could explode. Among the packing materials the police found an American newspaper. On 10 April another explosion occurred at the central police station in Liverpool, resulting in minor structural damage.

On 10 June 1881 two bombers were caught trying to dynamite the town hall in Liverpool, England. One of the two, James McGrath, although born in Glasgow of Irish parents, was living in New York. Both men were sentenced to life in prison. In that same month British authorities, while inspecting the cargo of a recently arrived steamer, *Malta*, discovered six sophisticated bombs hidden in a barrel marked cement. The dynamite had been manufactured in the United States.

On 20 January 1883 three explosions occurred in Liverpool. They blew up a gasholder (a relay storage tank used to supply gas for lighting), a shed in the railway yard, and a water viaduct. The three blasts injured about 20 people and caused some structural damage. The bombers escaped but the authorities could determine from the residue that the dynamite had been manufactured in America.

In mid 1882 another group of bombers arrived from the United States. They set up their dynamite factory in Cork, Ireland, to avoid detection by the British authorities. All of the necessary ingredients were purchased in Scotland and shipped to Ireland. Three of the dynamiters - Thomas J. Mooney, John Henry O'Connor and Terence McDermott (a British spy) traveled to London and on 15 March bombed the Local Government Offices in Whitehall not far from the House of Commons. The blast caused significant structural damage. A second bomb, made from the same batch, failed to properly explode at the building housing the *Times* newspaper in Printing House Square. Through information provided by McDermott the bombers and other conspirators were arrested in a few days. One agreed to turn Queen's evidence, deflecting suspicion from McDermott.

Others besides Rossa's followers were getting involved in the dynamite campaign. Members of *Clan na Gael* gathered in Chicago for what became known as the "Great Dynamite Convention." Dr. Thomas Gallagher of Brooklyn undertook a trip to England to lay the groundwork for a campaign. By early February another group of bombers had set up a dynamite manufacturing factory in London run by John Cadogan Murphy using the alias Alfred George Whitehead. All of Murphy's efforts to hide the location of his dynamite factory were to no avail. British spies in America learned enough details of the plot and Murphy's large purchases of pure glycerin led authorities to the factory. By early April eight would-be dynamiters were arrested including the manufacturer, Murphy, and the leader, Dr. Gallagher. They were tried between 11 and 14 June 1883; most were convicted and sentenced to life in prison.

Security among the American-Irish was tightened in the United States. On 30 October two bombs exploded on the Metropolitan Railway in London. The blasts caused significant property damage and numerous injuries, but none serious. The four American-Irish bombers - Harry Burton, James Gilbert Cunningham and two others - immediately fled to the United States undetected.

The same four bombers returned to London on 20 February 1884. On 26 February at 1 AM a bomb exploded in the Victoria station. Unexploded bombs were discovered in other railroad stations. The bomb components had been manufactured in America. Once again the bombers escaped back to the United States. To placate British outrage, President Chester Arthur instructed federal marshals to use extreme vigilance to prevent the illegal transport of explosives on board American ships.

Three dynamiters - Luke Dillon, William Mackey Lomasney and Harry Burton - returned to London a few months later. In the evening of 30 May two bombs exploded outside the Junior Carlton Club on St. James Square. Fourteen individuals were injured. A third bomb exploded at Scotland Yard at 9:20 PM. This last bomb caused significant structural damage and a few individuals were injured. Another bomb was discovered at Trafalgar Square near Lord Nelson's statue before it exploded. All three dynamiters escaped to New York.

In December 1884 Lomasney returned to London with two other dynamiters, a younger brother and John Fleming. Their target was the London Bridge. On 13 December at about 4:30 PM an explosion occurred under the bridge. Apparently there had been a premature detonation and all three of the dynamiters were blown apart. The bridge sustained only very minor damage.

The next pair of dynamiters - Harry Burton and James Gilbert Cunningham (also used the alias surnames Dalton and Gilbert) - was in transit at the time when the explosion under the London Bridge occurred. After finding accommodations in London and meeting a Fenian, they planted a bomb in a railway tunnel which exploded during the evening of 2 January 1885. Damage to the tunnel was minimal. Later in the month the dynamiters were joined by Luke Dillon and Roger O'Neil who just arrived from America. On Saturday 24 January Cunningham planted a bomb in the Tower of London. It exploded at 2 PM causing significant structural damage and injuring a dozen persons. Cunningham did not make good his escape and was captured.

Violence spilled back across the Atlantic. On 8 January Joseph Phelan, having been identified as a British spy, was seriously stabbed in New York while in the offices of Rossa's newspaper, the *United Irishman*. Shortly after that Mrs. Yseult Dudley, an Englishwoman, entered Rossa's office and shot him. His wound was superficial.

The next target in London was the Parliament building. Luke Dillon and Roger O'Neil acquired tickets made available to the public to tour the seat of government. While touring the building on 24 January they found a place unobserved by the increased security, and removed the dynamite belts they were wearing, lit the fuses and calmly continued exiting the building. Although the bombs were discovered, they exploded while being removed. Both of the bombers worked their way back to New York on tramp steamers.

Impact:

The attack on Parliament shocked the conscience of many Americans and lost significant public support for the Irish cause. In spite of that the outgoing Arthur administration was unable to obtain any legislation to deal with the problem of America-based Irish terrorists. And the plotting continued. A half-baked scheme known as the Jubilee plot (celebrating Queen Victoria's reign) was hatched but this scheme initially was orchestrated by the British to entrap potential conspirators.

As in the Fenian attacks of the 1860s, the Achilles' heel of the dynamiters was the inability of their organization to keep a secret. In defense of American-Irish security, the English spy system on both sides of the Atlantic was formidable.

How many of the dynamiters had established American citizenship prior to the attacks is unclear. However, those who were caught did not hesitate to claim American citizenship. P.J.P. Curran, an Irish nationalist and member of Parliament, observed, "The Irish make bad subjects but worse rebels."[4]

Biographies:

William Ansburgh (1861 - unk.) was born in Ireland. He immigrated to the United States as a young man. Ansburgh was arrested in London on 7 April 1883 and charged with felony-treason. He was found not guilty and released.

Thomas J. Clarke [alias Henry Hayward Wilson] (1858 - unk.) was born on the Isle of Wight. The family moved to northern Ireland and it considered this its native land. In 1881 Thomas immigrated to the United States. He was arrested with Dr. Thomas Gallagher. At the time of his arrest he had nitroglycerin in his possession. Clarke was tried, found guilty and sentenced to life in prison.

Luke Dillon (*ca.* 1848 - unk.) was born in Leeds, England. His parents had fled their during the potato famine of 1848. Luke was taken to the United States at the age of six and lived in Trenton, New Jersey, and Philadelphia, Pennsylvania. He joined the U.S. Army in 1867, fought Indians in Montana, and was honorably discharged in 1870.

Daniel Gallagher (unk.), a young brother of Dr. Thomas Gallagher, refused to undertake a dynamite mission in early February 1883 and returned to the United States.

Bernard Gallagher [alias James Campbell] (1854 - unk.), a young brother of Dr. Thomas Gallagher, was born near Glasgow, Scotland to Irish parents. He spent 1878 and 1879 in Glasgow working in an iron foundry, returning to New York at the request of his brother Thomas.

He was arrested in Glasgow and charged with felony-treason. Bernard was found not guilty and released.

Thomas Gallagher [alias Fletcher] (1850 - unk.) was born in Glasgow, Scotland, to Irish parents. Following the death of his father, the family immigrated to New York in 1868. Gallagher studied medicine and began a practice in Brooklyn, New York. He joined the Emerald Club, a Fenian society dedicated to the elimination of British rule from Ireland. Gallagher became the leader of the dynamite team sent to England. Gallagher was arrested in April 1883 and charged with directing a conspiracy to blow up public buildings in London. He was tried, convicted and sentenced to life in prison.

Edmund O'Brien Kennedy [alias Timothy Featherstone] (unk.), born in Ireland, took part in an attack on the police van in Manchester in 1867. He was captured and served five years in prison. Once released, Kennedy sailed to America.

John Kent [alias John Curtin] (1849 - unk.) was born in Fermoy, Ireland. He worked in a gasworks until 1872 when he immigrated to the United States. He was arrested 7 April 1883 and charged with felony-treason. He was tried, found guilty and sentenced to life in prison.

William Francis Mackey Lomasney [the "Little Captain"; alias J.G. Marshall] (1841 - 84) was born in Cincinnati, Ohio, to Irish parents. He was a small man and talked with a lisp. In 1865 he sailed to Ireland to take part in an aborted uprising. Lomasney was arrested. He was briefly jailed and then released on the condition that he leave the British Isles. In 1867 Lomasney returned to Ireland and took part in the Fenian uprising. On 6 March he was a leader in the capture of the Royal Irish Constabulary Barracks at Ballyknockane. Lomasney led subsequent raids throughout Ireland. He was captured on 7 February 1868 and initially charged with murder. Subsequently, he was convicted of treason felony. Lomasney was sentenced to 12 years in prison. He was released under a 1871 amnesty and returned to the United States where he opened a bookshop in Detroit.

William Joseph Lynch [alias William J. Norman] (unk.) worked in a factory in New York which constructed carriages. When arrested in London he had nitroglycerin in his possession. Lynch turned queen's evidence. Lynch disappeared following the trial.

John Cadogan Murphy [alias Alfred George Whitehead] (1860 - unk.) was born in Cork County, Ireland. He immigrated to New York and became a painter by trade. Selected for the dynamite team, Murphy was in charge of the manufacturing of dynamite in London. He was arrested on 3 April 1883. Murphy was tried, convicted and sentenced to life in prison.

John Henry O'Connor [alias Henry Dalton] (1843 - unk.) was born in Ireland. His family moved to London in 1851. O'Connor immigrated to the United States in 1873. He was arrested 3 April 1883 and charged with felony-treason.

Roger O'Neil (unk.) served in the Confederate army.

Jeremiah O'Donovan Rossa (1831-unk.) was born in Ireland. He became involved in the Fenian movement and was jailed in 1865. In 1869 Rossa was elected to the House of Commons from Tipperary (although not seated because of a conviction for treason-felony), and in 1871 he was an unsuccessful candidate for the New York state senate. An American judge, Richard L. Larremore, granted Rossa American citizenship in 1871 even though he had not met the five- year residence requirement.

QUOTATIONS:

[1] Joseph McKenna, *The Irish-American Dynamite Campaign*. Jefferson, NC: McFarland & Company, Inc., Publishers, 2012, p. 28.

[2] David M. Pletcher, *The Awkward Years*. Columbia, MO: University of Missouri Press, 1962, p. 246.

[3] McKenna, *The Irish-American Dynamite Campaign*, p. 13.

[4] McKenna, *The Irish-American Dynamite Campaign*, p. 3.

SOURCES:

Florence E. Gibson, *The Attitudes of the New York Irish toward State and National Affairs 1848-1892*. New York: Columbia University Press, 1951.

Robert Kee, *The Green Flag*. 3 vols. New York: Penguin Books, 1972.

Richard Knowles Morris, *John P. Holland, 1841-1914: Inventor of the Modern Submarine*. Columbia, S.C.: University of South Carolina Press, 1998.

Conor Cruise O'Brien, *Parnell and His Party 1880-90*. London: Oxford University Press, 1957.

Dynamite Fleet

1893-94

Goal:

This was a fight between the "haves" of Brazilian society over who was going to control the government and by extension the wealth of the nation.

Background:

Brazil abolished its monarchy in 1889. For the next few years an uneasy truce existed among political factions within the country. Finally on 5 September 1893 Admiral Custódio José de Mello led the Brazilian navy into rebellion against the government of General Floriano Peixoto who controlled the army. Complicating the military picture, the southern states of Brazil, which had some ground forces, rebelled against the government for their independence.

Leadership:

Within Brazil Admiral Mello and General Peixoto commanded their respective forces. Since the navy could not act decisively on land nor the army at sea, it became clear that whichever side could create a force capable of beating the other in its own domain, would win. The navy endeavored to forge a closer bond with the rebellious south while the army endeavored to buy a navy.

Brazilian government agents in North America and Europe were ordered to acquire warships. Rather than simply buy warships which would then need to be manned, Brazilian agents in the United States hired the premiere arms merchant of his day, Charles Flint, to create a navy. In years past he had acquired arms for both the Chileans and the Peruvians, who were enemies. This attested to his political dexterity. Flint created for the Brazilian government the "Dynamite Fleet". Flint gave command of his fleet to an old clipper ship captain, Ezekiel Baker. Typical of this breed, Baker was a strict disciplinarian, a risk taker and a superb sailor.

VOLUNTEERS:

The Dynamite Fleet's officers and crews were mostly Americans recruited in New York City. They numbered at least 200 men. Truthfully, these Americans were almost irrelevant to the endeavor's success. Intentionally, the fleet was more bark than bite.

COMPENSATION:

Flint demanded top wages for his services and probably rewarded well those who sailed the Dynamite Fleet to Brazil.

OPPOSITION:

The principal warships of the rebellious navy were the second-class battleship *Aquidaban* and the one-year-old protected cruiser *República*. In addition the navy had numerous smaller warships and captured merchantmen. On paper the ships that were available to the rebellious navy were formidable. The crews were another matter. The rebellious navy's manpower was so limited that the protected cruiser *Almirante Tamandaré* was manned by only 37 men during the height of the gun duels against the harbor's forts. Its normal complement was 400 men.

The Brazilian warship *Aquidaban* was the backbone of the naval revolt on 1893-94. The armored cruiser was the target of two plots concocted by American mercenaries. First, George Boynton Stone agreed to sink the ship by towing a non-self propelled torpedo into it. This was foiled when the British intercepted and captured the tug he was using to tow the torpedo. The tug was flying the British flag to make it immune from attack. Next, Charles Flint's "dynamite fleet" was to sink the Aquidaban with the "dynamite gun." By the time Flint's fleet arrived off Brazil the revolution had collapsed and the gun, of questionable accuracy, was never used.

Courtesy Brazilian Navy

STRATEGY:

Realizing that he had a few months at most to assemble a fleet, Flint decided to buy fast merchantships which he would armed with experimental weaponry. The primary weapon was the dynamite gun. This 50-foot-cylinder that was 15 inches in diameter could throw a 50 pound dynamite projectile about 3,000 yards. Here was the problem: the projectile was not very good at hitting its target. First, the cylinder could not be trained; you had to aim the ship at the target. Second, the projectile traveled at a slow speed, making it difficult to hit a maneuvering target. Flint also purchased the torpedo boat *Destroyer,* built on speculation by the acclaimed naval architect John Ericsson, who had constructed the *Monitor* of Civil War fame.

Just as important as the Dynamite Fleet was the propaganda campaign that Flint launched. It significantly overstated the destructive power of the new weapons.

OPERATIONS:

The Dynamite Fleet arrived off Brazil in early 1894. It was joined by far more practical, but less publicized torpedo gunboats that the government had purchased in Europe. Truly the fleet was a paper tiger. No one knew how to operate the Sims-Edison torpedoes; there were only a few rounds for the dynamite gun; and there were no boarding weapons on any of the ships. All this did not matter. In March the rebels deserted their ships for asylum on board two Portuguese warships.

IMPACT:

How much the Dynamite Fleet contributed to the collapse of the rebellious navy is difficult to calculate. If the fleet had arrived in Brazilian waters a few weeks after the rebellion began, the rebel flagship alone, the *Aquidaban*, could have blown it out of the water. But by March 1894 the rebellious navy was spent - it had no more fight left in it. The frivolity of the episode was captured by the poem of an American reporter:

> "Mello, Mello, where are you, old fellow?
> A Yankee ship and a Yankee crew is out on the sea to look for you
> To knock you all to hell-o
> We fly a flag of orange and green, Sir,
> The like of which we ne'er have seen, Sir,
> Our good ship's name, we cannot tell it,
> We haven't had time to learn to spell it.
> But what has a flag and a name to do

With a Yankee ship and a Yankee crew that's out on the sea to look for you
To knock you all to hell-o."[1]

Biographies:

Ezekiel C. Baker (1846-1914) went to sea at the age of 14 years and worked his way up to the rank of Captain. Known to be a strict disciplinarian, among other ships he was the captain of the clipper ship *Young America*. Two days out from Liverpool the crew mutinied and attacked him; Baker killed five crew members with an axe. The court of inquiry praised Baker for courageously protecting the property of the owner. Later he captained merchant steamships sailing New York and Brazil. Charles Flint hired Baker in 1893 to take the Dynamite Fleet, some eight ships, to Brazil. Flint gave Baker the title of "Grand Admiral."

Thomas T. Craven (unk.) was the son of Rear Admiral Thomas T. Craven. The younger Craven became a naval cadet in 1890 and resigned in 1891. He was hired by Flint with the rank of lieutenant, possibly due to the prestige associated with the family name. After his adventure with the Dynamite Fleet Craven reentered the U.S. Navy.

Quotations:

[1] Charles R. Flint, *Memories of an Active Life*. New York: G.P. Putnam's Sons, 1923. p. 99.

Sources:

Cláudio Moreira Bento, "A esquadra Legal ou 'esquadra de papelao: suas vitórias no Rio de Janeiro e em Santa Catarina." *Revista do Exército Brasileiro*. vol. 130; no. 4 (October/December 1993) pp. 63-68.

Robert L. Scheina, *Latin America's Wars*. 2 vols. Washington, D.C.: Brassey's, Inc., 2003.

Cape Code History. Eastham, Wellfleet and beyond. 15 Dec 2011. Electronic Genealogy. 12 July 2012. http://capecodhistory.us/genealogy/family/f174.html

Frederick Burnham and the Matabele Wars

1893-96

Goal:

To seek adventure and be well paid for services as a soldier of fortune.

Background:

In the post-Waterloo world Africa was up for grabs. Bold risk-taking industrialists staked out economic empires and were soon followed by their national flags. These European entrepreneurs and their companies, whether English, French, Portuguese, Dutch or whatever, exercised sovereignty. This was the age of colonial empires. The rule was a colony existed for the economic good of the mother country. The formula was simple. The colony supplied the rare materials at a low cost to the mother country and the colony absorbed the excess manufacturing of the mother country.

African peoples had not coalesced into nation-states and remained divided in ethnic tribes typically ruled by brutal strongmen. King Logengula of the Matabele tribe (a branch of the Zulus) was typical of these African potentates. He was a cruel, corrupt and corpulent monarch. To entertain his 68 wives he fed captured enemies to crocodiles. He was astute enough not intentionally to provoke the Europeans. But not all events were within his control. Logengula sent his warriors into neighboring Mashonaland, Whiteman's territory, to punish some cattle thieves. The warriors disobeyed his orders, massacred perhaps 400 Blacks and destroyed property belonging to Whites. This was enough to spark a war.

Frederick Burnham and the Matabele Wars, 1893-96

LEADERSHIP:

Overall leadership was in the hands of famed empire builder Cecil John Rhodes (1853-1902). His role was so important that eventually a nation - Rhodesia - would be named after him. Command was exercised by whomever Rhodes delegated it to. Burnham was one of those individuals, eventually holding the rank of major.

VOLUNTEERS:

There were two armies in the field. Rhodes purchased the services of 700 local White farmers and miners from Mashonaland plus adventurers like Burnham. Although these men lacked formal military training, they were all experienced with guns and used to living the frontier life. Their weapons even included five Maxim machineguns. The British government, not wanting to leave the matter entirely in Rhodes' hands, fielded 225 Bechuanaland Border Police and a 2,000-man Bechuana native contingent. They, too, were well armed. This became a race between these two forces to see who could get to Logengula first - Rhodes' force would win.

COMPENSATION:

Burnham almost certainly received the pay of a British officer, commensurate with the rank he held. The White volunteers from Masho-

Frederick Burnham (1861--1947) was a true cowboy. He worked as a buffalo hunter, ranch hand, prospector, Army scout and stagecoach guard. Burnham fought for the U.S. Army in the Indian wars in western America, for the British in the two Matabele wars in Africa, and again for the British in the Second Boer War.

Richard Harding Davis, *Real Soldiers of Fortune* (New York, 1911)

naland were to be paid in land, 6,000 acres each, and cattle captured from the Matabele.

Opposition:

Matabele tribesmen were fierce warriors and significantly outnumbered their combined enemies, although the Matabele army was weakened by a recent outbreak of small pox. The Matabele were armed with 1,000 rifles which had been delivered by Rhodes as part of a deal cut with King Logengula earlier. Most of the warriors were armed with spears and edged weapons.

Strategy:

The most effective offense for the Europeans was cavalry sweeps. The Matabele did not have many horses and had no defense against cavalry, particularly in open terrain. The most effective defense for the Europeans was the *laagers*. A *laager* was a square or rectangle created by placement of heavy wagons. This served as a makeshift fort. Wagons on the move could be transformed into a *laager* within five to six minutes. *Laagers* offered excellent protection against the Matabeles' massed infantry attacks.

Operations:

The First Matabele War was fought from July to November 1893. On 25 October 6,000 Matabele launched a night attack at the Shangani River. Burnham described the action:

"This was one of the most spectacular night fights I have ever taken part in; what with a double line of fire from the men lying on the top of the large African trek wagons and those crouching under the wheels, the roar of the Maxims [machineguns], and the continuous crack of several thousand hostile rifles that rimmed our entire *laager*. Over and above all the din of the firing rose the shrieks and yells of the friendly natives as they were swept against our *laager*, wily-nilly, to be shot down by our own Maxim guns. The firing continued until the light of day brought deadly accuracy to our rifles and enabled us to open the *laager* and with our mounted men sweep the grass and timber free of the enemy...."[1]

Hundreds of the attackers were cut down; only and one White trooper was killed and six White men were wounded. A week later another large Matabele force attacked the column. Again, the attackers lost about 1,000 men and the Whites only a few. On 4 November the attackers captured Logengula's capital, Buluwayo. The king died soon afterward, possibly of small pox.

The Second Matabe War raged from March to October 1896. It sparked the destruction Matabe society - its wealth (the confiscated land and cattle) and its culture (the end of the warrior heritage). Blacks throughout Matabeeland rose up and began butchering Whites and their Black servants. At the center of the uprising was the high priest M'Limo who claimed that he could turn bullets into water. The Whites fielded a 600-man volunteer force. Numerous bloody skirmishes occurred with neither side taking prisoners. White reinforcements, including government troops, arrived and the fighting now favored the Whites.

To strike at the heart of the enemy, Burnham received orders from the British commander regarding the troublesome high priest M'Limo: "Capture the M'Limo if you can. Kill him if you must. Do not let him escape."[2] In June 1896, accompanied by a British official, Burnham managed somehow to penetrate a tribal area and locate the priest in a ceremonial cave in a mountain. Burnham made a noise, attracted the priest's attention, and then fired at him, hitting M'Limo beneath the heart and killing him.

Burnham and his companion had concealed their horses in a clump of bushes. They succeeded in reaching the horses and galloping away, pursued by yelling, infuriated native warriors. Burnham and companion dodged, turned, retreated for two hours before finally reaching safety.

Impact:

The killing of the priest M'Limo in 1896 was an important element in ending the Second Matabee War (although a smaller allied tribe held out a while longer). Author Richard Harding Davis wrote: "The exploit was one of the chief factors in bringing the war to a close. The Matabeles, finding their leader was only a mortal like themselves, and so could not, as he had promised, bring miracles to their aid, lost heart, and when Cecil Rhodes in person made overtures of peace, his terms were accepted."[3] (Those persons interested in historic parallels will note the striking similarities of the killing of M'Limo and of terrorist leader Osama bin Laden in 2011 in Pakistan.)

African tribes, in spite of their numerical advantage, were no match for the mercenary armies of the European entrepreneurs or the national armies of the European nations. The first Matabele war had cost the Whites about 50 lives and 50,000 pounds in expenses. It had cost the Matabele thousands of lives. The second war caused the destruction of Matabele society.

Burnham was unique even among mercenaries because of the scope of his remarkable exploits and accomplishments. He succeeded in difficult and dangerous tasks that years later the special forces of the United States and other countries would learn to do. When he retired from the British army Burnham received a letter from the commander-in-chief, Lord Roberts, who cited "the thrilling enterprises in which ... you have been engaged, demanding ... the training of a lifetime, combined with exceptional courage, caution, and powers of endurance."[4]

BIOGRAPHIES:

Homer Ephraim Blick (1865-1947), an American, fought in the Second Matabele War.

James Shannon Blick [originally Blickensderfer] (1933-1916) was born in Blue Ridge, Pennsylvania. He fought in the Second Matabele War.

John Charles Blick (1875-1960), a native of Montana, fought in the Second Matabele War.

Judd Dunning Blick (1873-1933), a native of Montana, in 1895 he participated in the Barotseland expedition and fought in the Second Matabele War.

Frederick Russell Burnham (1861-1947) was born of a missionary family on an Indian reservation in Minnesota. Burnham began his adventurous career at the age of 12 as a mounted messenger for the Western Union Telegraph Company. He also worked as a buffalo hunter, cowboy, prospector and stagecoach guard. At the age of 14 he was employed as a scout and tracker for the U.S. Army. He participated in several Indian Wars. He became skilled at tracking, evasion, demolition, living off the land and navigation on land without a compass. He was also expert with the rifle and revolver. In the following years he became a deputy sheriff, did prospecting, worked in the cattle industry, did more scouting and tended an orange grove. Burnham also married his childhood sweetheart and had a son.

The Wild West, however, was not wild enough for Burnham. As he once said, " ... [W[hen the place is finally settled I don't seem to enjoy it very long."[5] Hearing of the building of explorer Cecil Rhodes' Cape Town to Cairo railway in Africa, Burnham on 1 January 1893 left San Francisco for Cape Town. He took his wife and young son with him. In South Africa he was employed by Rhodes' British South Africa Company as a scout and he headed north to what would become Rhodesia.

After fighting in the two Matabele wars Burnham and his family returned to California. They did not stay long. Gold had been discovered in the Klondike and the Burnham family took off for Alaska. War broke out between the United States and Spain in 1898 and Burnham heard about "Teddy" Roosevelt's Rough Riders. He rushed to join but before he could do so, the war ended. Burnham went back to prospecting. Next, Burham fought in the Second Boer War (1899-1902) once again on the side of the British (see Americans in the Boer War for later career).

Burham was injured in that conflict. Once he had recuperated, he engaged in a number of non-military tasks, including working for Rhodes again. He led an expedition to the Gold Coast Colony in Africa, surveyed the Upper Volta River, explored the Congo basin and discovered King Solomon's mines. He traveled to Mexico, where he opened copper and silver mines, helped divert the Yaqui River, and was one of the discoverers (1908) of Mayan ruins in the Yucatan Peninsula. During World War I a second attempt to serve alongside of Teddy Roosevelt fell through when Roosevelt's plan to raise a division of volunteers was unsuccessful. Burnham spent World War I directing exploration of the U.S. Southwest to find tungsten and manganese needed for the war effort. Frederick Burn ham's adventure-packed life would end at the age of 86.

Pearl "Pete" Ingram Miles (1871 - 11 December 1933), raised in Montana, survived the Shangani River patrol along with Burnham and William Gooding (an Australian).

Quotations:

[1] John S. Arvidson and F. Gerald Downey, "First Yank SOF in Rhodesia," pp. 66-74 *Soldier of Fortune* (May 1979) p. 68.
[2] Arvidson and Downey, "First Yank," p. 67.
[3] Richard Harding Davis, "Major Burnham, Chief of Scouts," pp. 191-228, *Real Soldiers of Fortune*. New York: Charles Scribner's Sons, 1911, p. 214.
[4] Davis, "Major Burnham," p. 224.
[5] Davis, "Major Burnham," p. 215.

Sources:

R. Ernest Dupuy and Trevor N. Dupuy. *The Harper Encyclopedia of Military History*. 4th edition. New York: HarperCollins Publishers, 1993.

Thomas Pakenham, *The Scramble for Africa, 1876-1912*. New York: Random House, 1991.

John Woolford, "The First Matabele War," *Military History* (May 2005) pp. 34-40, 70.

http://en.wikipedia.org/wiki/Three_Rivers,_California

Odyssey of Philo Norton McGiffin in Chinese Navy

1885-94

Goal:

The Chinese navy was being modernized. To help accomplish this, the services of a foreign naval expert were appreciated. For Philo Norton McGiffin this was an opportunity to use sea skills he had learned.

Background:

France and China were at war (the Tonkin Gulf War). Philo Norton McGiffin decided to use his skills in the service of the Chinese navy. He studied the Manchu language for a while in San Francisco, and then traveled to China, arriving in April 1885. The war had ended but he managed to be received by Viceroy Li Hung Chang, whom he asked for a naval appointment. The viceroy was skeptical but arranged for McGiffin to take an extensive naval examination (seamanship, navigation, gunnery, calculus, and so on). McGiffin did well on the exam. He was given a professorship and temporary command of a training ship. In the years that followed, McGiffin established a naval college modeled after the American college. He went to England to help supervise the construction of four warships. After ten years McGiffin applied for leave and it was granted. He may well have wanted to see if he could return to the U.S. Navy, a hope he always held. War, however, broke out between China and Japan, and McGiffin immediately withdrew his request.

China and Japan engaged in the first (1894-95) of two wars they would fight within a fifty-year period. Cause of this conflict was control of Korea. Despite the effort at modernization, the Chinese navy was not treated well by the government. The dowager empress helped herself to large amounts of navy funds to restore a palace.

LEADERSHIP:

Chinese Admiral Ting Ju Chang had been a cavalry officer. Philo Norton McGiffin described him as "a gallant soldier and true gentleman."[1] These attributes, however, could not make up for the admiral's lack of nautical knowledge. After a decade of service McGiffin was awarded the position of executive officer on the battleship *Chen Yuen* as war broke out. McGiffin was thrust into a position to make up for the deficiencies of the admiral and other Chinese senior officers.

VOLUNTEERS:

McGiffin was probably one of the few foreigners serving in the Chinese navy and undoubtedly the most influential. Like its army, the social structure of the Chinese navy was near-feudal and ill suited for modern war.

COMPENSATION:

McGiffin's initial pay in the Chinese navy was the equivalent of $143 per month. As he rose in rank this increased commensurately (he was paid in Mexican gold coins). He was also provided with servants and furnished houses.

OPPOSITION:

Following the opening of Japan by American Commodore Matthew Perry in 1853 the Japanese rapidly Westernized. The Japanese launched a massive campaign to modernize their armed forces. One might describe the Japanese Navy as being on steroids. The Japanese, an island people, enjoyed superior seamanship, and their gunnery was better. The Japanese fleet was commanded by Admiral Yuko Ito.

Philo McGiffin's (1860-97) pranks while at the U.S. Naval Academy cost him a career in the American Navy. Seeking employment elsewhere, he went to China and worked his way up to be the superintendent of the Chinese Naval College and later he commanded a Chinese battleship in combat against the Japanese.

Richard Harding Davis, *Real Soldiers of Fortune* (New York, 1911)

Philo McGiffin commanded the Chinese battleship Chen Yuen during the Battle of Yalu against the Japanese on 17 September 1894. Severely wounded, he travelled to New York for medical treatment. Apparently suffering from physical and psychological problems, McGiffin committed suicide in 1897.

Richard Harding Davis, *Real Soldiers of Fortune* (New York, 1911)

STRATEGY:

The Chinese navy tried - unsuccessfully - to block the movements of Japanese warships and troops. Japan's opening naval strategy was the destruction of the Chinese fleet.

OPERATIONS:

War broke out on 1 August 1894 between China and Japan. The Chinese had recently received two 7,430-ton battleships, the *Chen Yuen* and the *Ting Yuen*. McGiffin was assigned to the *Chen Yuen* as executive officer and second in command. On 17 September the Chinese and Japanese fleets engaged near the mouth of the Yalu River. Numerically the fleets were even; each had 12 vessels. But two of the smaller Chinese vessels fled (the captain of one was decapitated for his cowardice). The Chinese had two battleships and the Japanese had three 4,277-ton cruisers. The Chinese had more of the heavier guns. The Japanese, however, had the advantage of fast-firing artillery (twice the speed of the older weapons), greater total tonnage (36,000 to 21,000) and faster ships.

The battle lasted five hours. For four of those hours McGiffin was in command of the *Chen Yuen*. McGiffin later wrote, "Commodore Lin was our captain, but he was not to be seen at Yalu."[2] The Japanese concentrated their fire on the two battleships, sailing in a circle around the ironclads. The *Chen Yuen* was almost continuously on fire. McGiffin's skillful maneuvering of his vessel may have saved the Chinese ships from annihilation. McGiffin was caught by a blast from one of his cannon which burned an eye, burst both ear drums, left him temporarily unconscious and may have caused internal injuries. During the battle McGiffin was also hit by steel splinters. Not having a nearby port for repairs, Admiral Ito, his fleet low on ammunition, but not knowing the Chinese were also short, broke off the engagement. He also feared a possible night attack by Chinese torpedo boats. The Chinese had lost five vessels; the Japanese none. Vessels on both sides sustained considerable damage.

McGiffin brought his ship safely into port. Beset by his injuries he resigned his commission and travelled to New York for treatment. He kept his sense of humor, writing a friend, "I know that I will have ... my eye taken out (for a couple of hours only, provided it is not mislaid, and can be found."[3]

Before the Yalu battle, McGiffin had written his brother: "I don't want to be wounded. I hate to think of being dreadfully mangled and then patched up with half my limbs and senses gone."[4] Suffering psychological problems, unable to stand his pain any longer, on 11 February Philo McGiffin took his service revolver and killed himself. For his funeral he was dressed in a Chinese officer's uniform and a U.S. Navy guard unit rendered honors. Biographer/journalist Richard Harding Davis aptly summed up McGiffin's life: " ...[B]itter indeed must have been the reflections of the young wounded American, robbed, by the parsimony of his country, of the right he had earned to serve it, and who was driven out to give his best years and his life for a strange people under a strange flag."[5]

IMPACT:

In his handling of the battleship *Chen Yuen*, at one point luring a Japanese vessel into a virtual trap, McGiffin played a vital role in preventing the destruction of the Chinese fleet. But in spite of McGiffin's best efforts, the Chinese lost the war to the far better prepared Japanese.

BIOGRAPHIES:

Philo Norton McGiffin (1860-97) was known for his pranks at the U.S. Naval Academy, where he was a student. On one occasion he dropped cannon balls down a wooden staircase, causing considerate damage. Another time, he fired six cannon on the lawn of the Academy at midnight. McGiffin spent months confined in a prison ship. He also did a brave deed, running into the flames in a professor's home and rescuing a young daughter. For this McGiffin received a commendation from the secretary of the Navy. It took McGiffin five years to complete the four-year scholastic course. He did not, however, receive a commission. These were given only when officers' berths were available. McGiffin spent two years on board a warship and then was set adrift, given a year's pay.

QUOTATIONS:

[1] Richard Harding Davis, "Captain Philo Norton McGiffin," *Real Soldiers of Fortune*, pp. 121-44. New York: Charles Scribner's Sons, 1906, p. 143.
[2] John Laudermilk, "I Fought at Yalu," and James L. Yates, "Phio McGiggin Lore," pp. 22-27 *Naval History* - U.S. Naval Institute (September/October 1994) p. 26.
[3] Davis, "Captain Philo Norton McGiffin," p. 142.

[4] Laudermilk, "I Fought at Yalu," p. 27.
[5] Davis, "Captain Philo Norton McGiffin," p. 144.

Sources:

Dictionary of American Biography. 10 vols. plus sup. 1 thru 8. New York: Charles Scribner's Sons, 1936 & 1990.

Robert K. Douglas, *China*, vol. 6 of *The History of Nations*, edited by Henry Cabot Lodge. New York: P.F. Collier & Son Company, 1928.

R. Ernest Dupuy and Trevor N. Dupuy. *The Harper Encyclopedia of Military History*. 4th edition. New York: HarperCollins Publishers, 1993.

Americans in the Boer War

1899-1900

Goal:

For those fighting for the British, adventure and a payday; for those fighting for the Boers, adventure and the opportunity to fight the British Empire.

Background:

The British colonization of the southern tip of Africa took a circuitous route. During the 17th Century the Dutch established a colony at what is today Cape Town, a strategic location for travel to the Far East from Europe. This colony passed into British hands during the Napoleonic wars. As a consequence, the Dutch farmers (Boers - Afrikaner for farmers)) who lived there migrated north and east across the *veldt* (grasslands) defeating the indigenous peoples. By the 1850s the Boers had established the Orange Free State and the Transvaal to the north of Cape Town and in 1880-81 they fought a brief war against the British and won *de facto* independence. In 1886 the discovery of gold in the Witwatersrand region led to a massive influx of British and other foreigners into the Transvaal. In 1895 entrepreneur Cecil Rhodes, who controlled the Cape Town colony, clandestinely funded an expedition led by Dr. L. Starr Jameson on the pretense of rescuing British miners who were rebelling against the Boers. The Jameson raid was a disaster. The Boers captured the raiders and turned them over to the British for trial. Tensions increased and both sides armed themselves with modern weapons. Soldiers of fortune, spoiling for a fight, flocked to the region; significant numbers of Americans fought on both sides.

George Labram (ca. 1870-1899), an American mechanical engineer, poses with the 4" cannon the "Long Cecil" (named for the entrepreneur Cecil Rhodes) which he manufactured in Kimberley in the Orange Free State. In addition to the cannon, Labram designed and supervised the defenses of the besieged mining center. He was killed during the siege.

Courtesy wikimedia.org

LEADERSHIP:

For the British the overall command was in the hands of Field Marshal Frederick Sleigh Roberts, commander-in-chief of the British Forces South Africa. For the Boers the overall leadership was in the hands of the president of Transvaal, Paul Kruger. A number of Americans held field commands in the Boer army. The Irish Brigade was commanded by West Pointer John Blake and the American scouts were led by a former U.S. cavalry officer, John Hassel. Both men were experienced soldiers.

VOLUNTEERS:

Historian Bryon Farwell wrote, "[T]here were more Americans serving with the British side than with the Boers.... One congressman claimed that there were between two and three thousand Americans with the British, but he was guessing."[1] Many of the Americans arrived in South Africa accompanying the 100,000 horses and 80,000 mules purchased by the British from the United States. These Americans came as the animals' caretakers and stayed to fight.

American volunteers joined at least two combat units fighting for the Boers. Somewhere between 150 and 500 Americans served in the Irish Brigade (referred to by the Boers as "Irish Uitlanders" (outsiders) and "Wreckers Corps"). Anti-British sentiment ran strong among those Americans whose forefathers had immigrated to the United States from Ireland. Another smaller Boer unit dominated by Americans was the American Scouts. They numbered about 30 men. This was made up of adventurers who had fought elsewhere, including in Cuba against Spain.

COMPENSATION:

Apparently the Boers offered little or no pay to their volunteers Those fighting for the British received the standard military service pay.

OPPOSITION:

In 1899 "the sun never set on the British empire" - Great Britain was the most powerful nation in the world. In spite of that power, the British Empire had two challenges. First, much of its military power was dispersed throughout the world and second, many nations were envious of British wealth and power. British military units were rushed from India and other colonies to southern Africa.

STRATEGY:

The Boers set the tempo for the war. Their mounted infantry would find a strong defensive position blocking the British advance. When they were pressed they would fall back to a new defensive position. During the early months of the war the British sustained ten times the casualties of the Boers. Field Marshal Roberts wrote: "We have to deal with an enemy possessing remarkable mobility, intimately acquainted with the country, thoroughly understanding how to take advantage of the ground, adept in improvising cover, and most skilled in the use of their weapons."[2]

OPERATIONS:

The war began on 11 October 1899 and the highly motivated and fast-moving Boers struck first. Initially, the British employed the tried and true tactics developed during colonial wars against indigenous peoples: rigid formations and structured assaults. These tactics led to defeats.

The American Irish Brigade took part in fighting at Nicholson's Nek on 30 October 1899. The two sides were about equal in number, some 14,000 men each. The Boers gave the British a crushing defeat on the British. The British lost 1,210 men and the Boers only a few. Among the British troops captured were many Royal Irish Fusiliers. The Irish Brigade took part in the siege of Ladysmith between 2 November 1899 and 13 February 1900. The British successfully held out and were relieved. The brigade also fought at Colenso on 15 December 1899 which was another Boer victory. Outnumbered two to one, the Boers inflicted 30 times the casualties on the British (1,120 versus

38). At Spion Kop between 22 and 24 February 1900, again outnumbered five to one, the Boers defeated the British, inflicting more than 40 times the casualties on the British (1,440 versus 335).

In April 1900 a 58-man Irish-American unit arrived in the region. Most of the members called Illinois and Massachusetts home. They traveled under the ruse of being an ambulance unit. English Baptist Minister Henry James Batts wrote, "I would not like to meet them on a dark night."[3]

Throughout much of the early fighting the Boers fought a delaying action but ultimately, heavily outnumbered by the British, they suffered a series of defeats. Following the defeat at Komatipoort, the Boers were pushed back against the border with Mozambique. While the army escaped northward through the dry brush lands, by September 1900 most of the foreign volunteers sought sanctuary in the Portuguese territory.

Impact:

On 31 May 1902 the Treaty of Vereeniging ended the war. The Orange Free State and the Transvaal were annexed into the British Empire. In the end numbers mattered. The British had deployed 450,000 men (more than the entire Boer population - men, women, and children) to the region and the Boers fielded 40,000 men. This was the largest army the British had fielded to this point in history.

Apparently, the Irish Americans adapted well to their surroundings. Young Boer Roland Schikkerling wrote, "[Y]ou could not pick Patrick out of a herd of the wildest Boers..."[4] Historian Robert Kee wrote: "The pro-Boer Irish Brigade ... played ... a totally insignificant part in the war."[5] The brigade existed for one year (September 1899 - September 1900). The unit was disbanded by the Boers and the men surrendered to the Portuguese frontier post at Kamati. The Irish Brigade sustained more than 80 casualties, of which 17 died.

Biographies:

John Y. Filimore Blake (unk.), born in Missouri and was appointed from Arizona, graduated from West Point in 1880 and entered the U.S. Army as a Second Lieutenant. He fought in the Apache wars, commanding Navaho scouts. Resigning from the army on 19 August 1899 , he married a rich woman from Detroit, Michigan. Blake entered the railroad business and went bankrupt. In 1885 he traveled to South Africa and participated in the Matabele War in Rhodesia. Blake commanded the Irish Brigade for the Boers. When the British broke the siege of Ladysmith, Blake and other Americans distinguished themselves by saving one of the heavy artillery pieces. Blake was seriously wounded in the fighting along the Tugela River.

Frederick Russell Burnham (1861-1947) - (*see* entry Frederick Burnham and the Matabele Wars, 1893-96, for earlier career) - received a telegram while prospecting for gold in the Klondike; "Lord Roberts appoints you on his personal staff as Chief of Scouts. If you accept, come at once the quickest possible way."[6] He arrived just before the Battle of Paardeberg and began operating behind enemy lines. Burnham was twice captured and twice escaped. He was seriously wounded while blowing up the rail line which was the Boer link to the sea. Miraculously he made it back to British lines. Burnham was sent to London to recover from his wounds. He was given an audience with Queen Victoria and awarded the Distinguished Service Order, Britain's second highest military honor.

John Clement (unk.-1900), a railway engineer, was a friend on Lewis Seymour [*see* below]. He was second in command of her Britannic Majesty's Railway Pioneer Regiment and was given the rank of lieutenant. Like Seymour, Clement was killed on 14 June 1900 while working on the Sand River Bridge in the Orange Free State.

James "Arizona Kid" Foster (unk.) traveled to South Africa on board a mule carrier. He joined the British transport service and once at the front deserted to the Boers. He was known for his reckless bravery.

John Hassel (unk.), a former U.S. cavalry officer, was working in the Transvaal as a mining engineer when the war started. Fighting for the Boers, he saw early action at the siege of Ladysmith and the fighting along the Tugela River. Receiving permission to form a unit, Hassel advertised in an English-language Johannesburg newspaper and raised the 60-man American Scouts.

Maurice David Heany (unk.), of Irish descent, was reared and educated in Baltimore, Maryland. He travel to Africa and settled in Zambesi (Boer territory). Heany participated in the pro-British, failed Jameson Raid in 1895 and was captured by the Boers. He won his release from the Boers by the plea of being an American citizen.

O Ji Ja Tek Ka, "Burning Flower" (unk.), a Mohawk, traveled to South Africa and tried to join British forces but was rejected because he was an Indian. He worked in a horse depot.

James "Dynamite Dick" King (unk.) was born in the coal region of Pennsylvania and served in the American Scouts. He was one of two individuals who saved the wounded son of the former president of the Orange Free State during the Battle of Vaalkrantz. Looking to earn some money, King went to the British consul and threatened to blow up the Komatipoort railway bridge if he were not paid 3,000 pounds.

The consul checked with the British military and found the bridge to be well guarded. King was arrested and deported on a Portuguese warship.

George Labram (*ca.* 1870-1899) an American mechanical engineer, was employed by British-owned De Beers Consolidated Mines. Labram engineered the defenses of the besieged mining town Kimberley, in the Orange Free State which produced 90 percent of the world's supply of diamonds. Among other accomplishments he constructed a water-distribution system, manufactured a four-inch gun plus shells (named "Long Cecil" after Rhodes who was among those besieged in Kimberley). Labram built a 155-foot elevated observation tower and devised a telephone system connecting the defensive positions. Labram was killed by a Boer shell during the siege. Kimberley survived a four-month siege.

Lewis Seymour (unk.-1900), a railway engineer, fled to the Cape Colony when the war broke out. He volunteered to raise her Britannic Majesty's Railway Pioneer Regiment and was given the rank of major. Composed of more than 1,000 men, mostly foreigners, the regiment repaired bridges and track destroyed by the Boers. Seymour was killed on 14 June 1900 while working on the Sand River Bridge in the Orange Free State.

QUOTATIONS:

[1] Bryon Farwell, "Taking Sides in the Boer War," vol. 27, no. 3 pp. 20-24, 92-97 (April 1976) *American Heritage*, p. 92.

[2] Joseph Miranda, "The Boer War 1899-1902." no. 205, pp. 4-18 (September/October 2000) *Strategy and Tactics*, p. 4.

[3] Bryon Farwell, "Taking Sides in the Boer War," vol. 27, no. 3 pp. 20-24, 92-97 (April 1976) *American Heritage*, p. 92.

[4] Bryon Farwell, "Taking Sides in the Boer War," vol. 27, no. 3 pp. 20-24, 92-97 (April 1976) *American Heritage*, p. 92.

[5] Robert Kee, *The Green Flag*. 3 vols. New York: Penguin Books, 1972. vol. 2, p. 148.

[6] Bryon Farwell, "Taking Sides in the Boer War," vol. 27, no. 3 pp. 20-24, 92-97 (April 1976) *American Heritage*, p. 93.

SOURCES:

George W. Cullum, ed., *Biographical Register of the Officers and Graduates of the U.S. Military Academy*. New York: various publishers through Supplement 8, 1879-1940.

Jim Dingeman and Richard Jupa, "Under Foreign Flags: 20th Century Mercenaries, Partisans and Soldiers of Fortune: 1899-1914." no. 140 (February 1991) *Strategy & Tactics*. pp. 45-51.

Donald Mack, "The Boer War of 1899-1902." No, 178 (January/February 1996) *Strategy & Tactics*. pp. 20-35.

Thomas Parkenham, *The Boer War*. New York: Random House, 1979.

"Capt Heany Is Silent." *New York Times* (8 March 1896). http://query.nytimes.com/mem/archive-free/pdf

Odyssey of Lee Christmas

1897-1920

Goal:

To maintain General Manuel Bonilla in power in Honduras and to restore him when he had lost it.

Background:

The history of Central America has long been an ugly story of strongmen muscling their way to power and retaining it by brutal force.

Leadership:

General Manuel Bonilla became Lee Christmas' patron. Although Christmas was a natural leader on the battlefield, it was his benefactor who made the strategic decisions.

Volunteers:

During this period American would-be mercenaries flocked to Central America. Lee Christmas, like others, became a gun for hire.

Compensation:

Christmas would have received Honduran pay commensurate with his positions as a general and police chief. After one successful revolution Christmas paid "his" Hondurans 40 cents

A Nicaraguan revolutionary army is on the march in the 1920s. Uniforms are non-existent, sandals are the typical footwear, and the flag is home-made. This ill-prepared army is typical of those in Central America and the Caribbean during the late 19th and early 20th centuries. A few well-trained, well-armed and highly motivated mercenaries could turn the tide of battle one way or the other.

Authors' Collection

a day, and his Americans $1.20. Late in his career when he served as a "special agent" for the U.S. States Department Christmas had a salary of $200 per month with $4-per-diem for travel. Later the pay was cut to $100 monthly.

Opposition:

Military forces were a rag-tag affair in Central America. They were mostly made up of a few hired guns leading peasants who were armed with antiquated firearm. The peasants' most deadly weapon was the *machete* which they typically wielded with skill. Whichever side could lay its hands on a few modern weapons, such as machine guns, was the victor.

Strategy:

When in power, use military force to intimidate potential rivals and when out use that force to overthrow them. Given the postage-stamp size of Honduras, one or two well armed, highly motivated mercenaries could be the difference between winning and losing.

Operations:

In November 1894 Lee Christmas moved to Puerto Cortés, Honduras, and found employment as a railroad engineer. In the spring of 1897 he was driving a small locomotive ferrying bananas. At a place called Laguna Trestle he was captured by a band of rebels who had

FAME–FORTUNE–FRUSTRATION

Lee Christmas' (1863-1924) mercenary activities focused on Central America where he was a classic "hired gun." Unlike William Walker 50 years earlier, Christmas did not think in terms of empire-building and annexation to the United States. His adventures were primarily confined to Guatemala and Honduras.

Courtesy wikimedia.org

swept in from Guatemala. Years later he would write about the incident:

"A Revolution broke out on the 13 of April 1897 when he [Christmas] was captured by the Revolutionist[s] and forced to handle an Eng[ine] at the point of Bayonet ... he was then taken to a Drunken General and given to understand he would be shot."[1]

Christmas was not shot. Instead, whatever the reason - possible to save his life - he joined the rebels. He not only joined the rebels, he fought alongside them. The revolutionaries were attacked by a government force. Christmas grabbed a gun and helped drive the attackers back. As a reward he was given the rank of captain. Eventually, however, the rebels were forced to retreat back into Guatemala.

Christmas went to the United States, then returned to Honduras. This was a tumultuous time for him. He divorced, remarried, took a mistress, was the target of an assassination attempt because of his martial escapades and other endeavors (including investigating the murder of an American). He gave up railroading and bought an interest in a store. He evidently engaged in other activities. He was reported to have gone on a "mission in Guatemala" (purpose unknown) for $2,000 (a lot of money), paid by Honduran President Terencio Sierra.

After the fighting at Laguna Trestle Christmas enjoyed a reputation as a tough *yanqui* (he was said to chew on glass). In May 1902 Sierra appointed Christmas to a colonelcy and the post of director general of police of the capital, Tegucigalpa. Christmas had 200 men under his immediate command but in effect was top cop for the country.

A dispute over the presidency between Sierra and a general, Manuel Bonilla, evolved into a civil war. Christmas had known Bonilla and now sided with him, taking a number of his *gendarmes* with him. He was appointed second in command of one of the Bonilla forces. The unit in which Christmas served was a victory on 24 February 1903 at a town named Lamini in a battle that began at sunup and lasted for 12 hours. Later, Christmas helped Bonilla take Tegucigalpa. According to an observer of the civil war, Christmas "was in the fight to the finish ... one of the most skilled fighters on Bonilla's staff."[2] Upon becoming president, Bonilla made Christmas a *general de brigada* and restored him to his police post.

A border dispute between Honduras and Nicaragua led to war. In February 1907 Nicaraguan troops, equipped with Krupp cannon and Maxim machine guns, invaded Honduras. This was the first time the Maxims were used in Central America; they took a heavy toll. Christmas fought, was wounded and was captured. With the assistance of the local U.S. consul he was released. He traveled to Guatemala. He settled there and somehow managed to become head of the country's secret service. He also did railroad work.

In Guatemala Christmas reconnected with Bonilla, who had lost power as a result of the conflict with Nicaragua. With financing from *"El Amigo"* (Cuyamel Fruit Company executive Samuel Zemurray), Bonilla and Christmas led a revolution in 1910. It failed. They did better the following year with a reorganized force supplied with U.S. Army surplus Colt model 1895 machine guns. The rebels captured Trujillo and Ironia, and completed their victory at the Battle of La Ceiba on 25 January 1911. Christmas used his machine guns for fire support of the infantry with interlocking fields of fire, inflicting heavy casualties on the government forces.

Zemurray would later describe his interests in fostering a revolution:

> "I was doing a small business buying fruit from independent planters, but I wanted to expand. I wanted to build railroads and raise my own fruit. The duty on railroad equipment was prohibitive … and so I had to have concessions … [and be able to] import that duty free."[3]

Zemurray got what he wanted after the rebel victory. Thus was born the mighty United Fruit Company.

Bonilla did not return to the presidency immediately. The United States was playing a role in Honduran politics. U.S. warships were offshore and bluejackets on shore. A peace plan was worked out on board an American warship under which a provisional president took over. On October 1911 elections were held. Bonilla won and became president again in February 1912. Christmas had already been made police chief again. This was followed by his appointment as *comandante* of Puerto Cortés, a prosperous banana-exporting town. Christmas prospered, too, buying a hotel and part-ownership of a 1,000-acre coconut plantation.

In March 1913, however, Manuel Bonilla died, and Christmas was left without his benefactor. Facing charges of corruption, Christmas resigned his Puerto Cortés post. In 1915 he joined Manuel Estrada Cabrera's secret service in Guatemala. After an earthquake devastated Guatemala City Christmas was appointed "chief of sanitation police."

IMPACT:

Christmas' military feats significantly assisted Bonilla in his battles and allowed him to retain and later regain power.

Biographies:

Lee Christmas (1863-1924), born in Louisiana, began his career as a pilot on tugboats on Lake Pontchartrain and later became a brakeman for the Illinois Central System in 1879. He helped build the Louisville, New Orleans and Texas Railroad, and afterwards returned to passenger service as a baggage master. He then became a fireman and was later promoted to engineer. In 1891 he had an accident and in a subsequent physical exam it was found that he was color blind. He could not be an engineer again. This was probably the reason he decided to go to Honduras - seeking adventure and better pay for his railroad skills.

In his final few years the aging soldier of fortune would have difficulty settling down in peaceful conditions. He engaged in a number of business adventures; all failed. One of these entailed the exportation of fish oil and scrap from Honduras and Guatemala. In Guatemala he worked with an American lumber concern to provide pre-fabricated housing for quake victims. The Central Americans were not the only ones to be charmed by the Christmas aura: the U.S. State Department appointed him a "special agent," with the duty of investigating political and economic conditions in Central America.

In 1920 Christmas fell ill with sprue, a malarial disease. He returned to the United States penniless in March 1922. His health continued to deteriorate and on 24 January 1924 he died. Several of his buddy soldiers of fortune were pallbearers for him.

Quotations:

Lester D. Langley and Thomas Schoonover, *The Banana Men*. Lexington, Kentucky: The University Press of Kentucky, 1995. p. 48.
Langley and Schoonover, *The Banana Men*. p. 54.
Langley and Schoonover, *The Banana Men*. p. 143.

Sources:

Robert L. Scheina, *Latin America's Wars*. 2 vols. Washington, D.C.: Brassey's, Inc., 2003.
Barbara Tenenbaum, Editor in Chief. *Encyclopedia of Latin American History and Culture*. 5 vols. New York: Charles Scribner's Sons, 1996.
Internet, www.http//en.wikipedi.org/wiki/Lee_Christmas

ODYSSEY OF HOMER LEA

(1900-12)

GOAL:

Initially, to create an army to help the Pao Huang Hui society overthrow the dowager (a widow with a title derived from her dead husband) Empress Tzu-Hsi of China and restore the former Emperor Guangxu (her son) to power. Later, to replace the Chinese imperial dynasty with a republic.

BACKGROUND:

At the beginning of the 20th Century the privileged of China were at war amongst themselves. Should the centuries-old political structure be changed, and if so, how? For 40 centuries China had been under imperial rule. Ruling dynastic families came and went but the fundamental tenets of imperialism remained the same. All power was vested in the imperial family and those it chose to favor.

Imperial China was now under growing pressure from within and from without to change. Chinese students returning from abroad carried home revolutionary ideas. China had been recently defeated in a war by Westernized Japan, showing the need to modernize the army and navy. Foreign nations were seizing Chinese ports as commercial enclaves, giving rise to the anti-foreign Boxer Rebellion. Christian missionaries preached equality in a society based on inequality. Into this turbulent mix came Homer Lea.

LEADERSHIP:

Homer Lea, a hunchback (caused by a fall as an infant), was a mysterious figure whose self-promotion and persuasive personality won for him a highly visible role among two sets of

Fame–Fortune–Frustration

Homer Lea (1876-1912) became a hunchback due to a childhood accident. In spite of his small stature, Lea's intellect and bravado allowed him to rise to national status in China as a military strategist. His chief champion was none other than Dr. Sun Yat-Sen. Lea was also a successful author of both fiction and nonfiction works.

Courtesy wikimedia.org

rebels. First, Lea sided with the dowager empress' son against her. When this failed, he supported the champion of Chinese republicanism, Dr. Sun Yat-sen.

Volunteers:

Lea forged a diminutive volunteer army in the United States which, in the minds of some, gave credibility to the role he wanted to play in China.

Compensation:

Lea's expenses were paid by the rebel Pao Huang Hui society. He received monthly compensation, precise amount unknown. In addition, at various times he was given Chinese artifacts. When Lea set up his army-in-training in the United States, the American instructors received $125 to $150 monthly - the equivalent of U.S. Army officers' pay.

Opposition:

Lea's army, assembled to support the Pao Huang Hui society, never made it to China; hence it never faced combat. Later, although Lea was Sun Yat-sen's chief military advisor, only once did Lea apparently see any real fighting.

Strategy:

Initially, to organize, recruit and train an army on American soil that later was to fight in China. Whether Lea believed this to be practical or simply a ploy to get personal recognition is unclear. Later, he convinced Dr. Sun Yat-sen that he was an accomplished strategist and he became chief military advisor to the Chinese republican.

Operations:

The revolutionary Pao Huang Hui society's leaders decided to send Lea to China, paying his expenses. When he told a friend of his intentions to go to China, the friend warned that he might have his head cut off. Lea replied, "Fortunately, they'll have a hard time finding my neck [due to his handicap]."[1] On 22 June 1900 Lea sailed from San Francisco for China. His ship made several stops and the third week in July reached Hong Kong, where Lea was met by reformers. He then traveled to Singapore and there conferred with K'ang Yu-wei, founder and leader of the society. Later, in Hong Kong and Portuguese Macao Lea participated in planning for an uprising. The Chinese, however, were dubious about the brash, young American.

They gave him no important role. Instead, they sent him on a recruiting trip, with two aides/translators, through two provinces. He was promised a generalship. The recruiting effort was not successful but despite this Lea on 13 August 1900 was made a lieutenant general.

One of the local Pao Huang Hui commanders prematurely launched an uprising that same month - the famed Boxer Rebellion was part of it. The revolt was crushed. Lea intended to take command of a rebel garrison at Hankow but did not get to it before the garrison was destroyed. If he had reached it, he would have been executed with the other commanders. A plan of his to kidnap the empress did not jell. With the rebels in retreat, Lea became a fugitive.

Riding a palanquin, Lea traveled through rebellious southern China, conferring with local Pao Huang Hui officials. The he took a journey through parts of Asia. This included at least three months in Japan, where he talked with statesmen sympathetic to the Chinese revolutionary cause. With no command in sight, Lea late in March 1901 left Japan and returned to the United States planning to work on securing diplomatic recognition for the rebels. Instead, however, he remained in San Francisco and Los Angeles.

A subject of press attention, he told the *San Francisco Chronicle*: "I traveled over all the southern provinces of China ... organizing our forces. I had four narrow escapes from death, and was laid out once by a blow on the head. The officers of our army include 700 Americans and Europeans, and we are fully armed."[2] It was exaggerated accounts like this that built the heroic and mystical aura that surrounded Lea throughout his life. Lea continued his military studies at home. He became a popular speaker before church and civic groups. Wherever he went he carried his general's baton. He hatched a plan to recruit and train a mercenary force. The rebel society's leadership in Los Angeles accepted the plan. Lea, with help from the U.S. Army, obtained the services of a former cavalry sergeant, Ansel E. O'Banion.

Several other Americans with former military ties also joined what became known as the Imperial Reform Army. Early in May 1904 a company of about 35 men began training in Los Angeles. Lea chose uniforms for himself and his cadets that were similar to those of the U.S. Army. As a cover for his activities, Lea in November 1904 obtained a charter from the state of California for a school called the Western Military Academy. He got five civic leaders to serve on its board. Over the following year the school expanded to 25 more cities across the nation, including Sacramento, Denver, Boston and New York. Cadet corps ranged from 15 or so members to more than 100. So respectable was the academy that 500 of its cadets marched in the January 1905

Tournament of Roses parade in Pasadena, California. The *Los Angeles Times* reported that "they swung up the street like West Pointers, perfect alignment and cadence, rigid as German dragoons."[3] Lea had a meeting with President Theodore Roosevelt.

Lea, however, had to deal with major problems. For one, the U.S. Secret Service was investigating his activities, with O'Banion serving as a secret agent for the Service. Other probes were conducted by state and military officials. They were concerned that a foreign army appeared to be training on American soil - which Lea denied. The program in Fresno, California, was ordered shut down, as was the military portion of the New York City program. Another problem facing Lea was the efforts of Richard A. Falkenberg to take command of Lea's army. Falkenberg was a schemer, publicity seeker and would-be mercenary who had inveigled the rank of general from the rebels and had created his own army - on paper. Falkenberg wrote harassing letters about Lea to public officials.

In the face of continuing controversy, press attention and official disfavor, the cadet program was unraveling. According to a Lea biographer, by October 1905 "…[Lea's] own failures in addition to changes in party policy eventually led to the disbanding of the cadet-training organization entirely."[4] Lea was relieved of command. Remnants of the program lasted until May 1907. Thus ended Lea's first odyssey in Chinese affairs.

Lea's second China odyssey was linked to Sun Yat-sen, a Chinese physician and insurrectionist who favored a republic. Sun had been associated with a number of failed uprisings in China. In 1910, while Sun was on a fund-raising trip to the United States, Lea met with him twice. Lea became his confidant and military advisor. They subsequently had planning meetings and, also, Lea travelled to Washington and London to seek funds for the Chinese leader. Lea conferred with important personages but his mission failed because the U.S. and U.K. recognized the existing Chinese government.

In October 1911 a general, Li Yuan-hung, began a rebellion in central China which spread rapidly. Sun met with Lea in London in November and, encouraged by Lea, decided to go to China. Sun, his entourage and Lea and his wife stopped in a number of places, including France, where Sun failed in an effort to obtain support. On 21 December the party arrived at the British colony of Hong Kong and was greeted by revolutionary leaders from the mainland. Around this time Lea received a commission as a major general in the "Kwangtung army." Sun had been introducing Lea as "the greatest military theorist under heaven."[5] Sun evidently intended to make him army chief of staff. Sun and his group reached Shanghai on 25 December. They then proceeded to Nanking, where a national convention on 29 December made Sun the first president of the new Chinese republic. Homer Lea was the only foreigner at Sun's inauguration 1 January 1912.

Developments, however, did not favor Lea or Sun. Rebel officials resented the high status held by a foreigner. In addition, U.S. consular officials warned that Lea, in helping a revolutionary movement, was in violation of American law. Lea relinquished his official role but continued as Sun's confidant. In what was probably Lea's only combat experience, he participated in a military clearing-up operation between Nanking and Peking around late January 1912. Although remembered as the father of modern China, Sun was displaced as president by General Li Yuan-hung.

On 11 February Lea suddenly collapsed from a stroke. He went into a deep coma and was not expected to live. He recovered consciousness after three days but his left side was paralyzed and his vision was severely impaired. His doctors believed that it would be best for him to return to California. He did so and temporary recovered. Lea's days in China were over.

Impact:

Historically Lea is linked with China. The actuality is that nothing he did or said had any impact on China, apart from the advice he gave Sun Yat-sen. It was in the literary world that Lea did have a major impact. He wrote a novel and followed this with a work of nonfiction, *The Valor of Ignorance* (1909). He examined U.S. defenses and foresaw a war between the United States and Japan. As part of his research he spent months exploring backwoods areas of southern California where he thought the war would be fought. While doing this he narrowly escaped food poisoning. Two retired U.S. general provided a foreword and an introduction to the book, adding to its credibility. It was recommended reading for U.S. military officers. It was praised by the Kaiser of Germany and by a British field marshal and, later, by Lenin and by U.S. Secretary of War Henry L. Stimson. The book was published by the German general staff and it is believed to have influenced top Japanese commanders in World War II. Lea followed this volume with an equally prophetic work, *The Day of the Saxon* (1912), which predicted the breakup of the British empire.

Lea was viewed by some as a hero, by others as a charlatan, and always as a man of mystery. Throughout his career he had sought to command troops. In the end, his important work had been done not with the sword but with the pen.

BIOGRAPHIES:

Homer Lea (1876-1912) - occurrences during his early years affected Homer Lea through his life. As a result of a fall during his infancy, he became a hunchback. His love of China stemmed from frequent visits to Chinatown, which was near his high school in Los Angeles. In addition he had conversations with a Chinese clergyman who was a friend of his family. Lea learned Cantonese. He loved reading military history and particularly admired Napoleon, in part because Napoleon's short height was an example of greatness unfettered by physical size.

Lea attended Stanford University from 1897 to 1899. He got his first taste of military life when he joined a cavalry troop sponsored by local businessmen. The troop was instructed by a retired military officer. From his Chinese friends Lea learned of a recently organized secret society, the Pao Huang Hui (Protect the Emperor Society), set up to support a former reformist emperor, Kwang-hsu, who had been ousted by the dowager empress and made a prisoner. Lea joined the society and convinced its leaders of his military talents, learned through much study. He probably cited Napoleon to counter doubts about his handicap. He bolstered his position by falsely claiming to be a descendant of General Robert E. Lee, from whom he had inherited military expertise.

After disbandment in 1907 of the military training program Lea founded, and without an army to command, he turned to literary pursuits. He lectured. He wrote articles. He granted press interviews. In one of these, for the *Los Angeles Times* (February 1908), he prophesied that Japan "will undoubtedly declare war when it best suits her, and without warning."[6] He wrote a novel about China, The *Vermilion Pencil*. The book received highly favorable reviews and brought him national attention.

Lea's interest in China never flagged. He tried for posts as U.S. trade representative and as minister, but was unsuccessful. He also developed a new plan to foment an insurrection in China, the Red Dragon plan. A number of businessmen with interests in China were recruited. Even so, the plotters were unable to secure the funds necessary for the operation. Among those approached - unsuccessfully - was J.P. Morgan, who had lost a concession to build a railroad in China. On the personal side, in June 1911 Lea married Ethel Powers, a woman who had been helping him with his manuscripts. For their honeymoon the couple traveled to Wiesbaden, Germany, where Lea underwent treatment from a specialist for an eye ailment.

Lea's meeting with Dr. Sun Yat-sen sparked his second odyssey to China which ended in a stroke 11 February 1912. In mid-April he and

Ethel boarded a Japanese ship in Shanghai and arrived in San Francisco on 6 May. They set up residence in a small cottage in Santa Monica overlooking the ocean. Confined to a wheelchair, Lea resumed his literary activities, welcomed distinguished visiting Chinese, granted a press interviews - and went fishing.

By October 1912 Lea was able to walk again, although he suffered continuing pain. In China he was honored when the republican government prominently displayed his picture in a hall of fame commemorating the anniversary of the revolution. On 27 October, after an evening entertaining friends, Lea suffered another stroke. He did not recover. Lea was cremated and eventually, in 1969, his ashes and those of his wife (she died in 1934) were interred in a cemetery in Taiwan. He had wanted to be buried in China.

Edward Sinnott "Tex" O'Reilly (1881-1946) served in the Shanghai police force during at least part of the time Lea was in China. They may have lived together for a while. O'Reilly claimed to be a veteran of ten wars, including Asian and Central American conflicts (*see* Gringo Cowboys of the Mexican Revolution, 1910-17).

QUOTATIONS:

[1] Lawrence M. Kaplan, *Homer Lea - American Soldier of Fortune*. Lexington, Kentucky: The University Press of Kentucky, 2010. p. 33.
[2] Kaplan, *Homer Lea*, p. 56.
[3] Kaplan, *Homer Lea*, p. 84.
[4] Kaplan, *Homer Lea,* p. 127.
[5] Kaplan, *Homer Lea*, p. 175.
[6] Kaplan, *Homer Lea*, p. 142.

SOURCES:

Robert K. Douglas, *China*, vol. 6 of *The History of Nations*, edited by Henry Cabot Lodge. New York: P.F. Collier & Son Company, 1928.

Webster's American Military Biographies. Springfield, Massachusetts: G. and C. Merriam Company, 1978.

http://en.wikipedia.org/wiki/Homer_Lea

Gringo Airmen in the Mexican Revolution

1910-15

Goal:

The goal for the mercenary flyers was to support the ground forces of whichever side - revolutionary or government - they were on.

Background:

The Mexican Revolution (1910-17) was an extremely complex affair. Politically, the struggle pitted revolutionaries against the government. As the revolutionaries won and replaced the government, then the new revolutionary government was attacked by other revolutionaries who believed they had not received their fair shares. And this struggle against the new "king of the hill" occurred more than once. Although this sounds like no more than changing the "top man," at the same time Mexico was experiencing very profound social and economic changes. Soldiers of fortune, including Americans, flocked to this chaos. Some of these men brought with them new skills and weapons - flying and the airplane.

Leadership:

The Mexican revolution was a struggle among strongmen. They were in full charge and not infrequently executed or assassinated those who opposed them. Americans, like other foreigners, were hired guns and followed orders.

Volunteers:

The one skill these Americans had in common was the ability to fly. During these early days of aviation, this also meant the ability to keep your airplane in the air. Each carried baling wire and tape. All were trained at their own expense and thrived on excitement.

Compensation:

Although there were a multitude of employers - the government and various revolutionaries - in general the flying mercenaries had similar experiences at getting paid. Typically the advance payment was good and sustenance was provided (sometimes no more than eating out of the camp pot) but regular salaries were rarely forthcoming.

Early in 1913 to induce the French flyer Didier Masson to join their forces, rebels offered him pay of $300 per month plus $50 for each reconnaissance flight and $250 for every bombing run. They also bought for his use a $5,000 Martin pusher plane. The pay was probably just about standard for all mercenaries flying for the government and rebels. Masson quit flying for the revolutionaries on 5 August 1913, claiming he had not been paid in a month. Similarly, an American mercenary, Howard Rinehart, complained of his experience flying for Pancho Villa: "...[E]xpense money had been very liberal, but no salaries had been forthcoming. There was food...."[1]

Opposition:

The primary danger for these aviators was ground fire. Since many of the soldiers on both sides were undisciplined, the aircraft must have been enticing targets.

Strategy:

The flyers were used to scout enemy ground forces so their employers could accordingly plan the movement of their troops.

Operations:

Since these aviation mercenaries were flying for both sides and were "picked up" along the way, their operations were not a continuum but rather a series of vignettes. It is difficult to say which side - the "ins" or the "outs" - was the first to employ an aviator.

Moisant International Aviators was a flying circus led by flyers and brothers Bevins (1868-1910) and Alfred J. (*ca.* 1862-1929) Moisant. The company was composed of men from different countries. In February 1911 the group was barnstorming across the United States.

The company arrived in El Paso, Texas, at a time Mexican rebels were camped across the Rio Grande near the border town of Juárez. The Mexican government of Porfirio Díaz hired the flyers to scout the rebel positions from the air. Flying Blériot aircraft, the pilots scouted for several days, feeding reports to the Mexican army. To ensure, hopefully, their safety should anyone be forced to land, the pilots dropped oranges and cigarettes to the rebels. In appreciation, the insurgents did not fire at the aircraft. Thus Moisant's men may have been the world's first mercenary aviators.

The honor, however, may have belonged to the Englishman John L. Longstaff. Early in the revolution, flying a Farman biplane he carried weapons to the insurgents from Laredo, Texas, to Mexico at night. Perhaps this was the world's first air-borne contraband.

In early 1913 the rebels wanted to expand their stronghold from the northwestern state of Sonora. Their advance along the coast was blocked by three government gunboats dominating the port of Guaymas on the Gulf of California. The rebels decided to bomb these vessels from the air. It is unclear who came up with the idea but it fell to the Frenchman Didier Masson to execute it. His Martin biplane was jury-rigged into the first bomber used in the Western Hemisphere. The aircraft - named the *Sonora* - was equipped with a bomb rack, bombardier's seat and rudimentary bomb sight. Bombs were manufactured from 18-inch sections of iron pipe, packed with dynamite and steel rivets. The bombs had directional fins and detonators at each end. Piloted by Masson and with a Mexican captain serving as bombardier, on 30 May 1913 the *Sonora* flew at 2,500 feet over one of the warships, the *Guerrero*. Bombs were dropped. They missed, only splashing the ship's deck. Four successive attacks over days also failed, although Masson got to see panicked sailors jumping overboard. Finally the vessels put out to sea to avoid being sitting ducks any further.

American Aviator Dean Ivan Lamb drifted into Pancho Villa's encampment in the summer of 1913 and volunteered to fly. According to Lamb, Villa said, "You are so skinny, the wind she would blow you away."[2] Nevertheless Lamb got the job. He was assigned to do something about another mercenary American pilot, Phil Rader, who had been harassing Villa's troops for two months. Lamb cruised the skies in a Curtiss biplane, searching for Rader, flying a Christofferson. One day Rader descended on Lamb and the first dogfight in history began over Naco, Mexico (30 November 1913). The planes swooped and dodged. Somehow they managed to avoid colliding. The aviators fired at each other with pistols, reloaded, fired again. One bullet from Rader's pistol ripped into a wing of Lamb's craft. It was the only hit of the fight. Out of ammunition, the flyers withdrew. Rader was not seen again. The aerial combat was inconclusive, but the two fighters may have made history. Some historians believe this was a mock battle planned by the two aviators before the event.

The first air combat casualty occurred when Farnum Fish, in a Wright Flyer B, was on a scouting flight for Pancho Villa. He was at 500 feet when the government forces let loose a barrage of gunfire at him. He was hit; a single bullet had passed through his calf, continued through his thigh and came to rest in his shoulder. Fish managed to bring the plane in. He spent several days recovering and then returned to his home in Los Angeles, California.

Impact:

Although many "firsts" were claimed, the miniscule number of Americans flying in Mexico had no effect on the outcome of the fighting. And apparently none flew after 1915. Actually, the impact of these aviators was felt more outside Mexico. They were trailblazers in the use of aircraft in conflict.

Biographies:

Farnum Thayer Fish (1896-1978) was born in Los Angeles, California, the son of a wealthy physician. As a youth, he found trouble - he was arrested while trying to steal an automobile as a Halloween prank. Fish attended the Wright Flying School in Ohio in 1911. He flew at county fairs and air shows throughout the West. During World War I he served abroad as a flier in the U.S. Signal Corps.

Dean Ivan Lamb (1886-1956) was born in Cherry Flats, Pennsylvania, and served in the U.S. Navy. He then then became a pearler in The Philippines and a customs officer in China. He worked on the Panama Canal. After that he became a wandering soldier of fortune, participating in conflicts in Central and South America. He fought in Colombia, was deported from Venezuela and was wounded (around 1910) in a conflict in Nicaragua. Lamb worked on a Brazilian railroad and mined for minerals. Back in the United States Lamb went to flying school, soloing in May 1912. Then on to Mexico, Lamb was hired by Mexican General Benjamin Hill.

Lamb returned to the United States, bought a plane, became a barnstormer. He was in England when World War I broke out and he joined the Royal Engineers. He served in France until 1915, when he transferred to the Royal Flying Corps. He was credited with shooting down a number of enemy aircraft. Back in the United States after the war he became a pilot for the U.S. Air Mail Service (around November 1918). Lamb is credited with making the first non-stop air mail flight between New York and Chicago. After leaving the mail service, Lamb returned to mercenary work. In 1919 he fought in revolutions in Honduras and Guatemala. He established the Honduran air force in 1921; it would become the best in Central America. Lamb was also involved in a Brazilian civil war in 1924. He returned in the United States in 1925. He worked at various jobs associated with aviation and wrote two books. On the eve of World War II he served as intelligence officer in India for General Claire Chennault's Flying Tigers. With the United States entry into the war Lamb joined the U.S. Army Air Force in 1942, eventually rising to a lieutenant colonelcy.

In 1949 Lamb was interviewed by the FBI concerning information that he had gathered for Alger Hiss in 1933. (In 1948 Hiss was accused of being a Soviet Spy.) Lamb stated that he had reported his activity to Army Intelligence in 1934. Apparently, FBI chief J. Edgar Hoover was satisfied with the response.

Phillips Dwight Rader (unk.-1918), after flying in Mexico, flew as a test pilot for aviation pioneering firms, Dayton-Wright Airplane Company and the Glenn Curtiss Company.

Howard Max Rinehart (1885-1949), a flight instructor, signed up for Villa's forces in March 1915. He and other flyers acquired two planes for service in Mexico, one of which was smashed when high winds swept it across a field. The second plane, crated, was taken to Mexico. Rinehart flew messages for Villa but became unhappy at the lack of pay. After one of his flights, having deliberately damaged his plane, Rinehart was sent to Brownsville, Texas, to get spare parts. He did not return to Mexico. He had flown for Villa less than two months.

John Hector Worden (1885-1916) was a Cherokee Indian born in New York City and educated at the Carlisle Indian School in Pennsylvania. On visiting France he became interested in flying and took flying lessons. Back in the United States in 1911 he continued studying at the Moisant Aviation School in Garden City, Long Island. He received his license 14 November 1911. Worden became a flying instructor and then an exhibition flyer for the Moisant aviation company. He was given the task of flying aircraft to Mexico that the government had purchased. Mexican army officers persuaded him to fly scouting missions against the rebels, and Worden thus became the government's first aviator.

Returning to the United States at the end of 1912 he wrote an article on the use of aircraft against guerrillas that became classic in its genre. Worden continued flying in the United States. In May 1916, during an exhibition at a fair in Texas, he suffered a fatal heart attack at 2,000 feet and apparently died before his plane crashed.

Quotations:

[1] Sterling Seagrave and the Editors of Time-Life Books, *Soldiers of Fortune*. Alexandria, VA: Time-Life Books, 1985. p. 28.

[2] Seagrave, *Soldiers of Fortune*, p. 26.

Sources:

R. Ernest Dupuy and Trevor N. Dupuy. *The Harper Encyclopedia of Military History*. 4th edition. New York: HarperCollins Publishers, 1993.

Robert L. Scheina, *Latin America's Wars*. 2 vols. Washington, D.C.: Brassey's, Inc., 2003.

Wikipedia, The Free Encyclopedia. (2013, April 11). *Dean Ivan Lamb*. Retrieved from Wikipedia, The Free Encylopedia: http://en.wikipedia.org/wiki/Dean_Ivan_Lamb

Early Aviators. (2010, October 11). *Dean Ivan Lamb*. Retrieved from Early Aviators: http://earlyaviators.com/elambdea.htm

Early Aviators. (2006, March 31). *Phillips Dwight Rader*. Retrieved from Early Aviators: http://earlyaviators.com/eraderph.htm

Wikipedia, The Free Encyclopedia. (2013, September 13). *Farnum Fish*. Retrieved from Wikipedia, The Free Encyclopedia: http://en.wikipedia.org/wiki/Farnum_Fish

Early Aviators. (2007, June 26). *Farnum T. Fish*. Retrieved from Early Aviators: http://earlyaviators.com/efish.htm

GRINGO COWBOYS IN THE MEXICAN REVOLUTION

1910-17

GOAL:

To overthrow Mexico's habitual president, Porfirio Díaz. As author George Creel wrote, "True, Don Porfirio gave peace; but it was the peace of the grave, for he crushed every voice of protest with ruthless ferocity."[1]

BACKGROUND:

Porfirio Díaz had governed Mexico either as president or through puppets since 1876. In 1910 the mild-mannered rancher from northern Mexico, Francisco Madero, sparked a revolution that would rage for ten years. Nationally and internationally, individuals opposed to Díaz flocked to Madero's side. This was an eclectic group whose only common thread was hatred of the long-term dictator and the opportunity for adventure.

This was but the beginning of the Mexican Revolution which ended up being a five round affair - round one, Francisco Madero versus Profirio Díaz (1910-11); round two, Pascual Orozco versus Francisco Madero (1911-12); round three, Francisco Villa - Emiliano Zapata - Venustiano Carranza versus Victoriano Huerta (1913-14); round four, Francisco Villa - Emiliano Zapata versus Venustiano Carranza (1914-19); and round five, Alvero Obregón versus Venustiano Carranza (1920). In round one Francisco Madero was open to the use of mercenaries, even those from the United States. Beyond round one, revolutionary leaders were very suspicious of Americans and typically only employed a few who possessed specialized skills. (*see* Gringo Airmen in the Mexican Revolution, 1910-15).

LEADERSHIP:

Francisco Madero was the intellectual and political father of the revolution. However, he did not possess the military skills required to lead a violent revolution. Pancho Villa wrote (once he learned how to): "We contrived to launch our attack by military logic, circumventing Sr. Madero.... Sometimes a civilian chief is unable to see what is plain to the eyes of his military subordinate."[2] Madero's political skills were challenged by the fact that his two chief lieutenants, Pascual Orozco and Francisco "Pancho" Villa, developed an intense dislike for each other. Beyond round one, Mexican *caudillos* (strongmen) provided the leadership on both sides of the struggle.

VOLUNTEERS:

Mercenaries from all over the world drifted across the U.S.-Mexican border to take part in the early fighting and were welcomed by Francisco Madero. Newspaperman Timothy Turner observed: "About 70 of the members of this little army were Americans and Europeans, many of them experienced soldiers, many of them rank amateurs, but all, I was to learn, men."[3] Perhaps they were best personified by the Italian Giuseppe Garibaldi, the grandson of the famed Italian revolutionary. Dr. Ira Bush, soon to be Madero's chief medical officer, described the Americans:

> "Red-blood men from every walk of life - gunmen, cowboys, miners, men who had failed in life, young men just out of college or high school .... As long as I live I will never forget that bunch of daredevils who composed 'El Falange de Los Estranjeros,' 'The Foreign Legion,' in Madero's army."[4]

And as for weapons, it was a bring-your-own affair. Dr. Bush wrote:

> "Many of the *Insurrectos* had furnished their own guns, and as a result, there was every variety of calibers ..... The *Insurrecto* army also had no machine guns except one Colt gun brought to the border by a [former French] Legionnaire named Bulger."[5]

Among the *Maderistas* were perhaps 100 mercenaries, mostly Americans. As the revolution continued following the assassination of

Sam Dreben (unk.), born in Russia and raised in the slums of Philadelphia, served in the U.S. Marine Corps during the Spanish-American War (1898). He fought as a mercenary in Latin America and during the Mexican Revolution (1910-17). Dreben was skilled in the use of the machine gun.

Courtesy wikimedia.org

Fame–Fortune–Frustration

Madero (22 February 1912) the number of mercenaries fighting in Mexico dwindled. The primary revolutionaries, Francisco Villa, Venustiano Carranza, Alvaro Obregón and Emiliano Zapata, distrusted *Gringos* (term meaning an American, which for many Mexicans carried a derogatory connotation).

Compensation:

Many promises were made but few were kept. Many of the revolutionary leaders printed their own money which rose and fell in value dependent upon battlefield success.

Edward O'Reilly (1881-1946) wrote the book Roving and Fighting which touted his adventures as a soldier of fortune. He fought in Cuba and the Philippines while serving in the U.S. Army. Later O'Reilly served in China, Venezuela and Mexico as a soldier of fortune.

Edward S. O'Reilly, Roving and Fighting (New York: The Century Co, 1918)

Opposition:

Although the Mexican army under Porfirio Díaz was highly touted by the international and national press, this was more hype than reality. The army suffered from many problems. Chief among these were cronyism, corruption, class stratification (the officers were mostly from the well-to-do and the soldiers were forced conscripts) and too many years of soft barracks' life. The army did possess a few professionally trained officers. And, the government's best fighters were the *rurales* (federal police) but they were too few in number to put down a major revolution.

Strategy:

Although the revolution raged throughout Mexico, the critical battleground was the north. The terrain of northern Mexico was primarily deserts, mountains and grazing lands dotted by railroad towns. This was suited to movement by rail and cavalry.

Operations:

The beginning of the revolution was a spontaneous affair with groups here and there throughout Mexico self-igniting. The place where the uprising was the hardest to extinguish was in the north where distances were great and the government's military presence was small. The revolutionaries won and lost skirmishes. An early defeat for the revolutionaries took place at Casa Grande. Among the revolutionaries were some 75 Americans who formed their own company. They sustained some of the heaviest casualties - one-third were killed, one-third captured, and one-third escaped. The government troops made the American prisoners walk 200 miles to Chihuahua with their hands tied behind their backs.

It became clear that this part of the revolution would live or die on the outcome of the fight for the border town of Ciudad Juárez. About 3,000 *Maderistas* advanced on Ciudad Juárez. The border town was defended by 500 well equipped government troops. The fighting raged between 8 and 18 May 1911. It devolved into waves of *Maderistas* overwhelming the outer defensive perimeter by sheer numbers. Then dynamiters, many of them Americans, went to work. They blew holes in the walls of the interconnected houses thus bypassing fortified street blockades.

Following Madero's victory over Porfirio Díaz, the surviving revolutionary leaders began a process of elimination to see who would be the last man standing.

"Part of the Foreign Company Commanded by Major O'Reilly in Mexico." American mercenaries were prominent in the early fighting of the Mexican Revolution (1910-17) along the border. As the revolution dragged on, most of them dropped out of the fighting for various reasons.

Edward S. O'Reilly, Roving and Fighting (New York: The Century Co, 1918)

Impact:

Francisco Madero won round one (Madero versus Díaz) of the Mexican Revolution. Round two (Orozco versus Madero) was brief and although Madero won he was soon assassinated. As with rounds one and two, the critical battleground in round three (Carranza-Villa-Zapata versus Huerta) was again northern Mexico. Most American mercenaries were, for one reason or another, out of the fight by the time round four (Villa-Zapata versus Carranza) began. The mercenaries were few and mostly gone by mid-1914. They had played an important role in Madero's critical victory at Ciudad Juárez. If Madero had lost and been eliminated, the revolution would probably have taken on an entirely different character.

Biographies:

Ira J. Bush (unk.), a doctor, practiced medicine in El Paso, Texas. He stood out at 6'5" tall, fair-skin, brown-hair and blue-eyes. During the earliest fighting in 1910 he voluntarily crossed the border and treated the wounded of revolutionaries/bandits Pascual Orozco and Pancho Villa. Soon Francisco Madero made Dr. Bush *Coronel del Cuerpo Médico Militar del Ejercito Libertador*. The doctor adventured beyond medicine. The doctor's wife, Catherine Dunn, wrote, "Anyhow, my husband - the adventurer - with other members of the [Mexican] *junta*, on a night in April, 1911, kidnapped that [ceremonial] cannon from the very center of El Paso. With much secret plotting and several weeks' devious actions they actually managed to get the cannon and a ton of ammunition across the Río Grande and into the hands of the *Insurrectos*."[6]

Dr. Bush wrote, "I filled my bags with surgical dressings, buckled on my two six-shooters, and called a taxi. I realized that I was violating one of the rules of warfare by going armed on the battlefield .... My two six-shooters, "Tom" and "Jerry," with a belt full of cartridges concealed beneath my coat, gave me a feeling of security."[7]

[fnu] **Carpentier** (unk.) was an American of French origin. He helped manufacture a crude cannon and home-made shells for the Madero forces. The gun was used in the attack on Ciudad Juárez and almost immediately failed.

Oscar "Dynamite Devil" Creighton [true surname unknown] (unk. - 1911) was described as a bank robber who was skilled in the use of dynamite. He crossed the border with Giuseppe Garibaldi in 1911. He was given the rank of captain and served as a chief scout. He was killed in April.

Sam Dreben (unk.), a Jew, was born in Russian and raised in the slums of Philadelphia. He served in the U.S. Marine Corps during the Spanish-American War (1898) and fought as a mercenary in Latin America. He was a skilled machine gunner.

R.H. Ellis (unk.), a doctor, served as the medical chief of staff in

"Tin-Can Grenades Used at Santa Rosalia in 1911." Frequently soldiers of fortune were required to improvise their weapons, especially their artillery. This was true regardless of the continent or the century.

Edward S. O'Reilly, Roving and Fighting (New York: The Century Co, 1918)

Francisco Villa's army. In about 1914 he was appointed the surgeon general with the Yaqui Independent Brigade. Ellis and Villa remained life-long friends.

Tom Fountain (unk. - *ca.* 1911) was from New Mexico. It is unclear when he joined Pancho Villa's army. Apparently he was an experienced machine gunner. He was among Villa's forces that captured Parral and tarried too long when the force retreated. He was captured by the forces of Pascal Orozco and shot down by some intoxicated officers.

Roy Kelly (unk.) served in the U.S. Army in the Philippines as a scout. He was discharged due to a lung problem and settled in Texas for the climate. He served as a scout for the Madero forces during the early days of the revolution.

Jack Noonan (unk.) had been in Alaska during the gold rush. Apparently he had fought in several revolutions and run guns into Mexico during its revolution. Reporter Timothy Turner described him as: "modest, kindly, bland, and tough."[8]

Ivor Thord-Gray (unk.) was born in Sweden and educated in England where he became a British subject. It is unclear when he became an American citizen. He fought against the Zulus in Africa. When the Mexican Revolution broke out in 1910 Thord-Gray was in Shanghai, China. He sailed to San Francisco, California, and entered Mexico through El Paso, Texas, in late 1913. He repaired the firing pins in two 75mm field guns for a suspicious Pancho Villa and was made chief of artillery (two guns) with the rank of first captain. Thord-Gray fought for Villa against Huerta at the battle of Tierra Blanca (25-26 November 1913). Next, Villa asked him to smuggle arms from Arizona into northern Mexico (which he did) and then placed himself at the service of Carranza, who at that time was still on the same side as Villa. Thord-Gray was commissioned into Carranza's forces on 9 December 1913. He fought for Carranza at the battles of Tepic (12 February 1913), Hacienda Castillo (July 1913), La Piedad (28 July 1913), Irapuato (29 July 1913) and Temaxcatio (1 August 1913). Following these battles Thord-Gray was promoted to *coronel*. He survived a number of assassination attempts. He departed Mexico on 7 September 1914 to fight for the British in World War I.

Edward Sinnott "Tex" O'Reilly (1881 - 1946) lived in Texas and the Chicago area as a youth. He joined the U.S. Army at the time of the Spanish-American War (1898). After serving in Cuba, he fought in the Philippine Insurrection (1900). O'Reilly claimed to have served as an officer in the Chinese and Venezuelan armies. In Mexico apparently he joined the fighting in 1910 and rose to the rank of major within Poncho Villa's insurgent army. He departed in 1915 prior to Villa's defeat at Celaya. O'Reilly wrote a number of pieces for magazines and an autobiography which emphasized his feats of prowess.

Tracy Richardson (unk.) was raised on a farm in Missouri. He was employed as a machine gunner by Pascal Orozco. Early in the fighting he was shot through the lung at Bachimba and spent months recuperating in El Paso, Texas.

Jim Teel (unk.), used the alias Jim Harper, and was from El Paso, Texas.

Ben Turner (unk.), a machinist working in El Paso, Texas, joined the Villa forces in 1913. He fought at Laredo and Cornejos. At one point he was rescued from a firing squad for having shown mercy to a *federalista*. His savior was Villa's chief executioner Rudolfo Fierro, whom he had worked with on the South Pacific Railroad. By 1916 Turner was no longer fighting in Mexico.

Ben Viljoen (unk.), a former general in the Boer War, took up U.S. residency (and perhaps citizenship). Skilled in guerrilla warfare, he joined the revolutionaries in northern Mexico and served as Madero's military advisor.

Quotations:

[1] George Creel, *Rebel at Large Recollections of Fifty Crowded Years* (New York: G.P. Putnam's Sons, 1947), p.79.

[2] Martin Luis Guzman, *Memoirs of Pancho Villa*, trans. by Virginia H. Taylor (Austin: University of Texas press, 1975. p. 46.

[3] Timothy G. Turner, *Bullets, Bottles, and Gardenias*. Dallas, TX: South-West Press, 1935, p. 28.

[4] I.J. Bush, *Gringo Doctor*. Caldwell, ID: The Caxtion Printers, Ltd., 1939, pp. 195.

[5] Bush, *Gringo Doctor*, pp. 179-80.

[6] Jessie Peterson and Thelma Cox Knoles, editors. *Pancho Villa Intimate Recollections by People Who Knew Him*. New York: Hasting House Publishers, 1977. p.126

[7] Bush, *Gringo Doctor*, pp. 202-03.

[8] Turner, *Bullets, Bottles, and Gardenias*, p. 203.

Sources:

Ronald Atkin, *Revolution! Mexico 1910-20*. The John Day Company, 1970.

Edward S. O'Reilly, *Roving and Fighting Adventures under Four Flags*. New York: The Century Co., 1918.

Robert L. Scheina, *Latin America's Wars*. 2 vols. Washington, D.C.: Brassey's, Inc., 2003.

Robert L. Scheina, *Villa Soldier of the Mexican Revolution*. Washington, DC: Brassey's, Inc., 2004.

Thord-Gray, *Gringo Rebel*. Coral Gables, FL: University of Miami Press, 1960.

Paul J. Vanderwood, *Disorder and Progress*. Lincoln, NB: University of Nebraska Press, 1981.

EXPEDITIONS AGAINST NORTHERN MEXICO

1911

GOAL:

Those who launched an invasion from the United States against Baja California and the northern part of Sonora were a heterogeneous group. First, there were Mexican expatriates who wanted to overthrow the dictator Porfírio Díaz. Second, there were members of the leftist International Workers of the World (the Wobblies) who wanted to establish a socialist republic. Third, there were American filibusters who wanted to take advantage of the chaos in Mexico to loot and pillage the wealth of that nation's northwest states.

BACKGROUND:

Adventurous Americans long coveted Baja California and Sonora. In addition to the failed expeditions of William Walker (1853-54) and Henry Crabb (1857), there were the stillborn plans of Joseph Morehead (1851), J.K. Mulkey (1888), and Walker Smith (1890).

LEADERSHIP:

The 1911 invasion of northern Mexico resembled a pack of wolves attacking a victim in distress, Mexico. Each pack had its leaders and each seized opportunities as they presented themselves.

VOLUNTEERS:

Initially the invaders numbered only a score and were mostly Mexican expatriates. Soon, bandits, escaped convicts, mercenaries, U.S. Army deserters and Wobbly idealists flocked to the cause. Like vultures smelling blood, they were joined by adventurous Americans, and the invaders increased to a few hundred. As some became discouraged or frightened, they fled back into the United States, while others took their place.

COMPENSATION:

The invaders received some financial help from socialists who wanted to establish a socialist republic in Baja California. While he was recruiting in the United States, Ricardo Flores Magón offered pay of a dollar a day with a bounty of cash and land if he were victorious. But in reality, payment was whatever the mercenaries could carry off.

OPPOSITION:

The Mexican forces defending Baja California numbered 112 men. Twenty-two *Rurales* (rural police) patrolled the border from the Pacific Ocean to the Colorado River and 90 soldiers were garrisoned in Ensenada, Baja California.

STRATEGY:

For the American invaders this was a loot and hold operation.

OPERATIONS:

On 27 January 1911 Flores group - 17 Mexicans and two Americans - crossed into Baja California and on the 29th they captured Mexicali. They stole what they wanted and extorted money from businesses. Chief targets of the invaders were ranches owned by wealthy Americans John Cudahy of Chicago and H.G. Otis of Los Angeles. Both men were strong union protagonists, the enemies of the socialist backers of the expedition. Learning of the invasion, the government sent a force of less than 100 men marched northward from Ensenada. In mid February these poorly equipped and exhausted soldiers attacked the invaders, who had been reinforced by adventurers from the United States, and the Mexicans were defeated.

Next, the invaders attacked the border town of Algodones, which lies east of Mexicali on the Colorado River. The magistrate and 12 citizens who were defending the town were easily brushed aside. The filibusters, now numbering about 100, split into two columns. One marched south against Ensenada and the other west against the border town of Tecate, which it captured.

In the meantime, the Mexican government dispatched 500 men by sea to Ensenada. On 13 March an element of these troops defeated the filibusters near Tecate and on 8 April the main body of the Mexican force defeated the remaining filibusters near Mexicali. The leader of the mercenaries, Stanley Williams, was killed, and Carl ap Rhys Pryce was elected the new leader of the self proclaimed "Foreign Legion." Some of the surviving filibusters retreated into Mexicali and others fled across the border into the United States.

Reinforced from north of the border, Pryce again focused on Tecate, which he temporarily captured. The competing mercenary bands now agreed that they should attack Tijuana. This was a gambling town for American tourists and the region's largest population center with 2,000 inhabitants. Some two hundred mounted mercenaries (about one-quarter being Mexicans) attacked Tijuana but initially the defenders held out. Boldly, sub-lieutenant [fnu] Guerrero, leading 30 Mexicans, surprised the filibusters a little after midnight. Some of the filibusters panicked and fled back into the United States. The remainder, led by Pryce and reinforced by more invaders from the United States, finally succeeded in capturing Tijuana on 9 May.

Shades of William Walker in 1853, Pryce set up a (short-lived) Republic of Baja California, buried the dead (he read from the Episcopal Prayer Book), raised the Red flag of socialism over government buildings and collected taxes and instituted customs duties. He also destroyed all hard liquor in the town so as not to lose his men to booze - but he permitted looting, which he considered "the fair spoils of war."[1]

Not to be overshadowed, Mexican expatriates in San Diego, California, announced the capture of the town and released a proclamation denouncing the despotism of Mexico's habitual president, Porfírio Díaz. Yet another competitor, on 3 June publicist Richard Ferris proclaimed himself "Provisional President of Lower California" on 3 June.

In the meantime, the Mexican citizens of Baja California formed the "Defenders of the National Integrity" (*Defensores de la Integridad Nacional*). On 18 June 600 Mexican volunteers marched north from Ensenada. They attacked 100 filibusters at Tijuana on the 22nd. Thirty-one filibusters were killed; three Mexicans died and six were wounded. The surviving mercenaries in Baja California, including Pryce, fled back to the United States.

IMPACT:

While these events were playing out, the fate of Mexico had been decided elsewhere. On 10 May forces led by rebel Francisco Madero captured Ciudad Juárez hundreds of miles to the east. On 21 May Porfírio Díaz signed a peace treaty and on 25 May resigned as president of Mexico. Now, Mexico was no place for foreign invaders.

The failed "invasion" of Baja California could be described as one more nail in the coffin of Mexican mistrust toward the United States. Over the past 100 years Mexico had been invaded numerous times by adventurers, most frequently Americans.

Biographies:

"Dynamite" Bill (unk.) was the oldest man in the Second Battalion and an explosives expert. He cut nine-inch lengths from a rusty two-inch water pipe, filled these with dynamite, and closed the ends with fuses and wooden plugs. He thus made bombs and, in effect, gave the rebels short-range artillery.

Simón Berthold Chacón (unk.-1911) was an early leader of the mercenaries. He was born of German parents in Mexico, abandoned at birth and raised by a Mexican woman. He had worked as a truck driver in Los Angeles, drilling subversives in his spare time. A socialist activist, he was sort of a political commissar. Berthold died of gangrene in a bullet wound received in the battle for the gold-mining town of El Alamo.

Richard "Dick" Ferris (unk.-1933) was an American showman/businessman who had an ill-deserved reputation among the Mexicans as being a multi-millionaire. He was involved in various failed schemes regarding Mexico. He staged and performed with his actress wife in a successful play about that country. Probably his most successful enterprise was setting up the Los Angeles Yellow Taxi Cab Service.

"Melbourne" Hopkins (unk.) was second-in-command to Pryce.

James Jackson (unk.) treated rebel wounded. He claimed to be from the Red Cross but wasn't.

Louis James (unk.) took command when Pryce left and tried to establish a "Gaming Republic." The fast-talking publicist from Los Angeles, Dick Ferris, was to be president. Ferris, however, failed to show up and the affair ended in international laughter.

"Doc" Larkins (unk.) was a 24-year-old who claimed to have received medical training in Canada. He deserted the rebels when the ambulance wagon he was driving was hit.

[fnu] LeClare (unk.) was commander of one of three companies into which Pryce divided his force attacking Tijuana.

José María Leyya (unk.) was one of the initial leaders of the expedition. He later joined the Madero forces and at one point offered surrender terms to his former comrades.

Ricardo Flores Magón (1873-1922) was a family patriarch and expatriate who was the longtime opponent of the president of Mexico, Porfírio Díaz. In June 1912 he was arrested in Los Angeles for violation of the Neutrality Act. Tried and convicted, he served a 23-month sentence. After the United States entered WW I Flores was again arrested for radical writings, found guilty and sentenced to 22 years in jail. He died in prison on 21 November 1922, possibly murdered.

[fnu] **Milton** (unk.) was a large Afro-American who bodyguarded Pryce. He reputedly liked to bayonet Mexicans.

Monoricus Monterey (unk.-1911) was a Pryce follower who was kidnapped and killed while waiting to testify at Pryce's Long Angeles trial.

John Rombo "Jack" Mosby (1872-1941) was a deserter from the U.S. Marine Corps (February 1911) and a member of the International Workers of the World. He claimed to have been an artillery officer in the Boer War and a descendant of U.S. Civil War raider John Mosby; he wasn't the latter. He assumed command of the First Battalion when Berthold was killed.

Carl ap Rhys Pryce (1876-1955) was an international mercenary. He was born of a Welsh family in Madras, India, and studied at a Scottish school. Then, impelled by a lifelong yen for adventure, he went to South Africa, arriving in Salisbury, Rhodesia, on 1 May 1897. He enlisted in the Royal South African Police, a para-military force set up by the empire-builder Cecil Rhodes to crush rebellious tribesmen. In the decade that followed he also served in the Natal Police, the Imperial Light House and the South African Constabulary. He fought in the Matabele Rebellion and the Second Boer War. He won a decoration for his participation in the relief of the besieged town of Ladysmith in the latter conflict.

Pryce's next service was far from Africa. He went to Vancouver, Canada, and joined a militia unit, the 6th Duke of Connaught's Own Rifles. Being in the militia gave Pyrce time to engage in a commercial venture, a ship towing business. This lasted three years The concern was doing poorly and Pyrce took off again, this time south to Los Angeles. Penniless, Pryce joined an anarcho-socialist organization, the Industrial Workers of the World (the "Wobblies).

When Pryce returned from his Mexican adventure, he was arrested; a Mexican consul had asked that he be extradited. In Los Angeles in September 1911 Pryce was charged with violation of the U.S. Neutrality Act and with murder and arson. All charges were eventually dropped without a trial.

Pryce's career was not ended. He apparently helped write stories about Mexico and the West. The movie industry had started in Los Angeles and Pryce may have worked as an extra. Then, handsome, mustachioed, almost six feet tall, Pryce made it big - $25 per film - starring in seven one- and two- reelers, with minor roles in other films. One of the movies, "The Colonel's Escape," was loosely based on Pryce's own adventures in Mexico.

Pryce's military career was far from over. With war about to break out in Europe, Pryce in 1914 went to Canada and joined a Winnipeg unit. Then, as a lieutenant, he transferred to the Canadian Field Artillery so that he could go to Europe as part of the Canadian Expeditionary Force. In England he transferred again, this time to the Royal Field Artillery attached to the 38th (Welsh) Division. Then followed a transfer to command of a Welsh artillery brigade. This unit went to France and took up a frontline position, which it held for seven months, exchanging fire with German artillery. Pryce was promoted to captain. The battery then moved several times. On one occasion Pryce helped capture a German machine gun nest. He was awarded the Distinguished Service Order for bravery. On 3 June 1917 Pryce, now a major, was hit in the shoulder by shrapnel. He was invalided back to Britain, where he was given command of a reserve artillery brigade. He also met, wooed and married a war widow.

It is not known with certainty what Pryce did in the years immediately after WW I ended in November 1918. In January 1919 war broke out in Ireland between independists (the Irish Republican Army) and the British. It is believed Pryce may have served as an intelligence officer with the Black and Tans, a special police unit notorious for its terroristic tactics. The conflict ended with a truce in July 1921.

Pryce emerges in 1922 as commander of Company 6 of a paramilitary group composed mainly of former Black and Tans. The group was part of the Palestine Gendarmerie, which was charged with enforcing the mandate in Palestine that Britain had been granted in 1922 by the League of Nations. After training, Pryce and 762 officers and men sailed for the Middle East on 13 April 1922. Company 6 was based in Nazareth. Later Pryce was given command of a mounted squadron that patrolled borders. This detachment was disbanded in April 1925, and the following year so was the entire British section of the Gendarmerie. Pryce returned to England, the ageing lion's fighting days now over.

He dabbled in politics awhile as a member of the Conservative Party. His wife died in 1941. In retirement Pryce spent his time writing, fishing and doing family genealogical research. The old soldier died 20 November 1955 after a short illness.

Paul "Silent" Smith (unk.) was another company commander in the Tijuana attack.

[fnu] **Stone** (unk.) was a veteran of the Spanish-American War.

Stanley Williams (unk.-1911) - aka William Stanley, [fnu] Cohen,

Robert Lober - was a veteran of the war in the Philippines and a deserter from the U.S. Army's 9th Infantry Regiment. He was a member of the International Workers of the World. When the Magónista group split, Williams took command of the foreign faction, the "Second Battalion of the Liberal Army." He was killed in battle in April 1911.

Sam Wood (unk.-1911), a veteran of the Boer War, was the third commander of the mercenaries. He was killed in an attack.

QUOTATIONS:

[1] John Humphries, *Gringo Revolutionary*. Wales: Glyndwr Publishing, 2005, p. 133.

SOURCES:

Lowell Blaisdell, "Was it Revolution or Filibustering?" *Pacific Historical Review*. Vol. 23, no. 2 (May 1954) pp. 147-64.

Dwane Hal Dean, "The Last Filibusters," *Journal of the West*. Vol. 24, no. 2 (Apr 1985) pp. 113-14.

Robert L. Scheina, *Latin America's Wars*. 2 vols. Washington, D.C.: Brassey's, Inc., 2003.

"Carol Ap Rhys Pryce" [sic], "Simón Berthold" [Spanish], Wikipedia http://en.wikipedia.org/wiki/Carol_Ap_Rhys_Pryce

http://es.wikipedia.org/wiki/Simon_Berthold

"John Rombo 'Jack' Mosby," PhpGedView {Internet}

http://gedcom.augustacemetery-ohio.com/individual.php?pid=I4783

Yanks in the Royal Flying Corps, the Royal Naval Air Service and the Royal Air Force

1914-18

Goal:

To help Great Britain win in World War I.

Background:

Aviation was in its infancy when war broke out in Europe on 1 August 1914. With aircraft only a decade old, war required airplanes, their weapons and their tactics to mature rapidly. Whoever could field more advanced planes or improved weapons and tactics held a distinct advantage. And this technology-driven pendulum swung back and forth between the two protagonists.

Leadership:

Leadership did not come without its problems, particularly for the allies. First there were the international challenges. Initially, these were between France and Great Britain and then the United States once it joined the fight in April 1917. Then there were the intra-national difficulties as exemplified by those in Great Britain. Britain was plagued with an administrative dilemma related to the war in the air. For years the Royal Flying Corps and the Royal

Naval Air Service bickered over resources and priorities. On 1 April 1918 - closer to the end of the war than to the beginning - the two were merged into the Royal Air Force.

Volunteers:

It is unclear exactly how many Americans flew for the British air forces. We do know there were more than 30 American aces among them - those pilots each had a minimum of five kills. Given the difficulty in becoming an ace, it is reasonable to assume the number of Americans flying for the British was many fold the number of aces. What drove these Americans to war? There is not a simple answer. For many it had to be their love of flying as evidenced by the number who continued to fly after the war. After all, there were other less dangerous and more humane options open to them during the war, the ambulance services for one.

Compensation:

Undoubtedly the American flyers received the same pay as the British flyers.

Opposition:

The opposition was multi-faceted. First, there was the primitive nature of the aircraft. You were flying a match waiting to be ignited. You were sitting on top of a fuel tank in a wooden structure covered in cloth which had been stretched taut by soaking it in a highly flammable liquid called dope. Second was the weather, the cold and the wet in particular during the winter months. Your dress looked more like that of an arctic explorer than an emblem encrusted, flying knight. Finally, there were the German pilots, no better or worse than your compatriots. The one thing all pilots had in common regardless for whom they flew, that was they were risk takers. To make matters worse, Allied pilots were denied parachutes during the war.

Strategy:

Air combat was an individual art form. Some pilots chose to fly in packs, while others preferred to be lone wolves. Even though the technological advantage in aircraft swung back and forth between the Allies and the Central Powers, for the most part the best pilots remained the best pilots regardless of the aircraft.

Operations:

The majority of the American pilots entered the war through Canada. Most joined before the United States declared war on Germany on 1 April 1917, but not all. The Americans were scattered among numerous squadrons and flew a variety of aircraft. In 1917 some left the British service to join the American Air Corps, but not many did so.

Impact:

Much to-do is made of the heroics and sacrifices of *l'Escadrille Lafayette*. But its contribution to the war effort paled in comparison to that of the Americans flying for the RAF and its predecessors. Historian Ezra Brown wrote: "Of the 180 Americans who volunteered to fly for France before the United States entered the war, almost half died or were captured."[1]

Biographies:

Wilfred Beaver (1897-1986) was an American citizen living in Canada when World War I broke out. Following flight training with the RFC, he was assigned to No.20 Squadron in late 1917. Beaver flew the two-seat Bristol F2B *Brisfit*. He scored his first victory on 13 November when he shot down an Albatros D V near Houlthoulst Wood. He destroyed two enemy aircraft in December; two in early January 1918; six more between 3 February and 26 March; and eight between 25 April and 13 June - ultimately recording 19 confirmed kills.

Louis Bennett, Jr. (1894-1918), born in Weston, West Virginia, attended Yale University between 1913 and 1917. In 1916 he joined the Aero Club of America and unsuccessfully attempted to form an aviation corps that would be accepted into the Army Air Service. In 1917 Bennett traveled to Canada and joined the RFC. After sailing to England, he trained at the Central Flying School. In early 1918 he was assigned to No.40 Squadron, which was flying SE-5s. He accomplished his first kill on 15 August when he forced a Fokker D VII down. He became fixated with attacking balloons, which counted as kills. Bennett eventually tallied 12 kills - three aircraft and 9 balloons. On 24 August his SE-5 burst into flames after being hit by ground fire and Bennett jumped from some 100 feet to his death.

Charles A. Bissonette (1895-1971) as a youth lived in Los Angeles, California. He joined the RFC in 1917 and was sent to France. A member of No.64 Squadron, Bissonette flew SE-5s. He downed his first enemy aircraft, a Pfalz D III, on 17 March 1918 over Blache. He destroyed five more enemy aircraft through May, when he returned to England for a period of rest. Bissonette re-entered combat as a member

Charles Arthur Bissonette in RAF uniform in 1918
Courtesy wikimedia.org

of No.24 Squadron. He tallied six kills during the war.

Howard K. Boyson (1892-unk.) was born in Texas and lived in Chicago when he joined the RFC in Canada on 16 June 1917. After a short time he was assigned to No.66 Squadron, suggesting that he had had previous flight experience. Flying in Italy, his squadron was equipped with Sopwith *Pups* and later Sopwith *Camels*. Boyson shot down his first enemy aircraft, an Albatros D5, on 8 December 1917 over Valstagna. In May 1918 he shot down four more enemy aircraft. On 29 January 1919 he crash-landed his *Camel* and was injured. He was discharged from the service.

Sydney MacGilvary Brown (1895-1952) was from Brooklyn, New York, and was a student at Princeton University. He joined the RFC in July 1917 in Canada and was sent to England for additional training. He then went to France, where he was assigned to No.29 Squadron on 4 July 1918. Flying a SE-5a he scored his first kill on 12 August when he shot down a Fokker DVII. Throughout the war he downed three more aircraft and a balloon. Brown left British service in 1919.

Archibald Buchanan (1892-unk.), born on Long Island, New York, in 1917, joined the RNAS and was sent to England. Prior to completion of his training, the RNAS was merged with the RFC to become the Royal Air Force. Buchanan was assigned to No.210 Squadron on 11 June 1918. Flying over Belgium he scored his first kill, a balloon, on 30 June. Just prior to the end of the war, Buchanan was shot down and taken prisoner on 30 October. He was released within a few weeks. Throughout the war he had seven kills (six aircraft and one balloon).

Alvin Andrew Callender (1893-1918), born in New Orleans, Louisiana, was a member of the Louisiana National Guard, which was federalized during tensions with Mexico in 1916. Graduating from Tulane University, he joined the RFC in Canada on 19 June 1917. He was assigned as a gunnery instructor in Texas (British personnel were used to train U.S. volunteers). Callender was sent to England in January 1918 and assigned to No.32 Squadron flying SE-5s. He had his first kill, a Pflaz D III, on 28 May 1918. He was later shot down but survived. While escorting DH-9s bombers, Callender's unit was attacked by *Fokkers*. He was shot through the chest, crash-landed, and died. Callender had tallied eight kills.

Charles Gray Catto (1896-1972) was born in Dallas, Texas. While a medical student in Edinburgh, Scotland, he unsuccessfully tried to join a Scottish regiment when war broke out in August 1914. He returned to his studies until he was accepted by the RFC in June 1917. After training, Catto was sent to the Italian front, joining No.28 Squadron and then No. 45. His first kill was an Austrian *Aviatik* on 19 May 1918. He tallied six kills by the end of the war.

Eugene Seeley Coler (1896-1953) was born in Newark, New Jersey. He joined the RFC in Canada. Coler was assigned to No. 11 Squadron. Flying a Bristol F2B *Brisfit* he made his first kills on 9 May 1918 - three Pfalz D IIIs. He was wounded on 16 September. During the war he tallied 16 kills. During World War II Coler served in the U.S. Air Force in North Africa and England.

Frederick Warrington Gillet (1895-1969), born in Baltimore, Maryland, graduated from the University of Virginia and tried to join the U.S. Army Signal Corps. He was rejected by the U.S. Army Air Corps, apparently because of his age, so he traveled to Canada and joined the RFC. Gillet was assigned to No. 79 Squadron and flew the Sopwith *Dolphin*. Gillet's first kill was a balloon on 1918. Gillet's last three kills occurred on 10 November, the day before the armistice. By the end of the war his tally was 17 aircraft and three balloons. He was the second-ranking American ace.

William Becker Hagan (*ca.*1898-1918), raised in Brookline, Massachusetts, traveled to Canada and volunteered for the RAF. He died of pneumonia on 11 May 1918 while training in Toronto.

Frank Lucien "Buddy" Hale (1895-1944) was born in Syracuse, New York. He was with the New York National Guard, assigned to patrol the U.S.-Mexican border in 1914. Hale attempted to join the U.S. Signal Corps (responsible for aviation) but was rejected because he had not graduated from high school. Traveling to Canada, Hale joined the RFC in 1916. He trained pilots in Canada and in Texas. Sent to Europe, he was assigned to No. 32 Squadron in France, which flew SE-5s. He earned his first kill, a Fokker D VII, on 25 August 1918. During the war Hale had seven kills. He left the RAF in 1922. He served briefly in the U.S. Army Air Corps during World War II before being medically discharged.

Harold Evans Hartney (1889-1947) was born in Packenham, Ontario. He graduated from the University of Toronto. Hartney was sent to Europe in May 1915 as a member of the Saskatchewan 105th Fusilliers. He joined the RFC and was assigned to No. 20 Squadron. After a series of aerial victories, Hartney was forced down by an *Albatross* and seriously wound-

Charles Gray Catto in RAF uniform in 1918 Courtesy wikimedia.org

Frank Lucien Hale in RAF uniform in 1918 Courtesy wikimedia.org

ed. He recovered in England, and returning to combat, He transferred to the U.S. Air Corps with the rank of major. He scored one more kill while flying for the United States. He was credited with six kills during the war. He went to the United States, where he served in the office of the Chief on Air Staff until 1921. It is unclear when Hartney acquired his U.S. citizenship.

D'Arcy Fowlis Hilton (1889-1973), born in Youngstown, New York, sailed to England and joined the RFC in November 1916. He was assigned to No. 29 Squadron, which flew Nieuport 17s. Hilton's first kills occurred on 31 July 1917 - a balloon and an Albatross DV. In November he went to Canada and worked as an instructor. His war tally was seven aircraft and one balloon.

Malcolm Clifford Howell (1895-1976) was from New Jersey. He worked in his father's real estate business before joining the RFC. He was assigned in 1918 to No. 208 Squadron which was flying Sopwith *Camels*. He had a total of five confirmed kills.

August T. Iaccaci (unk.) was born in New York City. He and his brother Paul joined the RFC in Canada during 1917. Both were assigned to RFC No. 20 Squadron, which was flying Bristol F2B *Brisfits*. Based at Calais, France, he earned his first kill on 19 May 1918 when he shot down a Pfalz D III. After other successes, August was promoted to captain and made flight commander of No. 8 Squadron. He injured his eye and was sent to England to recover. He recorded 17 kills during the war.

Paul T. Iaccaci (1890-1965) was born in New York City. His career paralleled his brother's, both being assigned to No. 20 Squadron. Paul got his first kill, a Fokker Dr I triplane on 18 May 1918. Like his brother, Paul recorded 17 kills during the war.

Harold Albert Kullberg (1896-unk.), born in Somerville, Massachusetts, was rejected by the U.S. Air Corps because he was too short. Travelling to Canada, he entered the RFC in December 1917. He was assigned to No. 1 Squadron and initially stationed at Clairmarais, France. After 19 kills (18 aircraft and one balloon), on 19 September 1918 he was badly wounded but managed to land. Kullberg spent the remainder of the war recuperating in a hospital.

William Carpenter Lambert (1894-1982) was born in Ironton, Ohio. His job with Canadian Explosives Limited required him to live in Canada between 1914 and 1916. In 1917 Lambert joined the RFC and was assigned to No. 24 Squadron based at Conteville, France. His first day I combat, 1 April 1918, he forced down an Albatross DV. Over the next five months Lambert was credited with 18 kills (17 aircraft and one balloon). He was sent to England to recover from a ruptured eardrum. Given leave to go to the United States, Lambert was there when the war ended. He served in the U.S. Army Air Force during World War II.

Jens Frederick "Swede" Larsen (1891-unk.), born in Waltham, Massachusetts, joined the Canadian army and was sent to Europe in January 1915. He served in the Field Artillery. Larsen transferred to the RFC on 19 October 1916. He was assigned to the recently created No. 84 Squadron, which was flying SE-5as. Larsen earned his first kill, an Albatross D V, on 26 November. He achieved nine kills in the war.

Oliver Colin LeBoutillier (1894-1983) was born in Montclair, New Jersey. He earned his pilot's license as a civilian. Traveling to Canada, LeBoutillier joined the RNAS. He was assigned to No. 9 Squadron. On 26 May 1917, flying a Sopwith Triplane, he shot down an LVG over Ostend, Belgium. Following other victories, LeBoutillier was promoted to captain on 1 April 1918. He recorded ten kills during the war. Following the conflict he did barnstorming and flew in 18 films. LeBoutillier was one of Amelia Earhart's instructors and flew as a test pilot for Howard Hughes. During World War II he served as an aviation inspector in Colorado and Wyoming.

Emile John Lussier (1895-1974), born in Chicago, Illinois, was the son of French-Canadian parents. His family moved back to Canada and he joined the RFC in 1917. Early the following year Lussier was assigned to No. 73 Squadron. Flying a Sopwith *Camel*, he was credited with his first kill on 25 July 1918. Following other successes, Lussier was promoted to captain on 6 November. He was credited with 11 kills during the war. Lussier returned to the United States; when World War II broke out he entered the RCAF, serving as a wireless instructor until 1942. He then returned to the United States.

Francis Peabody Magoun (1895-1979) was born in New York City. Graduating from Harvard, he traveled to France and served in the American Field Service as an ambulance driver between March and August 1916. In February 1917 Magoun joined the RFC in London and was assigned to No. 1 Squadron on 17 November. Flying a new SE-5A, he shot down an *Albatross* D V on 28 February 1918. On 10 April Magoun was wounded by ground fire. He had five confirmed kills during the war. Following World War he returned to Harvard for graduate studies.

Osborne John Orr (1895-1918), born in Cleveland, Ohio, traveled to England and joined the RAF. He was assigned to No. 204 Squadron on 1 August 1918. He shot down two enemy planes over Holland on 12 August, his first kills. On 23 October Orr was shot down and killed. He was credited with five kills during the war.

Lieutenant Bogart Rogers, in the Air Service, United States Army, 1920s Courtesy wikimedia.org

James William Pearson (1895-1993) was from Nutley, New Jersey. He joined the RFC in 1917 and was assigned to No. 23 Squadron. Flying a Sopwith *Dolphin*, he shot down an *Albatross* on 30 May 1918, his first kill. Following other successes, Pearson was promoted to captain in October. He tallied 12 kills during the war.

Cleo Francis Pineau (1893-1972) was born in Albuquerque, New Mexico. His pre-war passion was motorcycle racing. He joined the RFC in Canada in December 1917. Following flight training Pineau was assigned to No. 210 Squadron. Flying a Sopwith *Camel*, he earned his first kill, a Fokker D VII, over Ostend, Belgium, on 6 September 1918. In October he was shot down behind enemy lines. Pineau was held prisoner until the end of the war. He was credited with six kills during the war.

Bogart Rogers (1898-1966) was from Los Angeles, California, and attended Stanford University. Traveling to Canada, he joined the RFC in 1917. In May 1918 Rogers was assigned to No. 32 Squadron. Flying an SE-5A he scored his first kill, a Fokker D VII, on 22 July. In August his squadron flew ground support during the Amiens offensive. Rogers was promoted to captain on 20 November, nine days after the war had ended. He was credited with six kills.

Oren J. Rose (1893-1971) was born in Platte County, Missouri. Traveling to Canada, he joined the RFC in 1917. Rose was assigned to No. 92 Squadron. Flying an SE-5A, he scored his first kill, a Fokker D VII, on 30 July 1918. Following a number of successes, he was promoted to captain. During World War I Rose was credited with 16 kills. Next he flew in Russia against the Reds. Rose served in World War II as a training officer.

Walter Karl Simon (unk.) joined the RFC in March 1918. He was assigned to No. 139 Squadron, which flew in Italy. Flying a Bristol F2B *Brisfits*, on 4 July he forced down an Albatross D III, his first victory. On 30 July Simon shot down five enemy aircraft. His final tally was eight kills.

Edgar Taylor (unk.-1918) was raised on Long Island, New York. He joined the RAF later in the war and was assigned to No. 79 Squadron. Flying a Sopwith FI *Dolphin*, Taylor forced down a Fokker D VII over France on 4 August 1918, his first kill. During that month he had five kills (one aircraft and four balloons). On 24 August his plane was hit by ground fire. He crashed behind enemy lines and died.

George Donald Tod (unk.) joined the RAF late and was assigned to No. 25 Squadron. Flying a Sopwith *Camel*, he scored his first victory on 9 May 1918, shooting down an *Albatross D V*. On 9 August he was shot down behind enemy lines near Vauxvillers, France. Tod survived and was rescued. He tallied five kills during the war.

E.S. Tooker - a.k.a. Norman Cooper - (unk.) was born in Schenectady, New York. He was a private in the 3rd Canadian Division Supply Column from June 1916 to August 1917. He then joined the RFC and was assigned to No. 73 Squadron, which was flying Sopwith *Camels*. He tallied six confirmed kills during the war.

Kenneth Russell Unger (1891-1979) was born in Newark, New Jersey. He was rejected by the U.S. Air Corps. He enlisted in the RFC in Canada. Unger was assigned to No. 210 Squadron. Flying a Sopwith *Camel*, Unger, he achieved his first kill on 26 June. During the war he was credited with 14 kills (13 aircraft and one balloon). After the war Unger flew as an airmail service pilot and during World War II he flew cargo planes as a lieutenant commander in the U.S. Navy.

Clive Wilson Warman (1892-1919), born in Norfolk, Virginia, enlisted in the Canadian army in August 1914. In April 1915 Warman was wounded at the Battle of Ypres. He next served in a transport unit before he was accepted by the RFC in August 1916. Warman served as an instructor and then was assigned to No. 23 Squadron. Flying a SPAD VII, he earned his first kill on 6 July 1917. Following 12 victories (10 aircraft and two balloons), Warman was badly wounded on 20 August, requiring hospitalization for a year. Following the war, he returned to Canada and was killed in an aircraft accident on 12 June 1919.

Harold Albert "Wilber" White (1889-1918) was from New York City and was the son on a Presbyterian minister. He graduated from the University of Wooster, Ohio, in 1912. White joined the RAF late in the war. He was assigned to No. 23 Squadron. On 28 June 1918, flying a Sopwith *Dolphin*, White earned his first kill, a Pfalz D III. His guns jammed on 10 October and White intentionally crashed his plane into a German fighter to save a novice pilot who was under attack. He had tallied eight kills before dying.

Quotations:

[1] Ezra Bowen, *Knights of the Air*. Alexandria, Virginia: Time-Life Books, 1981, p.24.

Sources:

J. Ward Boyce, ed. *American Fighter Aces Album*. Mesa, Arizona: The American Fighter Aces Association, 1996.

Norman Franks, *American Aces of World War I*. Oxford, England: Osprey Publishing, Ltd., 2001.

History of the American Field Service in France. Vol. 3. Boston: Houghton Mifflin Company, 1920.

Legion of Frontiersmen (25th Royal Fusiliers)

1915-17

Goal:

To help Great Britain defeat Germany in Africa during World War I.

Background:

On 12 February 1915 South African War veteran, Colonel D.P. Driscoll, received permission to recruit the 25th Royal Fusiliers (Service) Battalion in London. Author Brian Gardiner wrote: "The original intention had been to send it to France, but then someone, probably Driscoll himself, realized it would probably be better to send this motley collection of individualists to Africa, where they could do little harm and possibly a lot of good, than to the trenches, where their lack of discipline and training would make them more of a problem than a help."[1] The war was going poorly for the British in East Africa. Within three weeks Driscoll had exceeded the required strength of 1,000 men. The battalion also adopted the name that had been used by a group of fighters which Driscoll had assembled in Africa, the Legion of Frontiersmen.

The war in Europe extended to the Europeans' African colonies. The colony of German East Africa (the future Tanzania) was sandwiched between British East Africa (the future Kenya) and Portuguese East Africa (the future Mozambique).

Leadership:

Colonel D.P. Driscoll raised and commanded the 25th Royal Fusiliers (Service) Battalion. Apparently no Americans held any leadership positions.

Volunteers:

The volunteers were an eclectic collection of adventurers, soldiers of fortune and rich playboys. The 25th battalion was composed of 1,166 men. It is unclear how many were Americans but at least a few were.

Compensation:

The battalion received the regular pay of the British army.

Opposition:

Author H.C. O'Neill wrote: "Fighting in East Africa involved the overcoming of two enemies, nature and the Germans...."[2] The environment was particular harsh for those who were not acclimated to it. The German colonial troops were commanded by Paul Emil von Lettow-Vorbeck, who soon proved to be the best jungle strategist of World War I.

Strategy:

The British strategy was to attack the German colony's population centers, thus attempting to force the Germans into a face-to-face fight. The 25th Royal Fusiliers were one of many pawns which were employed. Although the British had the advantages of numbers and a dependable supply source, frequently the Germans' aggressiveness allowed them to slow the British offensive. Small detachments of *Askari* (German-trained African auxiliary troops) led by German officers would outflank the British and attack their logistics and communications.

Operations:

The Legion departed London and sailed for British East Africa in April 1915. At least some of the Legion was without basic training. Arriving at Mombasa on 4 May, the battalion was split on two. The half without any military training was sent to Nairobi for two months' training. The other half was divided into small detachments which were scattered among outposts to protect the Uganda Railway, which was being raided by German forces with devastating effect.

The scattered elements of the battalion - about 400 men - were reassembled at Victoria Nyanza and transported by rail to Kisumu, the western terminus of the Uganda Railway along with other British units. The objective was to destroy Bukoba, the German command post. On 22 June 1,600 men crossed Lake Victoria and planned to attack at night. The German's were alert so the attack was delayed until daylight. It took two days of hard fighting before Bukoba fell. The wireless, munitions and stores were blown up. Driscoll wrote in his diary: "I went into the town where the Fusiliers were looting hard. All semblance of discipline had gone, drunkenness was rifle and women were being violated."[3] This sordid conduct did not make it into the official histories. The men from the 25th Royal Fusiliers re-embarked in steamers and returned to Kisumu.

By August the battalion was scattered over a vast area in an attempt to deal with German raiding parties. The battalion headquarters was at Voi, in the eastern part of British East Africa. Two companies were at Maktau in the western part of the country and a company was stationed along the coast. On 3 September the Germans carried out a successful ambush, killing 31 members of the battalion.

On 5 March 1916 450 members of the 25th Royal Fusiliers joined in an advance on the town of Moshi inside the northern border of the German colony. Arriving too late to take part in the battle, the fusiliers marched southward to participate in the fighting at Kahe. On 20 March the fusiliers were ambushed. The 25th Royal Fusiliers entrenched themselves and beat off the German attack. The effective strength of the Frontiersmen was down to 200 men. The following day another intense fight took place at the Soko Nassai River. The outnumbered Germans retreated.

After a short rest the fusiliers and other units took control of the richest and most populous part of the German colony. British columns pressured the retreating Germans. On 24 June the Germans fought a delaying action at Kwa Direma. The 25th Royal Fusiliers were among the British forces that continued to chase the Germans through the bush country. A respite from the chase was big game hunting to provide fresh meat, which frequently was the only meat available. Author H.C. O'Neill observed, "[S]o terrible did the first [nature] prove, even to such hardened and splendid adventurers, that by Christmas, 1916, only 60 of the original unit remained in the field ...."[4] One hundred and fifty fresh recruits joined the battalion.

In January 1917 after a hard fight Behobeho was captured. As Captain F.C. Selous wrote: "[I]t has rained almost day and night all the time, and we have lived in a sea of vile sticky mud."[5] At the height of the rainy season the battalion was withdrawn to Cape Town. The Germans retreated into the southeast corner of their colony, a swampy area known to be unhealthy. The 25th Royal Fusiliers rejoined the fight in June. They attacked Ziwani. A battalion officer wrote: "They [the Germans] have vanished from the district entirely. During the fight the bees came for us in swarms and stung us badly. I saw some of the men running around not caring a penny for the bullets [being fired at them], but trying to beat off the bees."[6]

Once again, the British force was chasing the Germans through poorly map lands. The outnumbered Germans initially offered a stout defense at Tandamuti in early August before executing a well-planned retreat. Then in mid-August the British attacked the Germans at Narunyu. The climate, bugs and enemy took a heavy toll on the 25th Royal Fusiliers. The fusiliers were ordered to cover a temporary retreat. Suddenly they were overrun and cut to pieces. Author Brian Gardner wrote: "Most of the [50] survivors were of the original Frontiersmen who had been recruited - so it seemed to them - in a different century. Reported to be 'much debilitated', they were now withdrawn from the country."[7]

Impact:

The Legion of Frontiersmen became part of the carnage of World War I. Considering that almost the entire unit had been destroyed, its American volunteers must have suffered the same fate. Author Brian Gardner wrote: "Before the war was over, most of them [the 25th] were to die in a remote, inhospitable country ...."[8] Even after the occupation of German East Africa by British forces, the von Lettow-Vorbeck-commanded German forces continued to lead the British pursuers on a merry chase through Portuguese East Africa, back into German East Africa, and then into Rhodesia, not surrendering until the Armistice had been declared in Europe on 11 November 1918.

Biographies:

William Northrop Macmillan (1872-1925), was raised in St. Louis, Missouri. He traveled to Kenya in 1901 for big game hunting and hosted former President Theodore Roosevelt's 1911 African expedition. Macmillan volunteered for service in the 25th Royal Fusiliers and rose to the rank of captain, serving in the commissariat. Although he was an American, he was knighted by the King of England. Macmillan was noted for his enormous physique (his sword belt was 64" in diameter). He and his wife were noted philanthropists. They endowed the Macmillan Library in central Nairobi.

Quotations:

[1] Brian Gardner, *German East*. London: Cassell & Company Limited, 1963, p. 49.

[2] H.C. O'Neill, *The Royal Fusiliers in the Great War*. London: William Heinemann, 1922. p. 22.

[3] Gardner, *German East*, p. 64.
[4] O'Neill, *The Royal Fusiliers*, p. 288.
[5] J.G. Millais, *Life of Frederick Courtenay Selous*. New York: Longmans, Green and Co., 1919, p. 335-36.
[6] O'Neill, *The Royal Fusiliers*, p. 22.
[7] Gardner, *German East*, p. 155.
[8] Gardner, *German East*, p. 50.

SOURCES:

George H. Dodenhoff, "A Historical Perspective of Mercenaries," *Naval War College Review*. pp. 91-109 (March 1969), vol. XXI, No. 7.

Nigel Jones, "The Unexpected Guerrilla," *Military History* (November 2010), pp. 40-49.

http://en.wikipedia.org/wiki/Ol_Donyo_Sabuk

Odyssey of Kermit Roosevelt

(1917-41)

Goal:

To fight with the Allies in their wars with Germany.

Background:

The life of Kermit Roosevelt makes predestination creditable. He was fathered by Teddy Roosevelt (TR) who insisted that service to the nation was the highest possible calling an individual could have. TR imbued a sense of adventure in his six children. According to a biographer of Kermit, "The traditional character-building qualities of courage, honesty and devotion to duty ... were continually instilled [by TR] in his children."[1] It was these traits, said the biographer, that enabled Kermit to become "a multi-lingual intellectual, author, soldier, big-game hunter, explorer, world traveler, writer and corporate executive."[2]

Leadership:

An officer of junior and later middle rank, Kermit held no significant military commands.

Volunteers:

Volunteerism was the credo of the Roosevelt family.

Fame–Fortune–Frustration

Kermit Roosevelt (1889-1943) lived in the shadow of giants - his father (Teddy Roosevelt) and his cousin (Franklin Roosevelt). Kermit was inspired by his father to serve the nation: that was man's highest calling. Kermit fought for the British in World War I and endeavored to fight for them again in World War II. The second time the spirit was willing but the body was old and tired. Kermit was never able to get out from under the shadow of his famous family members.

Authors' Collection, Jon Peterson artist

Compensation:

Kermit's father (TR) made it clear. He was not going to support financially adult children. They had to earn their own way or marry rich. And, Kermit did marry rich. While fighting for Great Britain, Kermit earned British pay.

Opposition:

Kermit battled for the forces of "good" against those of "evil" as defined by TR. In both world wars Kermit fought against Germany and its allies.

Strategy:

To fight with English forces until the United States entered the conflicts.

Operations:

The outbreak of war in Europe in 1914 galvanized the young Roosevelt men to join the Allied war effort. Historian Edmund Morris wrote, "Kermit remained [without a military commission] - as ever - a man difficult to place.... Kermit's war, Roosevelt [TR] felt, should be far-ranging, profiting from his restlessness and flair for languages."[3] Kermit, in the early summer of 1917, took training at an officer training camp in Plattsburgh, New York. Then, probably with his father's aid, he obtained an honorary commission [equivalent of a brevet, or temporary, rank] as a captain from the king of England. He was assigned to the staff of Lieutenant General Sir Frederick S. Maud, fighting the Turks in oil-rich Mesopotamia. Traveling through the Red Sea Kermit exercised his muscles by shoveling coal on board ship. He arrived in Basra (1917) and joined the British forces in Samarra, about 100 miles north of Baghdad.

Kermit was now attached to the Royal Engineers and then to the Motor Machine-Gun Corps. He rode in Rolls Royce armored cars, one of which weighed an impressive four tons. He did reconnaissance work, engaged the Turks in skirmishes and battles and helped quell Arab uprisings. The British-Indian force to which he was assigned suffered not only from Turkish air and land attacks but also from heat strokes and muddy bogs. The heat was so great inside the armored cars that the pedals scorched the feet of the drivers. Kermit later wrote:

> "When the car became engaged the crew would get inside, pulling the steel doors shut. The slits through which the driver and the man next to him looked could be made still smaller

when the firing was heavy, and the peep-holes at either side and in the rear had slides which could be closed. The largest aperture was that around the tube of the gun. Splinters of lead came in continuously, and sometimes chance directed a bullet to an opening. One of our drivers was shot straight through the head near Ramadie."[4]

In March 1917 Kermit participated in a major and successful offensive on the Euphrates River front. Britons who had been captured were freed and 3,000 Turkish prisoners were taken, as well as a number of German officers. Also captured were ten artillery pieces, 600 animals, a large number of rifles and machine guns - and a gold convoy. Shortly after this attack, Kermit participated in another offensive, this time in Kifi in what is now Kurdistan. Kermit traveled many miles of desert, engaged in a series of skirmishes and watched a charge by sword-wielding Indian cavalrymen that resulted in 600 Turkish prisoners. Kermit also managed to liberate a Turkish officer's harem. The Britons had to endure severe weather conditions. Kermit wrote: "[A] veritable hurricane set in, with thunder and lightning and torrents of rain. The wind blew so hard that I thought the car would be toppled over."[5] He was awarded the Military Cross.

When the United States joined the war, Kermit was transferred to the American Expeditionary Force (AEF) in Europe, relinquishing his British commission on 28 April 1918. Presumably he immediately joined the AEF. In France he attended an artillery school and then was assigned, as a captain, to the Seventh Field Artillery in what was later the First Infantry Division. In October Kermit commanded a battery in the bloody Meuse-Argonne campaign. He participated in the attack on the city of Sedan shortly before the 11 November armistice. After that he was engaged in occupation duties and then, in January 1919, was assigned to a commission negotiating war damages.

Following World War I, Kermit enjoyed a successful commercial phase in his life. A second world war began in 1939 and Kermit again wanted to be involved. He began a new, erratic career which included getting officer commissions in two foreign armies. He became a British citizen and with the help of his friend Winston Churchill was commissioned a second lieutenant, then acting major, in the British army and assigned to the Middlesex Regiment.

On 30 November 1939 Finland was attacked by the Soviet Union. Kermit wanted to assist the Finns but Britain was officially neutral. Nevertheless an unofficial organization, the Finnish Aid Bureau, was set up to recruit volunteers and provide other assistance. With the help again of Churchill, Kermit was given command of the volunteer unit. He did, however, have to resign his British commission. On 7 March 1940 he was sworn in as a temporary Finnish colonel. Kermit did not see action. Ill health (flu, dysentery, other ailments) resulted in his being hospitalized.

He recovered enough to be able to rejoin the British army and to serve in the British expeditionary force in Norway. In June he distinguished himself assisting in the evacuation of Narvik while under fire. He next accompanied the Middlesex Regiment to Egypt. A recurrence of dysentery resulted in his being invalided in December. He went back to England. His ailments plus excessive drinking resulted in his muster out of the army in May 1941. He returned to the United States, where he entered a hospital for treatment of his ailments.

Kermit was in bad shape. He had lost considerable weight. In addition to his alcoholism he became a drug addict. His personal life was a mess; he engaged in an extramarital affair with a woman named Herta Peters. There was a security issue because of the possibility Peters was an enemy agent. In July 1941 Kermit went missing. Cousin (and President of the United States) Franklin D. Roosevelt, urged by Kermit's frantic wife, Belle, ordered the Federal Bureau of Investigation (FBI) to track him down. He was found in New York, probably living with Peters.

In April 1942 Kermit's brother Achibald signed him into a sanitarium, the Hartford Retreat in Connecticut. Kermit apparently agreed to this. After four months he was deemed sufficiently recovered and was released. The United States was at war and Kermit wanted to return to the military. FDR, who had a fondness for Kermit, appointed him a major in the U.S. Army and had him assigned to Fort Richardson in Alaska far from the temptations of New York City. FDR's chief aide, Major General Edwin M. Watson, held a different opinion of Kermit. The general said, "I know he's worthless … it makes me sick at the stomach."[6]

Beginning on 29 July 1942 Kermit was assigned, in succession, to two staff jobs. On 25 January 1943 he was hospitalized for treatment of hemorrhaging and then was transferred to a hospital in Vancouver, Washington. He was released on 17 April and on 20 April was ordered back to duty. After an apparent stay in Seattle, Kermit returned to Fort Richardson 18 May - despite the fact the fort's commanding officer told the War Department he did not want him back. On 4 June 1943 his inner demons overcame his warrior spirit and Kermit Roosevelt killed himself with a gunshot. The fact of his suicide was kept secret by the family and Pentagon for decades.

Impact:

Kermit Roosevelt's contribution for Great Britain in World War I was that of a valorous junior officer, like so many who served. Author Edmund Morris wrote that Kermit was "A proficient but not a natural soldier...."[7] His efforts on behalf of Britain in World War II were with no less enthusiasm but less accomplished due to age, poor health and addictions. The fact that his participation in both wars is difficult to document in spite of his famous name testifies to the absence of a noteworthy legacy.

Biographies:

Kenneth Kermit Roosevelt (1889-1943) was the son of one president, Theodore Roosevelt, and the cousin of another, Franklin Delano Roosevelt. Kermit was born in the residence on a 155-acre estate of the prominent Roosevelt family of Oyster Bay, New York. For his education Kermit began with private tutoring, then studied at the primary Albany Academy, followed by the elite Groton boarding school in Massachusetts and Harvard (1908). He was following in the footsteps of his cousin Franklin. Kermit completed his studies at Harvard in two and a half years (1912).

Kermit went on a bear hunt to South Dakota, and several years later a buffalo hunt in the same state. Now conservation-conscious like his father, Kermit shot no buffalo on his second hunt. Kermit also accompanied his father on a year-long African safari. He was the expedition's photographer. Kermit's athletic abilities were demonstrated when, his horse fatigued, he ran afoot over a mile after a wounded giraffe and caught it.

Kermit had no interest in politics. Deciding what to do after Harvard, he was given an opportunity for a job in Brazil. In June 1912, he was employed by the Brazil Railway Company working on a steam shovel. Living conditions were poor; mosquitoes and continuous rain aggravated the malaria from which Kermit suffered. And there was the threat of marauding Indians. In 1913 Kermit took more lucrative employment with a bridge-building firm, the Anglo-Brazilian Forging Steel Structural and Importing Company. He supervised the construction of a large span over the Paranapanema River about 200 miles west of Sao Paulo. He survived a drop of 40 feet onto rocks when another bridge upon which he was working collapsed.

In 1913-14 Kermit accompanied his father on another expedition, again serving as photographer. This time they exploded the upper reaches of the Brazilian jungle in the Amazon basin and the Rio Da Duvida (the River of Doubt). Kermit escaped drowning when a canoe he was in flipped in a whirlpool. In all, through many hardships, the expeditionaries traveled almost 6,000 miles.

After this South American adventure Kermit went to Spain to marry Belle Wyatt Willard, the daughter of the U.S. ambassador. They settled in Buenos Aires, Argentina, where Kermit became assistant manager of a bank. They eventually had four children. The eldest, Kermit Jr., "Kim," would one day win fame as a CIA operative successfully plotting the overthrow of a regime in Iran (1953).

After service in the British and American armies in World War I, Kermit returned to the United States in 1919. He set about establishing a new career in the world of commerce, specifically in coffee and shipping. With family and friends he established coffee shops in New York, possibly the first in the nation. First called "Brazilian Coffee House," later "Double R" (for Roosevelt and a partner), the firm prospered but was eventually sold (1928).

In shipping Kermit held a succession of ownership/management positions. In 1920 he formed the Roosevelt Lines. By 1933 he was directing eight steamship firms and Roosevelt Lines was managing some 64 steamers for other companies.

Kermit found time (1927) to help organize a private intelligence enterprise known simply as "The Room." Well-connected persons met in a rented New York townhouse and discussed world financial matters. Occasionally prominent persons (such as the explorer Richard E. Byrd and former intelligence agent Somerset Maugham) spoke to the group. Information gathered by the members was often transmitted to Kermit's cousin, FDR. On board "Rooms" co-founder Vincent Astor's 264-foot yacht *Nourmahal* Kermit and Astor cruised the South Pacific, sending back to FDR information on such things as island docking facilities and availability of fresh water.

Despite his management responsibilities Kermit also found time to engage in his lust for adventure. He hunted tigers in Korea (1922), in India (1923, with his wife) and in Nepal (1925, again with his wife). He participated in 1925 and 1928-29 in hunting and specimen-gathering expeditions through the Himalayan region and across Burma and into China. Kermit did this despite suffering from malaria, depression, bone and muscle pains and alcohol addiction.

Quotations:

[1] William E. Lemanski, *Lost in the Shadow of Fame,* Camp Hill, Pennsylvania: Sunbury Press, 2011, p. 12.

[2] Lemanski, *Lost in the Shadow of Fame,* p. 1.

[3] Edmund Morris, *Colonel Roosevelt*. New York: Random House, 2010, pp. 485-86.

[4] Kermit Roosevelt, *War in the Garden of Eden*. New York: Charles Scribner's Sons, 1919, p. 120.

[5] Roosevelt, *War in the Garden of Eden*, p. 174.

[6] Lemanski, *Lost in the Shadow of Fame,* p. 165.
[7] Morris, *Colonel Roosevelt*, pp. 565-66.

Sources:

Ebsco Industries, Inc. Biography Reference Center, 2012. Electronic Biographies. 6 March 2013. http://www.ebscohost.com/public/biography-refernce-center.

"Roosevelt, Theodore, Jr.", *Webster's American Military Biographies*. Springfield, Massachusetts: G. & C. Merriam Company, 1979.

Wikipedia, The Free Encyclopedia. Archibald Roosevelt. 12 November 2012. 6 March2013 http://en.wikipedia.org/wiki/Archibald_Roosevelt.

Wikipedia, The Free Encyclopedia. Kermit Roosevelt. 6 December 2012. 6 March 2013   http://en.wikipedia.org/wiki/Kermit_Roosevelt.

Wikipedia, The Free Encyclopedia. Quentin Roosevelt. 6 December 2012. 6 March2013. http://en.wikipedia.org/wiki/Quentin_Roosevelt.

Americans in the French Réserve Mallet

May-September 1917

Goal:

The French *Réserve Mallet* was a trucking corps that was "attached to no [French] Army Corps, but rather held in reserve for emergency duty whenever a crisis [occurred] ...."[1]

Background:

Following the U.S. entry into the war on 6 April 1917, Commandant [fnu] Doumenc (head of the French Automobile Service) inquired of the French General Headquarters if American drivers could be found to help transport war materials to the front. That fact that the United States had entered the war avoided the controversy as to whether these Americans were in violation of U.S. neutrality. Malcolm Cowley wrote: "while driving munition trucks we would retain our status of gentleman volunteers."[2]

Leadership:

This trucking corps was part of and answered to the French army.

Volunteers:

Some 800 Americans worked for the *Réserve Mallet*. Many came from the ambulance corps where there was a surplus of American volunteers and a shortage of ambulances. Many were college students or recent graduates. Their number was dominated by men from the Ivy

League schools. Harvard contributed 325 individuals, Yale 187, Princeton 181, and Cornell 105. In May 1917 a group of volunteers from Cornell University agreed to drive the trucks and others quickly signed-up.

Compensation:

The members of the French *Réserve Mallet* probably received modest compensation from the French army. Some of these volunteers were sponsored by Americans or American institutions at home which paid their expenses. Since these sponsors believed that the volunteers had gone to France to carry out humanitarian deeds (ambulance driving), at least some of the volunteers consulted their benefactors before agreeing to drive for the French army.

Opposition:

The primary danger was artillery and mortar shells raining down. Martin Sampson wrote, "There is nothing humdrum in driving under artillery fire."[3]

Strategy:

E. H. Pattison wrote, "we load up in the afternoon and then go and wait behind some hill or in some wood where the *Boche* sausages [observation balloons] can't see us, until dark, and then go to the depot and unload."[4]

Operations:

The first section of the *Réserve Mallet* entered service in May 1917. Among their assignments, these Americans hauled troops and war implements from the Aisne sector to the sad Chemin des Dames. The Americans drove 5-ton Pierce-Arrows. These were physically demanding trucks. They towed 37- and 75-mm cannons and hauled all types of munitions and logistics. By the time the *Réserve Mallet* was absorbed into the U.S. Army on 13 November 1917 at Soissons it had grown to sixteen *Transport Militaire* units and was manned by 800 men.

Impact:

Following the takeover of the *Réserve Mallet* by the U.S. Army, many of the volunteers chose to serve in front-line units. Driver Dunbar

Malcolm Cowley (1898-1989), like so many of the Americans with for the French Reserve Mallet, had traveled to France hoping to become a driver for an ambulance service. When this was not possible due to a shortage of ambulances, he and others joined this transportation corps which carried munitions and supplies to the front. Some 800 Americans worked for the French Reserve Mallet.

Courtesy wikimedia.org

Maury Hinrichs wrote that the *Réserve Mallet* "did more to help win World War I than all the ambulance men who ever served ...."[5] (The wounded carried to safety by those ambulance drivers would not agree.) Driver Frank O. Robinson wrote: "It is said that the *Réserve Mallet* hauled more ammunition during this time [May-September 1917] than the American Army fired during its whole participation in the war."[6]

Biographies:

Charles Patrick Anderson (*ca*.1896-1918) was from Chicago, Illinois, and attended the University of Illinois. He served in the *Réserve Mallet*, Sectons 133 and 526. Later, Anderson joined the U.S. Air Service and was killed near Conflans, France, on 16 September 1918.

Charles Bacon (*ca*.1896-1918) was from Waltham, Massachusetts, and attended Dartmouth College. He served in the *Réserve Mallet*, Section 184. Later, Bacon joined the artillery branch of the U.S. Army and was killed near Verdun on 24 October 1918.

Carlos Willard Baer (*ca*.1893-1918) was from Oxford, Ohio, and attended the University of Miami in Ohio. He served in the *Réserve Mallet*, Section 184. Later, Baer joined the U.S. Corps of Engineers. He died of pneumonia in Columbus, Ohio, on 6 April 1918.

Richard Varian Banks (*ca*.1894-1918) was from Ossining, New York, and attended Rensselaer Institute. He served in the *Réserve Mallet,* Section 526. Later, Banks joined the U.S. Army Air Service and was killed in a truck accident near Nancy, France, on 30 October 1918.

Robert Harris Barker (*ca*.1894-1918) was from West Bridgewater, Massachusetts, and attended State College of Rhode Island. He served in the *Réserve Mallet,* Section 184. Later, Barker joined the U.S. Army and was killed during the Marne offensive on 10 August 1918.

Merrill Manning Benson (*ca*.1896-1918) was from Sterling, Illinois, and attended the universities of Illinois and Wisconsin. He served in the *Réserve Mallet,* Section 526. On 16 October 1918 Benson died en route to the United States.

Richard Ashley Blodgett (ca.1897-1918) was from West Newton, Massachusetts, and attended Williams College. He served in the *Réserve Mallet,* Section 526. Later, Blodgett joined the U.S. Army Air Service and was killed near Lagney, France on 17 May 1918.

Alexander Bern Bruce (*ca*.1894-1918) was from Lawrence, Massachusetts, and attended Harvard University. He served in the *Réserve Mallet,* Section 526. Later, Bruce joined the U.S. Army Air Service and died in an aerial collision on 17 August 1918.

Benjamin Howell Burton, Jr. (*ca*.1896-1918) was from Colusa,

California, and attended the University of California. He served in the *Réserve Mallet,* 133. Later, Burton joined the U.S. Army and died in a base hospital near Toul, France, on 18 September 1918.

Stuart Carkener, 2nd (*ca.*1897-1918) from Kansas City, Missouri, and attended the University of Illinois. He served in the *Réserve Mallet,* 133. Later, Carkener joined the U.S. Army and served in the artillery branch. He was killed near Ronchères, France, on 30 July 1918.

Greayer Clover (*ca.*1897-1918) was from Richmond, Virginia, and attended Yale University. He served in the *Réserve Mallet*, 133. Later, Clover joined the U.S. Army Air Service and was killed in an accident on 30 August 1918.

Richard Steven Conover, 2nd (*ca.*1898-1918) was from Newport, Rhode Island and attended St. Paul's School. He served in the *Réserve Mallet*, 526. Later, Conover joined the U.S. Army and was killed near Cantigny, France, on 27 May 1918.

Malcolm Cowley (1898-1989), born in Belsaco, PA, he enrolled in Harvard University in 1915. Cowley left school and traveled to Paris in May 1917 and initially served as a truck driver for the American Field Service (one of the ambulance corps). In about July he began driving for the *Réserve Mallet*, Section 526. Following World War I he became a noted literary critic and was the author of numerous works and a spokes person for "the lost generation."

Henry Harrison Cumings (*ca.*1897-1917) was from Philadelphia, Pennsylvania, and attended Temple University. He served in the *Réserve Mallet*, Section 526. Cumings drowned when the transport *Antilles* sank on 17 October 1917.

George Eaton Dresser (*ca.*1899-1918) was from Chicopee, Massachusetts, and attended Andover College. He served in the *Réserve Mallet*, Section 526. Later, Dresser joined the U.S. Army and served in the tank corps. He was killed at Vauquois Woods, France, on 27 September 1918.

George Lane Edwards, Jr. (*ca.*1896-1918) was from St. Louis, Missouri, and attended Yale University. He served in the *Réserve Mallet*, Sections 133 and 211. Edwards was killed near Berry-au-Bac, France, on 24 October 1918.

William Armstrong Elliot (*ca.*1896-1918) was from Berkley, California, and attended the University of Berkeley. He served in the *Réserve Mallet*, Section 133. Later, Elliot worked as a civilian for the U.S. Navy's aviation unit. He died of typhoid in France on 4 September 1918.

Hugo Wing Fales (*ca.*1892-1919) was from Belding, Michigan. He served in the *Réserve Mallet*, Section 397. Fales was killed when a shell accidentally exploded on 2 May 1919.

Horace Baker Forman, 3rd (*ca.*1894-1918) was from New York City and attended Cornell University. He served in the *Réserve Mallet*, Section 526. Later, Forman joined the U.S. Army Air Service and he was killed on 14 September 1918.

Dunbar Maury Hinrichs (unk.) was from Glen Ridge, New Jersey, and a member of the Cornell University unit that was recruited for the *Réserve Mallet* on 2 May 1917. He drove in Section 526.

Ernest Armand Giroux (*ca.*1886-1918) was from Somerville, Massachusetts, and attended Dartmouth College. He served in the *Réserve Mallet*, Section 526. Later, Gioux joined the U.S. Air Service and was killed near Laventie, France, on 22 May 1918.

Warren Tucker Hobbs (ca.1895-1918) was from Worcester, Massachusetts, and attended Dartmouth College. He served in the *Réserve Mallet*, Section 526. Later, Hobbs joined the U.S. Army Air Service and was killed during aerial combat on 26 June 1918.

Charles Alexander Hopkins (*ca.*1896-1918) was from Newark, New Jersey, and attended Dartmouth College. He served in the *Réserve Mallet*, Sections 526 and 184. Later, Hopkins joined the U.S. Army Air Service and was killed in a training accident near Indre, France, on 30 January 1918.

Henry Howard Houston (*ca.*1895-1918) was from Philadelphia, Pennsylvania. He served in an American ambulance service and the *Réserve Mallet*, Section 133. Later, Houston joined a U.S. Army artillery unit and was killed near Arcis-le-Ponsart, France, on 18 August 1918.

Howard Crosby Humason (*ca.*1891-1918) was from New Britain, Connecticut. He served in the *Réserve Mallet*, Section 184. Later, Humason joined the U.S. Army Air Service. He died at in Dallas, Texas, from pneumonia on 21 October 1918.

Warren Thompson Kent (*ca.*1894-1918) from Clifton Heights, Pennsylvania, and attended Cornell University. He served in the *Réserve Mallet*, Section 251. Later Kent joined the U.S. Army Air Service and he was killed near Thiaucourt, France, on 7 September 1918.

Paul Warren Lindsley (*ca.*1897-1918) was from Marietta, Ohio. He served in the *Réserve Mallet*, Section, 184. Later Lindsley joined the U.S. Army Air Service and was killed in an aerial accident near Indre, France, on 5 October 1918.

Edward Hargrave Pattison (1896-unk.) was born in Troy, New York. He was a member of the Cornell University contingent which had recently arrived in France when it chose to a man to drive for the *Réserve Mallet.* He served in Section 526. Pattison next served in the U.S. Army Motor Transport Corps and then the U.S. Army field artillery. Graduating from Saumur in July 1918 Pattison was commissioned a Second Lieutenant in the U.S. Coastal Artillery Command, U.S. Army Reserve. For a while he was attached to French artillery intelligence. Following the war he attended Columbia University Law School in New York.

George Wells Root (*ca.*1896-1918) was from Middletown, Connecticut and attended the Massachusetts Institute of Technology. He served in the *Réserve Mallet*, Section 526. Later, Root joined the U.S. Army, the tank corps. He died of pneumonia in England on 25 December 1918.

Walter Laidlaw Sambrook (*ca.*1894-1918) was from Watervliet, New York, and attended Syracuse University. He served in the *Réserve Mallet*, Section 397. Sambrook died of pneumonia in Paris on 6 September 1918.

Kramer Core Tabler (*ca.*1895-1919) was from Parkersburg, West Virginia, and attended Marietta College. He served in the *Réserve Mallet*, Section 184. Later Tabler joined the U.S. Army Air Service. He died in a flying accident near Colombey-les-Belles on 16 May 1919.

William Henry Taylor, Jr. (*ca.*1899-1918) was from New York City and attended Andover College. He served in the *Réserve Mallet*, Section 526. Later Taylor joined the U.S. Army Air Service and was killed in aerial combat near St. Mihiel, France, on 18 September 1918.

Chester Robinson Tutein (*ca.*1895-1918) was from Winchester, Massachusetts and attended the Massachusetts Institute of Technology. He served in the *Réserve Mallet*, Section 526. Later, Tutein joined the U.S. Army Air Service. He was killed in an aerial accident on 17 November 1918.

Goodwin Warner (*ca.*1887-1919) was from Jamaica Plain, Massachusetts and attended Harvard University. He served in the *Réserve Mallet*, Sections 184 and 133. Warner died of pneumonia at Meaux, France, on 28 June 1918.

William Jewell Whyte (*ca.*1897-1918) was from Chicago, Illinois, and attended the University of Chicago. He served in the *Réserve Mallet*, Section 526. Later, Whyte joined the U.S. Army Air Service. He was killed in an aerial accident near Cazana, France, on 20 March 1918.

Jack Morris Wright (*ca.*1899-1918) was from New York City and attended Andover College. He served in the *Réserve Mallet*, Section 526. Later, Wright joined the U.S. Army Air Service. He was killed in a training accident on 24 January 1918.

Quotations:

[1] Kirkland H. Day, *Camion Cartoons*. Boston: Marshall Jones Co., 1919. p. vii.

[2] Malcolm Cowley, *Exile's Return, A literary Odyssey of the 1920s*. New York: The Viking Press, 1971, p. 37.

[3] Arlen J. Hansen, *Gentlemen Volunteers*. New York: Arcade Publishing, 1996, p. 154.

[4] Hansen, *Gentlemen Volunteers*. p. 154.

[5] Hansen, Gentlemen Volunteers, p. 155.

[6] *History of the American Field service in France*. Vol. 3. Boston: Houghton Mifflin Company, 1920, p. 20.

Sources:

R. Ernest Dupuy and Trevor N. Dupuy. The Harper Encyclopedia of Military History. 4th edition. New York: HarperCollins Publishers, 1993.

"Malcolm Cowley, holder of a French Fellowship, 1921-1923." n.d. Our Story- The Field Service. 12 June 2013. <http://www.ourstory.info/3/FF/c/Cowley.html>.

Krebs, Albin. "Malcolm Cowley, Writer, Is Dead at 90." 29 March 1989. The New York Times. 12 June 2013. <http://www.nytimes.com/1989/03/29/obituaries/malcolm-cowley-writer-is-dead-at-90.html?pagewanted=all&src=pm>.

Americans in the French Foreign Legion

1831-Present

Goal:

To enable France to utilize the services of foreign volunteers in a military force. This force would be ready at any moment to go anywhere in the world to further France's colonial policies or to assist a friendly foreign government in trouble.

Background:

On 9 March 1831 French King Louis Philippe established the *Légion Étrangére* (Foreign Legion) for service outside of France. The Legion would become the most legendary mercenary group in history.

Leadership:

The Legion has always been commanded by French officers. One of the best known was Captain Jean Danjou. He lost a hand in the Crimean War and replaced it with a wooden one. He was killed in a battle at a Mexican hacienda. The wooden hand was retrieved and has been a relic honored by the Legion ever since.

Volunteers:

The Legion was composed of men attracted to France or seeking military adventure or fleeing the law (now no longer the case as enlistment standards have been raised). Typical of

Fame–Fortune–Frustration

Eugene Bullard (1894-1961) was America's first Black combat pilot. That opportunity was afforded to him by the French. He had been turned away by the American-manned Lafayette Escadrille because of his race. Bullard had previously served in the French Foreign Legion, where he was seriously wounded. Remaining in France, he worked in the French underground during the early days of World War II where again was seriously wounded. Years later Bullard died in poverty.

Authors' Collection, Dan Burkhard artist

the multi-national composition of the Legion was a battalion at Dien Bien Phu in 1954 described by historian Bernard Fall as being "composed largely of Germans but with some Italians, Spaniards, and Yugoslavs."[1]

Although Americans were not among the most numerous nationalities present in the Legion, they were present and at times were more than just a handful. World War I broke out in August 1914, and within a month some 70 Americans had joined the Legion and some 20 more would join later.

COMPENSATION:

Starting salary for a legionnaire is 1,043 euros monthly (about $1,377). After that, pay is determined by ranks, length of service and place where serving. A veteran sergeant serving abroad may receive over 3,000 euros per month (about $3,960).

OPPOSITION:

The Legion fought peoples on four continents, among them the Chinese in Asia, the Mexicans in North America, the Berbers and Dahomeyans in Africa, and the Austrians and Germans in Europe.

STRATEGY:

The Legion was created specifically to fight for France in foreign lands. It was only when France itself was invaded that the Legion fought on French soil. Made up of volunteers from other lands, the Legion provided France with a tightly disciplined, highly trained force that could carry out France's policies. The Legion was a handy instrument that France could use to extend its policies without having to endanger young Frenchmen. It was a special force before there were special forces.

OPERATIONS:

The history of the Legion was the history of France. The Legion fought in all of France's small and large wars. Its beginning was not auspicious. In one combat with Berbers in Africa, the legionnaires fled. From then on the Legion would write a historic page in military history. In 1834 the government of Spain confronted an insurrection in Spain. The French government sided with the Spanish rulers and rented the entire Legion to them. The Legion proved to be the backbone of the government forces, distinguishing itself in a number of battles.

In an effort to build an empire in Africa France invaded Algeria in 1830. The war dragged on for seven years. The mountain citadel city of Constantine was besieged for a year. In October 1837 a breach was blasted open in the walls of the city and legionnaires barged in. They swept into the city; other French troops followed. Even so, the conflict continued until December 1847, when the Berber leader Abd el-Kader surrendered. He had inflicted the initial defeat on the Legion.

The Legion fought against the Russians in the Crimean War (1854-56), helping the allies to capture the key port of Sevastopol. The Legion battled in Italy (1859 against the Austrians), in Mexico (1863-67), in Indochina (1873-74, 1882-83 and 1945-54), in Dahomey (1890 and 1892-94), in China (1883-88), in Madagascar (1894-95), in Mandigo (West Africa - 1886, 1894-95 and 1898) and in Iraq (1991).

In Mexico (1863-67) the Legion had one of its most heroic actions. Late in April 1863 a convoy was sent to protect a wagon train. The unit was commanded by Captain Danjou; under him were two lieutenants and 62 men (and two mules). At a place called Camarone Mexican cavalry attacked; they were repelled twice. The legionnaires sought shelter in an hacienda. Soon about 2,000 Mexican troops were attacking. The siege lasted for about ten hours. Three Legionnaires survived. Ever since, 30 April has been Camarone Day to the Legion, marked by a parade and ceremony, including the display of Danjou's wooden hand.

France lost the first of three conflicts it would have with Prussia/Germany, the Franco-Prussian War (1870). As part of the peace agreement the Prussians were allowed to enter Paris. The Parisians rebelled and took to the barricades. This was a sad moment for the Legion; it was called upon to clear the streets for the Germans.

The Legionnaires fought the Germans in World War I (1914-18) and World War II (1939-45). Another sad episode for the Legion came during World War II in Syria when the Legion from Vichy France fought the Free French legion.

In the third conflict in Viet Nam (then Indochina) the legionnaires were among the defenders of the key town of Dien Bien Phu. When it fell on 7 May 1954 the French knew they had to withdraw from the country.

IMPACT:

Because of its hard training and strict discipline, plus a magnificent *esprit de corps*, the Legion has been one of the most effective forces in the French army.

Americans have made their contribution to the legend of the Legion. Of the 90-odd American volunteers in the Legion during World War I, 38 were killed in action of died of their wounds. Many of the survivors were wounded multiple times. Eight were decorated with the cross of the Legion of Honor, 21 with the *Medaille Militaire* and 52 with the *Croix de Guerre*.

BIOGRAPHIES:

James Jules Bach (unk.), from St. Louis, Missouri, was one of a small group of Americans in France who called themselves the "American Volunteer Corps." They joined the Foreign Legion in 1914, were given training and in October were sent to the front. Early in the following year Bach joined the Escadrille Lafayette. He was sent 23 September 1917 on a special mission to insert saboteurs behind enemy lines. Bach was captured, the first American taken by the Germans. He was tried twice, sentenced to death, but the sentence was not carried out. Bach remained a prisoner until the end of the war.

Eugene Jacques Bullard (1894-1961) became America's first Black combat pilot - but did not fly for the United States. He was born in Columbus, Georgia, seven of 11 children. His father was a Black who had been brought to the United States as a slave from Martinique and his mother was a Creek Indian. Bullard's mother died when he was five years old and he and his siblings were raised by their father. Bullard left home at the age of 8; he stated that this was sparked by a mob's unsuccessful attempt to lynch his father. He wandered through the southeast, searching for a means to travel to France where his father told him a Black man was treated as an equal. At the age of 12 Bullard stowed away on a merchant ship bound for Aberdeen, Scotland. He spent a few years doing odd jobs and at the age of 16 trained to be a boxer. As a successful fighter he traveled to the continent. Soon he became involved in vaudeville as a singer-dancer and settled in Paris.

When World War I broke out, Bullard joined the French Foreign Legion on 9 October 1914, his 19th birthday. He was assigned to the Moroccan Division which according to Bullard contained 54 nationalities. Between late 1914 and early 1916 he fought in some of the bloodiest battles - Somme, Artois Ridge, Mont-Saint-Eloi, Souchez, and Verdun. On 5 March 1916 he was seriously wounded and awarded the *Croix de Guerre* and *Medaile Militare*. He spend 8 months in a hospital recovering.

Unfit for combat duty in the infantry, Bullard joined the French flying corps. On a wager from a fellow soldier, he earned his flying wings on 5 May 1917. He wanted to fly for the *Lafayette Escadrille* but Dr Edmund L. Gros, one of the squadron's most influential patrons, block his entry because of Bullard's race. Instead, Bullard flew for the French *Escadrille* Spa. 93. He had a red bleeding heart pierced by a knife painted on his fuselage of his Spad with the inscription *"Tout le Sang qui coule est rouge"* (All Blood Runs Red). He flew his first combat mission on 8 September 1917. During the next month he had 2 confirmed kills and 2 unconfirmed kills. Bullard took part in twenty combat missions. He earned the nickname the "Black Swallow of Death."

When the United States entered the war Bullard requested a transfer to the U.S. Army air corps but his application was ignored. (On 23 August 1994 the U.S. Air Force posthumously commissioned Bullard as a second lieutenant.) In November 1917 Bullard was involved in a brawl with a French officer. This led to his transfer back to his old unit, the 170th Infantry Division where he was assigned to non-combat duties. Bullard was discharged from the French army in October 1919.

Bullard married in Paris and father three children (one dying shortly after birth). His marriage failed and he took custody of his two daughters. During the 1920s and 1930s he was a noted celebrity and nightclub owner. In July 1939 he joined a group that evolved into the French underground once World War II broke out. Bullard fled Paris with his daughters and fought in the defense of Orleans where he suffered a spinal wound. He and his daughters were smuggled into Spain and later evacuated to the United States. For the next 16 years Bullard worked at menial jobs in New York City increasingly in pain from his back injury. Bullard was one of the Blacks who were attacked at the Peekskill Riots in 1949.

In 1954 at the invitation of the French government he returned to Paris for the relighting of the Eternal Frame at the Tomb of the Unknown Soldier at the *Arc de Triomphe*. In 1959 Bullard was named a Knight of the Legion of Honor. At this ceremony he said:

> "The United States is my mother and I love my mother, but as for France is concerned, she is my mistress and you love your mistress more than you love your mother - but in a different way."[2]

During a 1960 visit to New York City, French President Charles de Gaulle publically embraced Bullard. Bullard died in poverty of stomach cancer. He was buried in the French War Veterans' section of the Flushing Cemetery, New York City.

Edmond C.C. Genet (1896-1917) was from Ossining, New York, and he was the great-great-great grandson of the "Citizen" Genet of France Revolution fame and the first Republican French minister to the United States. Wanting to be a naval officer, Genet sought appointment to the Naval Academy at Annapolis, Maryland. He failed the entrance math test, however, and could not enter the school. He did, however, join the navy and was ordered to the battleship *Georgia*. Genet thought that he would see action when the vessel was sent to Mexico, where hostilities were underway against the chieftain Victoriano Huerta. The conflict, however, was over by the time the *Georgia* arrived. After a stop in Haiti, the *Georgia* returned to the United States. Seeking adventure and influenced by his French heritage, Genet, while on leave, jumped ship and headed for France. He had written to his mother: "I never expect to come back - death seems nearer to me than any possible chances of going through the horrible ghastly conflict ...."[3] On 3 February 1915 Genet enlisted in the Legion. He fought in a number of battles. He wrote to a friend: "In an attack we made Sept. 28, out of our company of 250 there are not quite 60 left ...."[4] On 29 May 1916, after 16 months in the Legion, Genet enlisted in *l' Escadrille Lafayette*. On 16 April 1917, while flying low on patrol, Genet's Nieuport fighter was hit by anti-aircraft fire. The plane crashed and Genet was killed.

Siegfried Narvitz (1881-1916) was living in Paris and is believed to have been a professor of philosophy. He joined the Foreign Legion in August 1914 and fought with the *Régiment de Marche* until 4 July 1916 when he was killed at Belloy-en-Santerre during the Battle of Somme. The 35-year-old philosopher was killed by the same German machine guns that took the life of his fellow American, the poet Alan Seeger. They died on the same battlefield.

Paul A. Rockwell (1889-1985) and his brother, Kriffin, two South Carolinians, traveled across the Atlantic to France. There, on 21 August 1814, they enlisted in the Foreign Legion. They received training and at dawn on 30 September, as members of the Second Foreign Regiment, they entrained for the front. They went into action in December Paul was seriously injured by an exploding shell, which smashed his collar bone. He was invalided out of the Legion. He became a combat correspondent for the Information Bureau of the French army. After the war he became a reserve officer in the Legion. He held the rank of captain in anew unit of American volunteers, *L'Escadrille de Garde Cherifienne*. His brother became a distinguished pilot. (*see L'Escadrille Lafayette*)

Alan Seeger (1888-1916) was born in New York City. He early began to write poetry and in 1912 went to Paris to pursue his vocation. Within weeks of war breaking out in August 1914 Seeger joined the Foreign Legion. "I have joined up," he said, "in order that France, and especially Paris, which I love, should never cease to be the glory and beauty which they are."[5] Seeger fought in battles, and on 1 July 1916 he - now a lieutenant - and his unit were part of a major Allied offensive. They were to take the town of Belloy-en-Santerre, heavily fortified by the Germans. Seeger and his squad were enfiladed by six enemy machine guns. Most of the Legionnaires went down, including Seeger. His body was found the next morning. He had hoped to go to Paris to read before a statue of Lafayette and Washington his "Ode in Memory of the American Volunteers Fallen for France." Prescient ode lines:

> "When the slain bugler has long ceased to sound,
> And the tangled wires
> The last wild rally staggers, crumbles, stops,
> Withered beneath the shrapnel's iron showers: -
> Now heaven be thanked, we gave a few brave drops;
> Now heaven be thanked, a few brave drops were ours."[6]

Henrik Willem van Loon (1882-1944) was born in Rotterdam, The Netherlands. He came to the United States in 1902 to study at Cornell University, receiving his degree in 1905. He was a correspondent for the Associated Press during the Russian Revolution of 1905 and in Belgium in 1914 at the start of World War I. He later became a professor of history at Cornell University (1915-17) and in 1919 became an American citizen. From the 1910s until the death van Loon wrote numerous books, illustrating them himself. Most widely known among these is *The Story of Mankind a History of the World*, which won the first Newbery Medal in 1922.

David E. Wheeler (1873-1918) had been a prominent surgeon in Buffalo, N.Y. Evidently in search of adventure, he volunteered to work for the French Red Cross. There apparently was not enough excitement; in 1915 at the age of 42 Wheeler joined the Foreign Legion. During a battle at Champagne he won the *Croix de Guerre*. Wounded himself, he carried another wounded man from the battlefield under enemy fire. He was invalided home but then joined a Canadian regiment as a surgeon. He went back to France. When the United States entered the war he got permission to join the American forces. He became a surgeon in the U.S. First Division. While serving with this unit he was wounded in combat and died 18 July 1918.

QUOTATIONS:

[1] Bernard B. Fall, *Hell is a Very Small Place - The Siege of Dien Bien Phu*. Philadelphia: J.B. Lippincott Company, 1966, p. 82.

[2] William Chivalette, "Corporal Eugene Jacques Bullard. *Air & Space Power Journal*. http://www.airpower.maxwell.af.mil/apjinternational/apj-s/2005/3tri05/chivaletteeng.html 23 July 2013.

[3] Dennis Gordon, *Lafayette Escadrille Pilots Biographies*. Missoula, Montana: The Doughboy Historical Project, 1991. p. 144

[4] Gordon, *Lafayette Escadrille*. p. 145

[5] Jay Mallin and Robert K. Brown, *Merc: American Soldiers of Fortune*. New York: Macmillan Publishing Company, 1979, p. 64.

[6] Alan Seeger, *Poems of Alan Seeger*. New York: Charles Scribner's Sons, 1916. p. 173.

Sources:

R. Ernest Dupuy and Trevor N. Dupuy. The Harper Encyclopedia of Military History. 4th edition. New York: HarperCollins Publishers, 1993.

http://www.en.wikipedia.org

http://www.wsaww1.com/Eugene-Bullard

http://www.historyofway.org/articles/people_bullard_eugene

L'Escadrille Lafayette

1916-18

Goal:

To provide the French air service with additional power to combat German warplanes.

Background:

Hardly had World War I started when a group of Americans trooped into the office of the U.S. ambassador to France, Myron Herrick. They wanted to know if they would lose their U.S. citizenship if they joined the French armed forces. They would, the ambassador said, but he added that if they joined the French Foreign Legion, this probably would not happen. The legion did not require an oath of loyalty to France.

Declared the ambassador, "That is the law, boys, but if a were young and in your shoes, I know mighty well what I would do!"[1] On 21 August 1914, 43 Americans joined the *Légion Etragére*. It would not be long, however, before some of them ignored the risk of citizenship loss and transferred to the *Service Aéronautique*. Eventually about 209 Americans flew for France, known collectively as the Lafayette Flying Corps. Of these 38 served in the famed *Lafayette Escadrille*.

The *Escadrille* came about because several of the American flyers thought an American flying unit should be created. Among the Yanks was William Thaw II, scion of a wealthy Pittsburgh family who had won fame while at Yale by flying under four bridges over New York's East River. Another American was Norman Prince, from a wealthy New England family, a Harvard lawyer and a licensed pilot. The French government was reluctant at first to set up a special unit because of international law issues. But when several of the flyers on leave in the States received a good press, the decision was made to set up the unit.

Fame–Fortune–Frustration

K. Rockwell, Capt. Thenault, Norman Prince, Lt. DeLagge, Sgt. Cowdin, Sgt. Bert Hall, J.R. McConnell, and Victor Chapman. Lafayette Escadrille, World War I. Courtesy wikimedia.org

L'Escadrille Américaine was created 16 April 1916; later the name was changed to l' *Escadrille Lafayette* when the German ambassador to the United States complained that the name betrayed America's false neutrality. The insignia was an Indian with a feathered headdress (a Seminole until April 1917 and a Sioux after that date). The French picked seven volunteers for the new unit: five were the sons of millionaires; the others sons of a farmer and a Baptist minister. Two volunteers had already served in the French air service. To assist in setting up the unit, funds were sought and obtained from wealthy Americans with interests in France. Thaw's and Prince's fathers contributed and so did William K. Vanderbilt and J. Pierpont Morgan.

Leadership:

In command of the *Escadrille* at its founding were two French aviation officers, Captain Georges Thénault and Lieutenant Alfred de Laage de Meux, later killed in action. Thaw was the American vice commander.

Volunteers:

The American volunteers were young men of action, and some very rich. "Gallant" France was engaged in a deadly conflict with the "terrible" Huns, and these idealistic young American men joined the

L'Escadrille Lafayette, 1916-18

French armed forces to defend democracy or to find adventure or, probably, both.

The total personnel of the squadron was approximately 80 men. These included pilots, medical and armament officers, two mechanics for each plane, officers' orderlies and truck drivers. No more than 19 Americans served in the squadron at a time and throughout the 23 month existence of the unit.

The Americans flew the Nieuport 17, a sesquiplane (a compromise between a monoplane and a biplane). The plane, which entered service in May 1916, was a fast climber but had a tendency to lose its bottom wing in steep dives.

Victor Chapman (1890-1916), like a number of the Lafayette squadron's members, graduated from Harvard University. The privileged social status of many of the squadron's members attracted significant publicity to its activities. The squadron's ground routine was run more like an elite country club than a military base. Chapman had initially joined the French Foreign Legion before becoming a founding member of the squadron. He was killed in aerial combat.

Courtesy wikimedia.org

Compensation:

A pilot was paid nine sous plus a franc a day for flight pay. This totaled 20 cents daily in U.S. currency. In addition a pilot received 100 francs (20 cents) each month for his mess and other necessities. In addition, there were cash prizes for pilots who received decorations and/or downed enemy aircraft. These ranged between $50 and $300. But for some of the American flyers financial reward was not a factor since they came from very rich families.

The wealth of the squadron's American pilots and contributing philanthropists allowed them to convert their lodgings into the envy of other flying units. The flyers also enlisted the services of a French chef who had worked at the Ritz Hotel in New York. Pilot James McConnell observed: "At first sight [the squadron's ground personnel] seemed to outnumber the Nicaraguan army - mechanicians [sic], chauffeurs, armorers, motorcyclists, telephonists, wireless operators, Red Cross stretcher bearers, clerks."[2]

Opposition:

Unlike most fights between soldiers of fortune and their enemies, during World War I the "Hun" was as well armed and as well trained as the Americans, if not better.

The aircraft on both sides possessed superiorities and inferiorities when compared to their opponents. The challenge for the flyer was to exploit his aircraft's advantages while minimizing its shortcomings. An American pilot warned against the decision to attack a plane with a rear gunner from above: "If you want to go to heaven, the easiest way I know is to dive on a two-seater."[3] In view of the primitive technology of these planes, luck also played a major role.

Fame–Fortune–Frustration

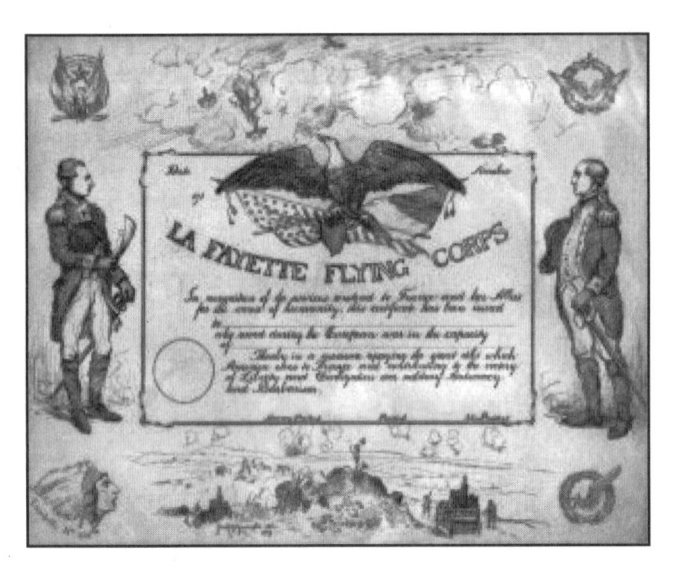

Lafayette Escadrille Service Certificate Courtesy wikimedia.org

Strategy:

As the fighting on land stagnated into trench warfare, the more creative individuals among the protagonists looked to the skies seeking a way to break the deadlock. Prior to the war both sides had had their air power prophets who had been ignored. As the fighting on the ground stalemated, the war in the air evolved from pilots dueling with pistols to dueling with machine guns. The new American-manned flying unit, officially designated Nieuport 124, was assigned to escorting a bombardment squadron. It was based at Luxeuil-les-Bains, a small town in northeastern France.

Operations:

On 13 May 1916 the squadron staged its first patrol, five of its six new Nieuport I7 fighters flying over enemy lines. They encountered anti-aircraft fire but no enemy aircraft. On 22 May the squadron drew its first blood. Pilot Bert Hall shot down a German Aviatik plane. Two days later Thaw downed a Fokker.

In the months ahead the aerial combat was intense, particularly over the carnage of the Battle of Verdun, where *l'Escadrille* participated. Gervais Raoul Lufbery, one of its pilots, described a fight with a German plane: "I began firing at him. Then we both circled, firing all the time. Suddenly, his machine seemed to turn all white. He was upside down. Then he caught fire. He fell .... Then I came home."[4]

Lafayette Escadrille Service Medal Courtesy wikimedia.org

Historian Dennis Gordon has described an action over the Verdun sector: A four-plane *Escadrille* scouting group, led by the squadron commander, spotted 12 German biplanes. The commander wanted to avoid contact but pilot Victor "Chapman broke out of the formation and dived to the attack. He fired upon and struck a Fokker which was seen to fall out of control. Soon a fierce battle ranged from a 4,000 meters [13,100 feet] to near ground level. The Americans, outnumbered three-to-one, fought heroically .... [F]irst [Kiffin] Rockwell, then Chapman, and finally Thaw were each forced out of the fight from wounds when each man's aircraft was repeatedly struck by fire...."[5]

IMPACT:

The American knights cruised the dangerous skies of France. During the 23 months of activity they flew over 3,000 combat patrols. Sometimes the Yanks won their battles. Other times they lost to the well-trained foe. The Americans scored some 39 confirmed victories and as many as 100 unconfirmed wins. (Under French rules only enemy aircraft downed over French-controlled territory were counted.) Six *Escadrille* pilots died in combat, one due to anti-aircraft fire and two in accidents. Five of the original squadron members did not survive the war.

Historian Ezra Bowen summed up the importance of the American squadron: "… [T]heir presence at the front tied the United States closer to the Allies and carried the promise of far greater American help to come."[6] The United States entered the war on 6 April 1917 and once its forces got to France, there would no longer be a need for a French-controlled American flying unit. On 18 February 1918 *l'Escadrille Lafayette* was disbanded. Twelve of its flyers joined the U.S. Air Service.

BIOGRAPHIES:

James Jules Bach (unk.), from St. Louis, Missouri, was one of a small group of Americans in France who called themselves the "American Volunteer Corps." They joined the Foreign Legion in 1914, were given training and in October were sent to the front. Early in the following year Bach joined the Escadrille Lafayette. He was sent 23 September 1917 on a special mission to insert saboteurs behind enemy lines. Bach was captured, the first American taken by the Germans. He was tried twice, sentenced to death, but the sentence was not carried out. Bach remained a prisoner until the end of the war.

Victor Chapman (1890-1916) graduated from Harvard University with an B.A. then studied art in Paris. He joined the Foreign Legion and was a founding American member of *l'Escadrille Lafayette*. He was killed in action.

Elliot Cowdin (1886-1916) graduated from Harvard University and joined the American Ambulance Service. He was a founding American member of *l'Escadrille Lafayette*. Cowdin was killed in action.

James Norman Hall (1887-1951) served in *l'Escadrille Lafayette*. When it was disbanded, he joined the American 94th squadron. He was forced to crash land in German territory and became a prisoner of war for the duration. Later, he and Charles Nordhoff (another member of the *l'Escadrille Lafayette)* co-authored *Mutiny on the Bounty*.

Weston "Bert" Hall (1885-1948) worked as a farm hand, a railroad section hand, a "human Cannon ball" at a circus and a seaman on a merchantship. While driving a taxi in Paris he enlisted in the Foreign

Legion. Hall was a founding American member of *l'Escadrille Lafayette* and had three kills.

Gervais Raoul V. Lufbery (1885-1918) was a French-born, U.S. naturalized citizen. His French mother and American father immigrated to the United States. At one time or another he had been a baker, stamp seller, hotel waiter, maker of casket handles, chocolate factory employee and ticker collector in the Bombay railroad station. Between 1902 and 1907 he traveled the world. Lufbury served with the U.S. Army in the Philippines and was the best marksman in his regiment. He was the mechanic for a barnstorming pilot in India and toured China and Egypt. Lufbury was in France in August 1914 when war broke out and joined the Foreign Legion. He then transferred to the French Air Service. From there he was transferred to the *l'Escadille Americaine* which became *l'Escadrille Lafayette*. He was the top ace in *l'Escadrille Lafayette* with 16 confirmed kills and numerous unconfirmed successes. Asked if he was not bothered many of his kills were unconfirmed, Lufbury replied: "What the hell do I care? I know I got them."[7] On 10 January 1918 he transferred to the U.S. Air Service and commissioned a major. During aerial combat on 19 June his fuel tank was hit and he jumped to his death. Lufbury was awarded British and French metals for valor.

James H. McConnell (1887-1917) as a youth, with a friend, drove an automobile from Chicago to New York City. He was educated as a lawyer. He joined the American Ambulance Field Service in France, then the French Aeronautical Service. McConnell was a founding American member of *l'Escadrille Lafayette*. He was killed in action.

Charles B. Nordhoff (unk.- 1947) from California, he went to France in December 1916 to drive an ambulance. When is contract expired in June 1917, he joined the French Foreign Legion and then transferred to the *l'Escadrille Lafayette*. Nordhoff and James Hall (another member of the *l'Escadrille Lafayette*) co-authored *Mutiny on the Bounty*.

Edwin C. Parsons (1892-1967), born in Holyoke, Massachusetts, graduated from the University of Pennsylvania. In 1912 he learned to fly with Glenn Curtiss in Los Angeles, California. Parsons trained pilots who flew for Pancho Villa during the Mexican Revolution. In 1915 he worked his way as an assistant veterinarian to France on board a ship that was transporting horses. Parsons served for a short while as an ambulance driver, entered the French Foreign Legion and transferred to service in French Air Service. On 25 January 1917 he was assigned to *l'Escadrille Americaine* N.124 (the future *l'Escadrille Lafayette*). On 3 September Parsons scored his first and only confirmed kill while flying for *l'Escadrille Lafayette* - he shot down a Rumpler C IV near the Argonne. Following the United States' entry into World War I, Parsons chose to remain in the French Air Service, downing seven more enemy aircraft. He received numerous French decorations including the *Medaille Militaire*.

After World War I, Parsons became one of the first FBI agents. Later he worked in Hollywood as a writer. In 1939 he joined the U.S. Navy and attended the rank of rear admiral before retiring in 1955.

Norman Prince (1887-1916) was educated as a lawyer. He learned to fly despite his father's abhorrence of aviation; he called planes "stinking chicken cages." Prince went to France and joined the Foreign Legion, then transferred to the French Aeronautical Service. He was a founding American member of *l'Escadrille Lafayette*. Prince flew 122 sorties against enemy planes in less than six months. He had the second largest number of kills - four. Prince was killed in action.

Kriffin Y. Rockwell (1892-1916), of French-Huguenot descent, was born in Newport, Tennessee. He entered Virginia Military Academy in 1908. Believing that he was more likely to see action at sea, he switched to the U.S. Naval Academy. Kriffin, now believing that war was not imminent, resigned from the Naval Academy and entered Washington and Lee University where his brother Paul was a student. In 1912 Kriffin traveled to the West Coast and ran an advertising agency.

On 3 August 1914 Rockwell wrote to the French consul-general in New Orleans offering to fight for France. Rockwell said, "I am very anxious to see military service and would rather fight under the French flag than any other, as I greatly admire your nation."[8] Before receiving a reply, Kriffin and his brother Paul travelled to France, where they joined the Foreign Legion. Displaying unusual energy, Kriffin was assigned to the First Foreign Regiment in March 1915. He participated in the storming of La Targette on 9 May and was hit by machine gun fire. Because his thigh wound probably precluded any further field service, and upon the recommendation of an American flyer friend, Rockwell applied for the French air service, was accepted, went into training and became a pilot. With six other Yank pilots Rockwell helped form *l'Escadrille Lafayette*. On 18 May he shot down the first kill by an American. Six days later Kriffin was wounded in the face. Between July and August he fought in 70 engagements. He would score one additional victory. On 23 September 1916 Rockwell himself was shot down and died. Rockwell was awarded the Cross of Chevalier and the Legion of Honor.

William Thaw (1893-1934) learned to fly in his teens and had a license at the age of 20. With funds from his father, he bought a flying boat, which he used to give rides to the Newport, Rhode Island, social set. Thaw traveled to Great Britain, planned to enter competitions in Monaco and Paris, but war broke out. He joined the French Aeronautical Service. Thaw was a founding American member of *l'Escadrille Lafayette*.

QUOTATIONS:

[1] Herbert Molloy Mason, Jr., *The Lafayette Escadrille*. New York: Random House, 1964. p. 5.
[2] Ezra Bowen and the Editors of Time-Life Books, *Knights of the Air*. Alexandria, VA: Time-Life Books, 1980. p. 100.
[3] Dennis Gordon, *Lafayette Escadrille Pilot Biographies*. Missoula, Montana: The Doughboy Historical Society, 1991. p. 17.
[4] Jay Mallin and Robert K. Brown, *Merc: American Soldiers of Fortune*. New York: Macmillan Publishing Company, 1979. p. 193.
[5] Gordon, *Lafayette Escadrille*. p. 35.
[6] Bowen, *Knights of the Air*. p. 98.
[7] Gordon, *Lafayette Escadrille*. p. 84.
[8] Gordon, *Lafayette Escadrille*. p. 48.

SOURCES:

C.F. Andrews, *The Nieuport 17*. Surrey: Profile Publications Ltd., 1965.

Peter M. Bowers, *The Nieuport N.28C-1*. Surrey: Profile Publications Ltd., 1966.

J. Ward Boyce, ed. *American Fighter Aces Album*. Mesa, AZ: The American Fighter Aces Association, 1996.

Dictionary of American Biography. 10 vols. plus sup. 1 thru 8. New York: Charles Scribner's Sons, 1936 & 1990.

Arlen J. Hansen, *Gentlemen Volunteers*. New York: Arcade Publishing, 1996.

Edwin C. Parsons, *I Flew with the Lafayette Escadrille*. Indianapolis: E.C. Seale & Company, Inc., 1963.

Sterling Seagrave and the Editors of Time-Life Books, *Soldiers of Fortune*. Alexandria, VA: Time-Life Books, 1985.

Americans in the French Service Aeronautique

1916-18

Goal:

To help France win World War I.

Background:

Joining the French *Service Aeronautique* was the final step in the morphing of American volunteerism for the French cause. Earlier iterations had been joining the French Foreign Legion, the French *Réserve Mallet*, and the French *l'Escadrille Lafayette*.

Leadership:

The *Service Aeronautique* was under the French high command, and its American flyers played no role in leadership decisions.

Volunteers:

The number of Americans serving in the *Service Aeronautique* was probably small. These included individuals who left the French *Réserve Mallet* when it was taken over by the U.S. Army and those who did not want to fly for the U.S. Army Air Corps once the French *l'Escadrille Lafayette* had been dissolved. There was also the unique circumstance of Eugene Bullard, a Black man, who was not permitted to fly for the *l'Escadrille Lafayette* because of his race and so he chose to fly for the French.

Compensation:

Undoubtedly, they received the same pay as the French flyers.

Opposition:

Although the war on the ground had turned in the Allies' favor following the failed German 1918 spring offensive, this was not true for the war in the air. By early 1918 the aviation technological pendulum, which had swung between the Allies and the Central Powers, now favored the Germans. Therefore, challenging the Germans in aerial combat was a very dangerous business.

Strategy:

In many regards aerial combat was literally and socially above trench warfare. Although planes did gang up on enemy aircraft, there were courtesies - almost medieval chivalry that were observed by both sides. This was especially true for the respect shown to a fallen opponent. A recruiting poster for the Royal Flying Corps proclaimed: "War in the air recalls the olden times, when knights rode forth to battle and won honor and glory...."[1]

Operations:

On 21 March 1918 Germany launched a massive ground attack on the Western Front in an attempt to defeat the Allies before significant numbers of American troops would enter the trenches. All remaining reserves were thrown into this last gamble to win. Supporting the attack were 730 aircraft. In March and April, German aircraft shot down 1,000 enemy planes. But by mid-July the German army was exhausted. On 8 August, reinforced by the Americans, the Allies launched their own ground offensive. As the German army retreated, Germany's air superiority waned. During the first four days of fighting, the Allies lost 144 planes and the Germans 30. Numbers and logistics began to decide who would be the winner. German aircraft were now outnumbered two-to-one, and they ran out of gasoline and bullets.

Impact:

The number of Americans flying for the *Service Aeronautique* were too few to have a significant impact.

Biographies:

Roger Marie Louis Balbiani (*ca.*1888.-1918) was a member of an

American ambulance service in 1914 and 1915. He joined the *Service Aeronautique*. Balbiani was killed in June 1918.

Frank Leaman Baylies (1896-1918) was born in New Bedford, Massachusetts. He graduated from Brown Preparatory School in Providence, Rhode Island. Between March 1916 and May 1917 he served in the American Ambulance Service in France. On 21 May Baylies joined the *Service Aeronautique*. In December he was assigned to *Escadrille* SPA.3, "*Les Cigognes*" (the Storks). His first confirmed kill was on 19 February 1918. His SPAD was shot down on 17 June by a Fokker tri-plane and he was killed. Baylies tallied 12 kills during the war.

Leif Norman Barclay (*ca.*1897-1917) was a member of an American Ambulance Service. He joined the *Service Aeronautique* and was killed in aerial combat near Belfort, France, on 1 June 1917.

Philip Phillips Benney (*ca.*1896-1918) came from Pittsburgh, Pennsylvania. He joined an American Ambulance Service in 1917. Next he entered the *Service Aeronautique* and was killed in aerial combat near Verdun on 26 January 1918.

James Alexander Connelly, Jr. (1895-1944) was reared in Philadelphia, Pennsylvania. He joined the French Foreign Legion in 1917. He transferred to the *Service Aeronautique* in November and was assigned to *Escadrille* SPA.157 on 15 January 1918. While flying for the French, Connelly scored seven kills (five aircraft and two balloons).

Eric Anderson Fowler (*ca.*1895-1917) was from New York City and attended Princeton University. He served in an American Ambulance Service in 1916 and 1917. Fowler joined the *Service Aeronautique* and was killed in an aircraft accident at Pau, France, on 26 November 1917.

Schuyler Lee (ca.1899-1918) from New London, Connecticut, and attended Andover Academy. He served in the *Réserve Mallet*, Section 526. Later, Lee joined the *Service Aeronautique*. He was killed near Montdidier, France, on 12 April 1918.

David Endicott Putnam (1898-1918), born in Jamaica Plain, Massachusetts, attended Harvard University. Putnam tried to join the U.S. Army Air Corps but was rejected because he was too young. Traveling to France, he joined the *Service Aeronautique*. Apparently he was administratively passed through *l'Escadrille Lafayette* on his way to being assigned to *Escadrille* SPA.94. On 19 January 1918 Putnam scored his first kill. He was shot down and killed by German ace Georg von Hantleman on 12 September. Putnam was credited with 13 kills (12 aircraft and one balloon).

Henry H. Houston Woodward (*ca.*1896-1918) was from Philadelphia, Pennsylvania. He joined an American Ambulance Service in

1917. He then served in the *Service Aeronautique*. Houston was killed in aerial combat over the Somme on 1 April 1918.

Quotations:

[1] Ezra Bowen, *Knights of the Air*. Alexandria, Virginia: Time-Life Books, 1981. p. 7.

Sources:

J. Ward Boyce, ed. *American Fighter Aces Album*. Mesa, Arizona: The American Fighter Aces Association, 1996.

Norman Franks, *American Aces of World War I*. Oxford: Osprey Publishing, Ltd., 2001.

History of the American Field service in France. Vol. 3. Boston: Houghton Mifflin Company, 1920.

Dennis Gordon, *Lafayette Escadrille Pilot Biographies*. Missoula, Montana: The Doughboy Historical Society, 1991.

Cooper's Kosciuszko Squadron

1918-21

Goal:

To assist the new nation of Poland in maintaining its independence from an assault by the Soviet Union.

Background:

World War I had ended on 11 November 1918 but eastern Europe remained in turmoil. The new Soviet Union wanted to retain control of the old Russian Empire which included Poland. Merian C. Cooper, who had been a pilot in the U.S. Army air force during World War I, offered Polish leader Marshal Jozef Pilsudski to establish an air squadron composed of Americans. Pilsudski accepted and Cooper went to Paris, resigned his U.S. Army commission and began recruiting demobilized American pilots. The Americans took over an existing Polish squadron on 16 October 1919.

Leadership:

Cooper founded the Kosciuszko Squadron. He chose another former American flyer, Major Cedric Fauntleroy, to command the unit. Painted on the sides of the aircraft were the American stars and stripes with superimposed, Kosciuszko's cap and crossed scythes.

Marion Cooper (1893-1973) not only flew against King Kong in the movie of the same name, he flew against Germany in World War I for the U.S. Air Corps; against Russia for Poland immediately after World War I; and against Japan for the Flying Tigers and for the U.S. Air Corps during World War II.

Courtesy wikimedia.org

Volunteers:

In all seventeen American pilots who had served in the U.S. Army during World War I joined the Kosciuszko Squadron.

Compensation:

The volunteers were paid by the Polish government.

Opposition:

The squadron was opposed by the air force of the new Soviet Union. It, however, proved to be little threat.

Strategy:

To support the Polish troops by attacking with bombs and Machine gun fire Soviet troops and railways.

Operations:

At first Marshal Pilsudski failed to see the support value of aircraft for his troops. The Kosciuszko was used to carrying messages. In April 1920, however, when the Polish army launched a major offensive, the squadron went into action. The Russian flyers, probably poorly trained, avoided contact with the Americans. Using machine guns and small bombs the Kosciuszko Squadron hit cavalry and ground troops. The railroads were a favorite target: lines, yards, and troop trains were attacked. One attack on a train enabled Polish prisoners who were on board to escape. The Americans also sank several troopships.

While on a routine mission, Cooper spotted a large white tent that looked military. He and his wingman machine-gunned the structure. They later learned that it had been occupied by Soviet airmen. The demoralized flyers fled - all the way to Kiev, 400 miles away.

In May the Russians began a counter-offensive. The Kosciuszko flyers were again in the thick of the fighting. They reported enemy movements, attacked enemy cavalry, and shielded Polish troops what were pulling back.

In one action, Fauntleroy spotted Soviet troops mining a rail line and preparing an ambush. In the distance a Polish troop train was approaching. Fauntleroy dived and flew in front of the train, waving frantically. The train stopped. Fauntleroy landed and warned of the trap ahead. Polish soldiers poured from the train and advanced on the Russians. Fauntleroy was later awarded the highest Polish military decoration, the *Virtuti Militari*.

Cooper's Kosciuszko Squadron, 1918-21

American volunteers, Merian C. Cooper and Cedric Fauntleroy, fighting in the Polish Air Force's Kościuszko Squadron Courtesy wikimedia.org

On 26 July 1920 Cooper's plane was shot down. He spent nearly nine months in a Soviet prisoner of war camp until he escaped to Latvia. Pilsudski gave him the *Virtuti Militari*.

On 18 October 1920 a truce was declared. All Polish units were withdrawn from the front. The Kosciuszko Squadron had flown 462 combat sorties in 682 flying hours and dropped 13,200 pounds of bombs. Three Americans died and four were wounded.

The Americans were demobilized on 15 May 1921. The squadron continued in service now manned by Polish airmen eventually seeing action in World War II.

Impact:

The participation of American air combat veterans was a decisive factor in giving Poland control of the air in its war with the Soviet Union. A Polish army command report stated: "Although very exhausted, the American are fighting as if possessed; without their help we would have broken down long ago."[1]

Biographies:

Merian C. Cooper (1893-1973) was a flyer in the U.S. Army. During World War I he was shot down and spent months in a German POW camp. After the war, he was assign to an American relief group in Poland. Cooper had a particular interest in Poland. His ancestral home in Georgia had sheltered two Polish officers, Tadeusz Kosciuskko and Kazimierz Pulaski, who assisted George Washington during the American Revolution. Following his tour with the Kosciuszko Squadron, Cooper eventually returned to the United States. He served in China (*see* Claire Lee Chennault) and then reentered the U.S. Army. Cooper served with the Fifth Air Force in the Pacific rising to the rank of brigadier general and on 2 September 1945 stood on the deck of the USS *Missouri* when Japan surrendered. Cooper also had an accomplished civilian career. He was a founder of Pan American Airways. He was a successful screenwriter, director and producer in Hollywood (his most famous film: King Kong, which included flying scenes - with Cooper, of course, flying the plane).

Cedric Errol Fauntleroy (1891-1973) (sometimes cited Faunt le Roy), was raised on a small plantation near Natchez, Mississippi, and worked as a dirt-track auto racer. When World War I broke out Fauntleroy joined the French Foreign Legion as a second-class private. He transferred first to the French air force and then to the famed "Hat in the Ring" squadron when the United States entered World War I, ultimately reaching the rank of major. During his service in Poland he was promoted to the rank of colonel and awarded Poland's highest military decoration, the *Virtuti Militari*. During World War II Fauntleroy supervised parachute production at Manti and San Diego, California.

Quotations:

[1] Jerzy B. Cynk, "Kosciuszko Squadron," *Air Pictorial* pp. 316-19 (September 1965) p. 318.

Sources:

Lynne Olson and Stanley Cloud. *A Question of Honor: The Koscuiszko Squadron - the Forgotten Heroes of World War II*. New York: Random House Digital, Inc., 2003.

Sterling Seagrave and the Editors of Time-Life Books, *Soldiers of Fortune*. Alexandria, VA: Time-Life Books Inc., 1985.

Lincoln Thomson, "Cute Maker Needs Workers." vol. 372 no. 9 [Salt Lake City] *The Desert News* (12 October 1943) p.7.

Odyssey of Marion Aten

1919

Goal:

To fight for the White Russians against the Reds.

Background:

The Great Russian Civil War raged 1917 to 1922 between the Reds (the Communists) and the Whites (a heterogeneous collection of those opposed to the Communists). Particularly intense fighting took place in southeastern Russia across the plains between the Black and Caspian seas. The British along with other World War I victors provided direct military aid, including men, to the Whites.

Leadership:

Major Raymond Collishaw, Great Britain's third most successful ace during World War I, recruited Royal Air force pilots, Marion Aten among them, to join No. 47 Squadron and fly in support of the Whites against the Reds. The Squadron was made up of 300 men.

Volunteers:

It is hard to say how many Americans flew in the revolution, but it was probably only a handful. And, apparently all of them flew for the Whites. It was dangerous work. Aten wrote: "The leaflet said that the Reds were very angry about the British airmen who were aiding the reactionary, Czarist White forces.... Should they capture any of us, our fate would be crucifixion, or worse."[1] For some of these American pilots, the Russian Revolution was a stopover between other conflicts.

COMPENSATION:

Apparently temporary Captain Aten and the other fliers and ground crews were paid by Great Britain. One of Aten's compatriots noted: "Combat pay too. A quid extra a day."[2]

OPPOSITION:

A motley collection of British- and French-built planes were used by both the Reds and the Whites. Enemy aircraft was not the primary danger to the protagonists. The primary threat came from poor maintenance and the lack of spare parts. Also, at times, ground fire could be intense.

STRATEGY:

Aircraft could have been a decisive weapon against enemy troops crossing the treeless plains of southeast Russia, if there had been enough planes, pilots and fuel - but there wasn't.

OPERATIONS:

Marion Aten and his squadron mates arrived in South Russia in the spring of 1919. Flying a British-designed Sopwith *Camel* he shot down a Red Air force, French-designed Nieuport in April. His second victory was over a German-designed Fokker triplane which broke apart and crashed during the chase. Between May and August Aten destroyed three more Red aircraft - two *Nieuports* and a Fokker *D VII*.

With the collapse of the White forces on the ground Aten fled Russia by train through the port city of Rostov just before the bridge over the Don River was blown up.

At least three other Americans flew in Russia at this time. In 1919 John S. Griffith and Frederick Lord flew for the Whites and Oren Rose flew for the Royal Air Force. Their hallmark of success had been their World War I accomplishments whereas Aten's call to fame was his successes - the downing of five enemy aircraft - during the Great Russian Civil War.

IMPACT:

The Great Civil War raged on well after the departure of Aten. The Whites failed because their leaders were disunited, inept and corrupt - more so than those of their enemy. Aten and his compatriots failed to make any impact on the outcome of the war.

BIOGRAPHIES:

Marion H. "Bunny" Aten (unk.- *ca.* 1961) was probably born in Texas, the son of a Texas Ranger captain. Marion went to Canada where he joined the Royal Air Force (RAF) apparently in 1914. During World War I he was assigned to No. 203 Squadron. Aten broke his arm badly in a flying accident and was in a hospital when the war ended. Following his service for the White Russians, Aten returned to England in 1921. Between 1922 and 1924 he flew for the Royal Air Force in the Kurdistan. He resigned in 1927 and came back to the United States. In 1961 Aten wrote an account of his adventures, *Last Train Over the Rostov Bridge*.

John Sharpe Griffith (1898-1974) was born in Seattle, Washington. He joined the Royal Flying Corps (RFC) in 1917 and was assigned to No. 60 Squadron. His first kill occurred on 9 March 1918 over Menin, Belgium. On 18 July he was wounded by anti-aircraft fire and was hospitalized for the remained of the war. During World War I, he was credited with shooting down seven aircraft and one balloon. In early 1919 Griffith traveled to Archangel, Russia, and flew for the Whites. He was credited with shooting down a balloon. He returned to the RAF and remained until 1921. Griffin served in the U.S. Army Air Corps in World War II and retired from the U.S. Air Force in 1956.

Frederick Ives "Tex" Lord (1900-67), born in Manitowoc, Wisconsin, joined the Texas National Guard in 1916 but was discharged when it was discovered he was under age. He traveled to Canada, lied about his age, and joined the RFC. He was assigned to No. 97 Squadron in March 1918. His first kill was an observation balloon on 28 May. Following a series of aerial victories, Lord was promoted to captain on 21 August. He was shot down and wounded on 17 October. The remainder of the war was spent in a British hospital. During World War I he was credited with 12 kills (11 airplanes and one balloon). Following the war, Lord flew for the Whites against the Reds. After some barnstorming, he flew for the Republicans in the Spanish Civil War. When World War II broke out, Lord rejoined his old squadron, No. 97. When his true age was discovered, he was assigned to ferry duty.

Oren J. Rose (1893-1971) was born in Platte County, Missouri. Traveling to Canada, he joined the RFC in 1917. Rose was assigned to Squadron No. 92. Flying an *SE-5A*, he scored his first kill, a Fokker *D VII*, on 30 July 1918. Following a number of successes, he was promoted to captain. During World War I Rose was credited with 16 kills. Next he flew in Russia against the Reds. Rose served in World War II as a training officer.

Quotations:

[1] Marian Aten and Arthur Orrmont, *Last Train Over the Rostov Bridge*. New York: Julian Messer, Inc., 1961, p. 92.

[2] Aten and Orrmont, *Last Train*, p. 10.

Sources:

J. Ward Boyce, ed. *American Fighter Aces Album*. Mesa, Arizona: The American Fighter Aces Association, 1996.

Nik Cornish, *The Russian Revolution: World War to Civil War 1917-1921*. South Yorkshire: Pen & Sword, 2012.

Norman Franks, *American Aces of World War I*. Oxford: Osprey Publishing, Ltd., 2001.

R. Ernest Dupuy and Trevor N. Dupuy. *The Harper Encyclopedia of Military History*. 4th edition. New York: HarperCollins Publishers, 1993.

Christopher Shores, *British and Empire Aces of World War I*. Oxford: Osprey Publishing, 2001.

Escadrille de la Chérifienne in the Riff War

1925

Goal:

To support France in its conflict with the Riff rebels in Morocco. Having fought for *la belle France* in World War I, Americans wanted to continue their adventurous lives by aiding France in its colonial war.

Background:

France and Spain were allied in the Second Riff War (1921-26) against the Riff Berbers who had the audacity to believe Morocco, their native land, belonged to them and not the Europeans. (The Riff is a large mountainous area in northern Morocco.) The Riffs revolted against the Sultan of Morocco, a puppet of the European governments.

Leadership:

French officered were in command of the American-manned flying unit. The Riffs were led by the excellent strategist, Muhammad Ibn ʻAbd al-Khattabi (1882-1963), better known as Abd el-Krim.

Escadrille de la Guarde Cherifienne in Morocco, 1925

Courtesy Wikimedia.org

Volunteers:

Sixteen Americans, plus one Canadian, became the *Escadrille de la Guarde Chérifienne* The official name of the force was the *Escadrille de la Chérifienne* (Squadron of the Sultan's Bodyguard), an element in the army of the Sultan of Morocco. No oath or enlistment papers were required. The purpose of the nebulous relationship was to circumvent U.S. law prohibiting Americans from serving in foreign militaries.

Compensation:

The aviators presumably received at least commensurate pay with that of French pilots.

Opposition:

The rebellious Riffs had about 80,000 men, some modern rifles, a few machine guns but no aircraft. They were, however, good marksmen, creating a danger to low-flying aircraft. The flyers in their planes fought against Riffs on their horses. The horses were probably a sturdier and more reliable means of transportation.

Strategy:

The flyers reconnoitered and bombed Riff concentrations.

Operations:

The flyers arrived in Morocco in August 1925 and were quartered in Casablanca. They were assigned Breguet bombers. Missions were typically limited to the early and late hours of the day because the mid-day heat was too intense for man and aircraft alike.

The first combat mission occurred on 6 September and involved low-level bombing and machinegun strafing. In addition to explosives, chemical bombs were also dropped on the Riff. The international press, encouraged by the international Communist movement (the COMINTERN), portrayed the struggle as a David (the Riffs) fighting a Goliath (the French and the Spanish). World public feelings led to the disbanding of the *Escadrille de la Chérifienne* in November 1925.

IMPACT:

In May 1926 the Riff surrendered unconditionally. The small group of *Chérifienne* flyers had no impact on the course of the war. The bombing apparatus was rudimentary, the Riffs were fast-moving and so the bombings did little damage. The *Chérifienne* logged 653 air hours in 470 missions during seven weeks of operations. The unit suffered no battle casualties. Abd el-Krim was vanquished not by tactics but by superior numbers and weaponry. His guerrilla operations are believed to have influenced Ho Chih Minh, Mao Tse-tung and Ernesto "Che" Guevara.

BIOGRAPHIES:

Curtiss Day (1892-1972) studied at the Wright Brothers School outside Montgomery, Alabama. He served as an instructor pilot during World War I before participating in the Riff War.

Paul Ayres Rockwell (1889-1995) was a veteran of the French Foreign Legion. He flew 37 missions for the *Chérifienne*. A relative of his, W.J.K. Rockwell, has written:

> "Rockwell was accorded the rank of captain and flew as a bombardier-observer against the forces of Abd-el-Krim. He did this with greatly mixed feelings, having no animosity toward the tribes and sympathizing with a people who were able to manage their own affairs when left alone. The culture of the people fascinated him, as did the terrain. The duties of observation could incorporate that last item. Concerning the bombing, he consoled himself considerably in the knowledge that the twenty-two and 110-pound bombs, 'aimed' and released in the most rudimentary fashion, were much more likely to produce great clouds of dust in the dry terrain than to obliterate human begins."[1]

QUOTATIONS:

[1] W.J.K. Rockwell, "Personal Diplomacy in Franco-American Relations." April 2007. *American Diplomacy*. Electronic Article. 7 August 2013. <http://www.unc.edu/depts/diplomat/item/2007/0103/rock/rockwell_personal.html>

Sources:

Dennis Gordon, *Lafayette Escadrille - Pilot Biographies*. Missoula, MT: The Doughboy Historical Society, 1991.

Scott Kraska, "*Escadrille de la Chérifienne* America's Second Lafayette Escadrille." *Military Trader* (February 2012) pp. 31-32

Four Americans Flying for China

1932-45

Goal:
To defend China from the invading Japanese forces

Background:
Japan staged an incident in Manchuria on 7 July 1937, invaded China and the two countries went to war.

Leadership:
The flyers played no leadership roles except within their aerial units.

Volunteers:
Whenever there has been a foreign war, some Americans have always volunteered for the "right" side. In the Sino-Japanese War at least four Americans fought for China, three of them Chinese-Americans. One American was killed in service. As a volunteer in the Chinese air force, Robert Short was the first American flyer to engage the Japanese in combat.

Compensation:
Short probably did not serve in the Chinese air force long enough to receive pay. Before that he was paid by the firm for which he worked, or received commissions from sales he made.

The Chinese-Americans probably received regular Chinese pay in accord with their ranks.

Opposition:

A lesson learned by the Japanese from World War I was the need to be technologically superior in critical industries. One industry that the Japanese concentrated on was military aviation. The world held the quality of Japanese products in low regard and few appreciated the advances being made by Japanese aviation. In 1931 Japanese aircraft and pilots were among the best in the world.

Strategy:

At the time Short joined the Chinese air force it was searching for a strategy to oppose the Japanese. The Chinese air force was in a dire state: its pilots inadequately trained, its U.S.- and Soviet-manufactured aircraft obsolete.

Operations:

A P-12 whose purchase Short had arranged was uncrated and assembled at an airfield outside Shanghai. The aircraft was armed with twin .30-caliber Browning machineguns which were fed ammunition by belts. The insignia of the Chinese air force was painted on the fuselage: a 12-point white star on a blue circle. Short took the aircraft up for a test flight. Later, on 12 February 1932, he set out for Nanking where he thought the air force was based. Somewhere along the route he was spotted by three Japanese Mitsubishi bombers. These were two-place planes doing reconnaissance work off the aircraft carrier *Kaga*. The Japanese closed in for the kill but Short climbed rapidly. He turned and dived on the foe, his shots hitting the wing plane and severely damaging the squadron commander's aircraft. The battle continued for about five minutes and then Short broke off the engagement.

In Nanking Short found that the air force had moved to Soochow. He flew there and his plane was placed under camouflage netting. On the afternoon of 22 February 1932 three Japanese bombers appeared over Soochow, flying at 2,700 feet. Short hurriedly took his plane out of hiding and rose to meet the Japanese. At first he apparently did not see three enemy fighter aircraft flying at 4,500 feet. They were Nakajima biplanes, also off the *Kaga*. Short dived on the bombers, his shots raking one of them and killing its gunner, the first Japanese to die in aerial combat. The enemy fighters closed the gap. Short came under heavy fire. His plane famed and crashed. Short was killed.

China gave the American hero the rank of colonel and a state funeral, with 4,000 people at graveside. On his tomb, in Chinese characters, was inscribed: "Greater love hath no man than this, that he lay down his life for his friends."[1]

"Arthur" Chen's first combat occurred 7 October 1937. Flying a Curtiss Hawk III he engaged an enemy bomber formation and shot down at least one. He shared credit on the 16th for another twin-engine bomber. His squadron switched to British-built Gloster *Gladiators*. Not much action for several months and then Chen shot down a Mitsubishi Type 96 on 31 May 1938. He was promoted to captain and became squadron commander. He again engaged bombers 10 June, claiming one destroyed and one damaged. Then, on 3 August he collided with a Type 96. He survived; the enemy craft didn't. He was promoted to major and became the group's vice-commandant. He shared in the probable destruction of a Type 97 on 19 October 1939. On 27 December he was badly burned in a dogfight and had to return to the U.S. for medical treatment.

"John" Wong was flying Boeing 248 monoplanes with the 17th Squadron when Japan invaded China in July 1937. Flying with squadron-mate "Buffalo" Wong, on 15 August he shot down a Mitsubishi G3M and was credited with a half-share in another Mitsubishi downing. On 22 September he shared in the destruction of two Ki-27 Nates. By June 1938 Wong was commander of the 17th Squadron, which now flew British Gloster Gladiators. On 16 June he downed one Ki-21 and shared in the downing of three more.

Shortly after war broke out between China and Japan, "Buffalo" Wong, flying a Boeing 248, shot down a Mitsubishi G3M (15 August 1937). He damaged another the following day and destroyed an A4N on the 23rd. On 19 September he was wounded combating eight Japanese E7Ks. By February 1938 17th Squadron was flying Gloster Gladiators. On 24 February in an air battle with A5M *Claude* fixed-gear fighters Wong shot down two enemy craft and shared in the destruction of a third. The next day he downed an A4N. He was transferred to the 29th Squadron as its commander. On 13 April he downed three enemy aircraft. On 16 November 1940, Wong, promoted to major, assumed command of the 5th Group. The group was flying Soviet-built I-15s. On 14 March 1941 Wong engaged in combat with Mitsubishi A6M Zeros. Severely wounded, he was shot down. He died in hospital two days later.

Impact:

These four flyers did not make much of an impact but they tried. "Firsts" are always difficult to know for certain, but Short had a strong claim to being the first American participant in the U.S. opposition to 20th Century Japanese expansionism. Like Irish-Americans in the 19th Century, these three Chinese Americans in the 20th Century continued the tradition of returning to the land of their ancestors to fight invaders.

Biographies:

Shui-Tin "Arthur" Chen (1913-unk.) was born in Portland, Oregon. He joined 15 young Chinese-Americans who began flying in the early 1930s. Upon completion of primary training, the group volunteered for service in the Cantonese air force. In December 1932 Chen, age 19, was accepted as a probationary pilot. He did flight training in Germany. He was posted to the 6th Squadron. Promoted to first lieutenant in September 1936, he was then assigned to the 28th Squadron as vice-commander. On 1 March 1945 he was discharged from the Chinese air force.

Robert McCawley Short (1904-32) was raised in Tacoma, Washington. He was an early breadwinner, helping to support his widowed mother and younger brother by employment as a messenger in a shipyard. Later he worked with a survey crew during the construction of the Cushman Dam. He took correspondence courses for self-improvement.

College was beyond financial reach. A friend suggested that Short, who was interested in aviation, enroll in the U.S. Army Air Corps Flying Cadet program. With 28 other candidates Short took written and physical exams. He was one of three selected. He was sworn in and began instruction on 1 March 1928, flying in a Consolidated PT-1 trainer. He was in the top five trainees of his class but was forced to discontinue because of family financial needs. He found jobs at southern California airports, including barnstorming, instructing, flying the mail and wealthy persons and a stint as a test pilot for the Lockheed company.

Short became involved in correspondence regarding work in China. He accepted an offer to fly an airmail route between two Chinese cities, and he travelled there. When he arrived, however, he found that the aircraft he was supposed to use were junk. He refused to fly them. Again he did other flying jobs and then was hired by the L.E. Gale Company, a firm which marketed U.S. planes in the Orient. Short traveled throughout China, as well as to Japan and The Philippines. He became a friend of Prime Minister T.V. Soong, who appointed him an adviser to the Chinese air force. Short arrangement for the purchase from the Boeing company in Seattle of a single-seat pursuit biplane with a powerful engine that gave it a speed of 200 miles per hour. The aircraft was the prototype of the P-12s which served the United States so well in World War II.

Short prophetically wrote to his mother concerning the pending conflict between China and Japan and America's future involvement: "... [Y]ou cannot realize the brutality and uselessness of it all and what the United States will have to contend with sometime in the years to come."[2]

Pan-Yang "John" Wong (unk.) was born in Seattle, Washington. He was part of the group of 15 young Chinese-Americans who volunteered for the Cantonese air force. After training and receiving his pilot's license in Portland, Oregon, he went to China in 1932. After the war he returned to the U.S.

Sun-Shui "Buffalo" Wong (1914-41) was born in Los Angeles, California, of emigrant parents. He was called "Buffalo" because of his short, stocky build. He began flight training in Los Angeles and won his wings as a teenager. He then went to China and continued his training at the Kwangtun Air Force Academy. Upon graduation he joined the 6th Squadron, later transferred to the 17th Squadron as deputy commander.

QUOTATIONS:

Martin Cole, "China's Aviation Hero," *Soldier of Fortune* pp. 22-25, 66-68 (April 1983) p. 68.

Cole, "China's Aviation Hero," p. 24.

SOURCES:

J. Ward Boyce, ed., *American Fighter Aces Album*, Mesa: Arizona: The American Air Fighters Association, 1960.

http://www.rtdouse.com/Robert_Short-American_Hero.html

http://www.republicanchina.org/Air-Battle-over-Shanghai-Suzhou-Hangzhou-1932.pdf

Odyssey of the Brown Condor

1935-36

Goal:

To assist Ethiopia in its defense against an invasion by the overwhelming forces of Italian dictator Benito Mussolini.

Background:

Italy invaded Ethiopia on 3 October 1935 without a declaration of war. Just before the invasion, studying in the United States at the time was Malaku E. Bayen, a doctor and cousin of Ethiopia's Emperor Haile Selassie. Bayen recruited Afro-Americans to fight for Ethiopia in the looming war, appealing to their loyalty to the African motherland. Bayen heard about John Charles Robinson, a Black pilot, and met with him twice; Robinson was interested, although he was considering an instructorship at the Tuskegee Institute. In April 1935 Selassie wired Robinson an official invitation to join in the defense of Ethiopia. He was offered an officer's commission on condition that Robinson remained in Ethiopia one year. Robinson agreed. He was secretly appointed "as a consultant in the development of the Royal Air Force."[1] He travelled to Ethiopia in May 1935. On the last leg of his trip Robinson met Selassie. Robinson's description of the event: "It was an unofficial visit. I was taken into his presence, bowed in and bowed out. Not a word was spoken."[2]

Robinson trained Ethiopian flyers. He met the emperor for a second time. Robinson later said, "He asked me if I liked the work I had been assigned to and I told him any work I did to help Ethiopia was to my liking."[3] Robinson became a good friend of Selassie's second son Makonnen, which helped the American in government matters. The Ethiopian "air force" consisted of nearly a dozen aged planes, including four French Potez 25 light attack aircraft, vintage World War I. Only three of the planes were fully operational. Robinson refurbished several of the aircraft, providing some with machine guns and others with bombing mechanisms. Despite a League of Nations' ban on arms trading, Robinson was able to obtain aircraft from abroad, including three Junker 52s, flown by German volunteer flyers. Robinson's pride was a biplane Beech[craft] 17L, with a top speed of 200 mph, able to outrace any Italian pursuit plane. Within a year Robinson had doubled the size of the Imperial Ethiopian Air Force. Robinson openly accepted the post of air force commander and was promoted to colonel - the only Black American to be a chief of a foreign air force. The "Brown Condor," as he became known, also served as Selassie's personal pilot.

John C. Robinson (1905-64) was a Black aviator who flew for Ethiopia's Emperor Haile Selassie against Italy's El Dulce Benito Mussolini. Robinson was the chief of the Ethiopian air force. In the financially-strapped air force he flew combat missions, was a courier, was the chief mechanic, trained new pilots and performed other duties as assigned. His humble background had prepared him to be a jack-of-all-trades.

Authors' copyright, Dan Burkhard artist

Leadership:

Italy was led by Benito Mussolini (1883-1943); Ethiopia by Emperor Haile Selassie (1892-1975). As the commander of the Ethiopian air force John Robinson was in charge of everything - aircraft acquisition, armaments, maintenance, pilot training and, once war broke out, flying combat and reconnaissance missions.

Volunteers:

American John C. Robinson was the most important volunteer on Ethiopia's side, but there were lesser known volunteers as well.

Compensation:

Robinson received pay commensurate with his rank within the Ethiopian military.

Opposition:

Measured against the leading air forces of the world, the Italian air force of 1935 was modest in quality and quantity but measured against that of Ethiopia, it was a giant.

Strategy:

Robinson had two basic tasks: to reconnoiter enemy troops and to carry orders from the capital to the front lines.

Operations:

The start of the war began dramatically for Robinson. In his words, paraphrased by a biographer:

> "When Italian planes attacked the Ethiopian towns of Adwa and Adigrat at the start of Rome's African campaign, Robinson was caught along with Ethiopian civilians and military in the wanton and bloody bombardment .... Staying there overnight, Robinson was awakened at dawn by the terrible noise of explosions .... Many people ran for cover in the city's outskirts. Others sought cover in the city's outskirts. Others sought refuge at the Red Cross hospital, imagining they would be protected there, but it too was shelled and was the scene of the heaviest casualties. Infuriated Ethiopian soldiers, anxious to engage the enemy in battle, ran out into the streets, waving their swords and challenging their adversaries to descend from the clouds and fight like men in hand-to-hand combat."[4]

Robinson and his flyers reconnoitered enemy positions. They ferried munitions and medical supplies to the front. They carried orders, messages and officials. Robinson served as the principal means of communications between the government and the front lines. He transported the emperor. On one occasion, carrying papers and flying a Potez, Robinson was attacked by Italian aircraft. Maneuvering in an effort to escape, Robinson managed to fire several rounds from his machine gun which he believed hit the foe. Out of ammunition, he headed back to base, pursued by the Italians. His barnstorming skills - flying low over hills - enabled him to escape.

In a later scrape with Italian aircraft Robinson was wounded in the left arm, but again escaped. On another occasion he was the attacker. He dived on and fired at a lone Caproni bomber, hitting it but not bringing it down. His luck held out in another way: the Italians were dropping mustard gas. Robinson survived three gassings, although his breathing was impaired for years to come.

As Italian troops advanced and bombers bombed, Robinson became increasingly disillusioned. Although he had obtained new aircraft, he lacked personnel. Most foreign volunteers left. Robinson hoped that flyer friends of his in the United States would come; they didn't. He continued training Ethiopians, ferrying Selassie, even doing mechanical work - despite his rank he was the best mechanic in the air force. Robinson also served as a journalist, sending dispatches to Black newspapers in the United States. An article - not by Robinson - in one such newspaper reported that Robinson "was in twelve actual flying battles and in one he narrowly missed shooting down the plane of Mussolini's son" (Vittorio)."[5]

IMPACT:

The war ended with the total defeat of Ethiopia. Robinson left the country and reached neighboring Djibouti 2 May 1936. A day later the emperor arrived in Djibouti. On 5 May the capital Addis Ababa fell to the Italians. *New York Times* reporter Herbert Matthews cabled: "ERA OF INDEPENDENCE THAT LASTED SINCE BIBLICAL TIMES ENDED FOUR THIS AFTERNOON WHEN ITALIANS OCCUPIED ADDIS ABABA."[6]

Robinson sailed for France and from there returned to the United States. En route possibly as many as six attempts were made to assassinate him, all unsuccessful.

BIOGRAPHIES:

John C. Robinson (1905-64) love of flying was sparked when, as a five-year-old in his town of Gulfport, Mississippi, he saw a plane landing in that town for the first time (December 1910). It was flown by legendary John Moisant, former soldier of fortune in Central America and now co-owner of an aerial exhibit company. As he grew up Robinson kept his eye on aviation, but as a Black man doors were closed to him.

Robinson learned mechanics and at the age of 14 - tall for his age - he became a truck driver. In 1920 he enrolled at the Tuskegee Normal and Industrial Institute in Alabama, a school noted for its technical programs. Robinson did well, excelling in mechanical science. He graduated in 1923 and then moved to Detroit, the nation's automobile capital, where he found work as a mechanic in a car garage. One autumn day in 1926 he wangled a flight in a Waco Nine at a local airport - his first time in the air.

Robinson's next step was to move to Chicago, where Blacks had a say in the city. Robinson married and opened a garage. He applied to the Curtiss-Wright Aeronautical School and was accepted. But when he arrived he was rejected because of his race. Nevertheless, determined to get his foot in the door, Robinson took a job as a janitor. At Curtiss his adroit use of charm and mechanical skill enabled him eventually to become a student (in 1929). Two years later he graduated as a master mechanic of aviation. Subsequently, he took another big step: by recruiting 20 potential Black students, he convinced the bosses to open a course in avionics for Black students. Robinson was, naturally, named the instructor for the course. He began taking flying lessons at Acres Airport. On 1 Jan 1930 he soloed and earned his pilot's license.

Robinson was determined to bring aviation to Blacks. He lectured, led discussions, formed flying clubs, opened an airfield and a flying school for Blacks, founded a Black Air Pilots Association.

Upon his return to the United States after the war in Ethiopia, Robinson was greeted as a hero, including press interviews on board the ship as he arrived. In Chicago he led an auto procession and then addressed a cheering crowd of over 8,000 people. In Washington, D.C., he made a speech before a large audience at a Baptist church. Robinson, however, was in need of rest and care. He had a broken collar bone. He suffered the effects of being gassed.

On 18 May 1936 the *New York Times* reported that Robinson had accepted the post of director at an aviation school to be established at the Tuskegee Institute. The problem was that Tuskegee possessed no aircraft, no landing field, no aviation facilities of any kind. Robinson was unable to reach satisfactory terms with Tuskegee. Instead, he set up his own aviation school, using funds that had been donated and money raised through barnstorming and speaking engagements. The John C. Robinson National Air College and School of Automotive Engineering officially opened in Chicago 28 September 1936. With Black and White students and well-qualified instructors, the school flourished.

Robinson and other advocates campaigned to have Black flyers join the U.S. Army Air Corps. Specifically, they wanted, as a first step, Blacks admitted into the Civilian Pilot Training program. Their efforts were successful; the program opened for Blacks in 1939. Robinson had on and off relations with Tuskegee. Although he was an inspiration, nothing jelled. Eventually Tuskegee did establish an aeronautical training program, and this produced the U.S. Army Air Corps' legendary Tuskege Airmen group of World War II. Robinson would liked to have flown with them. He hoped for a colonelcy but was offered the rank of second lieutenant, which he refused.

With the United States' entry into World War II Robinson became a civilian aviation instructor at Keesler Field in Mississippi and later at Chanute Field near Chicago. At War Department request he visited other military airfields and gave briefings on aerial warfare. In 1944 in Africa the British defeated the Italians in Ethiopia, capturing Addis Ababa in April. Robinson wanted to return to Ethiopia, and through the U.S. Lend-Lease Program was able to do so. He put together a group of aircraft technicians - becoming known as "The Brood" - and took them to Ethiopia, arriving at Addis Ababa 19 April 1944. Selassie wanted Robinson to rebuild the air force. Starting with two Cessna, Robinson began acquiring aircraft. He also established a school to train pilots. In addition, in 1947 Robinson set up the country's first airline, Sultan Airways, Ltd. Robinson became commander of the air force, again with the rank of colonel.

Robinson was living well in Addis Ababa but then his luck ran out. Sweden was one of the main providers of economic and military air to post-war Ethiopia. An influential Swede, Count Carl Gustaf von Rosen, had flown an ambulance plane during the war with Italy. Robinson and von Rosen came to a parting of the ways - racism the cause. There was an altercation. Robinson broke the Swede's jaw. Robinson was jailed. He was released by the country's Supreme Court in September 1947. Robinson resigned his air force position.

Robinson engaged in civilian flying activities in Ethiopia. On 13 March 1954 Robinson, with a co-pilot, he set out, with a co-pilot, in a training plane on a mercy mission to bring blood to an injured boy. The plane crashed; the co-pilot was killed and Robinson was badly burned. He was rushed to Addis Ababa's main hospital. For weeks Robinson struggled to live. He was visited by Emperor Selassie. Robinson died on 27 March 1954. He was given a military funeral. Hardly two months later, Selassie, on a visit to Chicago, made it a point to go to the little South Park Baptist Church, where Robinson had worshipped as a young man. The emperor thanked the congregation for "their beloved son."[7]

Quotations:

[1] Philip Thomas Tucker, *Father of the Tuskegee Airmen - John C. Robinson*. Washington, D.C.: Potomac Books, 2012. p. 71.
[2] Tucker, *Father of the Tuskegee Airmen*, p. 92.
[3] Tucker, *Father of the Tuskegee Airmen*, p. 97.
[4] http://ethiopundit.blogspot.com/2004/09/condors-and-eagles-from-harlem.html
[5] Tucker, *Father of the Tuskegee Airmen*, p. 179.
[6] Tucker, *Father of the Tuskegee Airmen*, p. 185.
[7] Tucker, *Father of the Tuskegee Airmen*, p. 258

Sources:

R. Ernest Dupuy and Trevor N. Dupuy. *The Harper Encyclopedia of Military History*. 4th edition. New York: HarperCollins Publishers, 1993.

ODYSSEY OF "THE FLYING BARBER,"

1933-36

GOAL:
To fly for pay and adventure - and for Italy's despotic ruler, Benito Mussolini (1883-1945)

BACKGROUND:
Dictator Benito Amicare Andrea Mussolini ruled Italy 1922-43. Prior to Italy's entry into World War II on 10 June 1940, Mussolini's boundless ambitions led to his endeavor to create a new Roman Empire. After having conquered Libya his next objective became the conquest of Ethiopia.

LEADERSHIP:
Mussolini's self-imposed title - *Il Duce* (the Leader) - left little doubt as to who was calling the shots

VOLUNTEERS:
In all probability Maresciallo Vincenzo Joseph Patriarca was the only American to volunteer for combat in Italy's war of conquest against Ethiopia.

COMPENSATION:
Patriarca's initial compensation was flying lessons in Italy which lured him back to the

mother country. When flying in Ethiopia he probably was paid the regular salary of an Italian airman. When he was recruited to fly in Spain, he received the equivalent of $200 per month.

Opposition:

Ethiopia had neither planes nor anti-aircraft guns. The greatest hazards to Patriarca and the other Italian flyers were the harsh environment, poor living conditions and the unreliability of their aircraft. Hazards in Spain were another matter. Here the Italian flyers were up against the Republican air force, which included highly motivated foreign soldiers of fortune. The Republican pilots were flying aircraft which at the least were the equal of the Italian planes.

Strategy:

Mussolini wanted militarily conquer Ethiopia and convert it into a colony. Air power was a particularly useful tool since Ethiopia was a very large country and possessed no way to counter its employment. In Spain, Mussolini wanted to help transform that nation into a Fascist state.

Operations:

Italy attacked Ethiopia in October 1935 in a war of conquest. That month Patriarca volunteered to serve in Mussolini's air force in Ethiopia. He was based in Massawa in the Italian colony of Eritrea on the Red Sea. He endured intense heat and suffered from stomach ulcers. The Italian air force gained international notoriety, subjecting poorly armed Ethiopian soldiers to bombing, often with canisters of poison gas. Patriarca did well and was promoted to sergeant.

The war ended; Ethiopia had been conquered. Patriarca considered returning to the United States. Perhaps he hoped that having combat experience, the U.S. Army Air Force would now accept him as a pilot. Meanwhile, in Spain civil war erupted in July 1936. The Nationalist rebels were led by General (later Generalissimo) Francisco Franco (1892-1975). Supporting Franco with troops, weapons, airplanes and airmen, were Mussolini and Germany's despot, Adolf Hitler. (France and Britain supported the Spanish Republican government.) While in Rome, Patriarca was again recruited by the Italian air force, this time to fly in Spain.

Based in Cáceres, Spain, in September 1936 he was now a sergeant using the name Vincenzo Bocalari. He flew planes in convoy with German Junker 52s taking Spanish soldiers and Moorish mercenaries to the Spanish mainland. On the 13th Patriarca and two mates were flying

Fiat CR.32s near the town of Talavera de la Reina. They intercepted and engaged a formation of Republican Breuget XIXs escorted by Nieuport Delage Ni.52s and Dewoitine D.371s. One Ni.52 was quickly shot down. Patriarca tangled with another Nieuport and clipped one of its wings. Both aircraft crashed. The other pilot was killed. Patriarca parachuted into Republican territory and was captured.

Patriarca feared that he would be tried and executed. American correspondents who saw him reported he was "despondent and weeping."[1] The U.S. Government was notified and diplomatic efforts began in an effort to get him released. Cited by the Soviet Union as proof of Italy's intervention in Spain, Patriarca became the center of an international fuss. Pressure in his favor built up. His father told the U.S. State Department: "My son didn't know better! His only interest is aviation! He didn't mean to kill!"[2] The Republican government agreed to exchange Patriarca for a Yugoslavian pilot captured by the Nationalists. Patriarca was soon on a vessel sailing across the Atlantic to the United States, arriving a week before Christmas 1936.

Impact:

Patriarca was a very minor figure in the combat events in which he participated. He had no impact whatsoever.

Biographies:

Maresciallo Vincenzo Joseph Patriarca (1913-93), whose Americanized name was Vincent Joseph Patriarca, was born 12 January 1913 in New York to Italian parents. (Later he would us the *nom de guerre* Vincenza Bocalare.) He wanted to fly, and his parents scraped together funds for him to take lessons at an aerodrome. The U.S. Government, however, raised the number of flying hours required to earn a license. The Patriarcas could not afford the additional costs. Vincent considered enlisting in the U.S. Army Air Force but figured that not having a college education, he would have "no chance of getting off the ground" and he did not want "to pull the chocks from the wheels only to watch someone else zoom off."[3]

In luck, Patriarca came across a notice in an aviation magazine inviting the sons of Italians living abroad to come to Rome for free training at an air school. The offer was part of an effort by Benito Mussolini to bring back families that had emigrated. The next morning Patriarca was outside the Italian consulate in New York when its doors opened. Arrangements were made and Patriarca was off to Italy. He was the first American to enter the air ministry's aviation school (November 1933). Because he was interested in aerobatics, he later transferred to an air school near Trieste associated with famer flyer Gabriele d'Annunzio. The school was known for its daredevil pilots.

Returning to the United States in 1936 following his exploits in Ethiopia and Spain, Patriarca did not remain. He declared that he had "not yet had enough adventure" and "barbering was no longer in his character."[4] In 1937 he returned to Italy and rejoined the *Regia Aeronautica*, the air force. During World War II, flying CR.42s, he served on the French, Albanian and Russian fronts. He engaged in aerial dogfights and ended the war with three biplane victories. He continued to serve in the air force after the war, flying P-51s and Vampires during the 1950s. He joined an acrobatic team that performed at air shows. Eventually, his flying days over, Patriarca went to work for the U.S. military in Naples.

Quotations:

[1] Judith Keene, "Franco's English Speaking Volunteers," Judith Keene and Gabriel Jackson, *Fighting for Franco: International Volunteers in Nationalist Spain during the Spanish Civil War*. London: Hambledon Continuum, 2001. pp. 97-99.

[2] Jay Maeder, "War Birds The Flying Barber, December 1936." *New York Daily News*. Electronic News Article. 21 May 2012. http://articles.nydailynews.com

[3] Keene, "Franco's English Speaking Volunteers," pp. 97-99.

[4] Keene, "Franco's English Speaking Volunteers," pp. 97-99

Sources:

"Biplane Fighter Aces - Italy." http://surfcity.kund.dalnet.se/italy patriarca.htm

Abraham Lincoln Battalion in the Spanish Civil War

1936-38

Goal:

To provide effective military support to the forces of the Republican government in its war with Nationalist rebels.

Background:

"... [I]n the town, where all the streets were full of Sunday crowds, the shells came with the sudden flash that a short circuit makes and then the roaring crash of granite-dust. During the morning, twenty-two shells came into Madrid.

They killed an old woman returning home from market, dropping her in a huddled black heap of clothing ....

They killed three people in another square, who lay like so many torn bundles of old clothes in the dust and rubble ...."[1]

Having ruled a united Spain for almost 450 years, the monarchy was deposed in April 1931. Years of political turbulence followed. Then, in July 1936 there was a clash in Spanish-held Morocco between troops of the Spanish Foreign Legion and a Communist-led mob. On 18 July garrisons in 12 mainland cities and five in Morocco rebelled. General Francisco Franco, former chief of staff who had been exiled to command of the Canary Islands by the then-Socialist government, flew to Morocco to take leadership of the rebel forces.

War had begun. It was to be an omen and small model of the forthcoming conflagration that would envelope much of the world. The conflicting ideologies were clear: the leftist Popular Front government (Republicans) against the rebel rightwing Fascists (Nationalists). The Communist Soviet Union supported the Republicans, providing tanks, artillery, planes and pilots. France sent planes and pilots. Fascist Italy and Nazi Germany backed the Nationalists, providing tanks, troops, pilots, and planes.

LEADERSHIP:

Trainer and first commander of the Abraham Lincoln Battalion was Robert Hale Merriam. The battalion would eventually have 12 commanders. The American battalions and those composed of other foreigners were grouped in the XV International Brigade, supervised by the Russians. Each battalion had a political commissar.

VOLUNTEERS:

Young men in various countries volunteered to fight for the Republicans. These included Americans, acting out of idealism or fleeing the Great Depression. Some were Communists; others had been recruited by Communists. A majority of the American volunteers, however, were not Communists. The first Yanks to arrive, late in 1936, were a group of 96 men who had crossed the Atlantic using false names. The passports of later American volunteers were stamped: "Not valid for travel in Spain." Most of these volunteers traveled to France and walked over the Pyrenees Mountains to Spain.

Many of the Americans had no military experience. Robert Steck recalled: "To show you how inexperienced we were, [when attacked by enemy planes] we dived under the trucks for cover, which were the very targets."[2] The Americans were given five weeks of training and the Abraham Lincoln Battalion (also known as the Abraham Lincoln Brigade) was created. Later it was joined by the George Washington Battalion. Fighting alongside the Americans were Irish volunteers who refused to be part of the English Battalion. The ranks of each American battalion eventually reached some 500 men. There was also a U.S.-Canadian Mackenie-Papineau (Mac-Pap) Battalion. Over 40,000 foreigners, including Americans, eventually fought for the Republicans.

American volunteers also served with the *Regimiento de Tren* (railway) and the John Brown Anti-Aircraft Battery. They staffed a well-equipped field hospital (funded by the American Medical Bureau to Save Spanish Democracy). Americans also flew military aircraft. (*see* American Flyers of the Republicans in the Spanish Civil War, 1936-38)

Alvah Bessie (1904-85), a member of the American Communist Party, fought against the fascist-supported Spanish Nationalist government as a member of the Abraham Lincoln Battalion in 1937-38. Bessie became a Hollywood screenwriter and was constantly hounded by the Federal Bureau of Investigation because of his affiliation with the Communist Party.

Courtesy wikimedia.org

Herman Bottcher (1905-44), born in Germany, fought in the Abraham Lincoln Battalion. J. Edgar Hoover was highly suspicious of everyone who served in the battalion, believing them all to be Communists or their sympathizers. Joining the U.S. Army during World War II, Bottcher earned two Distinguished Service Crosses before his long-denied U.S. citizenship was given to him. He was killed in the Leyte, Philippines, campaign.

Courtesy wikimedia.org

Compensation:

The Battalion volunteers probably received small sustenance sums.

Opposition:

The Nationalist army possessed many experienced soldiers. The 15,000-man Spanish Foreign Legion was well seasoned from years of fighting in Morocco. Many of the Italian troops had just come from fighting in Ethiopia, and many of the Germans were the nucleus of the new German air force and army.

Strategy:

On the ground, numbers mattered and the infantry remained the heart of the army. Tanks were introduced in larger numbers than in World War I, but they remained infantry-support weapons. The foreign volunteers, highly motivated, bore the brunt of the fighting for the Republicans.

Operations:

After being trained, on 16 February 1937 the Abraham Lincoln Battalion was taken to the trenches at Jarama. It helped repel a Nationalist assault and then went on the offensive. The battalion staged two attacks, suffering the death of 127 men and the wounding of about 193, including the commander, Merriman.

As the new recruits arrived, two new battalions were created: George Washington and (Mac-Pap) Battalions. There were occasions in the battles ahead when casualties were so heavy that the George Washington Battalion was temporarily absorbed into the Abraham Lincoln. The XV Brigade participated in the battles of Brunete, Zaragoza, Belchite and Ebro River. It also fought to keep open the supply road between Valencia and Madrid.

One of the most contested battlegrounds was the city of Teruel in eastern Spain, a strategic key to the capital, Madrid. Occupied early by the Nationalists, the city became the objective of a Republican offensive launched 15 December 1937. By 25 December the attack was largely successful. The fighting took place in snowy conditions, sometimes approaching blizzards. On 31 December the XV Brigade was moved to the front to help defend the city against a Nationalist counter-offensive. The brigade was subjected to intense artillery and ground attacks. On 15 February 1938 it spearheaded an assault on Nationalist communications lines. In March the Nationalists launched a 160,000-man offensive. The XV Brigade attempted to block the massive attack but was routed. Teruel fell. The Brigade was devastated; when it was eventually reconstituted it had less than 200 men.

Replenished with men from hospitals or who had been on leave or were newly recruited, the Brigade fought on - and continued to suffer heavy casualties. At one point its total ranks were 40 Yanks and 35 Spaniards. In September 1938 the Republicans pulled all foreign troops from the front lines in hopes that Franco would do likewise. He didn't. The Abraham Lincoln Battalion, which had been merged with the George Washington Battalion, was demobilized 21 September 1938.

IMPACT:

Two thousand eight hundred Americans fought for the Republicans in the Spanish Civil War. Of these approximately 1,000 were killed and 1,000 wounded. Americans played a significant role in the conflict. Their military units participated in most of the battles. The assistance rendered by these dedicated foreign soldiers was a morale booster for the Republicans.

In the United States the Abraham Lincoln Battalion was controversial. Some people believed it to be Communist as did the Director of the FBI J. Edgar Hoover. But prominent Americans gave it their support including Paul Robeson, Dashiell Hammett, Lillian Hellman, Helen Keller, Woody Guthrie, Dorothy Parker and Ernest Hemingway.

Edward Carter, Jr., was a member of the Abraham Lincoln Battalion during the Spanish Civil War. A Black man, he was recommended for the U.S. Medal of Honor during World War II. The medal was not conferred until the 1990s and then posthumously. Carter also had a short stint in the Chinese national army in the early 1930s.

Courtesy wikimedia.org

BIOGRAPHIES:

Alvah Bessie (1904-85) was born in New York City into a well-to-do family. He graduated from Columbia University in 1924. Bessie worked as a writer, married in 1930, and had two children. In 1936 he joined the Communist Party and worked for the Brooklyn *Daily Eagle*. His political views clashed with those of the editor of the newspaper and Bessie resigned in 1937. Next he worked for the Spanish Information Bureau, an instrument of the Spanish Republican government. His marriage foundered. In early 1938 he traveled to Spain with the objective of becoming a fighter pilot but was assigned to the Abraham Lincoln Brigade. He participated in the Ebro offensive between July and September. Additionally, Bessie worked as a correspondent for the International Brigade's publication *The Volunteer for Liberty*.

Following the Spanish Civil War Bessie returned to the United States, wrote for a Communist journal and eventually became a Hollywood screenwriter. In 1945 he was fired by Warner Brothers due to his support of striking studio workers. In 1947 Bessie was one of ten screenwriters who refused to answer questions from the House of Representatives' Un-American Affairs Committee and were accused of being Communists. The "Hollywood Ten" were found guilty of contempt and each served one year in prison. The ten were blacklisted by Hollywood film makers.

Hermann Friedrich Bottcher (1905-44) was born in Germany. Orphaned at an early age, he emigrated first to Australia and then to San Francisco where he lived with his aunt. Bottcher served in the Spanish Republican Army, was wounded several times and earned the rank of major. Following the attack of Pearl Harbor he joined the U.S. Army even though he was still a German citizen. He had lost the possibility of becoming a U.S. citizen due to his service in the Abraham Lincoln Brigade. Assigned to the 32nd Infantry Division, Bottcher earned two Distinguished Service Crosses and was promoted from staff sergeant to captain. He was awarded U.S. citizenship in December 1943 while serving in New Guinea. Reassigned to the 126th Infantry Division, Bottcher was killed toward the end of the Leyte campaign.

Edward Allen Carter, Jr. (1916-63) was born in Los Angeles, California. A Black, he was the son of missionary parents who relocated to Shanghai, China. Carter ran away from home, joined the Chinese army and rose to the rank of lieutenant. When it was discovered that he was 15 years old, he was dismissed. Carter attended a military school in Shanghai and could converse in four languages - English, German, Hindi and Mandarin. Soon, Carter found his way to Spain and served in the Abraham Lincoln Brigade. Following the defeat of the Republicans, Carter returned to the United States. He married in Los Angeles in 1940. Carter enlisted in the U.S. Army on 6 September 1941. He quickly rose to staff sergeant but was put under surveillance because he had been a member of the Abraham Lincoln Brigade. In 1944 Carter was sent to Europe. Due to the shortage of combat troops, the U.S. Army called for volunteers from all races for the Ground Force Replacement Command. Carter was demoted to a private to prevent a Black from commanding White troops. On 23 March 1945 Carter was recommended for the Medal of Honor for single-handedly destroying two enemy machine gun nests and a mortar crew but instead was awarded the Distinguished Service Cross due to his race. Recovering from serious wounds, he was restored to his grade of staff sergeant. In 1949 Carter attempted to re-enlisted but this was denied without explanation. He died of cancer in 1963. In the 1990s the U.S. Army commissioned a study to identify unrecognized African-American heroes of World War II. Carter was among those identified and was posthumously awarded the Medal of Honor.

Maury Colow (1917-93) was born in from Brooklyn, New York, and was Jewish. A member of the Abraham Lincoln Brigade, he fought on the Cordoba front. Following the Spanish Civil War, Colow, an artist, helped create the anti-Vietnam War movement among Spanish Civil War veterans.

Carmelo Delgado Delgado (1913-37) was raised in Guayama, Puerto Rico. He attended the University of Puerto Rico where he became friends with nationalist Juan Antonio Corretjer. Delgado became a member of the nationalist "Cadets of the Republic." Graduating, he moved to Spain and studied law at the Central University of Madrid. Once the Spanish Civil War broke out, he joined the Abraham Lincoln Battalion. In early 1937 Delgado was captured in the Battle of Madrid. Being a Puerto Rican nationalist, Delgado refused the help of the U.S. embassy and was executed by firing squad on 29 April 1937. He is believed to have been the first U.S. citizen to die in the Spanish Civil War.

David Doran (unk.) was killed at Gandesa on the Aragón front.

Leo Eloesser (1881-1976) graduated from the University of California at Berkeley in 1900 and earned a medical degree from the University of Heidelberg in 1907. Next, he voluntarily served at medical clinics throughout Europe. He became a noted thoracic surgeon and joined the Stanford Medical School in 1912. During the early years of World War I, Eloesser worked in Germany as a surgeon. Prior to the United States' entry into the war, he returned to the United States and became a major in the U.S. Army. Eloesser was chief of Amputation and Orthopedic Services at Letterman Hospital in San Francisco. He also worked with the poor and indigent. In 1916 Eloesser attended to Tom Mooney, who was tried and imprisoned for a 1916 bombing. This gave Eloesser celebrity status within the American left. Eloesser, at the age of 56, volunteered as a medic for the Republicans in the Spanish Civil War. Following World War II he led a medical team to China for the United Nations.

John Gates [a.k.a. Solomon Regenstriet] (1913-92), the son of Polish Jews, was born in Manhattan, New York, and joined the Young Communist League at the age of 17 years. He traveled to Ohio and unsuccessfully attempted to organize jobless youths. At the age of 24 Gates traveled to Spain and became the political commissar for the Abraham Lincoln Brigade. During World War II he served in the U.S.

Army. Initially, his service was confined to the United States due to his Communist affiliation. After the war Gates became the editor of the Communist newspaper *The Daily Worker* and one of seven national secretaries. On 28 July 1948 twelve members of the American Communist Party, including Gates, were convicted of advocating the overthrow of the American government and Gates was imprisoned from 1949 until 1955. Gates broke with the party in 1958 after a failed attempt to separate the American party from the control of Moscow. Toward the end of his life Gates served as a researcher for the International Ladies Garment Workers Union. He helped with issues related to workers' compensation, unemployment benefits and Social Security claims.

William Herrick (1915-2004), the son of Jews from Belarus, was raised in Trenton, New Jersey. His father died young; his mother was a charter member of the American Communist Party. Herrick and his mother moved to New York City. He then joined a utopian colony in Michigan. As a Communist, Herrick was involved in attacks on Trotskyites. Next he helped organize Black sharecroppers in Georgia. He served in the Abraham Lincoln Battalion during the Spanish Civil War and was seriously wounded. Returning to the United States he published the first of ten novels in 1967. He also wrote his memoirs.

Robert Hale Merriman (1908-38) attended the University of Nevada where he studied economics, played football (he was six feet two inches tall) and was a member of the Reserve Officer Training Corps (ROTC). He won a scholarship to study economics in Europe. When the Spanish Civil War broke out be volunteered to fight. Because of his military training, Merriman was chosen to lead the American volunteers. He was killed at Gandesa on the Aragón front.

Conlon Nancarrow (1912-97) was born in Texarkana, Arkansas. A free spirit, he was sent to military school to acquire discipline. Although Nancarrow's father encouraged engineering as a vocation, Nancarrow preferred music. Like a number of American artists, he became an adherent of the Communist Party. He traveled to Spain and fought as a member of the Abraham Lincoln Battalion. Wounded in the neck, he managed to escape ahead of the collapse of the Republican government. In 1940 he moved to Mexico City to avoid being harassed by the American government. He briefly returned to New York City in 1947 and then went back to Mexico City. Nancarrow became a highly successful musical composer.

Robert Steck (1914-unk.) attended the University of Iowa. In 1936 he worked with the Workers Laboratory Theater in New York. This was a group of socialists who used the arts to convey their interpretation of labor conditions. Steck crossed the Atlantic Ocean in February 1937 to France and walked to Spain and volunteered to fight in the civil war. While in the republican transportation corps Steck served as a political commissar, lecturing on the reasons for fighting. He later was a scout until captured. Steck was held until 16 March 1939. He served in the U.S. Army during World War II.

Robert George Thompson (1915-65) was born on Grant Pass, Oregon. He was a republican battalion commander during the Spanish Civil War. Thompson served in the U.S. Army during World War II and was awarded the Distinguished Service Cross for extraordinary heroism during the Guinea Campaign. On 28 July 1948 he was one of 12 members of the American Communist Party convicted of advocating the overthrow of the American government. Due to his World War II service, he was sentenced to three years in prison whereas his co-conspirators were sentenced to five years each. After Thompson was released he continued to work for the Communist Party and organized anti-Vietnam War protests. The U.S. Court of Appeals, District of Columbia Circuit, overrode a U.S. Army decision (under pressure from the U.S. Congress) and permitted Thompson to be buried at Arlington National Cemetery.

Paul White (unk.-1937), a member of the Abraham Lincoln Battalion, deserted to the French border. He changed his mind and voluntarily returned to the battalion. Despite this, he was charged with desertion and executed.

Milton Wolff (unk.) became commander of the Abraham Lincoln Battalion following the death of Robert Merriman at Gandesa.

QUOTATIONS:

[1] Ernest Hemingway, *By-Line: Earnest Hemingway*. New York: Charles Scribner's Sons, 1969, p. 259.

[2] Bryon Wells, "American Volunteers in the Spanish Civil War." *Military History*. pp. 50-57 (Apr 2001) p. 52.

SOURCES:

R. Ernest Dupuy and Trevor N. Dupuy. The Harper Encyclopedia of Military History. 4th edition. New York: HarperCollins Publishers, 1993.

Arthur H. Landis, *The Abraham Lincoln Brigade*. New York: The Citadel Press, 1967.

Jay Mallin and Robert K. Brown, *Merc: American Soldiers of Fortune*. New York: Macmillan Publishing Company, 1979.

James Neugass, "For Whom the Ambulance Rolls," *Military History* pp. 64-69 (February/March 2009).

Hugh Thomas, *The Spanish Civil War*. New York: Harper & Brothers, Publishers, 1961

J. Burns (1995). William Herrick and the Spanish Civil War. Retrieved from Penniless Press: http://www.penniesspress.co.uk/prose/william_herrick_and_the_spanish.htm

Ircam-Centre Pompidou. (2010) Conlon Narcarrow. Retrieved from Resources.ircam: http://brahms.ircam.fr/composers/composer/2365/

Stephen T. Martin, Hermann Johann Friedrich Bottcher. 2009. 7 August 2013. http://hermannbottcher.org/index.html

Ernest McPherson. Staff Sergeant Edward A. Carter Medal of Honor Recipient. 4 December 1998. 7 August 2013. http://www.militarymuseum.org/Carter.html

Manus O'Riordan. "Ireland and the Spanish Civil War." 18 November 2001. *Irish and Jewish Volunteers in the Spanish Anti-Fascist War*. 7 August 2013. http://irelandscw.com/ibvol-MoR1.htm

Richard F. Shepard, "Alvah Bessie is Dead at 81; Member of the Hollywood 10." 24 July 1985. The New York Times. Electronic Obituary. 7 August 1913. http://www.nytimes.com/1985/07/24/movies/alvah-bessie-is-dead-at-81-member-of-the-hollywood-10.html

J. Simkin (1997, September). John Gates. Retrieved from Soartacus Educational: http://www.spartacus.schoolnet.co.uk/SPgates.htm#source

Stanford University Medical Center (2000), August 8). Biographical Note. Retrieved from Register of the Leo D. Eloesser Papers: http://elane.stanford.edu/aid/20_Eloesser/index.htm#BN

Wikipedia, The Free Encyclopedia: http://en.wikipedia.org/wiki/Carmelo Delgado_Delgado

Wikipedia, The Free Encyclopedia: http://en.wikipedia.org/wiki/Robert_G._Thompson

American Flyers for the Republicans in the Spanish Civil War

1936-38

Goal:

In the face of an uprising by the "Nationalists," the Spanish Republican government appealed worldwide for pilots and planes to offset the influx of Italian and German pilots and planes that were assisting the insurrectionists.

Background:

The involvement of foreign air power in Spain began with General Francisco Franco's appeal to Adolf Hitler to transport by air his Nationalist army, which was isolated in Spanish Morocco, to the Spanish mainland. Beginning in July 1936 Junker trimotor transports moved 13,523 soldiers and 593,914 tons of material from Tetuín, Morocco, to Seville, Spain. Within a few months the Germans established the Condor Legion, a combat air force of 6,000 men with numerous aircraft. Franco also appealed to Italy's Benito Mussolini. He sent bombers and fighters as well.

Not to be out done, the Russians responded to the appeal from the Republicans. The first Red Air Force technicians arrived in southeastern Spain on 10 September 1936. By the end of the month 200 Soviet pilots and 1,500 technicians were in Spain along with their aircraft. The famous French novelist André Malraux organized an international squadron of French pilots and planes, but Great Britain and the United States pressured France not to get involved. Nevertheless, Malraux's *Escuadrilla España* went into action.

Lest important among those who travelled to Spain to fight in the air were the few true volunteers from America, Great Britain, France, and here and there. They came on their own without any support or approval from their governments.

LEADERSHIP:

The American Patrol was a component of a U.S.-Russian squadron commanded by a Spanish officer, Captain (later Colonel) Andrés García la Calle. La Calle had distinguished himself as a fighter pilot and had worked up from sergeant. Eventually an American, Frank Glasgow Tinker, Jr., was named commander - but only when the unit was in the air.

VOLUNTEERS:

The Americans who flew in Spain for the Republicans were not organized as a unit, with the exception of one small group, the American Patrol. The other American volunteers were dispersed within the Republican air force as mechanics, bombardiers, transport flyers and pursuit pilots.

COMPENSATION:

Who you were, what you could do, who recruited you - these factors resulted in a wide range in the pay the volunteers received. Early volunteers hired in the United States were paid $100 per week plus 300 *pesetas* monthly ($20). Harold "Whitey" Dahl, recruited in Mexico, received $1,500 monthly plus $1,000 for every enemy plane shot down.

OPPOSITION:

Germany and Italy were using Spain as a training ground for their pilots and a testing ground for their aircraft. One day your plane could be superior to that of the enemy and the next inferior as the opposition introduced a new model. Americans flew mainly Russian aircraft. The principal Soviet fighters were the Polikarpov I.15 biplane known as the Chato (the "snubnose") and the I.16 monoplane call the Mosca (the "fly"). These aircraft were very competitive in early 1937 but became less so as new models were introduced, particularly by Germany.

Frank Glasgow Tinker, Jr. (1909-39) was born in Louisiana and graduated from the U.S. Naval Academy in 1934. Frequently drunk, he was involved in brawls. Tinker resigned from the U.S. Navy and was recruited by the Spanish ambassador to Mexico to fly for the Spanish Republican government. Tinker shot down eight Nationalist aircraft during the Spanish Civil War, making him an ace. He died in Little Rock, Arkansas, apparently a suicide.

Courtesy wikimedia.org

STRATEGY:

Since most American pilots possessed little combat experience, their best strategy was to follow the orders of the more experienced European flyers. When the Patrol suffered a defeat, La Calle summoned the flyers, plied them with beer and told them bluntly, "The pilots disregarded the instructions and warnings which had been given to them."[1]

OPERATIONS:

The first Americans arrived in September 1936. They were found insufficiently trained to be suitable to serve as pursuit pilots, so the Republicans assigned them to other tasks. One of the volunteers later recalled: "Some of ... the Americans ... turned pretty bad .... One of them beat it with 7,000 *pesetas* he had taken from his outfit and some Spanish friends. Another turned yellow."[2] Three of the original volunteers eventually were able to become fighter pilots. The largest number of Americans arrived in December: ten men, with one more coming early in January 1937. In all, at least 21 Yanks served in the Republican air force, possibly more.

Four of the Americans were placed in a squadron of Russian-built Chato pursuit biplanes commanded by Captain La Calle. The squadron was based near Guadalajara and the Yanks were teamed with a Soviet group in *La Escuadrilla de Chatos*. The American unit became known as *La Patrulla Americana*. Its first mission was to bomb enemy gunpowder factories on the Jarama River. The Patrol scored its first victory when a flyer forced a German Heinkel fighter down to tree level and it crashed.

The Patrol's greatest action came on 18 February when it and its Russian team-mates tangled with 24 Heinkels. The odds were about three-to-one favoring the enemy. The Patrol went into a circular defensive formation taught by La Calle, but several flyers broke formation and were hit by the Heinkels. The Russians came to the rescue. When it was over, seven enemy aircraft were down, but so were three of the Patrol's planes. One American was killed, one was wounded but crash-landed, one parachuted and only one (Frank Tinker) made it back to his base.

One of the Republican air force's greatest successes occurred in March when a Nationalist motorized column, mostly Italian, was passing through the Guadarrama Mountains toward Guadalajara without air cover. Some 100 Russian planes attacked. The action was described by American Eugene Finick, a bomber pilot. "We tore that rolling, mechanized offensive to ribbons.... In two minutes' time the tanks and the road were a shambles. The tanks were blown up, overturned, piled up in knots."[3]

On 12 July Tinker was flying with Soviet wingmen when they spotted a Chato being attacked by three German fighters. Tinker and the Russians swooped to the rescue but were not able to save the Chato. Tinker shot down one enemy craft; the Soviet pilots downed a second.

It is believed no foreign flyers were hired after January 1937. Within months the first class of Spaniards trained in the Soviet Union would be coming home.

Impact:

Russian aid to the Republicans could not keep pace with the men and materiel being supplied by the Germans and Italians to the Nationalists. The Republican cause was doomed. The American volunteers were small in number. Their impact on the fighting was nil.

Biographies:

Bertram Blanchard "Bert" Acosta (1895-1954) was born in San Diego, California. Although an accomplished aviator, he was frequently in and out of trouble and survived a number of crashes. Acosta was arrested more than once for drunkenness. During his youth he constructed and flew both a glider and an airplane. At the age of 16 Acosta he studied engineering at the Throop Polytechnic Institute (later California Institute of Technology). He worked as a grease monkey and a flight instructor at Glenn Curtiss' flying camp near San Diego. During World War I Acosta trained Canadian cadets for Curtiss near Toronto. Acosta raced automobiles and did barnstorming. He set aviation records for both speed and endurance.

In 1928 Rodman Wanamaker assembled an elite team to fly the Atlantic and demonstrate the feasibility of transatlantic passenger service. In addition to Acosta as pilot the team included polar explorer Richard Byrd as commander as well as other notables. Delayed, Charles Lindbergh flew across first. A month later Acosta piloted the Fokker trimotor *America* which was forced to ditch off the Normandy coast. Regardless the crew was given a hero's welcome by the French.

Returning to the United States Acosta lost his pilot's license due to some wild flying stunts. He was jailed for nonsupport of his second wife and children and frequently was drunk. His daughters from his first marriage temporarily rehabilitated him and he joined the Republicans in the Spanish Civil War. Arguing over pay Acosta returned to the United States. During the last fifteen years of his life Acosta drank excessively and died of tuberculosis in New York City penniless.

James William Marion Allison (1905-46) shot down a Heinkel fighter on 18 February 1937, was wounded and did not fly again.

Albert "Ajax" J. Baumler (1914-73) was born in Bayonne, NJ. In 1936 he was dismissed as a U.S. Air Corps cadet for "failure to show proper flying proficiency"[4] when he forgot to switch fuel tanks and had to force land. Traveling to Spain, he joined the Republican government's Kosokov Squadron on 10 February 1937 and flew the Russian-built *Chato* fighter. Baumler shared his first kill with a Russian pilot when they downed a Fiat on 16 March. In July he was hospitalized with a throat infection and returned to the United States. In Spain he scored four and a half victories and two probables.

Baumler rejoined the U.S. Army Air Corps and commissioned a second lieutenant on 30 September 1938. In late 1941 he resigned to join the Flying Tigers in China (*see* Chennault and the Flying Tigers).

Hilaire du Berrier (1905-2002) served as an interpreter, pursuit pilot and pilot checking out recruits. He mistakenly fired at an Air France airliner, damaging it.

Harold Evans "Whitey" Dahl (1909-56) was shot down during the 18 February 1937 air battle. He was again downed on 12 July and captured. He was tried by a military court on 5 October and condemned to death. His case received international attention when his wife appealed to the rebel leader, General Franco, to spare his life. In her letter she included a photo of herself in a bathing suit. Dahl did receive a reprieve but was not freed until February 1940, nearly a year after the end of the war. He had five air victories.

Derek D. Dickinson (1897-1966) renounced his U.S. citizenship and joined the Spanish air force. He served longer than any other American, about 14 months, but was mainly a mechanic.

Eugene Finick (unk.) was among the first American volunteers to arrive in Spain. He was wounded during an aerial fight and hospitalized.

Benjamin David Leider (1901-37) was a New York newspaper reporter and a member of the Communist Party. He scored the first Patrol victory by forcing a Heinkel to crash. Leider was killed in the air battle on 18 February.

Frank Glasgow Tinker, Jr., (1909-39), born in Louisiana, joined the U.S. Navy in 1926 as a sailor. He was selected to go to the U.S. Naval Academy and graduated in 1934. Tinker was sent to flight school and then assigned as a reconnaissance pilot on the cruiser *San Francisco*. Frequently drunk, he was involved in brawls and plane crashes and resigned from the navy. In 1935 Tinker worked as a third mate on board a Standard Oil tanker. Apparently, he tried to volunteer to join the Ethiopian government as a pilot but was rejected because it had no aircraft at that time.

Using the *nom de guerre* Francisco Gómez Trejo, Tinker was recruited by the Spanish ambassador in Mexico to fly for the Republicans. For the first few weeks of January 1937 he was assigned to a light bomber squadron flying obsolete *Breguet* 19 bombers. On 23 January, along with other Americans, Tinker was assigned to the American squadron which was flying Russian-built *Chato* biplanes. On 14 March he shot down his first aircraft, an Italian Fiat CR.32 fighter, and six days later another CR.32. On 17 April Tinker shot down a German Heinkel 51 fighter from the Condor Legion over Teruel. On 3 May Tinker was reassigned to the 1st Escuadrilla de Moscas, commanded by a Russian, flying the Polikarpov I-16 *Mosca*. On 2 and 16 June he shot down two more CR.32s. And on 13 July, Tinker shot down a Messerschmitt Bf 109A and another on 17 July. He was the first American to shoot down the German legionary fighter. Tinker's final killed came on 18 July against a Fiat CR.32. Totally, Tinker shot down 8 aircraft.

Suffering from combat stress, Tinker returned to the United States where he spoke on the radio and wrote books concerning his exploits. Mystery shrouds his death. Purportedly he committed suicide by a gunshot to the head at the Hotel Ben McGehee in Little Rock, Arkansas on 13 June 1939. Next to his body was a letter of acceptance from the Chinese Air Force.

QUOTATIONS:

[1] Sterling Seagrave and the Editors of Time-Life Books, *Soldiers of Fortune*. Alexandria, VA: Time-Life Books, 1981. p. 59.

[2] Allen Herr, "American Pilots in the Spanish Civil War," *American Aviation Historical Society Journal*. (Fall 1977). p. 164.

[3] David Nevin and the Editors of Time-Life Books, *Architects of Air Power*. Alexandria, VA: Time-Life Books, 1985. p. 150.

[4] Seagrave, *Soldiers of Fortune*. p. 63.

SOURCES:

J. Ward Boyce, ed. *American Fighter Aces Album*. Mesa, AZ: The American Fighter Aces Association, 1996.

Dictionary of American Biography. 10 vols. plus sup. 1 thru 8. New York: Charles Scribner's Sons, 1936 & 1990.

Frank G. Tinker, *Some Still Live*. New York: Funk & Wagnalls Company, 1938.

http://imansolas.freeservers.com/Aces/Frank_Tinker.html

http://www.encyclopediaofarkansas.net/encyclopedia/entry-detail.aspx?entryID=4581>

http://en.wikipedia.org/wiki

Americans in the Russo-Finnish War

1939-40

Goal:

To defend Finland against the onslaught of the huge army of the Soviet Union.

Background:

In line with his expansionist policies and possibly to give the Soviet army combat experience in a war with what he probably perceived as a weak foe, Josef Stalin picked a fight with the Soviet Union's small neighbor, Finland. He made far-reaching demands on Finland. These included the demilitarization of the Mannerheim Line (90 miles of Finnish fortifications across the Karelian Isthmus just north of Leningrad), a 30-year naval base lease, and the cession of several islands in the Gulf of Finland. Moscow wanted the border moved back so Leningrad would not be within artillery range. Finland rejected the demands; negotiations broke down. Alleging (26 November 1939) that Finnish artillery had fired on Russian troops, the USSR broke diplomatic relations on 28 November. The Soviets bombed Helsinki and Viipuri, Finland's second city, on 30 November; war had begun. It would be known as the Winter War.

    White-clad Finnish soldiers skillfully and valiantly fought to defend their homeland. They battled the Russians for every snow-covered mile of Finnish territory. They were fighting a poorly led army. Temperatures dropped to minus 40 degrees Fahrenheit. A veteran of the Soviet army later recalled: "There were hundreds of us, but we were poorly equipped, and our dark clothes and machines stood out against the snow. Too many of the commanding officers were politicians rather than military. They could not even manage to feed us more than once a day, let alone lead us in battle. We had little air support."[1]

The initial Soviet attacks at Lake Ladoga, Suomussalmi, Salla and Ivalo were repulsed. The Soviet veteran described one action: ...[O]ur infantry was ordered to withdraw. The Finns saw our effort to retreat and bombed the river to break the ice. The infantry was sandwiched between the firing machine guns and the no longer frozen river. All those men froze to death out in the open fields."[2]

Beset by extremely low temperatures, throttling traffic jams and skiing snipers shooting from the woods, the attempted Russian attack moved slowly, or not at all. A Finnish soldier remarked: "So many Russians! Where will we bury them all?" Using their tactics of divide and destroy, the Finns in successful operations annihilated two Soviet mechanized divisions near the small town of Suomussalmi (the 163rd Division between 27 and 30 December and the 44th between 1 and 8 January 1940)

LEADERSHIP:

Field Marshal (Baron) Carl Gustav Emil Mannerheim (1867-1951), veteran of three wars. He effectively maneuvered his outnumbered troops to meet the overwhelming Soviet army. Soviet dictator Josef Stalin (1879-1953), while not at the frontlines, undoubtedly maintained a strong hand in the Red army's operations.

VOLUNTEERS:

At first the Finish government required foreign volunteers to bring their own weapons. This was not practical; men could not travel around Europe carrying assault guns. The policy was changed. Volunteers came from a number of countries, particularly Scandinavian nations. Over 8,000 Swedes formed their own unit. There were enough Hungarians, eager to fight the Russians, also to form their own unit. About 350 Americans, mainly of Finnish birth, were sent to training camps. At least one American became a driver in an ambulance corps.

COMPENSATION:

It is doubtful that the volunteers received more than subsistence pay.

OPPOSITION:

The Soviet forces had more than three times as many soldiers as the Finns (nearly one million), 30 times as many aircraft and 100 times as many tanks. Finland's heavily forested areas, however, virtually cancelled the Red army's overwhelming superiority in tanks. Furthermore, the Red army had been crippled by paranoid Soviet leader Stalin's "Great Purge of 1937," reducing the army's morale and efficiency shortly before the outbreak of the fighting. With more than 30,000 of its officers imprisoned or executed, including most of those of the highest ranks, the Red army in 1939 had a totally inadequate officer corps.

STRATEGY:

The Finns tried to repel every Soviet attack, and at first were successful. Moving swiftly on their skis they harassed the Russians guerrilla style. They would split off a "piece" of the Soviet forces and destroy it. They launched their own attacks.

OPERATIONS:

Little has been recorded concerning the participation by the American volunteers. A group of about 30 Americans were posted to the front in December. The group fought as a unit of its own and suffered some casualties. Never having shown any concern for human life, Stalin continued to hurl his troops against the devastating Finnish fire. On 1 February 1940 the Russians began a massive attack on the Mannerheim Line. Two armies consisting of 54 divisions launched four or five attacks each day, covered by air support and artillery bombardment. Wave after wave assault troops advanced through withering Finnish fire. Finally a breakthrough occurred 13 February and the Finns were rolled back.

Another company of Americans reached the front on 12 March and was supposed to take charge of the trenches on the 13th, but the order was reversed when the war ended that very day. Its troops exhausted, Finland capitulated.

IMPACT:

The presence of volunteers from a number of countries bolstered the ranks of the Finnish army. Probably more important to the army and the Finnish people, however, was the morale value of having Belgians, Danes, Estonians, Britons, Swedes, Americans and people from other nations fighting alongside them. There were some 12,000 foreign volunteers; of these about 50 were killed.

A far more important impact was the effect the war had on German dictator Adolf Hitler and his generals. They saw the ineptitude of the Soviet army and figured it would be a pushover if they attacked it. The weather, the skill of the Finnish warriors, the poor quality of the Soviet troops and their leadership enabled Finland to resist the Russians far longer than was generally expected (especially by Stalin). The Finns lost approximately 26,000 killed and 43,000 wounded In the peace treaty signed in Moscow on 13 March Finland ceded to the Soviet Union part of the Karelian Isthmus, Viipuri and several border territories to the Soviet Union. Soviet casualties were 126,000 killed, 264,000 wounded, and 39,000 missing. The conflict, however, was not truly over. Finland allied itself with Nazi Germany and in June 1941 warfare was resumed - the Continuation War - between Finland and Russia and became part of World War II.

Biographies:

Robert A. Winston (1907-74), born in Washington, Indiana, graduated from Indiana University in 1930. He worked for both the New York *Times* and the *New York News* between 1930 and 1935. Winston became a naval cadet and took flight training at Floyd Bennett Field, Brooklyn, New York, and the Pensacola Naval Air Station. He qualified as a carrier pilot landing on the carrier *Saratoga* (CV-3) in 1937. Winston was assigned to the carrier *Lexington* (CV-2) flying a Boeing F4B-4 biplane and then the *Enterprise* (CV-6) flying the Grumman F3F-2 biplane. Next, he served as an aviation instructor at Pensacola. Finishing his four year obligation, Winston entered the Naval Reserve.

During February and March, 1940, Brewster Aircraft Company sent Winston and a team of mechanics to deliver 44 Brewster Buffalo fighter planes through Sweden to Finland. The aircraft were reassembled at the Saab factory in Trolhattan, Sweden. Winston test flew each plane and helped familiarize the Finish pilots with the aircraft. He was award the Swedish Royal Order of the Sword and the Finish Mannerheim Medal and the Winter War Medal.

Next, Winston was sent to Belgium to assist in the delivery of Brewster aircraft to that country. Germany, however, invaded Belgium before the aircraft were delivered. Winston and the other Brewster employee fled to France and then through Spain and Portugal. He returned to the United States on the Pan American Clipper. Winston returned to duty in the U.S. Navy. He served as a pilot in the Pacific war, reaching the rank of Lieutenant Commander. He was credited with shooting down three Japanese aircraft and awarded the Distinguished Flying Cross and a Bronze Star among other medals. He wrote a number of books related to aviation.

QUOTATIONS:

[1] Rosemary C. Woodel, "Freezing in Hell," *Military History* pp. 50-56 (April 2003), pp.56.

[2] Woodel, "Freezing in Hell," 56.

[3] John Hughes-Wilson, "Snow and Slaughter at Suomussalmi," *Military History* pp. 46-52 and 69 (January-February 2006) p. 48.

SOURCES:

Kossila, T. (2012, April 7). *Foreign Volunteers In The Winter War*. Retrieved July 18, 2013, from Axis History: http://www.axishistory.com/axis-nations/finland/34-finland-general/finland-general/212-foreign-volunteers-in-the-winter-war

R. Ernest Dupuy and Trevor N. Dupuy. *The Harper Encyclopedia of Military History*. 4th edition. New York: HarperCollins Publishers, 1993.

http://www.vf31.com/pilots/winston.html

Yanks in the Royal Canadian and Royal Air Forces

1940-45

Goal:

In World War II the British military, desperately outclassed by the Germans' war machine, welcomed foreign volunteers to the ranks of its air force.

Background:

Initially this war was a European conflict; Great Britain, France and Poland against Germany and then Italy. During this phase (1939-41) the American volunteer flyers primarily fought over France, Holland and England. Then the war spiraled into the global conflict - World War II. The United States, the Soviet Union and Japan joined in. It was the democracies plus Russia against the Axis - Germany, Italy and Japan. During this phase (1941-45) the American volunteer flyers fought in all theatres.

Leadership:

Air Marshal Sir Hugh Dowding (1882-1970) commanded the Royal Air Force (RAF). His innovative techniques, including plotting of arriving German aircraft, helped the RAF with the crucial Battle of Britain against more experienced German pilots. As the war spread to the Mediterranean and the Pacific, Dowding's chief challenge was to send his limited resources to the right place and the right time.

Volunteers:

Charles Sweeney, a wealthy businessman living in London, began recruiting American citizens as a U.S. volunteer detachment in the French air force, echoing the World War I *Escadrille Lafayette*. With the fall of France these recruits joined the RAF. Sweeney and his rich society contacts bore the cost of processing and bringing the U.S. applicants to Great Britain for training.

As early as late 1939 a few American volunteers went directly to Europe to fight. Ten of these pilots flew with units under the command of RAF Fighter Command between 10 July and 31 October 1940, thereby qualifying for the Battle of Britain clasp.

Hundreds of Americans listed the RCAF and RAF. Young Americans (and other nationalities, too) had an opportunity to fight in defense of democracy. At the same time, service in the royal air forces fulfilled their craving for adventure. Of the more than 6,000 Americans who volunteered, 244 would eventually fly with the British. Three Eagle squadrons were created for the Americans. The first, Squadron 71, was formed in September 1940 and became operational 15 February 1941. Squadrons 121 and 133 followed. Sixteen Britons served as commanders.

Many Americans joined the RCAF was the fastest route to the war. For the most part, the American volunteers were scattered throughout British and Canadian squadrons and served in all theatres of conflict. Until 11 December 1941 the United States was officially neutral towards Germany. Special arrangements were made so that these volunteers did not lose their U.S. citizenship.

By the time the United States entered the war in December 1941, Sweeney and friends had processed and approved 6,700 applications from Americans to join the Royal Canadian Air Force or the RAF.

Carl Raymond Davis (1911-40) had an international background. He was born in South Africa to American parents. He was educated in England and learned to fly in New Jersey. Davis became a British citizen in 1932. Flying for the RAF during the Battle of Britain, he shot down eight German aircraft before being killed in aerial combat.

Courtesy wikimedia.org

Compensation:

An American pilot who transferred from the RAF to the U.S. Army Air Force noted; "Our pay increased from $150 per month to $350 per month."[1]

Opposition:

As the Battle for Britain began, the primary advantage held by the German Luftwaffe was combat experience. Many of Germany's pilots had gained experience flying against the Spanish Republicans and the Poles. Initially, the Germans had an aircraft production advantage but this evaporated as British plants soon caught up and even surpassed the German production. The principal German fighter, the Messerschmitt Bf109E, could out-climb and out-dive the British fighters (the Spitfire I and the Hurricane I) but the British planes were able to turn more tightly than the Bf109E could. Also in the Pacific, initially the Japanese held the advantages with more experienced pilots and superior planes. As the war progressed, these advantages rapidly disappeared.

STRATEGY:

Initially, the RAF had two primary tasks - to defend the homeland and France and to attack Germany. Once France fell, the RAF had two basic tasks: to battle daily incursions by German fighters and bombers and to be prepared to try to block a German invasion that was expected (but never came). Once Britain was safe from eminent defeat, the priority became to preserve the empire.

Pilot Officer C W "Red" McColpin of No 71 (Eagle) Squadron RAF, standing by his Supermarine Spitfire Mark VB at North Weald, Essex Courtesy wikimedia.org

OPERATIONS:

The armies of German dictator Adolf Hitler had swept across Europe in a *blitzkrieg* (lightning war). Only Great Britain stood in the way of a complete conquest. The British army had suffered disaster in France. The only forces able to block an invasion of the British Isles were the Royal Navy and Royal Air Force, and the Royal Navy would have been decimated without air cover.

The first task for the American volunteers was to help defend the British Isles from invasion. Every time enemy warplanes came over the English Channel the RAF rose to engage them. Dog fights occurred almost continuously. Eventually the balance of power began to change and the RAF was able to strike at enemy ground targets.

In May 1941 No. 71 Squadron suffered its first loss when pilot Stanley M. "Mike" Kolendorski was killed during a fighter sweep over Holland. On 2 July William J. Hall became the first Eagle pilot to become a POW when he was shot down during an escort mission. The squadron's first confirmed victory came on 21 July 1941 when William R. Dunn destroyed a Messerschmitt Bf 109F over Lille, France. In August the Spitfire Mk II replaced the Hurricanes the Yanks were flying, before quickly re-equipping with the latest Spitfire Mk V. The Americans soon established a high reputation, and numerous air kill claims were made in RAF sweeps over the continent during the summer and autumn of 1941.

On 19 August 1942 a disastrous 5,000-man raid was launched against the French port of Dieppe. This was the only occasion when all three Eagle squadrons saw action together. Seventy-one Squadron claimed a Ju88 shot down, 121 Squadron a single Fw190, while 133 Squadron claimed four Fw190s, a Ju88 and a Dornier Do 217 downed. Six Eagle Spitfires were lost, with one pilot killed and one taken prisoner. W. Brewster Morgan, one of the fliers over Dieppe, described the action:

> "It was daylight over the landing area, and before long a flight of Junkers 88s came in, escorted by fighters. I shot at one Ju-88 and was taking a head-on shot at a second Ju88 when another Spitfire appeared behind the German plane. It was on fire and I was afraid that I had shot down another Spitfire. I learned [later] that the other Spitfire ... [belonging to the squadron CO, Chesley G. Peterson] had been hit by the German tail gunner. The Ju88 went down, but I didn't claim it."[2]

Lance Wade pictured in the cockpit of his Spitfire Mk VIII, Triolo Airfield, Italy, November 12 1943

Courtesy wikimedia.org

When informed of the attack on Pearl Harbor, most of the Eagle Squadron pilots wanted to join immediately the fight against Japan. Representatives from 71 and 121 Squadrons went to the American embassy in London and offered their services to the United States. The pilots from 71 Squadron decided they wanted to go to Singapore to fight the Japanese, and a proposal was put to the RAF Fighter Command but it was turned down.

On 29 September 1942 the three squadrons were officially given over by the RAF to the fledgling Eighth Air Force of the U.S. Army Air Force and became the 4th Fighter Group. The Eagle pilots had earned 12 Distinguished Flying Crosses and one Distinguished Service Order. Only four of the original 34 Eagle pilots were still present when the squadrons joined the USAAF. Typical were the fates of the eight original pilots in the third squadron. Four died during training, one was disqualified, two died in combat, and one was a prisoner of war. About 100 Eagle pilots had been killed, were missing or were prisoners. Negotiations regarding the transfer between the Eagle Squadrons, USAAF and the RAF had to resolve a number of issues. The RAF wanted some compensation for losing three frontline squadrons in which it had heavily invested. Determining what rank each pilot would assume in the USAAF had to be negotiated, with most being given ranks equivalent to their RAF ranks. For example, a wing commander became a major. None of the Eagle Squadron pilots had served in the USAAF and they did not have U.S. pilot wings. It was decided to give them U.S. wings upon their transfers.

121st Fighter (Eagle) Squadron crest Courtesy wikimedia.org

But this was not the end of the saga of Americans fighting for the RAF. Many American pilots who had been assigned to other than the Eagle Squadrons continued to serve in British forces until the end of the war.

Impact:

When examining the American contribution to the RAF focus goes to the Eagle Squadrons. Through to the end of September 1942 the Eagle Squadrons claimed to have destroyed 73 ½ German planes. Seventy-seven American and five British members were killed. Seventy-one Squadron claimed 41 kills, 121 Squadron 18 kills, and 133 Squadron 14 ½ kills. But this was only a small part of the picture because it ignores the more numerous Americans who flew in British and Canadian squadrons.

The number of Yanks in the RAF and the RCAF was relatively small. But they did help fill desperate manpower needs. Also, having foreign fighters shoulder to shoulder with British subjects was undoubtedly a morale booster for the RAF flyers.

Few pages in military history present as much heroism as was displayed by the RAF in defending Great Britain against the Nazi German air force during World War II. British Prime Minister Winston Churchill declared, "Never in the field of human conflict has so much been owed by so many to so few."[3]

Biographies:

John F. Barrick (1918-unk.), born in Sweetwater, Texas, joined the RCAF and completed flight training on 14 June 1941. Receiving additional training in England, he was posted to India. His No. 67 squadron was assigned to the defense of Rangoon, Burma, along with the American Volunteer Group (the Flying Tigers). Sergeant Barrick shot down his first enemy aircraft, two *Nates*, on 7 February, 1942. He shot down three more enemy aircraft before he was shot down and wounded. Barrick recovered in India. He was commissioned a flight lieutenant and in 1944 as a member of No. 17 Squadron flew ground-attack missions in Burma. In May he was posted to Canada where he was assigned to training duties. Barrick was discharged from the RCAF on 2 October 1945.

John H. Curry (1915-unk.), born in Dallas, Texas, barnstormed in the 1930s. He joined the RCAF sometime in the early 1940s. In April 1942 he was sent to England and assigned to No. 601 Squadron. Curry was among pilots who flew *Spitfires* off the British carrier *Eagle* to reinforce the air defenses of Malta in the Mediterranean. On 26 June he had his first kill, an Italian Macchi 202 fighter. His squadron was relocated to Egypt. Between 26 June and 26 October Curry shot down six more aircraft. Beginning in 1943 he commanded No. 80 Squadron and flew ground support in Italy. On 2 March 1944 Curry was shot down but returned to service. He was discharged from the RCAF on

25 September 1945 and returned to the United States.

Carl Raymond Davis (1911-40) was one of a few Americans in the RAF before the Battle of Britain. In that battle he became an ace, claiming nine enemy aircraft destroyed (and one shared), four (and one shared) probably destroyed, and four damaged. Born in South Africa to American parents, Davis was educated in England at Cambridge and at McGill University in Canada, qualifying as a mining engineer. He then took flying lessons in New Jersey. He became a British citizen in 1932. Returning to the United Kingdom in 1935, Davis lived in London and joined the RAF, being commissioned in August 1936. Davis was called to fulltime service on 27 August 1939. On 27 November 1939 he flew one of six No. 601 Squadron Blenheims that attacked a German seaplane base on Borkum Island in the North Sea. On 11 July 1940 Davis shot down a Messerschmitt Bf110. He added two more Bf 110s on 11 August and three more on the 13th. Davis was awarded the Distinguished Flying Cross on 30 August 1940. The citation read in part, "He has shown great keenness and courage."[4] Davis downed five more aircraft before being killed when his Hawker *Hurricane* was shot down in combat with a Messerschmitt Bf109 over Turnbridge Wells on 6 September 1940.

William R. Dunn (1916-95), born in Minneapolis, Minnesota, at the age of 14 years he soloed in a Waco biplane. He worked as a cowboy before joining the U.S. Army in 1934 as an infantryman. Dunn was discharged in 1937. In 1939 he unsuccessfully attempted to join the RCAF, so he joined the Seaforth Highlanders who were sent to England in October 1939. In 1940 he was accepted by the RAF, received flight training, and was assigned to Eagle No. 71 Squadron. Pilot Officer Dunn shot down six Me-109s between July and August 1941. On 27 August he was downed and serious injured. Dunn transferred to the U.S. Army Air Force in June 1943 and remained in the service until 1973.

Charles E. Edinger (1916-unk.), born in Onaway, Michigan, joined the RCAF in 1941 and earned his wings on 6 February 1942. His first assignment was as a flight instructor and he was sent to England in July 1943. Flying a *Mosquito*, he shot down six German aircraft between 18 June 1944 and 25 December 1944. Edinger returned to Canada and was discharged on 26 October 1945.

Selden R. Edner (1919-49), born in Fergus Falls, Minnesota, joined the RCAF. Following flight training, he was assigned to Eagle No. 121 Squadron Flying a *Spitfire*, Edner had his first confirmed kill on 15 April 1942, a FW-190 over France. Following the transfer of the Eagle Squadrons to the U.S. Army Air Force in September 1942, Edner was commissioned a captain. Prior to being shot down in a P-51B on 8 March 1944 northeast of Berlin, Edner had tallied five kills. He was held as a prisoner until the end of the war. He was killed in a flying accident in Greece on 21 January 1949.

William M.L. Fiske (unk.-1940), was a graduate of Cambridge University in England and a leading personality in the American bobsled teams that won the Olympic championships in 1928 and 1932. He was a member of RAF No. 601 Squadron. He died in hospital on 17 August 1940 after bringing his damaged *Hurricane* fighter back to his base. Fiske was the first American to give his life in the Battle of Britain.

David Charles "Foob" Fairbanks (1922-75) was born in Ithaca, New York. In February 1941 he joined the RCAF and received his wings on 21 November. Fairbanks was a flight instructor until February 1943. Sent to England, he was assigned to No. 501 Squadron. On 8 June he had his first kill, a Me-109. Flying a Hawker *Tempest V*, he shot down two V-1 rockets over England. He was promoted to squadron leader and tallied 12 ½ kills before being shot down and captured in February 1945. Fairbanks was liberated in April and released from the RCAF in October.

Edward L. Gimbel (1916-77), born in Chicago, Illinois, joined the RCAF on 9 October 1940 and received his wings in September of the following year. He was assigned to Canadian No. 401 Squadron. Between January 1943 and March 1945 Gimbel shot down five enemy aircraft and was promoted to captain. On 16 April he was shot down over Czechoslovakia and captured. He was freed in May and released from the RCAF.

Paul G. Johnson (*ca*. 1920-44), born in Bridgeport, Connecticut, he joined the RCAF on 11 October 1941. Between then and June 1943 he underwent training. He was assigned to Canadian No. 421 Squadron. In 1944 Johnson had five kills. On 18 July his *Spitfire* Mk. IX hit a tree during a strafing attack. Attempting to return to base, he lost control and was killed in the crash.

Ripley O. Jones (1915-41), born in Cooperstown, New York, earned a flying certificate in England during 1936. He graduated from Harvard in 1938 and became a U.S. Navy pilot in 1939. Jones was assigned to the battleship *Texas*. When war broke out in Europe, he resigned his commission and joined the RCAF. He was among the pilots who flew *Spitfires* off the U.S. carrier *Wasp* to Malta on 9 May 1942. Flying in the Mediterranean, he tallied six German and Italian aircraft. While flying from Malta he crashed into a lead enemy bomber, a Ju-88, killing himself and the German crew on 17 October.

George C. Keefer (1921-85) was born in New York City to Canadian parents. He studied engineering at Yale University and joined the RCAF in 1940. He was assigned to No. 274 Squadron and flew in North Africa. On 7 December 1941 he shot down a MC.202, his first kill. In June 1942 Keefer accomplished an unusual feat when he landed behind enemy lines to rescue a downed South African pilot. During the war he held a number of commands. His final tally was 13 confirmed kills. Keefer was released from the RCAF in 1947 and became vice president of Canadair.

Vernon C. "Shorty" Keogh (*ca.* 1912-41) was born in Brooklyn, New York. He earned a civil pilot's license and was also a professional parachute jumper with over 500 jumps, performing at air shows across America. He travelled to France and joined the French air force towards the end of the Battle of France. France fell and Keogh went to England with friends, Americans Andrew Mamedoff and Eugene Tobin. The trio joined the Royal Air Force in 1940. Koegh was the smallest pilot in the entire RAF. He was 4'10" tall, hence the nickname. He had to use two cushions in his Spitfire to see out of the cockpit. Keogh flew many missions during the height of the Battle of Britain in August and September. He was credited with one shared "kill", a Do17 on 15 September. He was assigned to Kirton airfield in Lincolnshire on 18 September 1940. He was a founding member of Eagle No. 71 Squadron along with Arthur G. "Art" Donahue, Andrew Mamedoff and Eugene Tobin.

John J. Lynch (unk.-1956) was a native of California. He joined the RAF and was assigned to No. 232 Squadron in September 1941. He was re-assigned to No. 121 Squadron and then No. 71 Squadron, both American Eagle Squadrons. In late 1942 Lynch was promoted to flying officer and assigned to No. 249 Squadron operating from Malta. While flying for the RAF in the Mediterranean he was credited with 13 kills. He then transferred to the U.S. Army Air Force. Lynch was killed off Okinawa while flying an F84G on 9 March 1956.

Andrew B. "Andy" Mamedoff (1912-41) was born in Thompson, Connecticut, where his White Russian family had settled in the early 1910s. As a young adult he learned to fly and even had his own plane with which he performed in air shows. With a friend, Eugene Tobin, he also flew other friends at Mines Field in California before the war. He was attempting to set up charter services in Miami, Florida, immediately prior to World War II. Mamedoff went to Europe, initially to fight for Finland against the Russians, but arrived too late for that war. He joined the French air force towards the end of the Battle for France. As France fell, however, he went to England with his friends and fellow Americans Eugene Tobin and Vernon Keogh. They joined the Royal Air Force in 1940. Mamedoff was posted to the RAF base at Middle Wallop and joined No. 609 Squadron on 8 August 1940. On 18 September 1940 he was a founding member of Eagle Squadron 71 along with "Art" Donahue, Eugene Tobin and Vernon Keough. Mamedoff was posted to Duxford in August 1941 to another Eagle squadron as flight commander. On 8 October 1941 he was flying with No. 133 Squadron on a standard transit flight from Fowlmere airfield in Northern Ireland in his *Hurricane*. He didn't arrive at his destination. The wreckage of his plane was found near Maughold on the isle of Man and his body was later recovered.

Jackson B. Mahon (1921-unk.), born in Santa Barbara, California, learned to fly and joined in RAF in 1941. He was assigned to Eagle No. 121 Squadron. Mahon was shot down and captured while flying protection for the Dieppe landing on 19 August 1942. By that date he had five kills. He was incarcerated in *Stalag Luft III* and worked on the tunnels documented in the movie "The Great Escape." Mahon escaped prior to the mass escape but was re-captured at the Czechoslovakian border. He attempted yet another escape and was again re-captured. Mahon was freed in 1945 at the end of the war. After the war he managed the career of movie star Errol Flynn.

Carroll Warren "Red" McColpin (1914-unk.) was born in Buffalo, New York, and graduated from Golden Gate University. An experienced civilian flyer, he joined the RAF in November 1940. McColpin was assigned to various squadrons, including Eagle No. 121 Squadrons, No. 71 and then No. 133. While flying for the RAF he tallied five kills. McColpin transferred to the U.S. Army Air Corps on 25 September 1942. He held various commands both in the United States and Europe. McColpin retired as a major general in August 1968.

Chesley G. "Pete" Peterson (1920-90) was born in Idaho but moved to Utah in his childhood. He enlisted in the Utah National Guard in 1937. In 1939 he joined the U.S. Army Air Corps and was selected for air cadet training. He moved to Los Angeles, California, after being dropped from flying school and was working at Douglas Aircraft when he became interested in flying for the RAF. Peterson arrived in England in late 1940 and was assigned to Eagle No. 71 Squadron. In time Peterson was promoted to flight lieutenant and given command of No. 71 Squadron. Peterson completed 42 missions while flying with the RAF. When he was given command of No. 71 Squadron, he was only 21 years old and was the youngest squadron commander in the RAF. In 1942 Peterson accepted a transfer to the U.S. Army Air Force along with the rest of the members of the Eagle Squadrons. He was assigned to the 4th Fighter Group as executive officer and as a major. Later he was promoted to colonel at the age of 23, the youngest colonel in the USAAF. He remained in the service until retiring as a major general in 1970.

Donald Mathew Pieri (unk.), a native of Texas, joined the RCAF early in World War II. He was sent to Europe in 1944. Pieri tallied six enemy aircraft before being shot down by his own ricocheting cannon shells. Made a prisoner, he was released at the end of the war.

Reade F. Tilley (1918-unk.), born in Clearwater Florida, he joined the RCAF in June 1940. He was assigned to Eagle No. 121 Squadron. In early 1942 Tilley was transferred to No. 691 Squadron. He was among those pilots who flew *Spitfires* from the U.S. carrier *Wasp* to the besieged island of Malta in March. Once again he was re-assigned to an Eagle No. 126 Squadron. On 3 August he was promoted to flying officer and on 13 October 1942 he transferred to the U.S. Army Air Force. During World War II he had seven kills. Tilley retired with the rank of colonel in March 1971.

Eugene Q "Red" Tobin (1917-41) was born in Los Angeles, California. Tobin initially went to Europe with his friend Andrew Mamedoff to fight in Finland against Russia, but was too late for that war. He was a qualified pilot, having learned to fly in the 1930s. He and Mamedoff had been flying friends at Mines Field in California before the war. They joined the French air force towards the end of the Battle of France, but as France fell Tobin went to England with his friends and fellow Americans and joined the RAF in 1940. On 8 August 1940 Tobin was posted to No. 609 Squadron at Middle Wallop airfield. His first mission was on 16 August. He flew numerous missions during the Battle of Britain in August and September. He was credited with two shared "kills," an Me 110 on 25 August and a Do 17 on 15 September. Tobin was posted to Kirton airfield in Lincolnshire on 18 September 1940 and was a founding member of Eagle No. 71 Squadron along with "Art" Donahue, Andrew Mamedoff and Vernon Keogh. On 7 September 1941 Tobin went into combat with Me 109s on No. 71 Squadron's first sweep over France. His was one of three *Spitfires* shot down. He crashed into a hillside and was killed.

Lance C. Wade (1915-44) was born in Broaddus, Texas. He learned to fly as a civilian in 1933. He attempted to join the U.S. Army Air Corps but was rejected because he lacked a college education. He joined the RAF in December 1940 and earned his wings on 1 April 1941. Wade was among the RAF pilots who flew *Hurricanes* from the British carrier *Ark Royal* to reinforce Malta on 14 September 1941. Flying in the Mediterranean he tallied 14 kills. In late 1942 Wade was loaned to the U.S. Army Air Force and he toured training centers in the United States. In December 1942 he returned to the Mediterranean and scored nine more enemy aircraft. He was promoted to wing commander. On 12 January 1944 Wade died when the liaison aircraft he was flying in crashed at Foggia, Italy. With 23 confirmed kills, Wade was the highest-scoring American in the RAF.

Claude "Weavy" Weaver III (1923-43), born in Oklahoma City, Oklahoma, joined the RCAF after graduating from high school. He received his wings on 10 October 1941. In June he was sent to No. 185 Squadron based on Malta. Between 17 and 24 July 1942 Sergeant Weaver shot down five enemy aircraft, making him an ace (five kills) at the age of 18. He shot down five more enemy planes before having to bail out of his *Spitfire* due to engine trouble. He was captured by the Italians. Weaver and a fellow American flying escaped to Allied-controlled territory. He received a commission as a pilot officer at Buckingham Palace. On 21 January 1943 he was shot down. As he bailed out his parachute became entangled in the aircraft's tail and he was dragged to his death.

Henry Paul Michael Zary (unk.) was born in New York City. He joined the RCAF and was sent to England in 1943. As a member of No. 421 Squadron he flew in France following the Normandy landing. He tallied five kills before the end of the war.

Quotations:

[1] Luther Y. Gore, "So Much Owed to So Few." *Military History* 47-52 pp. (October 1985) p. 47.

[2] Gore, "So Much Owed" p. 47.

[3] James Holland, *The Battle of Britain*. New York: St. Martin's Press, 2010, p. 476.

[4] "Eagle Squadrons," Wikipedia, The Free Encyclopedia. 18 June 2013. <http://en.wikipedia.org/wiki/Eagle_Squadrons>

Sources:

J. Ward Boyce, ed. *American Fighter Aces Album*. Mesa, Arizona: The American Fighter Aces Association, 1996.

Robert L. Popp, "Yank in the RAF," *Military History* pp. 35-40 (June 1991).

Christopher Shores, *Duel for the Sky*. Garden City, NY: Doubleday & Company, Inc., 1985.

Five Yanks with the British in North Africa

1941-43

GOAL:

To fight with the British against the German army in North Africa.

BACKGROUND:

In 1941 a back-and-forth battle for North Africa raged between the German *Afrika Korps* and the British 8th Army.

LEADERSHIP:

Erwin Johannes Eugen Rommel ("the Desert Fox") and Bernard Law ("Monty") Montgomery, both of whom would become field marshals, moved men and tanks across a giant wasteland trying to outmaneuver the other. Both were masters of their trade.

VOLUNTEERS:

Perhaps inspired by the hundreds of American college students who went to Europe during World War I to fight Germany, five American college students chose to make common cause with the British effort in North Africa.

COMPENSATION:

These Yanks were paid at British officer rates.

Opposition:

In 1941 Germany was at the peak of its military power. General Rommel's earlier successes in North Africa caused his troops to be highly motivated.

Strategy:

The ultimate prize for the *Afrika Korps* was the capture of the Suez Canal. This would have significantly crippled the British war effort. Conversely, British strategy was to prevent this from happening.

Operations:

Five American college students decided that they wanted to join the British 7th Armor Division - the famed "Desert Rats" fighting in North Africa. A Dartmouth campus magazine which John Brister helped found editorialized in 1941:

> "Now we realize that we do conscientiously object to war. But we realize too that America must fight Hitler.... We're ready. Ready to fight. Ready to destroy. Ready, if necessary to be destroyed."[1]

The five Americans sailed on 10 July 1941 from Halifax, Canada, on board a 3,489-ton vessel through U-boat infested waters. They arrived in Manchester, England, on 1 August. From there they were taken to a basic training camp in Winchester, England, where they spent a little over three months and became lance corporals. After this it was seven months at an officer cadet training unit in Perham Down. As celebrities of a sort, they were feted at a farewell dinner by U.S. Ambassador John Winant and British Foreign Secretary Anthony Eden.

In June 1942 the Yanks received commissions in the British army and later in the month they boarded a ship in Glasgow, Scotland, that would take them to Africa. In Africa Rommel's *Afrika Korps* was crashing through British defenses and pushing the British 8th Army back toward the Suez Canal. The only way for the British to transport men and materiel to the 8th Army was around the Horn of Africa via the British colony at South Africa. The Yanks sailed on board the freighter *Doña Aurora*. The convoy was attacked by a German submarine wolf pack but the *Doña Aurora* survived the perilous voyage.

After over a fortnight of relaxation and fun and eating foods not available in England (such as chocolate) the Yanks sailed again. They were on board a former liner, the *Duchess of Atholl*, overcrowded with

4,000 troops. The vessel sailed up the east coast of Africa; there were no U-boats here. The *Duchess* arrived in Suez, Egypt, on 2 September 1942. The Americans were taken on a 12-hour rail journey to an "infantry depot" on the rim of a lake. After four hours of acclimation - long hikes and physical exercise - they were ordered to join battalions near the front - Brister and Durkee were in the First Battalion and Cox, Bolte and Cutting in the Second (7th Armoured Division). Field Marshal Rommel's army had advanced to 150 miles of Cairo and the Suez Canal. Slowed by a long supply line the German troops were stopped in July 1942 at a coastal town, El Alamein. The British had a new commander, Lieutenant General Montgomery.

In mid-summer the opposing forces were in battle lines that stretched approximately 20 miles between the town of El Alamein and the Qattara Depression. Montgomery ordered an attack and the First Battle of El Alamein (1-27 July 1942) began. The 7th Armoured Division's First Battalion was to the south, and the Second further north. The Allied (British and Commonwealth) troops tried to force their way through wide minefields. They were constantly attacked by German aircraft and artillery. The platoon commanded by Brister used its three-inch mortars to attack a German outpost 800 yards away. After two hours the Germans raised the white flag, which the Britons respected while the Germans removed their wounded. Then the fighting resumed until the enemy fled. The Second Battalion took the surrender of a group of about two-dozen German soldiers. The first Battle of El Alamein ended in a stalemate.

While the opposing armies maneuvered for advantage, the Yanks suffered their first casualty. Cox fell with a bullet in his back from an enemy machine gun. He also contracted jaundice at the hospital where he was being treated. Eventually he returned to active duty.

Then, in the Second Battle of El Alamein (23 October - 4 November 1942) the Allies broke the Axis line. Rommel pulled back his forces. His men were exhausted, their ranks depleted. Rommel conducted a stubborn retreat. On 19 April 1943, while on a reconnaissance, Cox was shot three times and died. The next casualty was Cutting, an arm and both legs pierced by machinegun fire, and two front teeth lost. Bolte was the next casualty, his right thigh hit by an artillery shell fragment; he lost most of a leg. The British eventually drove the Germans all the way back to Tunisia. As the Allied forces pressed forward, the Yanks suffered their fourth and fifth casualties. Shells from a Messerschmitt 109 smashed into Durkee's knee. Brister had an ear drum punctured when a mine exploded under his Jeep. He also suffered from athlete's foot. He probably considered himself lucky in view of the injuries incurred by his friends. But then his luck ran out. On 27 April as the British advanced, an artillery shell killed Brister instantly. He did not know that his request for transfer to the U.S. Army had just been granted.

In early November 1942 the British had been joined by over 100,000 American troops who had disembarked in North Africa. The war had ended for the five young Americans who had fought under the British flag. Two had died; three were disabled.

Impact:

The five Yanks, perhaps inspired by their World War I predecessors, were too few to have any military impact. But their presence provided a psychological boost to the British.

Biographies:

Charles G. "Chuck" Bolte (unk.-1994) was a Dartmouth college student.
    John Frederick "Jack" Brister (1920-43) was a Dartmouth college student.
    Robert Hill "Rob" Cox (1919-43) was a Harvard college student.
    Heyward Cutting (unk.) was a Harvard college student.
    William Porter Durkee (unk.-1982) was a Dartmouth college student.

Quotations:

[1] Rachel S. Cox, *Into Dust and Fire*. (New York: New American Library, 2012), p. 33.

Sources:

Wikipedia, The Free Encyclopedia. *El Alamein*. 10 June 2013. Electronic Encyclopedia. 17 June 2013. <http://en.wikipedia.org/wiki/El_Alamein>.

CLAIRE LEE CHENNAULT AND THE FLYING TIGERS

1941-42

GOAL:

To defend the supply line over the Himalayan Mountains, which enabled China to receive arms and provisions in its war with Japan.

BACKGROUND:

Following World War I, Japan became increasingly aggressive in subjugating China to its will. This aggression intensified during the 1930s and it began increasingly clear to the Chinese government that war with Japan was imminent. The government of Generalissimo Chiang Kai-shek was painfully aware that China's air force was woefully inadequate. The general tasked his highly competent wife, Madame Chiang, to find a solution. She brought in flyers from a number of countries, including the United States. One of the Americans was a friend of Captain Claire Chennault of the U.S. Army Air Corps and he asked Chennault to suggest additional pilots, which Chennault did. Then the friend relayed an offer from Madame Chiang for Chennault himself: come to China for three months and inspect the Chinese air force and test-fly any aircraft he wished to inspect. Pay would be $1,000 per month, plus expenses - far more than Chennault had earned in U.S. service. Chennault accepted the offer and soon after retiring was on his way to China. All hell broke loose on 7 July 1937 when Japan invaded China. Chennault offered his services to Chiang, who "gratefully accepted."[1]

The ill-trained Chinese flyers and ill-maintained aircraft were no match for the Japanese

Fame–Fortune–Frustration

Claire Chennault (1893-1958) was one of many American pioneer aviators who sought flying opportunities outside the United States, in part because they thought that aviation was being stifled by the U.S. military. Chennault believed that the U.S. Army Air Corps was obsessed with bombers. He accepted a position to modernize the Chinese air force in 1937 and became best known as the creator of the "Flying Tigers."

Authors' Collection, Jon Peterson artist

war machine. Chennault tried to set up an international flying unit, but this failed due to the lack of qualified personnel. So, a Chinese general and Chennault were sent to Washington to seek aid. In Washington was Ambassador T.V. Soong, Madame Chiang's brother. He was a friend of one of President Franklin Roosevelt's closest aides, Thomas G. "Tommy the Cork" Corcoran. Chennault and Corcoran met. Corcoran believed the flyer was a fanatic but eventually they became friends. Legend has it that Roosevelt was swayed by Alfred E. Houseman's *Epitaph on an Army of Mercenaries*. A portion:

"Their shoulders held the sky suspended; They stood, and earth's foundation stay; What God abandoned, these defended, And saved the sum of things for pay."

The war in China was going poorly. Japan succeeded in isolating China from outside help by occupying its ports and coastal areas. To counterbalance this, the Chinese constructed a critical supply route known as the "Burma Road" over the Himalayan Mountains ("the Hump") between British-occupied Burma and southern China. The Japanese were attempting to close the road through air power.

Leadership:

Recently retired U.S. Air Corps captain, jet-jawed Claire Chennault, was somewhat of a daredevil and an advocate of fighter aircraft in a service that championed bombers. He wrote a book, *The Role of Defensive Pursuit*. He had commanded a pursuit squadron in Hawaii and had been the leader of an acrobatic team, "Three Men on a Flying Trapeze." Chennault also had developed tactics for dogfighting and for spotting distant enemy aircraft.

Volunteers:

On 15 April 1941 President Roosevelt signed an order permitting U.S. servicemen to resign their commissions and service and volunteer to serve in China. Thus, with Roosevelt's support, Chennault cut through Washington's red tape. Recruiters for the American Volunteer Group (AVG) spread out through the American military aviation community. The first contingent of volunteers sailed from San Francisco in July 1941, some carrying passports identifying them as missionaries. The American Volunteer Group (better known as the Flying Tigers) was officially founded on 1 August 1941 in Burma

Claire Lee Chennault and the Flying Tigers, 1941-42

Pilots of the 1st American Volunteer Group in China
Courtesy wikimedia.org

with its headquarters at Kunming, China. The force was divided into three pursuit squadrons - "Adam and Eve," "Panda Bears" and "Hell's Angels."

Chennault obtained 98 P-40B fighters which had been originally ordered by Sweden and recruited 96 pilots and some 250 mechanics and support personnel.

COMPENSATION:

Pilots were paid $600 monthly; squadron commanders $750. There was a $500 bonus for destroying a Japanese plane.

OPPOSITION:

Up to the arrival of the American Volunteer Group, the Japanese had no air opposition worth mentioning. Experts throughout the world held Japanese air power in low regard. Chennault was one of the few who had seen Japanese aviation in action and knew that its aircraft and pilots were among the very best in the world.

STRATEGY:

The American Volunteer Group was given the responsibility of defending the "Burma Road" and its logistical infrastructure. Chennault, knowing that his P-40Bs would encounter the more maneuverable and faster Japanese "Zero", taught his pilots to fight in pairs and to dive through the formations of "Zeros" to take advantage of the P-40s' better diving speed and to exploit the fact that the "Zeros" lacked armor and self-sealing fuel tanks.

OPERATIONS:

On 20 December 1941 the American Volunteer Group (known as the "Flying Tigers" because of the teeth painted on the noses of their P-40 aircraft), based in Kunming, China, engaged in its first combat. The Japanese had been bombing Kunming for a year. Then, on the 20th, the Japanese bomber crews, unaccustomed to meeting resistance, were startled to see aircraft coming to attack them. The ten Japanese twin-engine "Sally" bombers, without fighter protection, jettisoned their bombs and tried to flee. Six of the bombers were shot down. One P-40 fighter ran out of gas and crashed; the pilot was saved.

The AVG continued their campaign to defend the Burma Road, combating Japanese aircraft, bombing and strafing enemy troops and installations. In one incident the Americans dropped bombs on the top of a mountain gorge, sending a landslide onto enemy troops. The Japanese pressure was unrelenting and AVG aircraft maintenance primitive. By the end of February 1942 the Japanese had successfully closed the Burma Road. The AVG fell back into Burma.

Next, the Japanese invaded Burma, the objective being the capital, Rangoon. Although outnumbered, the AVG, allied with British RAF flyers, fought to defend the city. The AVG could not put up more than 29 aircraft at a time, sometimes only five. But the Japanese paid dearly. In the ten-week period prior to the fall of Rangoon on 8 March 1942, the AVG had 217 confirmed kills and 43 probables. Five Americans were killed; one was taken prisoner; and 16 aircraft were lost. In addition to the air combat, the AVG provided support to British troops fighting on the ground. Later, British Prime Minister Winston Churchill declared: "The victories of these Americans over the rice paddies of Burma are comparable in character, if not in scope, with those won by the RAF over the hop fields of Kent in the Battle of Britain."[2]

Following the entrance of the United States into the war on 7 December 1941, some ACG personnel were absorbed into the U.S. Army Air Force as the China Air Task Force. Still commanded by Chennault, the CATF continued the work of the "Flying Tigers." Other flyers served in the China National Air Transport, which flew supplies over "the Hump" for the Chinese government. Others returned to the U.S. Army Air Force, the Marines and Navy, which they had left.

IMPACT

The "Flying Tigers" briefly delayed the Japanese from closing the Burma Road. But these few months were among the most critical in World War II. The Allies desperately needed time and heroes. The AVG gave them a little of both at a critical moment.

In less than seven months the "Flying Tigers" had destroyed 299 enemy aircraft, plus 153 probables. Thirty-two P-40s were lost in combat and 61 on the ground. Thirteen "Flying Tigers" were killed in action; ten died in accidents and three were captured.

BIOGRAPHIES:

Percy R. Bartelt (1912-86) born in Waseca, Minnesota, graduated from the University of Iowa and received an ROTC commission. He was stationed at Fort Riley, Kansas, and was assigned to the Corps of Engineers. He resigned his commission and volunteered for the U.S. Navy's pilot training program. Bartelt received flight training at Pensacola, Florida, and was assigned to Squadron VF-3 on board the carrier *Saratoga*. In the summer of 1941 Bartelt resigned his naval commission and volunteered to fly for the Flying Tigers. He received flight training in the P-40 Tomahawk at Toungoo, Burma, and was assigned to the 2nd Pursuit Squadron. Between 23 and 24 January 1942 he became an ace, shooting down five Japanese aircraft. Dissatisfied with conditions in the Flying Tigers, he returned to the United States in April. Bartelt was re-commissioned in the U.S. Navy on 29 September.

William E. Bartling (1914-79) born in Ft. Wayne, Indiana, graduated from Purdue University with a degree in chemical engineering. He entered the U.S. Navy and received flight training. He resigned his commission in 1941 and joined American Volunteer Group in China. Bartling got his first kill on 23 January 1942 and racked up four more before the Flying Tigers were disbanded.

Albert "Ajax" J. Baumler (1914-73) was a U.S. Army Air Corps veteran who had previously flown as a mercenary for the Republican government during the Spanish Civil War (1936-38) and then rejoined the U.S. Army Air Corps. In late 1941 he resigned his commission and joined the Flying Tigers. He was in transit to China when the Japanese attacked Pearl Harbor on 7 December 1941. The Clipper aircraft he was on board turned around at Wake Island and returned to the United States. Baumler re-entered the U.S. Air Corps. In June 1942, as a U.S.

Army officer, he was assigned to China and flew several missions with the Flying Tigers. He shot down a Ki-27 *Nate*, before the Flying Tigers were disbanded and replaced by U.S. Army Air Corps personnel.

Charlie R. Bond, Jr. (1915-unk.), born in Dallas, Texas, served in the ranks of the Texas National Guard between 1936 and 1938. After failing to gain admission to West Point, Bond received his wings at Kelly Field, Texas, in 1939. He was assigned to the Ferrying Command and flew bombers destined for the RAF between the United States and Montreal, Canada. In June 1941 Bond resigned his commission and in a few months joined the American Volunteer Group in China. Flying for the 2nd Squadron, on 29 January 1942 he shot down two *Nates* and damaged a third. His final tally was seven confirmed and three probables. Following the disbanding of the Flying Tigers, Bond returned to the United States and re-joined the U.S. Army Air Corps. He retired in 1968 with the rank of major general.

Gregory "Pappy" Boyington (1912-88), born in Coeur d'Alene, Idaho, graduated from the University of Washington in 1934 with a degree in aeronautical engineering. On 11 March 1937 he was commissioned in the U.S. Marine Corps and received his wings. Boyington resigned his commission in 1941 and joined the American Volunteer Group in China. He flew for eight months and shot down two Japanese aircraft. He resigned from the Flying Tigers in March 1942 and returned to the United States. Boyington re-joined the Marine Corps and had a distinguished career during World War II. He was credited with 24 kills and 4 probables. Among his decorations was the Medal of Honor.

George T. Burgard (1915-78) was born in Franklin, Pennsylvania, and graduated from Bucknell University. During the 1930s he worked in the newspaper business. In December 1939 he joined the U.S. Army Air Corps and received flight training at Kelly Field, Texas. Burgard resigned his commission in September 1941 and joined the American Volunteer Group in China. He was assigned to the 1st Pursuit Squadron and scored his first kills on 21 February 1942, shooting down two *Nates*. When the Flying Tigers were disbanded on 4 July 1942 Burgard returned to the United States. His tally was 10 confirmed kills. In the United States he flew as a commercial pilot for American Export Airlines.

Claire Lee Chennault (1893-1958) was born in Commerce, Texas. He wanted to go to the U.S. Naval Academy in Annapolis, Maryland, but when he learned of the strict discipline to which the plebes were subjected, he decided he did not want to attend after all. Chennault studied at Louisiana State University where he was in the ROTC. After leaving college, he remained a civilian. He had a number of jobs, including teaching at a rural school.

When the United States entered World War I in April 1917 Chennault enlisted in the Army. He wanted to be a pilot but at the age of 26 was considered too old. Nevertheless, he talked flight instructors into giving him lessons in their free time. He did get a non-flying assignment as a supply officer to an air squadron. After a serious bout with the flu during the epidemic of 1918, Chennault succeeded in being assigned to flight school.

He went into the Aviation Service of the Signal Corps. He proved himself to be an outstanding fighter pilot. His strong advocacy of the effectiveness of fighter planes brought him into conflict with superiors who favored bomber aircraft. Chennault's health deteriorated. By 1937 he suffered from damaged ear drums, chronic bronchitis and low blood pressure. He was grounded. On 30 April 1937 Captain Chennault retired from the Air Corps.

Chennault was recalled to active duty with the U.S. Army Air Corp as a colonel in April 1942. He was retired for a second time on 8 July 1945 just before the surrender of Japan. Chennault was an unconventional commander, he had to deal with military politics. A sad moment came when he was not invited to be present at the surrender of the Japanese in September on board the USS *Missouri*. Knowing all that Chennault had contributed to victory, General Douglas MacArthur, who was present, asked, "Where is Chennault?"[3] Chennault advocated Free World assistance to Asian anti-Communist movements.

Marian C. Cooper (1893-1973), a the founder of the Kosciuszko Squadron which fought to preserve Polish independence following World War I, showed up one day carrying his bed roll and announced he wanted to join a fighting group. He proved to be an excellent tactician, at times riding in the noses of bombers on forays he had planned.

Robert P. Hedman (1916-95), born in Webster, South Dakota, on 19 December 1939 joined the U.S. Army Air Corps. He received flight training at Kelly Field, Texas and was assigned to the 1st Pursuit Squadron. He resigned his commission and joined the American Volunteer Group, arriving in Rangoon, Burma, on 20 July 1941. He was assigned to the 3rd Pursuit Squadron. On 25 December he shot down five Japanese aircraft - four *Sally* bombers and one *Oscar* fighter. He was credited with a sixth kill before the Flying Tigers were disbanded on 4 July 1942. Hedman next flew over the Himalayas for the China National Air Corporation. He returned to the United States in December 1944. Between 1945 and 1977 Hedman flew for the commercial Flying Tiger Airlines, out of Long Beach, California.

David L. Hill (1915-unk.), born in Kwangjo, Korea, was the son of Presbyterian missionaries. He graduated from Austin College in Texas and joined the U.S. Navy. In 1938 he received flight training and was assigned to the carriers *Saratoga* and later the *Ranger*. Hill resigned his commission in the summer of 1941 and joined the American Volunteer Group. He was made a flight leader and later he commanded the 2nd Pursuit Squadron. He earned his first kills on 3 January 1942 when he shot down two *Nates* at Tak, Thailand. At the time the Flying Tigers were disbanded he had tallied 12 kills. Hill then joined the U.S. Army Air Force and had a distinguished career, retiring in 1968.

Frank L. Lawlor (1914-73), born in Winston-Salem, North Carolina, graduated from the University of North Carolina in 1935. Two years later he joined the U.S. Navy and completed his flight training in July 1938. Lawlor was stationed at San Diego and then assigned to the carrier *Saratoga*. In July 1941 he resigned his commission and joined the American Volunteer Group. On 23 January 1942 he shot down two I-97 *Nate* fighters, his first kills. During his service with the Flying Tigers he downed five planes and one probable. Lawlor returned to the United States and re-entered the U.S. Navy, from which he retired in 1961.

Robert Laing Little (1916-42), born in Spokane, Washington, joined the U.S. Army Air Corps and received his flight training at Kelly Field, Texas. Little resigned his commission in May 1941 and joined the American Volunteer Group. He was assigned to the 1st Pursuit Squadron and was made flight leader due to his experience in P-40 aircraft. On 29 January Little was credited with his first confirmed kill, a *Nate*. During February he tallied nine additional kills. On 25 April Little was shot down by enemy ground fire and was killed.

William D. McGarry (1916-90), born in Los Angeles, California, studied at Loyola University and then Chainads Art Institute. He joined the U.S. Army Air Corps and received his wings at Kelly Field, Texas, on 20 December 1940. On 13 July 1941 McGarry resigned his commission and joined the American Volunteer Group. He arrived in Rangoon, Burma, in January 1942. He was credited with his first kill on 26 January. McGarry shot down seven more enemy aircraft before he was knocked down by enemy ground fire on 24 March while attacking the Chiang Mai Airdrome in northern Thailand. Captured, McGarry remained in a Thai jail until repatriated in May 1945.

Robert H. Mooney (unk-1941), from Kansas, on 26 December 1941 shot down an enemy aircraft. He was then involved in a head-on collision with another enemy plane. Mooney maneuvered to avoid falling into the town of Xiangyun. His plane crashed outside the town and he died within a few hours.

Robert H. Neale (1914-94), born 1914 in Vancouver, British Columbia, studied at the University of Washington but left to join the

U.S. Navy in 1938. He received his wings at Pensacola, Florida, the next year and was assigned to the carrier *Saratoga*. He resigned his commission and joined the American Volunteer Group. Neale arrived in Burma on 16 August 1941 and was made vice squadron leader of the 1st Pursuit Squadron. During January and early February 1942 he shot down five enemy aircraft. He was awarded the command of the squadron on 6 February. He tallied 13 kills and six probables before the Flying Tigers were disbanded. This made Neale the AVG's top-scoring ace. He returned to the United States and flew for American Overseas Airlines until 1950.

John Van Kuren "Scarsdale Jack" Newkirk (1913-42), born in New York City, attended Rensselaer Polytechnic Institute and Columbia School of Mines. He was commissioned in the U.S. Army and served for three years before resigning. Newkirk then entered the U.S. Navy, was awarded his wings and assigned to the carrier *Yorktown*. In the summer of 1941 he resigned his commission and joined the American Volunteer Group. He was appointed commander of the 2nd Pursuit Squadron. He shot down his first enemy aircraft on 3 January 1942. Before being shot down by ground fire and killed over Chieng-mai, Thailand, on 24 March, Newkirk had tallied seven confirmed kills and one probable.

Charles H. Older (1917-unk.), born in Hanford, California, graduated from the University of California in 1939. He joined the U.S. Marine Corps and received flight training at Pensacola, FL. Older resigned his commission and joined the American Volunteer Group. He was assigned to the 3rd Pursuit Squadron and earned his first kill on 23 December 1941. He was credited with ten kills by the time the Flying Tigers were disbanded. Older returned to the United States and joined the U.S. Army Air Corps. Perhaps he is best remembered for being the presiding judge in the Charles Manson trial in the 1970s.

Edmund Fryer Overend (1914-71), born in Portland, Oregon, graduated from San Diego State College in 1939. He joined the U.S. Marine Corps and received his wings on 20 January 1941. In the summer of that year he resigned his commission and joined the American Volunteer Group. He was assigned to the 3rd Pursuit Squadron and earned his first kill on 23 December. On Christmas Day Overend crash landed near Rangoon, Burma, after his plane was hit by fire from an enemy bomber. During his service with the Flying Tigers he was credited with five kills and one probable. In October 1942 Overend returned to the United States. He worked as a test pilot for Douglas Aircraft and then re-joined the U.S. Marine Corps in March 1943. He was assigned to the Pacific theatre and shot down three more Japanese aircraft.

Robert W. Prescott (1913-78), born in Fort Worth, Texas, worked in his father's trucking business until 1934. Moving to Los Angeles, California, he attended Compton Junior College and Loyola School of Law. Prescott entered the U.S. Navy and earned his wings at Pensacola in 1939. In September 1941 he resigned his commission and joined the American Volunteer Group in China. Prescott was assigned to the 1st Pursuit Squadron. He shot down his first enemy plane on 25 February 1942. His final tally was five and a half kills. Following the disbanding of the Flying Tigers, Prescott returned to the United States. He flew for Trans-World Airlines. Returning to China, he next flew for the China National Aviation Corporation - flying supplies from India over the Himalayas into China. Once again he returned to the United States and played a leading role in the creation of the commercial airlines, the Flying Tigers, on 25 June 1945.

Camile Joseph Rosbert (1917-unk.), born in Philadelphia, Pennsylvania, was a graduate of Villanova College. He joined the U.S. Navy in 1938 and received his wings on 22 April 1940. Rosbert joined the American Volunteer Group in the summer of 1941. He was assigned to the 1st Pursuit Squadron and stationed at Rangoon, Burma. He achieved his first kill on 25 February 1942 when he shot down a Ki-27 *Kate*. While flying for the American Volunteer Group, Rosbert had six confirmed kills and one probable. In secession, Rosbert flew for the China National Aviation Corporation - the Himalayas run - and then the commercial Flying Tigers out of Long Beach, California. Returning to China he joined the Chennault-led Civil Air Transport Corporation and became vice president of the airline.

John Richard "Dick" Rossi (1915-unk.), born in Placerville, California, attended the University of California at Berkeley. He was commissioned in the U.S. Navy and earned his wings at Pensacola, Florida, in 1940. Rossi resigned the next year and joined the American Volunteer Group. On his first combat flight over Burma he shot down a *Nate* fighter. While flying for the Flying Tigers he had six kills and six probables. Following the disbanding of the American Volunteer Group, Rossi joined the China National Air Corporation. He flew some 750 supply-trips over the Himalayas. Next he flew for the Chennault-led Civil Air Transport Corporation. He returned to the United States in 1948 and flew for the commercial airline, the Flying Tigers.

Robert J. "Sandy" Sandell (1916-42), born in Kansas City, Kansas, was commissioned a pilot in the U.S. Army Air Corps. He resigned his commission and joined the American Volunteer Group in the summer of 1941. While flying in the air defense of Rangoon, Burma, Sandell recorded five kills and one probable. He was killed on 7 February 1942 while testing a P-40B at Rangoon.

Robert H. "Snuffy" Smith (1918-unk.), born in Oneida, New York, joined the U.S. Army Air Corp and received his wings in late 1940. He resigned his commission and joined the American Volunteer Group in 1941, having only one hundred hours of flight time in fighter aircraft. During his time with the Flying Tigers he recorded five kills and one probable.

Robert Tharp Smith (1918-95) born in York, Nebraska, attended the University of Nebraska. He joined the U.S. Army Air Corps in 1940. He resigned his commission in mid-1941 and joined the American Volunteer Group. He was assigned to the 3rd Pursuit Squadron and took part in the air defense of Rangoon, Burma. Smith was credited with his first kill on 23 December 1941. While serving in the Flying Tigers he was credited with nine kills and three probables. He re-joined the U.S. Army Air Corps following the disbanding of the Flying Tigers.

QUOTATIONS:

[1] Anna Chennault, *Chennault and the Flying Tigers.* New York: Paul S. Eriksson, Inc., 1963. p. 53.

[2] Jay Mallin and Robert K. Brown, *Merc: American Soldiers of Fortune.* New York: Macmillan Publishing Co., 1979. p. 208.

[3] Anna Chennault, *Chennault and the Flying Tigers.* New York: Paul S. Eriksson, Inc., 1963. P. 270

SOURCES:

J. Ward Boyce, ed. *American Fighter Aces Album.* Mesa, Arizona: The American Fighter Aces Association, 1996.

Flying Tigers, *The Hump, A History We Created.* n.p.: China Intercontinental Press, 2002.

Thomas Parrish, ed. *The Simon and Schuster Encyclopedia of World War II.* New York: Simin and Schuster, 1978.

Sterling Seagrave and the Editors of Time-Life Books, *Soldiers of Fortune.* Alexandria, VA: Time-Life Books, 1985.

Wikipedia, The Free Encyclopedia. Claire Lee Chennault. 22 June 2013. Electronic Encyclopedia. http://en.wikipedia.org/wiki/Clair_Lee_Chennault.

Yanks in the China National Aviation Corporation

1942-45

Goal:

The China National Aviation Corporation (CNAC) had one primary customer - the Chinese National government and their chief concern was supplying General Claire Chennault, head of the American Volunteer Group (the Flying Tigers) and later commander of the China Air Task Force and his air war against the Japanese.

Background:

The government of China and Curtiss-Wright Corporation founded the China National Aviation Corporation (CNAC) in 1929. The airline was taken over by Pan American Airways in 1933. CNAC was headquartered in Shanghai until mid-1937 when the Japanese invaded China. Next its headquarters moved to Hong Kong and then to Calcutta, India, as the Japanese advanced. In December 1940 Captain Hugh "Woodie" Woods surveyed a route across the Himalayas from Calcutta, India, to Chungking, China.

Leadership:

The China National Aviation Corporation (CNAC), a subsidiary of Pan American Airlines, was civilian-owned and in business to make money.

Volunteers:

Some 300 pilots flew for the CNAC, but for many the work too dangerous and demanding and they did not remain long. Five nations were represented among the pilots but overwhelmingly they were American civilians. Many had previously flown for the parent airline, Pan American. Sixteen pilots had flown for the Flying Tigers before this group was disbanded on 4 July 1942. The CNAC pilots flew two-engine, C-46, C-47 and C-53 cargo planes.

Compensation:

CNAC pilots were the highest paid pilots in the world. They earned between $1,200 and $2,500 a month. Provided they stayed out of the United States for two years, this was tax free. On top of that, pilots could make a fortune on the money exchange market and many of them did that. A pilot could exchange U.S. dollars for Chinese currency on the streets of Kunming, China, at a rate as high as one to 300. He could then exchange the Chinese currency back to U.S. dollars in Calcutta, India, at a rate of 30 to one. Thus, he increased his wealth tenfold.

Opposition:

The chief enemy was the world's most challenging weather. Next came the altitude, flying over some of the world's highest peaks, maxing at 19,500 feet. And finally, there was the enemy's aircraft. Additionally, the CNAC pilots were mostly flying fuel-trucks (principally carrying some 850, 55-gallon drums of aviation fuel), alone (no convoys), mostly without fighter protection and without defensive guns.

Strategy:

Luck was the primary component in the strategy of flying "The Hump" in wartime. Pilot Fletcher Hanks wrote: "Flying the Hump is like a game. ... dead reckoning is the only method of navigation .... The degree of error determines if the pilot survives. Sometimes a thirty-degree error in drift for three hours will result in an error of 200 miles .... It is no wonder that most crashes are due to errors in dead reckoning."[1]

Planes did not return empty. Valuable cargos such as tungsten ore were flown out. Not all out-bound cargoes were legal. Enterprising mechanics would smuggle gold out of China by casting airplane parts out of the precious metal and substituting them for the aluminum ones.

Operations:

Operations over The Hump began on 1 April 1942. CNAC flights originated from northeast India (the Dinjan, Chabua or Ledo airfields). They flew eastwardly (north of the Burma Road) to China (the Chengtu, Chungking or Kunming airfields), the trip averaging 550 miles. Operations continued following the disbanding of the Flying Tigers on 4 July 1942. Typically the CNAC made 150 trips per month over the Himalayas. In December the U.S. Air Transport Command (ATC) took control of The Hump operations. CNAC continued to fly but now its aircraft were required to get clearance to fly in ATC's jurisdiction.

In January 1943 CNAC operated 20 aircraft manned by 50 pilots; the planes carrying an average of 37 tons. At this same time the ATC operated 146 aircraft manned by 750 pilots; the planes carried an average of 13 tons. Significant mistrust developed between the CNAC and the ATC, causing a poor relationship. Among areas of dispute were that the ATC controlled the fuel, oxygen and spare parts and apparently frequently hoarded these for its reserves. Also, the work schedule was more demanding for the civilian pilots than for those in the military. Typically, CNAC pilots flew every day whereas the ATC pilots flew twice a week. The earning potential of the CNAC civilian pilots, however, was much greater than that of the army pilots of the ATC.

Beginning on 1 November 1944 CNAC aircraft were tasked with dead-dropping (no parachute) rice to Chinese units on the return flights from China. Typically this involved flying 200 feet above the ground.

Impact:

CNAC played an important role in keeping Nationalist China in the war. Losses among the CNAC pilots were heavy because the flying was dangerous. Lieutenant General William H. Turner, USAAF, wrote in 1944, "Flying the Hump had the same casualty rate as flying bombers from England into deepest Germany." [2] The CNAC sustained 81 deaths, 27 of those being pilots. Thirty-seven out of 91 aircraft were lost and many were damaged.

Biographies:

George "Andy" Anderson (unk.-1944) crashed into Digboi Mountain and was killed on 12 December 1944. All three crew members were killed.

Samuel Anglin (unk.-1943), flying a C-53, was shot down by a Japanese fighter on 11 August 1943. The two Chinese crew members also died.

Leo B. Atwater (unk.-1944), flying a C-47, probably crashed on the Patkai Range on 15 May 1944. Two Chinese crew members were also killed.

Sherwin Ball (unk.-1945), flying a C-47, crashed on 7 January 1945 killing all three on board.

James Carville (unk.-1943) crashed while flying a C-47 on 19 November 1943. Two others died in the crash.

Russell Coldren (unk.-1945), flying a C-47 from Kunming to Tengchung, crashed during bad weather on 6 January 1945. Four Chinese crew members also died.

Bert Coulson (unk.), flying a C-47, ran out of fuel over the Hukawng Valley on 31 August 1944 and successfully bailed out. The other two crew members died.

John J. Dean (unk.-1942) was flying a C-47 from Kunming, China, to Dinjan, India, when it disappeared on 17 November 1942. In addition to Captain Dean, the co-pilot J.S. Brown and a Chinese radio operator were also lost.

Jim R. Fox (unk.-1943) had previously flown for Pan Africa Airlines, crashed and was killed while flying The Hump on 11 March 1943. Two Chinese crew members were also killed.

Ridge Hammill (unk.-1945), flying a C-47, crashed shortly after takeoff from Dinjan on 9 May 1945. The Chinese co-pilot also died.

Fletcher Hanks (1917-unk.), born in Oxford, Maryland, graduated from Lehigh University in 1941. Hanks learned to fly and was hired by United Airlines. He received additional training at the Boeing School of Aeronautics. In the early 1940s he flew for Pan American Airlines and Pan Alaskan Airlines. Hanks then joined the China National Aviation Corporation. Between November 1943 and the end of the war he flew 347 round trips over the Himalayas.

George Huang (unk.-1945), flying a C-47, crashed on 16 January 1945. All three crew members died.

Paul Kessler (unk.-1944), flying a C-47, crashed on 18 June 1944. The other crew members survived.

M.K. Loh (unk.-1943) crashed while flying a C-47 on 18 December 1943. Two others died in the crash.

Thomas Loomis (unk.-1944), flying a C-47, crashed on 8 June 1944. All three on board were killed.

M.K. Mah (unk.-1944), flying a C-47, crashed on 1 August 1944 killing all three on board.

Richard Marchant (unk.-1944), flying a C-47 from Calcutta to Dinjan, crashed killing all twelve on board.

Einar I. "Micky" Michelson (unk.-1944), flying a C-47, crashed.

He and a Chinese co-pilot were killed. Michelson had been a Flying Tiger.

Arthur Privensal (unk.-1943), flying a C-53, crashed while attempting to land at Kunming. Two Chinese crew members were also killed.

Joe R. Rosbert (unk.) crashed while flying from China to Dinjan, India, on 7 April 1943. He and his co-pilot, Charles R. Hammell, survived but their Chinese radio operator died.

Mike J. Schroeder (unk.-1943), flying a C-47, was shot down by a Japanese fighters on 13 October 1943. Two Chinese crew members were also killed.

James Scoff (unk.-1944), flying a C-47 from Dinjan to Sui Su Fu, China, crashed during bad weather on 7 October 1944. The crew of three was killed.

William "Hal" Smith (unk.-1945), flying a C-47 from Kunming to Hsinching, crashed on 9 April 1945. All three crew members died.

Albert Olafur Thorwaldson (unk.-1945), flying a C-47, crashed near Myitkyina, Burma, on 14 January 1945. Four crew members including Thorwaldson were killed; two Chinese food droppers survived.

Orin M. Walsh (unk.-1943) was believed to have crashed on the Patkai Range during a storm on 13 March 1943. Also lost were two Chinese crew members.

William D. Warren, Jr. (unk.-1945), flying a C-47, crashed during bad weather on 6 January 1945. All three crew members were killed.

Al Wright (unk.-1943) crashed while flying a C-47 on 18 December 1943. Also killed in the crash were pilot Charles Cook and a crew member.

QUOTATIONS:

[1] Fletcher Hanks, *SAGA of CNAC #53*. Bloomington, Indiana: Author House, 2004, p. 50-51.

[2] Hanks, *SAGA of CNAC #53*. unnumbered foreword.

SOURCES:

Chick Marrs Quinn, *The Aluminum Trail*. Privately published, 1989.

Flying Tigers, *The Hump, A History We Created*. n.p.: China Intercontinental Press, 2002.

Wikipedia, The Free Encyclopedia. CNAC History. 26 June 2013. Electronic Encyclopedia. http:///www.cnac.org/history01.htm

CLAIRE CHENNAULT AND CIVIL AIR TRANSPORT (CAT)

1946-50

GOAL:

To maintain a major and continuing flow of military and civilian supplies to the areas of China controlled by the Nationalist government.

BACKGROUND:

The Japanese had attacked China in 1937. In the hills of Yunnan Province the Communists, led by "Chairman" Mao Tse-tung, established their own fiefdom, allied with the Nationalists led by Generalissimo Chiang Kai-shek. After the war with Japan ended, the Nationalists and Communists engaged in a new conflict.

After the Flying Tigers were absorbed into the U.S. Army Air Force on 4 July 1942 General Chennault felt there was a need for an independent transport flying service in southeastern Asia. With Whiting Willauer he created the Civil Air Transport in 1946. CAT received funds from Chinese backers and probably from Chiang's Nationalist government. In 1946 the new company obtained a contract to fly supplies for the United Nations Relief and Rehabilitation Administration (UNRRA), headed by the famous and feisty former mayor of New York City, Fiorello LaGuardia. LaGuardia overruled subordinates who were doubtful about the project.

LEADERSHIP:

Creator and leader of Civil Air Transport was Brigadier General Claire Lee Chennault (1893-1958), who had set up and led the legendary Flying Tigers. He was assisted by Whiting Willauer (1906-62), a pilot, former diplomat, topnotch administrator and expert in supply transportation.

Volunteers:

The fliers of CAT were former pilots in the Flying Tigers and Royal Air Force. But the Flying Tigers were no more and the RAF was withdrawing from the region. The aviators joined CAT for adventure and good pay. Chief pilot and later chief of flying operations was Eric Shilling, former Flying Tiger and pilot for a small air firm.

Compensation:

The work the mercenaries did was perilous. To and from dangerous areas, they hauled refugees, ammunition, jungle fighters, pigs, chickens, tons of rice and secret agents. Their salaries sometimes reached $40,000 yearly.

Opposition:

The Communists had no or few aircraft to interfere with CAT's work. It was Mother Nature, the age or condition of the aircraft, and the ground facilities which were the enemies. CAT purchased 25 old C-47 cargo planes from a surplus dump in Hawaii. A third of the aircraft were to be cannibalized for spare parts.

Strategy:

The responsibility of CAT was to maintain the aerial-supply line to the Nationalists open and fully operating. Anna Chennault wrote, "CAT was really a prototype of the Berlin airlift (which saved Berlin in 1948-49)...."[1]

Operations:

CAT crisscrossed through thousands of miles of Chinese air space. It carried just about everything, from machinery to agricultural products. By 1948 it had become, according to Chennault's wife, the largest freight line in the world. She described the airline:

> "It literally carried anything anywhere. In early days people often shared accommodations with cattle, sheep and pigs. No one seemed to mind although a pilot occasionally looked behind the cockpit into the velvety eyes of a cow thoughtfully surveying the cloud banks. On many occasions pilots and ground personnel were quartered in tents, pilots doubled as

James B. "Earthquake McGoon" McGovern, Jr. (1922-54) apparently he and his co-pilot, Wallace Buford, were the only Americans to die in combat during the defense of Dien Bien Phu. His C-119 was shot down while dropping a howitzer to the besieged French. This 300-pound pilot was known for his sense of humor.

Authors' Collection, Dan Burhard artist

passenger agents weighing freight and collecting fares; nor was the pay princely .... [I]t operated with generally over-loaded planes in some of the worst weather in the world with no navigational ground aids but its own."[2]

By mid-1948 CAT was flying four million ton-miles of cargo each month. A big and growing problem, however, was that the Communist troops were conquering more and more territory. CAT airlifted food, weapons and ammunition to besieged Nationalist garrisons. It dropped food and medicines to encircled civilians. It flew to safer areas treasures, machinery and key personnel. In 1949, when Chiang was forced to leave the mainland, CAT helped ferry his troops to Formosa.

By 1950, with the defeat of Chiang's forces and their loss of most of the country, CAT faced severe financial difficulties. The U.S. Central Intelligence Agency (CIA) formed a private Delaware company, the Airdale Corporation, which set up s subsidiary called CAT, Inc. This corporation purchased nominal shares of the Civil Air Transport. CAT maintained a civilian appearance by flying scheduled passenger flights while simultaneously using other aircraft in its fleet to fly covert missions. In 1950 the CIA bought CAT outright. It was no longer a mercenary organization but an instrument of U.S. policy.

CAT continued to make history. It flew more than 15,000 missions during the Korean War. It dropped supplies to the beleaguered French troops at Dien Bien Phu. (Famed pilot Captain "Earthquake McGoon" McGovern also dropped beer and cigarettes bought with his own funds.) In 1959 CAT morphed into Air America, which participated in the Vietnam War.

Impact:

After the struggle that had been going on for decades - only delayed by an uneasy truce to fight the Japanese (1937-45) - the Communists eventually defeated the Nationalists. Chiang was able to maintain control of only the island of Formosa (now Taiwan). CAT was an important factor in helping the Nationalists fight the Communists. CAT helped slow the communization of China - delayed it for "a full year," in the view of Mrs. Chennault.[3] An example of what CAT accomplished was the city of Taiyuan. Besieged, the city was able to hold out for nine months thanks to CAT, which airlifted rice, supplies and ammunition. Fifteen air strips were constructed in turn as enemy artillery destroyed them.

Biographies:

James B. "Earthquake McGoon" McGovern, Jr. (1922-54) served in China in 1944 as a member of the 14th U.S. Army Air Force's 23rd Fighter group. He was credited with shooting down four Japanese *Zero* fighters and destroying another five on the ground. He switched to CAT, probably when Japan was defeated. Known for his sense of humor (perhaps necessary: he weighed about 300 pounds), on one occasion he dropped empty beer bottles that whistled like bombs as they fell and sent the enemy running for cover. On 5 May 1954 a barrage of Viet Minh gunfire at Dien Bien Phu brought down McGovern's C-119 while he was parachuting a howitzer to the French. He was killed, as was his co-pilot, Wallace Buford. They were the only Americans to die in combat in the war.

Eriksen Emerson "Erik" Shilling (1916-2002) graduated from the Army Air Corps Flying School in 1938. Initially flying for the U.S. Army Air Corps, in 1941 he resigned his commission and joined the Flying Tigers in southeast Asia. He became a flight leader on a pursuit squadron. When the Tigers were absorbed into the U.S. Army Air Force, Shilling went to work for the China National Aviation Corporation, a firm owned by the Nationalist government and Pan American Airways. He made some 350 dangerous round trips over the Himalayan "Hump," carrying military supplies. In 1946 he began working for CAT. This was followed, in the late '50s, by a career in commercial aviation, and as a racer and builder of planes.

Quotations:

[1] Anna Chennault, *Chennault and the Flying Tigers.* New York: Paul S. Eriksson, Inc., 1963. p. 277.

[2] Chennault, *Chennault and the Flying Tigers.* p. 274-75.

[3] Chennault, *Chennault and the Flying Tigers.* p. 277.

Sources:

Sterling Seagrave and the Editors of Time-Life Books, *Soldiers of Fortune.* Alexandria, VA: Time-Life Books Inc., 1985.

Two Yanks Fighting for Israel

1948

GOAL:

To protect the new state of Israel from being crushed by Arab neighboring countries.

BACKGROUND:

Between 1945 and 1948 a guerrilla war raged throughout Palestine between the Arabs and the Jews, with the British occupation army caught in the middle. The United Nations decided to partition the land between the two factions. Early in 1948 the British chose to remove their occupation troops on 14 May 1948, some four months ahead of the date called for under the U.N.'s plan. On that same date, Jews in Palestine declared themselves to be an independent state. The Jewish Agency (the *de facto* Israeli government led by David Ben-Gurion) had been preparing for this eventuality. Aside from agreeing that they did not want a Jewish state in their midst, the Arabs had only vague plans as to how to deal with the British withdrawal. In January 1948 the Arab Liberation Army (ALA), troops from Egypt, Transjordan and four other Arab countries, launched a series of raids from Syria into Palestine and the fighting became widespread.

LEADERSHIP:

Jewish men and women who had led the struggle for independence became the leaders of the new state. But there was a scarcity of trained military leaders. Recently retired U.S. Colonel David "Mickey" Marcus filled much of that void. On 28 May he was named the commander of the Israeli forces defending Jerusalem, with the rank of brigadier general. Not in a leadership but nevertheless in a significant role, skilled American fighter pilot Rudolph Augarten flew in the nascent Israeli Air Force.

Volunteers:

Israel quietly sought to recruit skilled war veterans in the United States. Both "Mickey" Marcus and "Rudy" Augarten were highly qualified. Marcus was a senior officer with both administrative and combat experience. Augarten was a frontline fighter pilot.

The way Augarten was recruited into the Israeli cause is known. It was reminiscent of the volunteers for France from Harvard University during World War I. In early 1948 Augarten attended a lecture at the Harvard library by representative Abba Eban of the new state of Israel. Traveling to Manhattan, Augarten visited the offices of Land and Labor for Palestine (a front for recruiting experienced fighters). Given Augarten's wartime record, the recruiters asked if he could leave for Palestine immediately. He hesitated due to the objection of his parents but as the fighting in Palestine intensified, Augarten decided to go.

A Czech-assembled fighter (Avia S-199) built from German parts flown by an American for Israel attacks a British-built Spitfire belonging to Egypt. The successful attack occurred on 16 October 1948 and the pilot was Rudy Augarten. Improbable events like this are what make fact more incredible than fiction.

Authors' Collection, Phyllis Saroff artist

Compensation:

Both Marcus and Augarten received retirement pay from their service in the U.S. Army and U.S. Army Air Forces, respectively. It is not known what pay they received from Israel.

Opposition:

Although the Arab armies of Egypt, Transjordan, Iraq, Syria, Saudi Arabia and Lebanon were impressive in a parade, many were facades. Mostly, these militaries had been constructed to keep their elites in power. Little attention had been paid to tactics and logistics and emphasis had been placed on population control.

The major exception was the Transjordanian 10,000-man Arab Legion. It was commanded by the British soldier of fortune Major General John Bagot Glubb, better known as Glubb Pasha.

STRATEGY:

Marcus faced two great challenges. First was to devise a military strategy for a nation which was disunited politically and geographically. The single factor which tenuously bonded the Israeli political factions together was their desire to create the nation of Israel. A number of these Israeli political forces possessed their own fighters, which were more akin to terrorists than guerrillas. Marcus began to transform the Haganah, the main Israeli band and other armed groups into a modern fighting force. He wrote a training manual covering the aspects of modern warfare, including organization and logistics.

Israelis experienced a classic *levee en mass* - every ablebodied individual was expected to participate in the struggle against the numerically overwhelming Arab forces. In Palestine alone the 1,200,000 Arabs outnumbered the Jews two to one. And there were millions of Arabs in the surrounding countries. All Jewish young men were expected to fight. Creating an army, however, was no easy task. Some building blocks existed, such as the Irgun and the Stern Gang (Jewish fighters who had employed terrorist tactics against the British and Arabs) and well-trained settlement guards. In some respects the qualities that made the Irgun and the Stern Gang good clandestine fighters were the antithesis of what made a good army. Frequently, they acted brashly with little consideration for losses and the big picture. Molding these elements into an army was a huge challenge.

Geographically, Israeli was not an entity but rather pockets of populations that were tenuously connected by roads which were under constant threat by the Arabs. And the Arabs were everywhere, both within and without the new nation, making a classic strategy of fronts and interior and exterior lines of communications nonexistent.

Vastly outnumbered, Marcus championed the continuous offense, attacking whenever an opportunity presented itself, and counter-attacking following each Arab attack to keep the enemy forces off balance.

Rudy Augarten (1922-2000) was an accomplished fighter pilot who chose to fly for the very young Israel Air Force. Demonstrating his versatility, Augarten flew a Spitfire, a P-51 Mustang and an Avia S-199 in just a few days. This last plane was made of left-over parts from the Third Reich air force. It had a Messerschmitt BF-109 frame, engines from a Junker Jumo-211, and war-surplus guns. It had a tendency to shoot off its own propeller.

Authors' Collection, Jon Peterson artist

Fame–Fortune–Frustration

David Marcus (1901-48) was one of many West Point graduates who fought for other countries. Following World War II he took up the cause of an independent Israel and paid with his life. He was shot in error by a sentry. There were three primary motivators among soldiers of fortune - ideology, excitement and money. If numbers of mercenaries matter, the strongest of these was ideology.

Authors' Collection, Jon Peterson artist

Operations:

Prior to declaring independence, the highly organized Jewish forces positioned themselves to seize the British-garrisoned towns as those troops evacuated. Fighting raged along the borders of the new country from the Negev Desert to Jerusalem. And Jerusalem, parts of which were held by both Arabs and Jews, became a hotly contested prize. The key to the prize became the Tel Aviv-Jerusalem Road which ran through Arab controlled territory. The Arab Legion held a thick-walled police station along the road and was able to block Jewish reinforcements from breaking through to the new capital of Israel, Tel Aviv. Marcus was appointed Supreme Commander of the Jerusalem Front and given the rank of colonel. Forces under Marcus' command were unable to crack the Arab defenses blocking the road, but he did succeed in protecting the builders of a bypass through the mountains to the south. Tragically for the Jews, Marcus, who spoke no Hebrew, was killed on 11 June by a Jewish sentry when Marcus ignored a challenge.

As an Israeli pilot, Rudy Augarten's first stop was Czechoslovakia for flight training. Israel had purchased some Czech-assembled Avia S-199 fighter planes. Ironically, these were "Frankensteins" made from left over parts of the Third Reich's aircraft. They had German Messerschmitt BF-109Gs frames, engines from Junker Jumo-211s, and war-surplus weapons. As with any jury-rigged piece of complicated machinery, the Avia S-199 had more than its share of technical problems. The plane was nicknamed the "Nazi Revenge."

In July 1948 Rudy Augarten joined the sole Israeli fighter squadron, No. 101. Since Israel had more pilots than planes and fuel was in short supply, Augarten had to wait his turn to fly. On 16 October, flying an Avia S-199, he shot down an Egyptian Spitfire. Five days later, flying one of Israel's new Spitfires, Augarten downed another Egyptian Spitfire. On 11 November he brought down an Egyptian Dakota and on 17 November another Spitfire. Again flying a Spitfire, Augarten damaged a Macchi which was landing at the El Arish airfield. When a truce in January 1949 ended the conflict, Augarten helped train the first two groups of future Israeli pilots.

Impact:

How much difference can two weeks of work by one man, David Marcus, make in a conflict involving tens of thousands? The historian Trevor Dupuy wrote: "Colonel Marcus had demonstrated a combination of energy and ability which marked him as one of the outstanding leaders of the Haganah. His death was a disaster."[1] How is that possible? Having the advice and leadership of a trained foreign officer, Marcus was of major importance to the Haganah as it transformed itself from a clandestine guerrilla force into a modern army.

Augarten's success as a fighter pilot provided a psychological boost to the Israelis. He flew combat missions for Israel in the Czech-assembled Avia S-199, the British-built Spitfire, and the American-built P-51, demonstrating remarkable flying skills.

Biographies:

Rudolph "Rudy" Augarten (1922-2000) was born in Philadelphia, Pennsylvania. He enlisted in the U.S. Army in January 1941 and transferred to the Army Air Forces in July. After training he joined the 371st Fighter Group In England. On 10 June 1944 he was hit by flak and bailed out behind enemy lines in France. After evading capture for four weeks, he was taken. He escaped and managed to get back to his squadron. On 3 October he downed two Me-109s. He was discharged from service as a captain. In the spring of 1948. With war having broken out in the Middle East, Augarten offered his service to Israel, arriving there in July 1948 and joining its fighter squadron. After the war he went to Harvard, where he had previously studied, and he graduated in 1950. He then went back to Israel and rejoined the air force. Augarten, as a lieutenant colonel, was the commander of the air base at Ramat David. Augarten then returned to the United States. He worked as a real estate salesman and was employed as an engineer by Rockwell International.

David "Mickey" Marcus (1901-48) was born in New York and appointed to the U.S. Military Academy from that state. He graduated from West Point in 1920 and served in the U.S. Army until 1926 and then joined the reserves. During the 1930s Marcus worked as a federal attorney in New York and in the New York Department of Corrections. In 1940 he returned to active duty in the U.S. Army. Two years later, he was named commandant of the U.S. Army's Ranger School. On the eve of D-Day Marcus parachuted into Normandy with the 101st Airborne Division. During World War II he served as adviser to President Franklin Roosevelt at the Yalta Conference and to President Harry Truman at the Potsdam Conference. By V-E Day he was a full colonel and chief of planning for the War Department's Civil Affairs Division. Marcus helped draw up German and Italian terms of surrender. Later he headed the War Crimes branch involved in the

Nuremberg Trials. In early 1947, at the age of 46 years, after serving 13 years in the army, Marcus returned home to a promising law practice in New York and assured his wife, Emma, a schoolteacher, he would settle down. They did not have any children.

Quotations:

[1] Trevor N. Dupuy, *Elusive Victory: The Arab-Israeli Wars: 1947-1974*. Garden City, New York: Military Book Club, 1978, p. 66.

Sources:

Arab-Israeli Air Wars 1947-67. Madrid, Spain: Osprey Publishing Ltd., 2000.

Eric Bogomolny,. *Rudy Augarten- Avenging the Holocaust*. 11 November 1999. Electronic article. 18 July 2013. <http://www.elknet.pl/acestory/augarten/augarten.htm>.

Colonel J. Ward Boyce, Ed., *American Fighter Aces Album,* Mesa, Arizona: The American Fighter Aces Association, 1960.

George W. Cullum, ed., *Biographical Register of the Officers and Graduates of the U.S. Military Academy*. New York: various publishers through Supplement 8, 1879-1940.

Martin Gilbert, *Israel - A History*. New York: William Morrow and Company, Inc., 1998.

John Laffin, *Arab Armies of the Middle East Wars 1948-73*. Oxford: Osprey Publishing Limited, 2005.

Jay Mallin and Robert K. Brown, *Merc: American Soldiers of Fortune*. New York: Macmillan Publishing Company, 1979.

Los Angeles Times. "Rudolph Augarten; World War II Fighter Pilot." 13 September 2000. *Los Angeles Times*. Electronic Obituary. 18 July 2013. <http://articles.latimes.com/2000/sep/13/local/me-20405>.

Zoom Info. "Rudolph Augarten." 7 July 2002. *Zoom Info*. Electronic Obituary. 18 July 2013. <http://www.zoominfo.com/CachedPage/?archive_id=0&page_id=301933946&page_url=//www.harvard-magazine.com/on-line/010258.html&page_last_updated=2002-07-07T05:21:06&firstName=Rudolph&lastName=Augarten>.

ODYSSEY OF WILLIAM MORGAN

1958-60

GOAL:

To rid Cuba of the Fulgencio Batista dictatorship

BACKGROUND:

Fidel Castro and his band were the best-known of the rebels fighting Batista during the Cuban Revolution. There were, however, other groups. Largest of these was the *Segundo Frente Nacional del Escambray*, operating in the Escambray Mountains of central Cuba, (Front second to Castro's first front in the Sierra Maestra Mountains of eastern Cuba.

LEADERSHIP:

Commander of the *Segundo Frente* was Eloy Gutíerrez Menoyo, one of whose brothers had died in an unsuccessful attack on Batista's Presidential Palace (March 1957). Rapidly rising to second in command was an American, William Morgan.

VOLUNTEERS:

The ranks of the *Segundo Frente* were young local men who primarily came from the cities, often fleeing Batista's police.

Fame–Fortune–Frustration

William Morgan (1928-60), although not highly educated, rose to the rank of comandante in the Cuban Revolutionary Army. He was possibly the most influential American serving the Cuban revolutionary cause. A veteran of the U.S. Army, he came to Cuba to fight the Fulgencio Batista dictatorship. His downfall and execution were due to his turning against the tightening Fidel Castro dictatorship.

Authors' Collection, Dan Burkhard artist

Compensation:

The guerrillas received little or no compensation. Food and weapons were provided by the group.

Opposition:

Fight against theses guerrillas was Batista's army. This consisted of some 30,000 men, drawn from the poorest and least educated sectors of society. Like most Latin American forces at the time, this was a barracks army. The officers did not have the slightest inkling of how to combat guerrillas. (Ironically it was because of this conflict and of Cuba-sponsored movements in other Latin American countries that the U.S. developed counter-insurgency doctrines, which it then imparted to the Latin American armies.)

Strategy:

To wear down Batista's army through hit and run guerrilla tactics, while using the mountains as a hideout and staging area.

Operations:

The guerrillas would attack army patrols and pull back into the rugged terrain when confronted with superior forces. The *Segundo Frente* eventually may have numbered close to 2,000 men and women, more than the better known Castro forces.

Impact:

The fighting of the guerrilla bands, together with operations by underground rebel organizations, resulted in the defeat of the Batista army. Batista fled Cuba on 1 January 1959. Castro rapidly seized power, leaving other rebel groups largely in the cold. Castro soon turned to Communism; Morgan and Gutíerrez were anti-Communists. They eventually became involved in an anti-Castro plot sponsored by Dominican dictator Rafael Trujillo. Castro learned of the plot and Morgan and Menoyo openly switched sides.

The was no place for Morgan in the Castro regime. He turned to frog farming in the Escambray. But he also surreptitiously became involved with a new, anti-Communit guerrilla group in the mountains. He evidently shipped weapons to them. Morgan was arrested and tried (he went to the trial singing the U.S. Army's song "As the Caissons Go Rolling Along"). He was found guilty and sentenced to death. Morgan was executed on 11 March 1960, with Fidel and his brother Raúl possibly watching.

Biographies:

Jack Nordeen (unk.), an American, apparently was a polio victim. He served with the anti-Batista guerrillas.

William Alexander Morgan (1928-60) served briefly in the U.S. Army. He joined the anti-Batista rebels in February 1958. His military training was welcomed by the *Segundo Frente*. He would late say, he joined the guerrillas because a friend had been tortured and killed by the Batista police. In a letter written to his mother the day before he died, Morgan criticized the new rulers of Cuba. He stated: "... [N]o man has the right to impose his will or his beliefs on others. All men have an innate right to a better life for themselves and for their families. I have spent my time in Cuba trying to help them [the Cubans] achieve this."[1]

Quotations:

[1] "*Sale a la luz ultima carta de William Morgan ....*" Miami, FL: *El Nuevo Herald*, 29 April 2012, p. 1

Sources:

Interviews between William Morgan and Jay Mallin Sr., 1959-60.
Jay Mallin and Robert K. Brown, *Merc: American Soldiers of Fortune.* New York: Macmillan Publishing Company, 1979.

ODYSSEY OF
HENRY WHARTON

1966-68

GOAL:

To fly arms, munitions and supplies to the Ibos in the newly declared African nation of Biafra.

BACKGROUND:

Apparently Wharton's involvement in the decolonization of Africa began with a flight to the Congo (today Zaire) in late 1961. He joined other risk-taking pilots to fly for the United Nations and probably humanitarian non-governmental agencies. In 1962 Wharton unsuccessfully attempted to set up his own airline. He purchased three DC-4s and tried to register them in Liberia. Arrested, he escaped from Liberia and fled to Europe disguised as an airline pilot. Wharton followed this pattern of buying a few aircraft and establishing new airline companies on a number of occasions, making it very difficult to unravel his past. When the Ibos of southern Nigeria declared their independence in June 1967 Wharton began supplying them by air.

LEADERSHIP:

Wharton led by example. Unlike many other arms merchants, he took significant personal risks by delivering the weapons and munitions himself.

Volunteers:

Wharton hired a few other aviators who were willing to run risks for pay.

Compensation:

Wharton told *The London Sunday Times*: "I never miss a chance to make some money and do a bit of lucrative business."[1] Reportedly, in 1966 Wharton received some $22,000 for each roundtrip flight between Portugal and Biafra. Each aircraft crew member earned about $1,000 per flight.

Opposition:

When flying contraband to Biafra, Wharton's two greatest military threats were ground fire and Nigerian, Russian-built MiGs flown by Egyptian pilots. He knew that the Egyptian pilots did not like to fly low and seldom at night. Ground fire was very difficult to avoid. As the war between Nigeria and Biafra progressed, the territory controlled by Biafra shrank, bringing Nigerian anti-aircraft guns closer to the Biafra airfields. Wharton's secretary, Gitta Harder, a former stewardess, described an attack by ground fire on a transport plane.

> "On one flight to Biafra the ground fire was heavy and I could see the tracers coming up at us. It looked just like a war film. Our most dangerous hop is from the Spanish-governed island of Santa Isabel, 150 miles off the Nigerian coast. Lagos has a large number of spies there who know exactly when our planes are taking off."[2]

Strategy:

Wharton had two opponents, one on the ground and the other in the air. On the ground there were the officials of the international aviation community who regulated the aviation flight industry, and in the air there was Nigeria, the country from which Biafra had declared its independence. Wharton confounded the international aviation community by purchasing a number of aircraft of the same model and changing their tail numbers to conform to the registration papers accepted at a given airfield. He moved planes from place to place, using the pretext that the aircraft was simply getting airborne to test its engines, thus adding to the confusion. Wharton's strategy to deal with Nigeria, whose airspace lay between Biafra and its supply sources in Europe, was to fly a circuitous route frequently in the dark and to maintain radio silence.

Operations:

Wharton's activities are very difficult to unravel. With the help of the embassy in Paris of the newly created government of Burundi, Wharton acquired a Canadair DC-4. The first verifiable arms smuggling operation by Wharton occurred in 1966 before the Ibos declared their independence. Author Peter Marson wrote:

> "[I]n the early evening of 11 October [Wharton] crashed 40 miles west of Garoua, on the bank of the Benoue River, in northern Cameroun [a few miles short of Biafra], apparently short of fuel. The aircraft's true destination was subsequently revealed to be Nigeria, and the arms on board were part of a large consignment that had been arranged between Paul Favier, arms dealer, and a group of Ibo-Nigerians in Geneva. The Ibos' struggle against the Federal Nigerians had begun."[3]

Wharton was seriously injured and spent some months in the custody of the Cameroun government. Eventually he escaped and returned to Europe. The Ibos declared their independence from Nigeria in June 1967 and founded Biafra. Once again Wharton gathered together some used cargo aircraft and began flights between Lisbon, Portugal, and Port Harcourt, Biafra. Not all arrived safely. Apparently the MiGs shot down at least one aircraft and forced down a second, a DC-7 in Lagos. Cargoes during the early operations were arms and ammunitions. The Red Cross and other relief organizations purchased space for humanitarian cargos. Wharton acquired more aircraft to meet the increasing demand for cargo space.

In January 1968 the Biafrans diverted a Nigerian aircraft to Enugu. It was transporting a large shipment of Nigerian banknotes which the Biafrans seized. Before the Nigerian government changed its currency, making that in the hands of the Biafrans worthless, Wharton's airlines flew at least three plane-loads to Switzerland to exchange it for a more useful currency.

Wharton continued losing his aircraft to a variety of circumstance. In January 1968 his only Super Constellation fitted with a wide cargo door crashed at Port Harcourt, Biafra, while carrying medical supplies for the Vatican. A month later a second Super Constellation, piloted by Wharton, was impounded at Malta for flying with false documents and without a license. Out on bail, he escaped in a small boat bound for Lisbon. Almost as fast as Wharton acquired more planes, they fell from service. Another of his Super Constellations, which had been delayed at Bissau, Portuguese Guinea, due to hydraulic problems, blew up the night of 2 June; sabotage was suspected.

Now Wharton's air fleet was temporarily down to three Super Constellations. During the night of 30 June a Super Constellation crashed during a storm while approaching a new airfield at Uli, Biafra. All on board were killed. Lost as well were 10 ½ tons of medical supplies. Wharton remained flexible and acquired more planes. Spanish authorities at Fernando Poo, an island off Biafra and a staging place for supply runs, began to question the registration of Wharton's aircraft. To solve the problem the one registration number the Spanish would accept was painted on the fuselage of whatever aircraft was flying into Fernando Poo.

Wharton's business dealings were always tenuous. Beginning in August 1968 he flew relief supplies to Biafra for a group of German churches. In September one of his Super Constellations developed motor problems and had to dump a cargo of anti-tank weapons and a large quantity of Biafran banknotes into the Atlantic Ocean before limping back to Biafra. Also, the Biafrans were suspicious that Wharton was dealing with the Nigerians. This finished his association with the Biafran government. On 12 January 1970 Biafra collapsed and Nigeria regained control of the rebellious province.

Beginning in July 1970 Wharton and his aircraft were engaged in charter flights bringing fresh fruit into Europe. In early 1971 he moved this base of operations to Miami, Florida, his charter aircraft flying to Central and South America.

IMPACT:

What sets Wharton apart from most arms dealers was that he personally delivered many of his cargos, sometimes under dangerous conditions, making him by our definition a soldier of fortune.

BIOGRAPHIES:

Bob Harnett (unk.) was an American and a competitor in the arms business. He was based out of Geneva, Switzerland.

August Martin (unk.), an American pilot who was Black, was killed along with all on board a Wharton-owned Super Constellation on 30 June 1968 while the aircraft was approaching Uli, Biafra. Martin's wife was among the casualties.

Henry Arthur "Hank" Wharton (1916 - unk) [on occasion cited as Warton] was born in Gratz, Germany (since 1945 Grodzisk, Poland) as Heinrich Wartski in 1916. He immigrated to the United States in 1937, joined the U.S. Army in 1941, and became a U.S. citizen. He fought in the Pacific theatre and worked in military intelligence. He was fluent in German and Spanish. In 1947 he earned a commercial pilot's license. Beginning in the late 1940s Wharton flew for numerous non-mainline airlines throughout Europe and to developing areas of the world, including Israel and India.

Quotations:

[1] Anthony Terry, "Arms Smuggler Keeps Biafra's Supplies Coming," 16 July 1968. *Fulton History - The Geneva Times.* Newspaper Article. 13 August 2012. http://fultonhistory.com/Newspaper%2011/Geneva%20NY20Daily%Times/Geneva%20NY%Daily%20Times%201968Jul-Aug%201968%20Grayscale/Geneva/20Daily%20Times%201968%20Jul-Aug%201968%20Grayscale%20-%200253.pdf

[2] Anthony Terry, "Arms Smuggler," cited above.

[3] Peter Marson, "Prop Personality - Hank Wharton," 2006 Airliners at Basel-Mulhouse-Freiburg, pp. 26-32, p. 28. Electronic article. 13 August 2012. http://www.bsi-mlh-planes.net/download/Hank_Wharton_Propliner_24.pdf

Sources:

R. Ernest Dupuy and Trevor N. Dupuy. *The Harper Encyclopedia of Military History.* 4th edition. New York: HarperCollins Publishers, 1993.

Anthony Mockler, *The Mercenaries.* New York: The Macmillan Company, 1969.

CRIPPLED EAGLES FIGHTING IN THE CHIMURENGA WAR FOR RHODESIA

1966-80

GOAL:

To help the White minority retain control of Rhodesia.

BACKGROUND:

Like other struggles throughout Black Africa which began during the Cold War, the fight in Rhodesia had as much to do with race, tribalism and colonialism as it did with ideology. Rhodesia was established by and named for the entrepreneur Cecil Rhodes in the 1890s. It became a self-governing British colony in 1923. Opposed to de-colonization based on the terms of majority rule, Ian Smith, the leader of the Rhodesian Front Party, a Unilateral Declaration of Independence published on 11 November 1965 from Great Britain. Initially, the White- minority government feared British intervention, which never materialized. Instead Great Britain, followed by other nations, imposed an economic sanction. Only White-controlled South Africa supported the White-minority government of Rhodesia. At the same time, the Communist bloc was seeking opportunities to spread revolution. Increasingly, it saw Black Africa as a fertile opportunity.

LEADERSHIP:

Ian Smith was in firm control of the White-minority government of Rhodesia. Mercenaries, including Americans, were fully integrated into the Rhodesian army and did not fight as a unit. The political leadership of the Blacks was splintered; tribal and ideological differences prevented unification. Joshua Nkomo led the Zimbabwe African Peoples Union (ZAPU) and Ndabaningi Sithole led the Zimbabwe African Union (ZANU).

Volunteers:

Throughout this 14-year war a steady flow of mercenaries arrived in Rhodesia to fight for the White-minority government. Journalist Xandre Anderer wrote:

> "The Rhodesians managed to recruit about 1,400 foreign nationals for their cause. Volunteers came from across the globe: Britain, Ireland, South Africa, Portugal, Hong Kong, Canada, Australia, and New Zealand.... It is believed that some three hundred Americans served in the Rhodesian Light infantry...."[1]

According to a footnote by Professor James Taulbee, "The four hundred or so Americans serving in the Rhodesian army in the late 1970's called themselves the 'Crippled Eagles,' because they felt the United States government harassed them."[2]

Compensation:

A British South African Police (colonial name held over) superintendent told Robert K. Brown, "We pay all travel expenses in advance or reimburse the volunteer once he arrives.... If he cannot find employment or desires to return home, the Rhodesian government will repatriate him at government expenses."[3] Once in country, all mercenaries were paid the same as Rhodesians serving in the military and were required to enlist in the Rhodesia army. They were subjected to Rhodesian training and discipline.

Opposition:

Approximately 3,500,000 Blacks populated Rhodesia. As throughout Black Africa, the colonial powers drew national boundaries based on their interests which frequently brought African tribes into conflict with each other. This was true in Rhodesia.

Some 275,000 Whites and Asians also populated Rhodesia. The Rhodesian army was well trained to fight bush war. Many of its members had fought for the British in counter-insurgency warfare in Malaya. The White forces were organized around the Rhodesian Security Force (RSF). Its mission was to coordinate military and paramilitary forces. Field units included the all-White Rhodesia Light Infantry

(RLI), the mixed-race Rhodesian African Rifles (RAR) and the Special Air Service's regiments (SAS).

STRATEGY:

The Black-majority fighters (called "terrs" - short for terrorists - by the White-minority government) planned to hide in remote areas of Rhodesia and strike at the White infrastructure. Initially, the only safe haven and source of weapons for the Black-majority fighters was Rhodesia's northern neighbor, Zambia. The Black-majority received its weapons from the Communist bloc. Communist China befriended the ZANU and the Soviet Union championed the ZAPU.

The strategy of the White-minority government was to prevent infiltration from Zambia and, failing this, to counter-strike Black forces with lightning speed. Since Rhodesia was facing a total embargo, it had to purchase weapons and munitions illegally through third parties.

OPERATIONS:

The Chimurenga War (named by the Black-majority to associate the conflict with anti-British uprisings of the 1890s) began on 28 April 1966 when seven Black-majority fighters were killed by the British South African Police (a colonial title retained by the Rhodesian police).

Initially, the RSF's counter-tactics were very successful. In 1968 a significant Black-majority force operating in the farming area Sipolilo was discovered by the RSF and over 100 guerrillas were killed or captured. In July the RSF intercepted three bands of Black-majority fighters, totaling 91 fighters, attempting to infiltrate from Zambia. The RSF killed or captured 80 of the Blacks.

On 15 August 1967 the fighting broadened. The ZAPU announced a military alliance with the underground South African National Congress (SAANC), native to Rhodesia's neighbor to the south. To counter this union, White South African forces deployed into Rhodesia. The Rhodesian Black-minority remained disunited.

Beginning in the 1970s the RSF created new units. It began using helicopter attack teams known as Fire Force. The RSF employed locally-configured French-built Alouette III helicopters. Typically one or two gunships would accompany transport helicopters and rapidly strike against any recently discovered enemy force. The success rate of this tactic was very high. The RSF also formed the Selous Scouts. Manned mostly by Blacks, they disguised themselves as Black-majority fighters in order to infiltrate the enemy. And the RSF formed the Grey Scouts. These were horse-borne infantry, giving added mobility in less accessible areas.

By late 1972 Black-majority fighters' attacks increased. The White-minority government reacted by moving the rural population into protected villages, similar to the American strategic hamlet strategy employed by the United States in Vietnam. This government effort, however, was overwhelmed by the rural population. Finally, on 23 March 1973 the ZAPU and the ZANU created a joint military command. The next year a liberal coup in Portugal led to the disintegration of the Portuguese colonial empire in Africa. A Black-majority movement seized power in Mozambique, which bordered Rhodesia on the east. This opened another invasion route for the Blacks.

By 1975 the White-minority was under increasing pressure and began secret talks with Black-majority factions. Initially these talks led nowhere. The following year the Black-majority fighters threatened the rail line between Rhodesia and South Africa, the White-minority's lifeline. White emigration grew, forcing the government to increase the length of military conscription from nine to 12 months.

The White-minority government decided to carry the fight into neighboring Mozambique. In August 1976 a column of four armored cars and ten trucks attacked a Black-majority camp across the border. Catching the enemy by surprise, the 85-man force inflicted 2,000 casualties, including civilians. In May 1977 a 700-man force again crossed into Mozambique, attacking terr camps. On the 28th American Captain John Murphy led a 110-man unit against camps at Jorge do Limpopo. They seized the airport at Mapai. Dakota aircraft flew in, were loaded with captured weapons and flew out. One aircraft was shot down. Murphy moved on to Mabalane, 125 miles away, and destroyed railroad bridges. These military victories turned into a political disaster. The White government in South Africa feared that these attacks into Mozambique could lead to a widening of the war and withdrew its 50 helicopter pilots who had been flying for the Rhodesians.

In spite of military successes the position of the White-minority government was becoming increasingly untenable. White emigration had increased to 2,000 persons per month, and with the exception of South Africa, no country in the world would help the White-minority Rhodesian government. On 24 April 1979 it allowed elections but excluded the Black-majority fighters. The international community refused to recognize the results. Militarily, the Black-majority fighters in neighboring Mozambique and Zambia were growing significantly stronger. Finally, all sides signed the British-negotiated Lancaster Peace Settlement. On 12 December 1979 a British governor (Great Britain had never recognized Rhodesian independence) returned to the Rhodesian capital as an interim measure. Elections 14-29 February 1980, open to all persons, turned Rhodesia into Zimbabwe under Black rule. Within a few years most of the remaining Whites emigrated.

Impact:

The two advantages possessed by Black-majority fighters - numbers and staying power - won out in the end. It is estimated that the Rhodesian army lost less than 2,000 men whereas the terrs lost 40,000 fighters. Journalist Anderer placed the number of American lives lost at seven. The White-minority government could claim that it had won every major military encounter. But this was irrelevant. Historian James C. Gordon concluded: "Most Black Rhodesians never took up arms, but neither were they strong supporters of the White government. They were caught in the middle."[4]

Biographies:

[fnu] **Bowers** served in the U.S. military in Korea. He was a pilot in Rhodesia with the rank of lieutenant.

John Coey (unk.), from Ohio, was killed in action while serving as a medic in the Rhodesian Light Infantry.

Chris Johnson (unk.) from Houston, Texas, served in the U.S. Marines and then in the French Foreign Legion for five years. He joined the Rhodesian forces.

Mike Kelso (unk.) enlisted in the U.S. Army in 1973 and served in the 82nd Airborne Division. In 1977 he joined the Rhodesian army and fought as a member of the Rhodesian Light Infantry for 15 months. During that time he made six combat jumps. Kelso observed that by 1979: "The war was lost. Everybody knew. I went home on leave and never went back."[5]

Buddy Lilley (unk.) served as a U.S. Marine and had two tours of duty in Vietnam between 1966 and 1970. He traveled to Rhodesia in September 1979 brining his personal weapons with him. At a flight stopover in Johannesburg, South Africa, a customs official asked what was in the heavy suitcase. Lilley responded, "Tools." The customs officer smiled and replied, "I understand."[6] Arriving in Rhodesia, Lilly signed up as an armed security guard for the Forest Management Service. He participated in a number of fire-fights with the terrs. He returned to the United States at about the time of the February 1980 elections.

Bruce McNair (unk.) had tried his hand at being a race car driver, deep-sea diver, and professional hunter before going to Rhodesia. He was rejected by the Rhodesian Army's Officer Candidate School due to his age. McNair joined the British South African Police (the name a holdover from colonial days). On 18 September 1973 the Land Rover was destroyed by a mine and he escaped with minor injuries.

John Murphy (unk.) was a U.S. Marine Corps veteran of Vietnam. He obtained the rank of captain while fighting in Rhodesia.

Bob Nicholson (unk.) was from Fortune, California. He served eight years in the U.S. Army, which included four years in Vietnam. He joined the Rhodesian forces in June 1975.

Michael "Reb" Pierce (unk.), a musician who worked in Hollywood, California, had no combat experience. He traveled to Rhodesia on his own initiative *cerca* 1979. Pierce served in Winkler's Armored Car Regiment and returned to the United States *cerca* 1980.

Frank A. Sweeney (unk.), from Tenafly, New Jersey, served in the Rhodesian Light Infantry and attained the rank of corporal.

Waine Walker (unk.), from Virginia, attained the rank of corporal. He commanded a Rhodesian military police unit, Umfali, at the border with Mozambique.

Jeffery Wassermann (unk.), from Houston, Texas, served in the Rhodesian Light Infantry.

Margaret Wassermann (unk.), Jeffery's wife, served in the Rhodesian Women's Army.

Michael Williams (unk.), holding the rank of major, commanded One Squadron, Grey's Scouts, a cavalry unit.

Darryl Winkler (unk.), a Vietnam War veteran, held the rank of major and commanded a Rhodesian Armored Car Regiment. He returned to the United States after the war.

QUOTATIONS:

[1] Xandre Anderer, "War Continued ... Vietnam Veterans in the Rhodesian Bush." vol. 32, no. 2 (March/April 2012) pp. 33-34, *The VVA Veteran*, p. 34.

[2] James L. Taulbee, "Myths, Mercenaries and Contemporary International Law," *California Western International Law Journal*. vol. 15 (1985) pp. 339-63, p. 342.

[3] Robert K. Brown with Vann Spencer, *I Am Soldier of Fortune*. Philadelphia: Casemate, 2013. p. 112.

[4] James C. Gordon, "The Chimurenga War: The Rhodesian Insurgency 1966-1980." No. 238 (September 2006) pp. 40-51 *Strategy & Tactics*, p. 44.

[5] Anderer, "War Continued," p. 34.

[6] Buddy Lilley [assisted by Dr. Martin Brass], "A Former Marine and Vietnam Vet Becomes a MERC." *Soldier of Fortune,* Vol. 37, No. 5 (May 2012), p.28.

Sources:

Martin Brass, SOF and Mercs Fight Terrorists in Rhodesian Bush War." *Soldier of Fortune.* Vol. 37, No. 2 (February 2012) pp. 42-50, 55.

Robin Moore, "The Soldiers of Fortune," *New York Times* (28 July 1978) p. A23.

United States. House of Representatives. Hearing before the Special Subcommittee on Investigations of the Committee on International Relations, 94th Congress, 2nd Session. *Mercenaries in Africa.* 9 August 1976.

Yuri Zhukov, "Twentieth-Century Mercenaries." *Soviet Military Review.* (May 1978) pp. 48-49.

Angola Fiasco

1976

Goal:

To save Angola from Communism.

Background:

Following World War II Africa became increasingly tumultuous. Revolutionary Che Guevara declared that Africa was "one of the most important, if not the most important, battlefields against all the forms of exploitation in the world, against imperialism, colonialism, and neocolonialism."[1] Following the United States' withdrawal from Vietnam in 1974 Cuban Premier Fidel Castro, no pawn of the Soviet Union, wanted to take the offensive against the capitalists and spawn revolution throughout the world.

    The fighting in Angola between colonial and anti-colonial forces began in 1961 and grew increasingly complex. By 1974 five armies (the Portuguese, the South African, and three disparate revolutionary factions) were fighting against each other. Fidel Castro risked sending combat troops to Angola before having a Russian endorsement. In October Cuban troops landed in significant numbers and within six months they spearheaded an offensive by the Popular Movement for the Liberation of Angola (MPLA), which pushed the opposition into the bush land.

Leadership:

Irishman Michael "Mad Mike" Hoare was the leader of the anti-Communist mercenaries fighting in Angola but for the Americans who arrived at the eleventh and a half hour this was irrelevant because the anti-Communist forces were already defeated. On the other side, the military leadership for the Communist forces was, by strength of arms, the on-scene spokesperson for Fidel Castro.

VOLUNTEERS:

Although mercenaries had been fighting in Angola since 1961, they were overwhelmingly Portuguese, French and English. The Central Intelligence Agency (CIA), which funded anti-Communist factions in Angola, was opposed to American soldiers of fortune being used.

COMPENSATION:

The American mercenaries, who were freelancers outside the control of the CIA, received promises and nothing more. They even paid their own airfare to get to Africa.

OPPOSITION:

The MPLA was the umbrella organization for the Communist forces. The Cubans were the critical military muscle. Many of the Cubans were field-tested veterans. Practically all had seen guerrilla combat in Cuba and elsewhere in Latin America.

STRATEGY:

By the time the Americans arrived, all that remained for the Communists forces was to push the anti-Communist forces out of their last stronghold, Sao Salvador. The mercenaries' tactics, as described by author Anthony Mockler, no longer worked against the more seasoned Cuban troops, "By now the enemy had come to anticipate the white mercenaries' suicidal frontal assault tactics ...."[2]

OPERATIONS:

The American mercenaries spent less than one week in the field. Most of them had flown into "Leo" (Leopoldville and now Kinshasha), Zaire (formerly the Congo) on 7 February 1976 and traveled by land to the northeastern Angolan town of Sao Salvador, which was threatened by the MPLA. After a brief fire-fight outside Sao Salvador, among 13 mercenaries captured were three of the Americans and other Americans were killed.

IMPACT:

The American mercenaries were on a fool's mission. They did not grasp the political or military circumstances. They entered a fight that was already lost. At the insistence of the Cubans, the 13 captured mercenaries were tried in Luanda, Angola, during June 1976 by the victorious Popular Movement for the Liberation of Angola (MPLA). The *Procurador Popular*, charged:

> "You came to a country that was not your own from a land far away, you came voluntarily, you came with guns. What are guns for? For killing. You were paid for killing. You are a hired killer, a paid assassin, guilty of aggression and invasion, guilty of crimes against peace, guilty of crimes of mercenarism."[3]

The trial began on Friday, the 13th of June, for 13 defendants (three of whom were Americans) and ended on 28 June. And they paid the price: three were sentenced to 16 years in prison (including American Acker); three to 24 years in prison; three to 30 years in prison (including American Grillo); and four to death by firing squad (including American Gearhart).

Biographies:

Gary Martin Acker (ca. 1955 - unk.). served in the U.S. Marine Corps between 1972 and 1975 and was trained in the use of machine guns. He along with five other American mercenaries flew into Zaire (formerly the Congo) on 7 February 1976. Captured, he was sentenced to 16 years in prison. He was released in 1982 during a prisoner exchange.

George Bacon III (unk. - 1976) graduated from Georgetown University and served in the Green Berets during the Vietnam War. In the early 1970s he traveled to Zambia and unsuccessfully tried to join the anti-Communist Union for the Total Independence of Angola (UNITA). One author speculated that his effort was probably blocked by the CIA. Bacon, along with five other American mercenaries flew into Zaire (formerly the Congo) on 7 February 1976. He was killed that same month outside Sao Salvador.

David Bufkin (unk.), a crop-duster from Kerman, California, became a self-appointed mercenary recruiter. He spent one day in Africa and then returned to the United States to recruit more mercenaries. Returning to Africa in February 1976, Bufkin was forced by some of his recruits to go to Sao Salvador where he was charged with misappropriating FNLA (National Front for the Liberation of Angola) property. He was found guilty and sentenced to fight at the front without pay.

Daniel Francis Gearhart (*ca.* 1942 - 76), in debt due to medical bills, ran the following ad in the winter 1975 issue of *Soldier of Fortune* magazine: "Wanted. Employment as mercenary on full-time or job contract basis. Preferably in South or Central America but anywhere in the world, if you pay transportation. Contact Gearhart, Box 1457, Wheaton, MD, 20902."[4] Gearhart flew into Zaire on 7 February 1976. He was arrested a few days after arriving in Angola. He did not participate in any of the fighting. Gearhart was sentenced to death by firing squad. He was executed on 10 July 1976.

Gustavo Marcelo Grillo (ca. 1950 - unk.), a U.S. permanent resident national, was sentenced to 30 years in prison. He was released in 1982 during a prisoner exchange.

Tom Oates [also cited as Tom Otis] (unk.), a former sergeant of the Los Angeles Police Department, was retired on a disability.

Eugene Scaley [also cited as Eugene Scalon] (unk.) upon arriving in "Leo" on 7 February 1976, along with five other American mercenaries, took refuge in the U.S. embassy in Zaire and requested to be repatriated.

Lobo do Sol (unk.) was employed by David Bufkin and ran the mercenary recruiting effort. Do Sol, along with five other American mercenaries flew into "Leo" on 7 February 1976.

Quotations:

[1] Robert L. Scheina, *Latin America's Wars*. 2 vols. Washington, D.C.: Brassey's, Inc., 2003. p. 327.
[2] Anthony Mockler, *The New Mercenaries*. New York: Paragon House Publishers, 1987. p. 210.
[3] Mockler, *The New Mercenaries*. p. 210.
[4] Mocklet, *The New Mercenaries*. p. 180.

Sources:

Gary Acker, "Angolan Reflections: A Mercenary's Road to Hell." *Soldier of Fortune* (February 1986) 100-05, 130-33.

James C. Gordon, "A War that Never Ends: The Conflict in Angola." *Strategy & Tactics*. (May/June 2005) no. 228. pp. 20-30.

United States. House of Representatives. Hearing before the Special Subcommittee on Investigations of the Committee on International Relations, 94th Congress, 2nd Session. *Mercenaries in Africa*. 9 August 1976.

Odyssey of Michael Echanis

1977-78

Goal:

To protect the Somoza regime in Nicaragua.

Background:

Anastasio "Tacho" Somoza and his son Anastasio "Tachito" Somoza had long ruled Nicaragua with iron fists. U.S. President Franklin Roosevelt reportedly had questioned Secretary of State Cordell Hull, "Isn't that man [Tacho] supposed to be a son-of-a-bitch?" The secretary reported replied, "He sure is but he is our son-of-a-bitch."[1]

Leadership:

The Somozas had absolute control of the army and the police. The leadership of the Sandinista rebels was increasingly influenced by Fidel Castro in Cuba.

Volunteers:

Mike Echanis, aided by an American friend, Charles Sanders, trained the Somoza forces. As a consequence, they were reasonably competent when compared to other Central American militaries.

COMPENSATION:

In all probability, Echanis was paid well by the Somoza regime. Also, he received a disability pension from the U.S. Government.

OPPOSITION:

The Sandinista National Liberation Front (named for the guerrilla leader who had fought the U.S. Marines when they occupied the country in 1912 to 1933) was initially disorganized due to the disputes among the leaders of various factions. Through the intervention of Fidel Castro, these disputes were resolved (sometimes by assassination). Increasingly Castro provided training and arms.

STRATEGY:

The Somozas used the full power of their military forces, frequently employing sheer terror, to combat the rebels.

OPERATIONS:

In the fall of 1978 an uprising took place. Businessmen opposed to Somoza staged a general strike and Sandinista rebels attacked police and military posts in the capital, Managua, and several cities, occupying parts of some cities. The National Guard went into action and spearheading its counter offensive was *Los comandos*. Echanis did not live to see the (temporary) victory of the government forces.

The Sandinistas finally succeeded in toppling Tachito Somoza when international circumstance allowed them to change strategy. Costa Rica, whose leadership detested Somoza, virtually ceded to the Sandinistas a strip of land along the border from Nicaragua. The rebels used this as a base to launch a conventional land offensive against Somoza's troops. As the rebels advanced, Somoza fled in July 1979. He was later assassinated while in exile in Paraguay.

IMPACT:

More was at stake in the struggle in Nicaragua than the Somoza dynasty. With the overthrow of that government and assumption of power by the Sandinistas, Communist Cuba got its first ally in Latin America.

Like many post-World War II American soldiers of fortune, Mike Echanis (1950-78) served in Vietnam. He was severely wounded and spent eight months in a hospital recovering. Echanis became interested in the martial arts. He wrote three books on knife and stick fighting. In the late 1970s Echanis trained the Nicaraguan presidential bodyguards and an elite unit of the Nicaraguan army. He was killed in a small plane crash, the cause unknown.

Authors' Collection, Jon Peterson artist

Biographies:

Michael D. "Mike" Echanis (1950-78) loved excitement. As a teenager he drove cars wildly, crashing several. He made pipe bombs and in one case blew up someone's VW. The United States was in a war in Vietnam. Echanis wanted to participate. He joined the Army. He did his basic training, then went to airborne school, and then joined the Special Forces. He shipped out with a Ranger unit. His stay in Vietnam, however, would be short. His until was ambushed and Echanis was hit four times. He spent the next eight months in a San Francisco hospital. He was awarded the Bronze Star.

Discharged from the Army, Echanis was crippled and underweight. He took steroids and began a hard program of physical rehabilitation. He also honed his mental facilities and power of concentration. As a youth he had been interested in the martial arts. Once he was fit again, he began training in the arts, eventually becoming proficient. He wrote three books on knife and stick fighting. He developed a system of combat which the professional magazine *Black Belt* described as "the most effective ... in the modern world."

Echanis went to work for the Department of defense, training Army and Navy special forces. Echanis came to the attention of Major Anastasio "Tachito" Somoza, son of Nicaragua's president who was taking courses at the center of Army special forces, Fort Bragg, and would soon be president himself. Somoza convinced Echanis to come to Nicaragua and train its forces.

Echanis trained the civilian presidential bodyguards. He also organized and trained (1977) a special unit of the National Guard, the country's army. The training was rugged and ranged from martial arts to dealing with a sniper. Echanis was the *de facto* commander of the unit, which was known as *Los Commandos*. He was killed while riding in a small plane which plunged to earth. There were reports that there had been an explosion on the craft. Had the Sandinistas planted a bomb on board?

Quotations:

[1] Robert L. Scheina, *Latin America's Wars*. 2 vols. Washington, D.C.: Brassey's Inc., 2003. 2: 184.

Sources:

Jay Mallin and Robert K. Brown, *Merc: American Soldiers of Fortune.* New York: Macmillan Publishing Company, 1979.

DOOMED EXPEDITION TO DOMINICA

1981

GOAL:

To overthrow the government of Mary Eugenia Charles.

BACKGROUND:

Dominica became independent from British colonial rule in 1978. For its first year it was governed by the corrupt regime of Patrick R. John. In July 1980 Mary Eugenia Charles was elected the Caribbean's first female prime minister.

LEADERSHIP:

Patrick R. John led the conspiracy and Michael Perdue was in charge of the would-be mercenaries.

VOLUNTEERS:

The invasion force was composed of eight Americans and two Canadians, six of whom were members of the Ku Klux Klan and neo-Nazi organizations. They were armed with Israeli-manufactured Uzi machine guns, plastic explosives and dynamite.

COMPENSATION:

Each of the would-be mercenaries was promised $3,000 and a percentage of the criminal enterprises Perdue planned to set up.

Opposition:

Dominica, a tiny, impoverished Caribbean island with a population of some 70,000 inhabitants, was protected by a small police force armed with antiquated weapons. Literally, it was a "banana republic" with bananas making up 70 per cent of its exports.

Strategy:

The conspirators planned to reinstate by force the former prime minister, Patrick R. John. He was in secret contact with two officials of Dominica's 100-man police force. The main strike was to be against the capital's police station

Operations:

The operation was still-born. One of the would-be mercenaries, while intoxicated, revealed the details of the attempted coup to a Canadian reporter. The would-be mercenaries were arrested on 27 April 1981 north of New Orleans, Louisiana, while they were on their way to board a chartered boat.

Impact:

Three of the would-be mercenaries were tried for violating the U.S. Neutrality Act and for violating firearms statutes. Stephen Black and Joe Hawkins were found guilty. Both were long-time members of the Ku Klux Klan. The others agreed to plea-bargains.

Mocking the scheme, federal authorities referred to the operation as the "Bayou of Pigs." Prime Minster Charles, astonished by the plot - particularly its finances - said, "I don't know if anyone in Dominica has that much money .... If there is someone who wants to waste money out there, I wish he'd give it to me so I could fix the roads."[1]

Biographies:

Christopher Anderson (*ca*. 1940 - unk.) was from Oklahoma City, Oklahoma.

Stephen D. Black (unk.) was from Birmingham, Alabama, and Grand Wizard of the Knights of the Ku Klux Klan.

Joe D. Hawkins (*ca*. 1944 - unk.) was from Smith County, Mississippi.
George T. Malvaney (*ca*. 1959 - unk.) was from Jackson. Mississippi.
Michael S. Norris (*ca*. 1960 - unk.) was from Tuscaloosa, Alabama.
Robert W. Prichard (*ca*. 1951 - unk.) was from Raleigh, North Carolina.
Michael E. Perdue (*ca*. 1949 - unk.) was from Houston, Texas.
William B. Waldrop, Jr. (*ca*. 1948 - unk.) was from Braxton, Mississippi.

QUOTATIONS:

[1] "Bayou of Pigs," *Time* vol. 117, issue 19 (11 May 1981) p. 22.

SOURCES:

Facts on File Yearbook 1981. New York: Facts on File, Inc., 1981.

"Klansmen Are Among 10 Indicted In Plot on Caribbean Island Nation," *New York Times* (8 May 1981) p. A16.

Andrew H. Malcolm, "Toronto Paper Details Intrigue to Invade Dominica: Defends Not Alerting Police," *New York Times* (17 May 1981) p. 4.

James Larry Taulbee, "Raiders of the Leased Art: A Note on Mercenary Coup Strike Force," *Conflict*, vol. 7, no. 2 (1987), pp. 197-210.

DOOMED EXPEDITION TO HAITI

1982

GOAL:

To overthrow the government of Jean-Claude (Baby Doc) Duvalier. It was the latest of efforts to out the Duvaliers through expeditions launched from Miami, Florida.

BACKGROUND:

The Duvalier family had ruled Haiti since 1957, first through the father, Francois (Papa Doc), and the son, Jean-Claude (Baby Doc). In 1963 the Magloire family joined a failed coup attempt and ultimately fled the country. Four years later the Magloire family unsuccessfully endeavored to launch an invasion of Haiti from a Bahamas island. For almost 20 years the family plotted its return from exile.

LEADERSHIP:

Haitian exile Roland Magloire, leader of the Council for the National Liberation of Haiti (CNLH), was the instigator of the expedition. He was the nephew of former Haitian President Paul Magloire, who had ruled Haiti between 1950 and 1956. Military command of the plot was entrusted to Benjamin Weissberg.

VOLUNTEERS:

Ads were run in the *Miami Herald* seeking individuals with military experience to help a small multinational corporation with security. Out of the almost 300 responses, 16 men were chosen. In addition to the 16 would-be mercenaries (10 Americans, five Haitians, and one Canadian), some 250 Haitian "boat people" were recruited from the slums of Belle Glade and were trained in the Everglades. This training was taking place in the same camps used to train Cuban exiles.

COMPENSATION:

Magloire raised some $75,000 from the Haitian immigrant communities in Chicago and Miami.

OPPOSITION:

The Haitian army was composed of a few thousand men. The principal opposition to a mercenary-led uprising would be the Leopards. These were some 600 men trained in counter-insurgency operations by a Miami-based private company.

STRATEGY:

First, some 50 exiles were to infiltrate Haiti. They would prepare for the invasion by blowing up power lines and disrupting communications. This group would then broadcast a coded message that signaled for the invasion. The mercenaries would land a short distance north of Port-au-Prince. One of the would-be mercenaries said: "We weren't going to storm the presidential palace .... We weren't that stupid. But you don't have to take the capital to take the country. We were just going to take a little and let it have a snow ball effect."[1]

OPERATIONS:

On 13 March two chartered cabin-cruisers, the *Sassoon* and the *Wanderlust III*, sailed from Miami, Florida, for Cay Sal, a tiny island about 30 miles off the coast of Cuba. The boats were packed with the essentials - 61 assault rifles, shotguns, pistols, 17 CS gas grenades, 16,000 rounds of ammunition, frozen steaks and Jack Daniels whiskey. The boats were boarded by the U.S. Coast Guard 10 miles off the Florida coast and their occupants arrested for violating U.S. neutrality laws.

IMPACT:

Military analyst Gwynne Dyer concluded: "There are well over a quarter million Haitians in exile, but they do not represent a mortal danger to the regime in themselves ... the relatively few opponents of the government acting from exile are decisively hampered in trying to found an anti-Duvalier guerrilla movement by the gulf that separates them - mostly middle class by Haitian standards, and with a large mulatto contingent - from the world of the Haitian peasant."[2]

One American law enforcer said, "Baby Doc's Leopard Battalion would have strung them [the 16 would-be mercenaries] up by their toes."[3]

Biographies:

Robert Martin (*ca.* 1951 - unk) served in the U.S. Marine Corps.

Benjamin Weissberg (unk.) served three tours of duty in Vietnam rising to the rank of captain in the U.S. Special Forces.

Quotations:

[1] Art Harris, "The Fizzle: Alleged Plot Against Haiti Ended in Choppy Seas," *The Washington Post* (23 March 1982) p. A9.

[2] John Keegan, *World Armies*. New York: Facts on File, 1979, p. 286.

[3] Harris, "The Fizzle," *The Washington Post* (23 March 1982) p. A9.

Sources:

Facts on File Yearbook 1982. New York: Facts on File, Inc., 1982.

Doomed Expedition to Ghana

1986

GOAL:

To overthrow the dictator of Ghana, Chairman (later President) Jerry John Rawlings (1947-).

BACKGROUND:

Rawlings was turning Ghana into a Marxist state. He was particularly friendly with Cuba's Communist leader, Fidel Castro.

LEADERSHIP:

The mastermind and chief funder of the expedition was Godfrey Osei, a former businessman in Ghana whose properties had been seized by Rawlings. Commander of the expedition was American John Early.

VOLUNTEERS:

Eight Americans, all former military men, embarked on an expedition to oust Rawlings from power. At their later trial, they claimed to have been recruited by an American, Ted Bishop, and a Ghanajan, Godfrey Osei.

COMPENSATION:

Mercenary leader John Early was paid $12,000. The men received $5,000 to $7,000 each.

Opposition:

The 20,000-man-strong paramilitary forces - the General Police, the People's Militia and the National Civil Defense Force - provided the security for the Rawlings' regime.

Strategy:

To stage a seaborne assault on Ghana's capital, Accra. The operation envisioned sailing to the Ivory Coast, where 100 exiled Ghanaian soldiers were believed waiting. They would be armed by the expeditionaries and then the two groups would attack Accra. The assault would begin at 0200 on a Sunday, 23 March. Ghanaian government troops were paid on Saturday; it was figured they would be drunk that night. There was, however, no communications with the soldiers in the Ivory Coast. Nor did the mercenaries have any intelligence from Accra.

Operations:

The operation began with discussions between Godfrey Osei, the former businessman, and Pierre Duvall, a 17-year veteran of the French Foreign Legion. Osei wanted to overthrow the government of former flight lieutenant and now dictator Jerry Rawlings. Osei and Duvall planned to create a mercenary force to oust Rawlings. Osei claimed to have "$175,000 now and I can get more. A lot if we need it."[1] He paid Duvall $5,000 immediately. Among the sources of Osei's funds: the Chinese Mafia in New York who wanted to establish a banking base in Ghana.

At some point Osei and Duvall broke. Leadership of the mercenary group fell to John Early. Seven Americans with military backgrounds were recruited. On 12 February 1986 Early and the seven flew from Miami, Florida, to Buenos Aires, Argentina. They were met at the BA airport by an Argentine official and an American named Ted Bishop, an arms dealer who had become attached to the group (possibly working for the CIA). Bishop and the Argentine intelligence officer, Luis Kabut, would provide the necessary boat, weapons and equipment.

Apart from the steaks and night life for which Buenos Aires is famous, things did not go well for the mercenaries during their two-week stay in the city. They were shown the vessel they were supposed to use. It was the rusting hulk of a World War II Liberty ship, its bridge controls useless.

The mercenaries were provided with arms, including 150 Argentine-manufactured FN assault rifles, four FN MAG 58 general purpose machine guns and various hand guns. Critical elements were missing, however, such as explosives, armor-piercing rockets and tracers (and this was to be a night operation!). Equipment was faulty (ammunition pouches didn't fit on belts) and medical supplies were inadequate (Band-Ads, aged sulfa powder and hydrogen peroxide). The mercenaries found that their Argentine companion, together with Bishop, were helping themselves to funds when they made purchases.

Early had spoken of a broad plan of action but did not inform the individual mercenaries what they were supposed to do. When asked a question, he would tap a shoulder as if it displayed rank insignia and say, "Let's pretend I'm in charge."[2]

Finally a boat was produced: the 120-foot ocean-going tug *Nobistor*. An Argentine captain and crew were signed up. The group sailed around 1 March 1986. They did not know that the Ghanaian regime had learned an attack might be forthcoming. As the *Nobistor* approached land, the captain, Eduardo Gilardoni, demanded payment of a sum of money. Early checked by radio and was told the money would be paid. According to a journalist who later would interview the mercenaries, Early did not inform the captain. The expedition ended. Did Early fear they were moving into a trap? Or was Early acting on secret orders from the United States to abort the expedition? Or was he planning to pocket the money?

The *Nobistor* turned around and again sailed across the Atlantic to Rio de Janeiro, Brazil, reaching there 10 March. Due to a harbor pilots' strike, the vessel could not be docked. The mercenaries contacted the U.S. consulate. That same day, 14 March, a patrol boat came alongside and 15 Federal policemen brandishing shotguns and automatic weapons boarded the *Nobistor*. The mercenaries were arrested. One of them later would describe what happened: "They [the police] went bananas. It was like they found a bunch of toys. Pistols disappeared into pockets, and they started loading the weapons into private cars."[3]

A hellish period began for the mercenaries. They spent about 45 days in a filthy, mosquito-plagued prison and then they were told they were going to be brought to trial. They were taken to a brief court hearing and then two weeks later to another. They were found guilty of contrabanding. In July Early and the ship's captain were given five-year sentences. The other men, four years each. They were taken to another prison, *Agua Santa* (Holy Water). Food was noxious, medical attention non-existent. In August the men were transferred to still another prison, *Helio Gomez*. Life was just as terrible as in their pervious prisons.

In October a court of appeals overturned the men's convictions. They were released, only to be seized by the Federal police again, and again imprisoned. Argentina had requested their extradition and the Brazilian Supreme Court was considering this. In November the mercenaries were flown to Brasilia, the capital, and placed in a more civilized prison. The Supreme Court ruled in favor of the Argentine request.

The men planned an escape. They had been able to receive some packages from the United States, including from editor Robert K. Brown and the magazine *Soldier of Fortune's* staff. They now received a most welcome package. The wife of one of the mercenaries sent them four hacksaw blades hidden in a box of powdered milk. With this they cut a hole in the ceiling of the shower room. Through this, one night four of the men were able to escape.

Three of them, in a circuitous route through Bolivia (where they received funds from *Soldier of Fortune's* Brown) made it to the United States. The four man used a different route. The four mercenaries who had remained behind, including Early, were extradited to Argentina. There they put up between $7,000 and $9,000 each for bail and were permitted to leave the country. The long misadventure was over.

Impact:

The expedition was a disaster and had no impact whatsoever. It was a tale of stealing, treachery, incompetent leadership, a rotting boat, inadequate weapons, a shady American, the Chinese Mafia, an Argentine intelligence officer on the take and inadequate operational plans. The boat's captain, Argentine Eduardo Gilardoni, and expedition leader John Early were sentenced to five years in prison. The seven other Americans, including the four who had escaped, were sentenced to four years in prison.

Biographies:

John Dee Early (unk.) served in the U.S. Army and spent almost five years in Vietnam in the early '70s in the Special Forces. He rose to the rank of captain. Once out of the U.S. service, he worked as a teaching assistant at an Illinois college and then was recruited by a representative of the Rhodesian government. Rhodesian was embroiled at the time in a racial civil war between the White government and Black revolutionaries. Early went to Africa in May 1976 and enlisted in the Rhodesian air force and then the Selous Scouts. He is believed to have deserted from the Scouts upon facing court-martial for having shot up a pub.

Quotations:

[1] Pierre Duval, "Soldiers of Misfortune," pp. 34-39, 99-100. Boulder, CO: *Soldier of Fortune* (April 1987) p. 35.

[2] John Coleman, "Soldiers of Misfortune - Part 2," pp. 62-67, 97-98 Boulder, CO: *Soldier of Fortune* (May 1987) p. 66.

[3] John Coleman, "Soldiers of Misfortune - Part 3," pp. 54-61 Boulder, CO: *Soldier of Fortune* (June 1987) p. 55.

Sources:

John Cronin, "Soldiers of Fortune - Mercenary Wars," http://mercenary-wars.net/biography/john-early.html

Facts on File Yearbook 1986. New York: Facts on File, Inc., 1986.

Ghana A Country Study. 3rd edition. Washington, CD: Federal Research Division, 1995.

Doomed Expedition to Suriname

1986

Goal:

To overthrow the government of Lieutenant Colonel Desi Bouterse.

Background:

Dutch Guyana, home to numerous ethnic groups, was granted independence by the Netherlands in 1975 and assumed the name Suriname. In 1980 its civilian government was displaced by a military coup which declared a socialist republic. Following the coup two factions fought to control the entire nation, which is about the size of the state of Georgia. Creole (Afro-European) Desi Bouterse controlled the coastal area and about 80 per cent of the population. Roddy Brunswijk, a Bush Negro (descendant of escaped slaves), controlled the interior and about 20 per cent of the population. Brunswijk's mixed-blood supporters were known as Amerindians.

Leadership:

Tommy Denley, a former customs agent, led the aborted attempt. Apparently he had ties to the Amerindian rebels.

Volunteers:

The invasion force was made up of 13 Americans. Apparently their most lethal weapons were M-16 rifles.

COMPENSATION:

Evidently Denley's payoff was to take control of the banking system in Suriname. Reportedly, the American mercenaries were promised one million dollars each if they successfully overthrew the Bouterse government.

OPPOSITION:

The government's armed forces numbered about 1,000 men.

STRATEGY:

Denley planned to pose as a banker who was willing to lend money to the Bouterse regime. Bouterse and his ministers were to be taken hostage.

OPERATIONS:

On 28 July 1986, 13 Americans were arrested in Louisiana on their way to a small airport about 50 miles northwest of New Orleans and a 14th American near Lafayette, Louisiana.

IMPACT:

At his trial, Denley implicated the Dutch government and the Dutch company, the Ansus Foundation of Amsterdam. Nine of the 13 would-be mercenaries pleaded guilty to misdemeanor weapons' charges in exchange for their cooperation. They received suspended sentences. Three of the conspirators received six to 18 months in prison. On 5 November Denley was sentenced to 30 months in prison.

In the United States the men were charged with violating the U.S. Neutrality Act. The regional commissioner in New Orleans for U.S. Customs, J. Robert Grimes, stated, "We may have saved their [the American mercenaries] lives."[1]

BIOGRAPHIES:

Tommy Denley (unk.) was originally from Grenada.

QUOTATIONS:

[1] Philip Shenon, "U.S. Seizes 13 in Louisiana in Plot to invade Suriname," *New York Times* (29 Jul 1986) p. A3.

SOURCES:

Facts on File Yearbook 1986. New York: Facts on File, Inc., 1986.
John Keegan, *World Armies*. New York: Facts on File, 1979.

AMERICAN SONS OF KOSOVO

1996-99

GOAL:

To liberate Kosovo from Yugoslavia.

BACKGROUND:

In the 1990s, Kosovo, the southern province of Yugoslavia, was populated by 90% ethnic Albanians and 10% ethnic Serbs. The two ethnic groups had been on opposite sides during four wars in the 20th Century. Exacerbating the tensions was religion - the ethnic Albanians were mostly Muslims and the Serbs mostly Christians. As in many places in the world, both saw themselves as minorities. The Serbs living in Kosovo were a minority to the ethnic Albanians and the ethnic Albanians living within Yugoslavia were a minority to the Serbs.

In 1989 Slobodan Milosevic, an ethnic Serb who controlled Yugoslavia, revoked Kosovo's autonomy. In April 1992 he initiated military interventions to unite ethnic Serbs in areas neighboring Yugoslavia in order to create a "Greater Serbia." In Kosovo he enforced his decisions by placing ethnic Serbs in positions of authority. Milosevic had a reputation for cruelty. As the leader of Yugoslavia he had recently fought unsuccessful bloody wars against the breakaway provinces of Bosnia, Croatia and Slovenia.

Following the Dayton Accord in 1995, which ended the fighting between Serbia and Bosnia, the three-dozen-man Kosovo Liberation Army (KLA) was created by a few university students and farmers. On 6 February 1996 the KLA fired grenades into six Serb housing settlements that were scattered throughout Kosovo; there were no injuries. Throughout the spring and summer the KLA attacked police patrols and stations everywhere in Kosovo. The Milosevic regime responded with mass arrests, beatings and torture.

In November 1996 Milosevic's Socialist Party suffered significant political defeats in Serbian municipal elections. Milosevic was forced to recall many of the security forces from Kosovo to deal with street protests. On 16 January 1997 a car bomb in Prishtima, Kosovo, seriously wounded the Serb rector of the local university. Milosevic ordered the security forces back into Kosovo with instructions to eliminate the ethnic Albanian terrorists by any means necessary, including "ethnic cleansing" (the extermination of anyone who was not an ethnic Serb).

Leadership:

Numerous factions vied for control of the Kosovo insurgency. Among these were the followers of pacifist Ibrahim Rugova; the leaders of the Marxist Popular Movement for the Liberation of Kosovo (LPK) which was based in Switzerland; and the Brooklyn, New York, owner of Triangle General Contractors, Florin Krasniqi. It was Krasniqi's efforts that led to the creation of the Atlantic Brigade.

Volunteers:

Journalist Stacy Sullivan has written, "Florin [Krasniqi] would recruit hundreds of young Americans of Albanian heritage to fight in the [KLA] guerrilla forces." These Americans formed what would become known as the Atlantic Brigade of America. Sullivan continued, "Some were born in the United States and did not even speak Albanian. Others were immigrants who had come in the early 1990s when they received draft papers to fight with the Yugoslav army against Bosnia and Croatia.... Most of the volunteers didn't have any military experience at all."[1]

Florin Krasniqi (ca.1979 - present) organized the American Kosovo community in the struggle of Kosovo for independence from Serbia. WSith the issue falling between the end of the Cold War and the beginning of the War on Terrorism, Krasniqi clandestinely acquired weapons and recruited volunteers for the cause. America had in the past been the base of operations for those wanting to free their former homelands from outside rule.

Authors' Collection, Phyllis Saroff artist

Compensation:

New York City-based 100,000 ethnic Albanians (mostly from Kosovo) were the source of most of the funds, equipment, and arms sent to the KLA. Apparently, much of the money was filtered through the Homeland Calling Fund, a charitable organization. Reportedly $30,000,000 was raised. The individual members of the Atlantic Brigade received very little.

Opposition:

The Yugoslavian armed forces were overwhelmingly superior to the few thousand Kosovo fighters. The army numbered more than 150,000 men. In addition Yugoslavia possessed 500,000 reservists and a large force of security police. The military were equipped with 450 combat aircraft and 200 helicopters. The down sides for Yugoslavia were three: first, it had problems with all its neighbors; second, it had serious internal security issues; and third, initially the Kosovo fighters employed guerrilla tactics against the Yugoslavian military; its heavy military equipment had little utility.

Strategy:

The Kosovo Liberation Army (KLA) believed that success was dependent upon keeping its membership secret, employing guerrilla tactics, courting popular support, finding safe havens, and developing outside sources for finances and weapons. The preferred targets were police patrols and stations. Initially, the favored weapon for ambush was the AK-47 assault rifle. The preferred locations for attacks were railroad crossings and bridges; both required the police to slow down and afforded little cover. As the fighting progressed, high-power sniper rifles became popular on both sides. Krasniqi observed: "If you can kill an enemy from 2.2 or 2.5 kilometers away that means your enemy is terrified. They cannot sleep, they cannot get their heads out of the tanks."[2]

With the collapse of the economy in neighboring Albania in January 1997 weapons flooded the region's black market. Florin Krasniqi stated: "Kalashnikovs were going for ten dollars each. The villagers were giving us ammunition for free."[3]

Operations:

On 14 March 1999 NATO planes began a bombing campaign against Yugoslavia to force it to stop "ethnic cleansing" and to withdraw from Kosovo. Many believed that this would lead to a rapid collapse of the Yugoslavian war effort. But the bombing dragged on for days, then weeks, and then months.

On 17 April 1999 the 200-person Atlantic Brigade of America departed from the New York area on board Miami Air for Albania. The airline had been told that it was transporting aid workers. Two previous chartered flights had been cancelled when those airlines learned that they were transporting future fighters. On landing in Albania Florin Krasniqi smiled and told the pilots, "Congratulations, you've just transported the first American contingent of fighters for the Kosovo Liberation Army."[4]

The KLA propaganda machine billed the Atlantic Brigade as a crack unit which had been trained by the U.S. government. This was to boost the morale of local fighters. The brigade was moved by bus to the port city of Durres where it received the full attention of the world press. The soldiers sporting their new uniforms, it was easy to sell the brigade as an elite unit when it was compared to the soldiers, friend and foe alike, wearing battle-worn fatigues.

On 20 April the Atlantic Brigade took an oath of alliance to the KLA; those who were U.S. citizens probably did not realize that taking an oath to a foreign country was prohibited by U.S. law. The brigade was clandestinely moved to a training camp in Burrel. This was a dismal place - long abandoned by the Albania army. It was overflowing with trash and garbage and had been stripped of all plumbing and cooking facilities.

NATO's war against Milosevic was not going well. On 23 April NATO bombers hit Serbian state television, killing 10 people, mostly technicians. Next, NATO bombed a refugee column mistaking it for a military unit. NATO politicians began vetoing targets their militaries wanted to bomb. The Kosovo-ethnic Albanian fighters were running out of ammunition while the Atlantic Brigade and other would-be-fighters were restrained in Burrel, Albania.

The Atlantic Brigade was joined by 800 Kosovo Albanian émigrés. Boot camp drudgery dragged on and on; food was scarce; no weapons were provided; and daily the soldiers in the camp learned of new atrocities being committed by the Milosevic regime. On 26 April one of the Americans refused to take part in the calisthenics and other brigade members joined the protest. The camp guards fired their weapons in the air and Gani Shehu, the brigade commander, gave the brigade members a choice - train and wait for weapons or leave. Some 20 Americans chose to leave. The next day their names were read before the assembled brigade and they were declared cowards.

By 27 April the number in the camp had grown to 3,000 volunteers with more expected. Guards surrounded the camp to keep the volunteers in and refugees and press out. The conditions in the camp had not improved - there was little food and no plumbing. Finally on the 29th AK-47s and assorted support weapons were given to the volunteers for training.

On 2 May the Atlantic Brigade rioted. A member of the brigade had been beaten by the guards for having sneaked out of camp. A hundred members stormed the military police post. The police fired their AK-47s, killing a Macedonian recruit. The volunteers broke into the arsenal, armed themselves and endeavored to storm the police station.

The fighting lasted for several hours. Another volunteer was killed and three were seriously wounded. The next day a few hundred volunteers deserted, including some Americans.

Word of the conditions in the camp spread back to the United States. Those at home who had contributed to the KLA were outraged. They were equally frustrated that NATO's bombing campaign had been ineffective. Out of desperation, Florin Krasniqi concocted a scheme to get additional weapons fast. He purchased $2,000,000 worth of weapons on credit from arms dealers in Montana, Nevada and Michigan. Krasniqi and fellow expatriates drove four U-Haul trucks filled with guns non-stop across the United States. In spite of a driving accident at a motel in New Jersey, the scheme went undetected by U.S. authorities. Without the knowledge of any charity organization, the weapons were concealed in a humanitarian shipment and flown into Albania on 11 May.

Finally in mid-May the Atlantic Brigade and other volunteers left Burrel and climbed the south slope to the summit of Mount Pastrik. The peaks delineated the border between Kosovo and Albania. The brigade was in the thick of intense fighting with the Serbs who held the north slope. Both sides sustained significant causalities. Whoever controlled the mount controlled the southern entrance into Kosovo. As the fighting continued, finally the NATO air campaign had the desired effect and on 9 June Milosevic capitulated.

Impact:

Florin Krasniqi observed, "It is a thin line between a thug and a freedom fighter."[5] A peace agreement specified that Kosovo would remain part of Yugoslavia until its status was determined in the future. The Serb forces had to withdraw from Kosovo; NATO was permitted to keep 50,000 peacekeepers in Kosovo; and the KLA would disarm and disband. Since June 1999 Kosovo has been governed by the United Nation's Interim Administration Mission in Kosovo (UNMIK). Its authority is based on UN Security Council Resolution 1244.

Author Stacy Sullivan observed: "But in truth it didn't matter what Florin [Krasniqi] or the rest of the KLA thought. The rebels had not won the war. NATO had."[6]

Inside Kosovo some 10,000 ethnic Albanians were killed and approximately 1,000,000 were driven away. Some 150,000 ethnic Serbs fled Kosovo and about 50,000 remained. The destruction of the region's infrastructure was massive.

Biographies:

Agron Bytyqi (unk.-1999) was a construction worker from Hampton Bay, Long Island. He and his two brothers Mehmet and Ylli joined the Atlantic Brigade. They participated in the battle for Mount Pastrik. In July, following the fighting, the three brothers were arrested while traveling through Yugoslavia and a year later their bodies were found in a mass grave in the Yugoslav National Forrest near the town of Petrovo Selo.

Haxhi Dervisholl (unk.) was a roofer employed by Florin Krasniqi. He volunteered for the Atlantic Brigade. He was seriously wounded, losing a leg during the battle for Mount Pastrik. Krasniqi arranged for Dervisholl to be airlifted to the United States.

Isa Kodra (*ca*. 1980-unk.) was a sergeant in the U.S. National Guard and one of the few members of the Atlantic Brigade with any military training.

Florin Krasniqi (unk.) immigrated to the United States from Kosovo in late 1988 and owned Triangle General Contractors in Brooklyn, New York. Unlike the typical fund raiser, organizer and arms supplier, Krasniqi ran significant personal risk by regularly traveling to Kosovo and Albania to support the Kosovo insurgency.

Florim Lajqi (*ca*. 1979-unk.) immigrated to the United States at the age of three. He grew up in the Bronx and played quarterback for Lehman High School. Lajqi quit Manhattan's John Jay College to join the Atlantic Brigade. He participated in the battle for Mount Pastrik.

Linda Muriqi (*ca*. 1983-unk.) was born in Peja, Kosovo. Her father was a member of the Democratic League of Kosovo and was frequently beaten by the Serb police. In 1992 he was given political asylum in the United States and the family joined him in New York City in 1995. Linda attended Columbus High School and earned the reputation of being a rough kid. Linda's father returned to Kosovo and joined the KLA shortly after the massacre of 51 ethnic Albanians most of them members of the Jashari family) in Prekaz on 5-7 March 1998. Linda dropped out of high school and joined the Atlantic Brigade. It tried to turn her away because of her age but she stated, "I'm going and there is nothing anybody can do to stop me."[7] She participated in the battle for Mount Pastrik.

Giles Pace (*ca*. 1944-unk.) a native of Chicago, Illinois, graduated from high school and joined the U.S. Army. He served two tours in Vietnam in the 82nd Airborne Division, earning a Bronze Star with V device and a Purple Heart. He was discharged due to shrapnel wounds in his legs. Pace worked as an iron worker and at an atomic power plant. He has stated that he had untaken security work in Africa, Central Asia, the Middle East and the Balkans. Pace intercepted Florin Krasniqi at the Rome airport as he was flying to Albania in 1999. Pace asked to go with him to help the KLA. Although suspicious, Krasniqi took Pace along. Pace proceeded to teach KLA members how to use explosives, how to fabricate portable bunkers, how to improvise an anti-tank vehicle, and most importantly, he taught Krasniqi how to smuggle weapons. Pace then wrote Krasniqi volunteering his services, asking to be compensated only for his expenses. Krasniqi never answered the letter. Many associated with the KLM believed Pace to be an operative for American intelligence.

Gani Shehu (*ca*. 1968-unk.), a lawyer by education, fought in the defense of Junik, Kosovo, in 1998. He was shot in the head, was treated, survived and underwent additional surgery in Texas. He was the commander of the Atlantic Battalion.

Bruno Ukaj (*ca*. 1975-unk) immigrated from Vranoc, Kosovo, in 1993 to avoid the Serbian draft. Prior to joining the Atlantic Brigade, he was the manager of a Pisa Pizza in New York City. Ukaj participated in the battle for Mount Pastrik.

Quotations:

[1] Stacy Sullivan, *Be Not Afraid, for You Have Sons in America*. New York: St. Martin's Press, 2004. pp. 6 & 241.
[2] "The Brooklyn Connection: How to Build a Guerrilla Army." A Film by Klaartje Quirijns, 2005.
[3] Sullivan, *Be Not Afraid*, p. 125.
[4] Sullivan, *Be Not Afraid*, p. 246.
[5] "The Brooklyn Connection: How to Build a Guerrilla Army." A Film by Klaartje Quirijns, 2005.
[6] Sullivan, *Be Not Afraid*, p. 275.
[7] Sullivan, *Be Not Afraid*, p. 244.

Sources:

"Civil War in Former Yugoslavia," John Laffin, *The World in Conflict*. War Annual 6, pp. 203-19. London: Brassey's, 1994.
Seth Robson, "Vietnam vet in Haiti eager to share war experiences." *Stars and Stripes*. (21 March 2010).

United Arab Emirates and its Mercenary Army

2011-Present

GOAL:

To defend the United Arab Emirates against internal and external threats.

BACKGROUND:

One of the consequences of the American withdrawal from Vietnam in 1974 was that the U.S. military evolved from a primarily conscription service to an all volunteer force. It soon became apparent that the expense of a large number of volunteers would become prohibitive in the out years due to escalating costs for retirement and medical benefits. A way had to be found to significantly reduce the number of people in the military. One solution was to outsource to private contractors roles other than combat. Thus the birth of the modern private military companies came about.

In 1997 Erik Prince, a former U.S. Navy SEAL, founded Blackwater Worldwide, which in little more than a decade evolved into the world's largest private military company, earning billions of dollars from the U.S. government. Within that decade American private military companies, like Blackwater, faced ever increasing pressure due to international and nation law.

Since 1949 international law has defined two entities during conflicts, the military and the civilians. It wrestled to specify their rights and responsibilities. Enter now a third player - the private military company. What were its rights and responsibilities under international law? To this day, international law is murky as it relates to mercenaries.

U.S. national law also struggled to deal with Americans who work for private military companies operating outside the United States. The U.S. Supreme Court has ruled that many rights afforded to American citizens stop at the nation's borders. Blackwater, finding itself increasingly confronting international and national legal challenges, its principal owner, Erik Prince distanced himself from this legal quagmire by selling Blackwater (now Xe Services) to a group of investors in late 2010. In 2011 again its name was change, this time to Academi.

Prince reemerged into the shadowy world of mercenaries. According to a correction printed by the New York *Times* on 7 June 2011, "He [Prince] worked to oversee the effort and recruit troops [for Reflex Reponses based in the United Arab Emirates]."[1] Reflex Reponses, referred to R_2, was tasked by the UAE to create an 800-man battalion made up of mercenaries. It was licensed in March 2011 with 51% of the company owned by citizens of the UAE.

LEADERSHIP:

Great effort has been taken to hide who is in charge of Reflex Responses.

VOLUNTEERS:

The volunteers come from a multitude of countries. The countries which have been identified include Colombia, France, Germany, Great Britain, South Africa and the United States. At least some of these individuals are highly trained military professionals and most have served in countries allied to the United States. Some of the volunteers came from Executive Outcomes, a former South African mercenary firm. Others were recruited through Thor Global Enterprises, based on the Caribbean island of Tortola in the British Virgin Islands.

COMPENSATION:

Apparently some of the volunteers were lured from danger spots such as Afghanistan and Iraq with significant pay raises.

OPPOSITION:

Yet to be determined - but the following report by journalists Mark Mazzetti and Emily B. Hager suggests who one opponent might be: "[M]r. Prince's subordinates were following his strict rule: hire no Muslims."[2] Also, the UAE has a longstanding dispute with Iran over a chain of islands in the Persian Gulf. Mostly uninhabited, they are currently occupied by Iran. The islands might be a key to oil reserves.

Strategy:

Possibly these mercenaries are to used as shock troops to lead the UAE military into combat.

Operations:

In November 2011 dozens of Colombians, posing as construction workers, flew into the United Arab Emirates. The impact on the Colombian military was sufficient for the Colombian Minister of Defense to become alarmed over the exodus of highly-trained troops.

Impact:

Foremost, one must conclude that the United Arab Emirates does not believe that its own military is capable of defending the country, at least, not without help from these mercenaries. It is unclear whether the Americans involved have secured the necessary license from the U.S. departments of Defense and State to train foreign troops.

Biographies:

Ricki ("CT") Chambers (unk.) worked for the Federal Bureau of Investigation and has been associated with Erik Prince for years. He did not remain with R_2 for very long.

Erik Dean Prince (1969-) was born in Holland, Michigan. After graduating from Holland Christian High School he toured Europe with his father. Prince received a B.A. from Hillsdale College. While attending the college he served as a volunteer firefighter and as a cold-water diver for the Hillsdale County Sheriff's Department. In 1990 Prince worked as an intern in the White House and then with California Congressman Dana Rohrabacher. In 1992 he was commissioned in the U.S. Navy through the officer candidate program. Prince then became a Navy SEAL and served in Haiti, the Middle East, and the Balkans. He left the navy in 1995 when his father died.

Quotations:

[1] http://www.nytimes.com/2011/05/15/world/middleeast/15prince.html
[2] http://www.nytimes.com/2011/05/15/world/middleeast/15prince.html

Sources:

James Larry Taulbee, "Myths, Mercenaries and Contemporary International Law." *California Western International Law Journal.* Vol. 15 No. 2 (1985) pp. 339-63.

UPI.com. *Colombia worries as troops join Arab mercenary force.*

7 June 2013. Electronic Article. 12 June 2013. <http://www.upi.com/Business_News/Security-Industry/2013/06/07/Colombia-worries-as-troops-join-Arab-mercenary-force/UPI-90811370626017/#ixzz2VYn4UzbS>.

Wilkie, Christina. *Iraq War Contractors Fight On Against Lawsuits, Investigations, Fines*. 20 March 2013. Electronic Article. 12 June 2013. <http://www.huffingtonpost.com/2013/03/20/iraq-war-contractors_n_2901100.html?>

http://en.wikipedia.org/wiki/Erik_Prince

Concluding Observations

American mercenaries were the best of America and they were the worst of America. Some fought only for money, some fought only for principal, and others fought simply because they liked fighting. Many were more famous in foreign lands than their own country and others more infamous. A few American mercenaries got rich - John Coe changed sides for half a million dollars in gold in 1854 when half a million was real money. George Boynton Stone won and lost a few fortunes. But many received only promises - the Crippled Eagles fought in Rhodesia for the hope of stemming Communism in spite of scorn from their own government. The majority of American mercenaries received payment that they could have earned in far less dangerous professions.

There are no typical American mercenaries. They came from all walks of life. They ranged from high school dropouts to Ivy League graduates. At least one was an accused bank robber (Oscar Creighton) and another was the son of a president (Kermit Roosevelt). The Porter family contributed three generations - grandfather David (War of 1812 hero), father David D. (Civil War hero), and son David E. (drunkard). Others were field-hands, and yet others possessed knowledge of cutting edge technologies.

American mercenaries also came in all shapes and sizes. Homer Lea was a 5'3" hunchback who weighed 100 pounds. William Walker, the most notorious of the filibusters, was a 5"2" soft-spoken, steel-eyed 120 pounder. The one-legged Charles Gilman rejoined Walker in Central America. Pancho Villa said of Dean Lamb, "You are so skinny, the wind she will blow you away." W.N. Macmillan possessed a 64" girth. James "Earthquaker McGoon" McGovern, Jr., was a 300 pound pilot. And 4'10" Vernon "Shorty" Keogh had to use cushions to see out the cockpit of his Spitfire fighter.

On occasion, American mercenaries fought on opposite sides. During the Mexican revolution American pilots Phil Rader and Dean Lamb, flying for opposing factors, dueled with each other in the skies over Mexico. In the 1930s American pilot Maresciallo Patriarca fought for Italy against Ethiopia while another American pilot, John Robinson, fought for Ethiopia against Italy.

There are discernible patterns.

Naval officers who lost the opportunity to fight for the United States (either because the Navy was contracting or they were no longer welcome) were well represented among the mercenaries - John Paul Jones to Russia; David Porter to Mexico; William P.A. Campbell, Charles I. Graves, Wilburn B. Hall and Beverly Kennon to Egypt; William Tucker and John Reed to Peru; and Philo McGiffin to China.

A few mercenaries were West Point graduates - Alexander Welch Reynolds (class of 1838), William Crittenden (class of 1845), Charles Pomeroy Stone (class of 1845), Charles W. Field (class of 1848), William McEntyre Dye (class of 1853), Eugene Oscar Fechét (class of 1868), Chancellor Martin (class of 1868), Richard H. Savage (class of 1868), John Blake (class of 1880) and David Marcus (class of 1920).

Many American aviators would go almost anywhere to fly (and fight) - China, Ethiopia, England, France, Italy, Mexico, Morocco, Poland and Spain.

Many American mercenaries found employment as newspapermen

- William Barret Travis (1930s) the *Claiborne Herald*
- Theodore O'Hara (1850s) Louisville, Kentucky, *Times*
- William Walker (1850s) San Francisco, California, *Commercial Advertiser*
- Jeremiah O'Donovan Rosa (1880s) New York, New York, *United Irishmen*
- Robert Winston (1930s) New York, New York, *Times*
- John Gates (1940s) New York, New York, *The Daily Worker*.

Many American mercenaries were hired because they mastered new technologies - the observation balloon, the torpedo, dynamite and the machine gun.

Ideology was more of an influence than one might suspect. Journalist Robin Moore writes, "Mercenaries are probably the last romantics. They fight for a cause, but many would be lost without a cause for which they could use their combat experience."[1] Ideology was the prime motivation for those in L'Escadrille Lafayette (1916-18), the Spanish Civil War (1936-38), the Crippled Eagles in Afghanistan (1966-80), and the American Sons of Kosovo (1996-99). These causes represented both the political right and the left as well. Although we typically think that newly arrived immigrants "checked their historical baggage at Ellis Island and left it behind," that was not true for the Irish and the ethnic Albanians from Kosovo. There were some American-Irish who would travel half way around the world to fight Englishmen.

How many Americans became mercenaries is unknowable for many individuals took great pains to hide their nationality for fear of losing their citizenship. The number could be at least ten thousand. At first blush this seems like a wild over-estimate. But if we consider that there were at least a couple thousand Americans fighting in Spain in the 1930s, perhaps a similar number of American-Irish waiting to invade Canada in the 1860s, at least one thousand Americans fighting in the Boer War, another thousand fighting for Great Britain and France during World War I, some 400 fighting in Rhodesia in the 1970s, a similar number with William Walker in Central America in the 1850s - ten thousand does not seem totally unrealistic.

Just as memorable as the number 10,000, so were the deeds of three Black men who not only fought their enemies but also racial prejudice at the same time. Both John Charles Robinson and Eugene Jacques Bullard wanted to fly for America but were denied because of the color of their skin. In the end Robinson was recognized by Ethiopia and Bullard by France as national heroes. Edward Allen Carter, Jr., a veteran of both the Chinese Nationalist army and the Spanish Republican army, fought for the United States in World War and earned the Medal of Honor in 1945 which was posthumously awarded to him some fifty years later.

Hardly has a decade gone by since independence when a new group of American mercenaries has not arisen. What does this book suggest about the future? Understand that history does not repeat itself because the space-time continuum never remains constant. If nothing else, technology is constantly evolving and influencing this continuum. Having said that, we can learn from history especially if we pay particular attention to the changing elements as they impact on the constants.

So, what does the past of American mercenaries suggest about the future? First, when the current American military down-sizes, some former American soldiers will choose to become mercenaries - fight for other governments or entities. Second, some former service personnel will find employment in the high tech fields such as cyber/counter cyber operations, drone operations, IED (improvised explosive devices) disposal, and field-combat triage. Third, others will find work in logistics which is becoming increasingly dangerous since the distinction between front- and rear-line service is increasingly blurring. As in the past these future American mercenaries will be motivated by numerous factors including money, excitement and ideology.

With globalization and the rapid growth in the demand for "skilled" security forces, there will continue to be an expansion of private, international security companies eager to fill the void for any country or entity. The popularity of these private security resources blur the traditional definition of "mercenary" and may require consideration of a new category of soldiers for hire. The demand for these qualified veterans to be employed by foreign entities will continue to grow well into the future.

[1] Robin Moore, "The Soldiers of Fortune," *New York Times* (28 July 1978) p. A23.

INDEX

Abbreviations

ca. cerca

[fnu] first name unknown

A

Abd al-Khattabi, Muhammad: 273
Acker, Gary Martin: 370-71
Acosta, Bertram B. "Bert": 304
Adair, John: 319
Addendrum, Soren: 127
Adolphus, Gustavus: 97
Alexiano, Panaiotti: 2
Allen, Ezra S.: 107-09
Allen, James: 108
Allison, James William Marion: 304
Anderer, Xandre: 362, 365-66
Anderson, Charles Patrick: 240
Anderson, Christopher: 376
Anderson, Evelina: 20
Anderson, Frank: 75
Anderson, George "Andy": 376

Anglin, Samuel: 340
Ansburgh, William: 159
Arnold Benedict: xiii
Arranda, Anastasio: 93
Arthur, Chester: 158
Astor, Vincent: 236
Aten, Marion H. "Bunny": 268-72
Atwater, Leo B.: 341
Augarten, Rudolph "Rudy": 348-52
Austin, Stephen F.: 28

B

Bach, James Jules: 248, 257
Bacon, Charles: 240
Bacon, III, George: 370
Baer, Carlos Willard: 240
Baez, Buenaventura: 139-40
Baker, Edward D.: 134
Baker, Ezekiel C.: 163, 165
Baker, William Charles M.: 32
Balbiani, Roger Marie Louis: 262

Ball, Sherwin: 341
Banks, N.P.: 92, 95
Banks, Richard Varian: 240
Barclay, Leif Norman: 240
Barker, Robert Harris: 240
Barrick, John F.: 316
Bartelt, Percy R.: 331
Bartling, William E.: 331
Bassel, James: 128-29
Batista, Fulgencio: 353-55
Batts, Henry James: 180
Baugh, John Joseph: 32
Baumler, Albert J. "Ajax": 305, 331
Bayen, Malaku E.: 282
Baylies, Frank Leaman: 263
Baylor, Jr., John Walker: 32
Baynard, William: 123
Beaver, Wilfred: 219
Ben-Gurion, David: 347
Bennett, Jr., Louis: 219
Benney, Philip Phillips: 236
Benson, Merrill Manning: 240
Berrien, John: 76
Berrier, Hilaire du: 305
Bessie, Alvah: 293, 295-96
Bevins brothers: 197
Bin Laden, Osama: 169
Bishop, Ted: 381-83
Bissonette, Charles A.: 218, 220
Black, Stephen D.: 376
Blake, John Y. Filimore: 178-81, 400
Blennerhassett, Harman: 7, 9
Blennerhassett, Margaret: 8
Blick, Homer Ephraim: 170
Blick, James Shannon: 170
Blick, John Charles: 170
Blick, Judd Dunning: 170
Blodgett, Richard Ashley: 240
Bocalari, Vincenzo: See Patriarca,
    Maresciallo Vincenzo

Bolte, Charles G. "Chuck": 325-26
Bonaparte, Napoleon: 88
Bond, Jr., Charlie R.: 332
Bonham, James Butler: 32
Bonilla, Manuel: 184-88
Bottcher, Hermann F.: 294, 296
Bouterse, Desi: 386-87
Bowen, Ezra: 257
Bowen, Francis: 119, 123
Bowers, [fnu]: 365
Bowie, James: 28-29, 32-33, 35
Boyington, Gregory "Pappy": 332
Boynton, George: See Stone,
    George Boynton
Boyson, Howard K.: 220
Breckinridge, John C.: 53, 58
Brister, John F. "Jack": 324-26 346
Brooks, Theodore: 121
Brooks, William C.: xiii
Brown, Ezra: 219
Brown, J.S.: 341
Brown, Robert K.: ix, 362, 384
Brown, Sydney MacGilvary: 220
Brown, William: 22, 24, 66
Brown Condor: See Robinson,
    John Charles
Bruce, Alexander Bern: 240
Bruin, Peter: 9
Brunswijk, Roddy: 386
Buchanan, Archibald: 220
Buchanan, James: 53, 80
Bufkin, David: 370-71
Buford, Wallace: 344, 346
Bulger, [fnu]: 203
Bullard, Eugene J.: 246-51, 261, 401
Burgard, George T.: 332
Burgevine, Henry Andres: 86-88
Burgoyne, John: 4
Burke, Richard O'Sullivan: 114-15
Burnet, [nfu]: See Stone, George Boynton

Burnham, Frederick Russell: 166-70
Burr, Aaron: xiii, 6-11
Burton, Jr., Benjamin H.: 240-41
Burton, Harry: 157-58
Bush, Ira J.: 203, 206
Butt, Walter Randolph: 100-03
Byrd, Richard E.: 236, 304
Bytyqi, Agron: 393
Bytyqi, Mehmet: 393
Bytyqi, Ylli: 393

C

Cabal, Conway: 11
Cabrera, Manuel Estrada: 187
Calderón de la Baca, Angel: 53
Callender, Alvin Andrew: 220
Callo, Joseph F.: 4
Campbell, James: See Gallagher, Bernard
Campbell, William P.A.: 129, 400
Carlos (pretender to Spanish throne): 138-39
Carpentier, [fnu]: 206
Carranza, Venustiano: 202, 204-07
Carter, Jr., Edward A.: 295-97, 401
Carville, James: 341
Castro, Cipriano: 144
Castro, Fidel: 353-54, 368-69, 372-73, 381
Castro, Raúl: 355
Catherine II (czarina of Russia): 1, 5
Catto, Charles Gray: 218, 221
Chaille-Ling, Charles: 129
Chambers, Richi "TC": 397
Chapman, Victor: 254-57
Charles, Mary Eugenia: 375
Chartrand, René: 98-99
Chennault, Anna: 344-45
Chennault, Claire: 200, 268, 327-38, 343-45, 350
Chiang Kai-shek: 327, 343, 345
Chiang Kai-shek, Madame: 327-28

Christ, Jesus: 84, 92, 95
Christmas, Lee: 184-88
Church, George Earl: 93
Churchill, Winston: 233, 316, 330
Clark, James F.: 103
Clarke, Thomas J.: 159
Clement, John: 181
Cloud, Daniel W.: 33
Clover, Greayer: 241
Coe, John Halstead: 25, 50, 64-66
Cochrane, Thomas: 24
Coey, John: 365
Cohen, [fnu]: See Williams, Stanley
Coldren, Russell: 341
Cole, Byron: 71, 73
Coler, Eugene Seeley: 221
Colston, Raleigh Edward: 129
Collishaw, Raymond: 269
Colow, Maury: 297
Condon, Edward Meagher: 114
Condon, Patrick: 115
Connelly, Jr., James Alexander: 263
Conover, Richard Steven: 241
Conrow, A.H.: 98
Cook, Charles: 342
Cook, Hamlin: 14
Cooper, Merian C.: 265-68, 333
Cooper, Norman: See Tooker, E.S.
Corcoran, Michael: 110
Corcoran, Thomas G. "Tommy the Cork": 328
Corretjer, Juan Antonio: 297
Coulson, Bert: 341
Cowdin, Elliot: 254, 257
Cowley, Malcolm: 238-41
Cox, Robert Hill "Rob": 325-26
Crabb, Henry A.: 78-80, 210
Craven, Thomas T. (father): 165
Craven, Thomas T. (son): 165
Crawford, Lemuel: 33

Creel, George: 98
Creighton, Oscar (Dynamite Devil): 206, 399
Crespo, Joaquín: 143-44
Crisp, D.H.: 41
Crittenden, John: 62
Crittenden, William Logan: 61-62, 400
Crocker, Timothy: 75-76
Crockett, David "Davy": 29, 31, 33
Crossman, Robert: 33
Cudahy, John: 211
Cumings, Henry Harrison: 241
cummings, e.e.: xv
Cunningham, James G.: 157-58
Curry, John H.: 316
Curtin, John: See Kent, John
Curtiss, Glenn: 200, 258, 304
Cutting, Heyward: 326

D

Dahl, Harold E. "Whitey": 302, 305
Dalton, Henry: See O'Connor, John Henry
Danjou, Jean: 245, 247
D'Annunzio, Gabriele: 291
Davidson, George R.: 76
Davis, Carl Raymond: 313, 317
Davis, Charles H.: 75
Davis, Jefferson: 51
Davis, Richard: xvi
Davis, Richard Harding: 167, 169, 171, 173-76
Day, Curtiss: 275, 279
De Gaulle, Charles: 249
De Laage de Meux, Alfred: 254
Dean, John J.: 341
Deasy, Thomas: 114
DeKay, George Colman: 23, 25
Delgado Delgado, Carmelo: 297, 300

Denley, Tommy: 386-87
Dennison, James A.: 128, 129-30
Derrick, Henry C.: 130
Dervisholl, Haxhi: 393
Despallier, Charles: 33
Devoy, John: 154
Díaz, Porfirio: 198, 202-05, 210, 212
Dickerson, Mahlon: 19
Dickinson, Derek D.: 305
Dillon, Luke: 158-59
Do Sol, Lobo: 371
Doheny, Michael: 110
Donahue, Arthur G. "Art": 319-20
Doran, David: 297
Dos Passos, John: xv, 11
Doubleday, C.W.: 71, 73, 76
Douglas, Robert: 85, 90, 176, 195
Doumenc; [fnu]: 238
Dowding, Hugh: 312
Dreben, Sam: 203
Dresser, George Eaton: 241
Driscoll, D.P.: 226, 228
Dudley, Yseult: 158
Dufour, Charles: 59, 62-63
Dunlap, William W.: 130
Dunlop, Richard G.: 39
Dunn, Catherine: 206
Dunn, William R.: 314, 317
Dupuy, Trevor: 171, 176, 201, 244, 252, 272, 287, 299, 311, 351-52, 360
Durkee, William Porter: 325
Duvalier, Francois "Papa Doc": 378
Duvalier, Jean-Claude "Baby Doc": 378
Duvall, Pierre: 382
Dye, William McEntyre: 130, 400
Dyer, Gwynne: 379

E

Earhart, Amelia: 223

Early, John Dee: 381-85
Early, Jubal: 92, 95
Eban, Abba: 348
Echanis, Michael D. "Mike": 382-74
Eden, Anthony: 324
Edgerton, Samuel: 41
Edinger, Charles E.: 317
Edner, Selden R.: 317-18
Edwards, Jr., George Lane: 241
El Ghazi, Hassan "the Capudan Pasha": 2-3
El-Kader, Abd: 44, 247
Elliot, William Armstrong: 241
Ellis, R.H.: 206-07
Eloesser, Leo: 297, 300
Ericsson, John: 164
Escobedo, Mariano: 94
Evans, Robert: 33
Ewing, James L.: 33

F

Fairbanks, David C. "Foob": 318
Fales, Hugo Wing: 318
Falkenberg, Richard A.: 192
Fall, Bernard: 246, 251
Farwell, Bryon: 178, 182
Fauntleroy, Cedric Errol: 265-68
Fauntleroy, William Keener: 33
Favier, Paul: 358
Featherstone, Timothy: See Kennedy, Edmund O'Brien
Fechét, Eugene Oscar: 130, 400
Fernando VII (king of Spain): 17
Ferris, Richard "Dick": 212-13
Field, Charles W.: 130
Fierro, Rudolfo: 208
Fillmore, Millard: 60
Finick, Eugene: 303, 305
Fish, Farnum Thayer: 199, 201

Fisher, S. Rhodes: 38-39
Fisk, James "Jim Jubilee Junior": 138, 145
Fiske, William M.L.: 318
Fleming, John: 158
Flint, Charles: xiii, 146-47, 150-51, 162-65
Flores Magón, Ricardo: 211-14
Flynn, Errol: 320
Ford, Patrick: 156
Forman, Horace Baker: 242
Forsyth, John H.: 34, 39, 42, 80
Foster, James "Arizona Kid": 181
Fountain, Tom: 207
Fowler, Eric Anderson: 263
Fox, Grace: 48, 50
Fox, Jim R.: 341
Franco, Francisco: 289, 291-92, 301, 305
Franklin, Benjamin: 4
French, Marcellus: 75
French, Parker: 76
Fry, Joseph: 119-23

G

Gaines, Edmund: 10
Gallagher, Bernard: 159
Gallagher, Daniel: 159
Gallagher, Thomas: 157, 159-60
Gardner, Brian: 229-30
Garfield, Bobby: xiii
Garibaldi, Giuseppe (grandfather): 73, 77
Garibaldi, Giuseppe (grandson): 203, 206
Garrand, James W.: 34
Garrett, James Girard: 34
Garrison, Cornelius: 72-74
Gates, John: 297-300, 400
Gearhart, Daniel Francis: 370-71
Genet, Edmond C.C.: 249-50
Gilardoni, Eduardo: 383-84
Gillet, Frederick Warrington: 221
Gilman, Charles: 76, 399

Gimbel, Edward L.: 318
Giroux, Ernest Armand: 242
Glubb, John Bagot "Glubb Pasha": 349
Gómez Trejo, Francisco: See Tinker, Jr., Frank Glasgow
Gooding, William: 171
Gordon, Charles George "Chinese": 89, 129, 133
Gordon, Dennis: 252, 256, 260, 264, 276
Gordon, James C.: 365, 371
Grace, W.R.: 146-53
Grant, Ulysses S.: 91, 95, 121, 132
Grau, Miguel: 148, 152
Graves, Charles I.: 131, 400
Green, Francis L.: 94
Green, George M.: 91, 93-94
Griffith, John Sharpe: 270-71
Grillo, Gustavo Marcelo: 370-71
Grines, J. Robert: 387
Gros, Edmund L.: 248
Guangxu (emperor of China): 189
Guerrero, [fnu]: 212
Guevara, Ernesto "Che": 275, 368
Guthrie, Woody: 295
Gutierrez Menoyo, Eloy: 353-54
Guzman Blanco, Antonio: 139-40
Gwynne, James C.: 34

H

Hagan, William Becker: 221
Hager, Emily B.: 396
Hahn, Albert: 93
Hale, Frank L. "Buddy": 219, 221
Hall, James Norton: 257-58
Hall, Weston "Bert": 254-58
Hall, Wilburn B.: 131, 400
Hall, William J.: 314
Halleck, Henry: 95
Halpin, William: 115
Hamilton, Alexander: 6-7, 10

Hammell, Charles R.: 342
Hammett, Dashiell: 295
Hanks, Fletcher: 339, 341-42
Harcourt, William: 155
Harder, Gitta: 357
Harnett, Bob: 359
Harper, Jim: See Teel, Jim
Harris, Eli: 14-15
Harrison, William B.: 34
Hartney, Harold Evans: 221-22
Hassel, John: 178, 181
Hawkins, Charles: 18
Hawkins, Charles E. 41
Hawkins, Joe D.: 376
Hawkins, Joseph Mark: 34
Hawkins, Thomas T.: 56-58
Haydon, F. Stansbury: 108-09
Hays, John M.: 34
Heany, Maurice David: 181, 183
Hedman, Robert P.: 333
Hellman, Lillian: 295
Hemingway, Ernest: xv-xvi, 295, 297
Henderson, James Stuart: See Stone, George Boynton
Henningsen, Charles Frederick: 76
Henry, Thomas: 83
Herreshoff, Nat: 146-47, 150, 152
Herrick, Myron: 253
Herrick, William: 298, 300
Hersee, William Daniel: 34
Hill, David L.: 333-34
Hilton, D'Arcy Fowlis: 222
Hinrichs, Dunbar Maury: 240
Hinton, A.C.: 41
Hippolyte, Dominique: 143
Hitler, Adolf: 289, 301, 309, 314, 324
Hoare, Michael "Mad Mike": 368
Ho Chih Minh: 275
Hobbs, Warren Tucker: 242
Holland, John P.: 155-56, 161

Hing Hsiu-ch'uan: 84-85
Hoover, J. Edgar: 200, 294-95
Hopkins, Charles Alexander: 242
Hopkins, Esek: 4
Hopkins, Melbourne: 213
Houseman, Alfred E.: 328
Houston, Henry Howard: 242
Houston, Samuel "Sam": 27-35, 39-41
Howell, Malcolm Clifford: 222
Howell, William D.: 35
Huang, George: 341
Huerta, Victoriano: 202, 205, 207, 250
Hughes, Howard: 223
Hull, Cordell: 372
Humason, Howard Crosby: 242
Hungerford, Daniel E.: 93-94
Hunt, Cornelius: 131

I

Iaccaci, August T: 222
Iaccai, Paul T.: 222
Inglis, James: 25
Irgins, Henry: 130
Isabella II (queen of Spain): 53
Ito, Yuko: 174
Iturbide, Augustín de: 15

J

Jackson, Andrew: 7, 19, 27
Jackson, James: 213
James, Louis: 213
Jameson, L. Starr: 177, 181
Jefferson, Thomas: 6-10, 118
Jenifer, Walter H.: 127, 131
John, Patrick R.: 375-76
John (king of Abyssinia): 127
Johnson, Andrew: 115
Johnson, Chris: 365

Johnson, Paul G.: 318
Johnson, Thomas: 131
Johnston, Albert Sidney: 58
Jones, John Paul: 1-5, 400
Jones, Ripley O.: 318
Juárez, Benito: 89, 91-97

K

Kabut, Luis: 382
K'ang Yu-wei: 190
Kearny, Philip: xv, 43-47
Kee, Robert: 117, 161, 180-81
Keefer, George C.: 319
Keller, Helen: 295
Kelly, Roy: 207
Kelly, Thomas J.: 113-15
Kelso, Mike: 365
Kennedy, Edmund O'Brien: 160
Kennon, Beverly: 131, 400
Kent, John: 160
Kent, Warren Thompson: 242
Keogh, Vernon C. "Shorty": 319-21, 399
Kerr, Joseph: 35
Kerr, Nathaniel: 35
Kessler, Paul: 341
Kewen, Achilles: 76
King, James "Dynamite Dick": 181-82
Kinnear, John F.: See Stone, George Boynton
Kodra, Isa: 393
Kolendorski, Stanley M. "Mike": 314
Kosciuskko, Tadeusz: 265-68, 333
Krasniqi, Florin: 389-94
Kruger, Paul: 178
Kullberg, Harold Albert: 222

L

Labram, George: 178, 182
Lafitte, Jean: 14

Lagos, Hilario: 64
LaGuardia, Fiorello: 343
Lajqi, Florim: 393
Lake, Harvey: 94
Lamar, Mirabeau: 42
Lamb, Dean Ivan: 198-200, 399-400
Lambert, William Carpenter: 222
Lamson, Robert S.: 131
Larkins, Doc: 213
Larremore, Richard L.: xv, 155, 161
Larsen, Jens Frederick "Swede": 223
Lawlor, Frank L.: 334
Lay, John: 146, 150
Lea, Homer: 189-95, 399
LeBoutillier, Oliver Colin: 223
LeClare, [fnu]: 213
Lee, Robert E.: 51, 194
Lee, Schuyler: 263
Leider, Benjamin David: 305
Lenin, Nikolai: 193
Lewis, William Irving: 35
Leyya, José María: 213
Li Hung Chang: 172
Li Yuan-hung: 192-93
Lilley, Buddy: 365-66
Lincoln, Abraham: 95, 109, 134
Lindbergh, Charles: 304
Lindsley, Paul Warren: 242
Linn, William: 35
Little, Robert Laing: 334
Lober, Robert: See Williams, Stanley
Lockett, Samuel H.: 126, 128, 131
Lockridge, S.A.: 76
Logan, John A.: 58
Logengula (king of Matabele tribe): 166-68
Loh, M.K.: 341
Lomasney, William Mackey ("Little Captain"): 158, 160
Long, David: 77

Long, James: 13-15
Longstaff, John L.: 198
Loomis, Thomas: 341
López, Francisco Solano: 106-08
López, Miguel: 98
López, Narciso: 51-63, 73, 76-77, 118
Lord, Frederick Ives "Tex": 270-71
Loring, William Wing: 126-27, 132-33
Lorraine, Lambton: 121
Loshe, Charles F.: 131
Louis Philippe (king of France): 245
Lowe, Thaddeus: 106-09
Lufbery, Gervais Raoul V.: 256, 258
Lussier, Emile John: 223
Lynch, John J.: 319
Lynch, William Joseph: 160

M

MacArthur, Douglas: xv, 333
MacDermot, Jim "Red": 112
MacFarlane, George: See Stone, George Boynton
Machen, [fnu]: 18
MacIver, Henry Ronald Douglas: xiv, xvi
Macmillan, William Northrop: 229
Macomb, Alexander: 46
Madero, Francisco: 202-08, 212-13
Madison, James: 36, 118
Magloire, Roland: 378-79
Magoun, Francis Peabody: 223
Magruder, John Bankhead: 98
Mah, M.K.: 341
Mahon, Jackson B.: 320
Malone, William T.: 35
Malraux, André: 301-02
Malvaney, George T.: 376
Mamedoff, Andrew B. "Andy": 319-21
Mannerheim, Carl Gustav Emil: 307-10
Manson, Charles: 335

Mao Tse-tung: 275, 343
Marchant, Richard: 341
Marcus, David "Mickey": xiv, 347-52, 400
Marques de Caxias: 108
Marshall, J.G.: See Lomasney, William Mackey
Marshall, John: 10
Marshall, William: 35
Marson, Peter: 358, 360
Martin, August: 359
Martin, Chancellor: 132, 400
Martin, Robert: 380
Marx, Karl: 87
Mason, Alexander M.: 132
Massey, Gordon: 115
Masson, Didier: 197-98
Maud, Frederick S.: 232
Maugham, Somerset: 236
Maximilian, Ferdinand (emperor of Mexico): 91-99
Mazzetti, Mark: 396
McCafferty, John: 115
McCann, John McFarland: 58
McColpin, Carroll Warren "Red": 314, 320
McConnell, James H.: 254-55, 258
McCorkle, David Porter: 100-01, 103
McDermott, Terence: 157
McDonald, C.J.: 73-74
McDowell, William: 35
McGarry, William D.: 334
McGlashan, Peter Alexander: 76
McGiffin, Philo Norton: 172-76, 400
McGovern, Jr., J. B. "Earthquake McGoon": 344-46, 399
McKenna, Joseph: 117, 155, 161
McKinstry, Justus: 69
McNair, Bruce: 365
McNulty, George William: 93-94
Mead, Cowles: 9

Mei, Chang: 89
Mejía, José Antonio: 41
Mello, Custódio José de: 142-43, 162, 164
Merriam, Robert Hale: 293
Merry, Antony: 6, 11
Michelson, Einar I. "Micky": 341-42
Miles, Pearl "Pete" Ingham: 171
Milosevic, Slobodan: 388-92
Milton, [fnu]: 214
Mitchell, Agnes: 46
Mix, Tom: xvi
M'Limo (high priest): 169
Mockler, Anthony: 360, 369, 371
Moisant, Alfred J.: 197
Moisant, Benins: 197
Moisant, John: 285
Montgomery, Bernard Law "Monty": 323, 325
Monti, Martin J.: xiii
Mooney, Robert H.: 324
Mooney, Thomas J.: 157, 297
Moore, Edwin: 39-42
Moore, Willis A.: 35
Mordvinov, Nicholas (count): 2
Morehead, John C.: 67
Morehead, Joseph: 210
Morgan, J.P: 72, 74, 194, 254
Morgan, James M.: 132
Morgan, W. Brewster: 315
Morgan, William: 353-55
Morison, Samuel Eloit: 2, 5
Morris, Edmund: 232-37
Mosby, John R. "Jack": 214, 216
Mott, Thaddeus P.: 132
M'Tesa (monarch of Uganda): 129
Mulkey, J.K.: 210
Muriqi, Linda: 393
Murphy, John: 364, 366
Murphy, John Cadogan: 157, 160
Musselman, Robert: 35

411

Mussolini, Benito: 282

N

Nancarrow, Conlon: 300
Napoleon I (emperor of France): 88, 194
Napoleon III (emperor of France): 91, 96
Narvitz, Siegfried: 250
Nassau-Siegen (prince): 1, 3
Neale, Robert H.: 334-35
Neill, James Clinton: 35
Nelson, Edward: 35
Nelson, George: 35
Newbiggin, Thomas: 111
Newkirk, Jan Van Kuren "Scarsdale Jack": 335
Nicholson, Bob: 366
Nkomo, Joshua: 362
Noonan, Jack: 297
Nordhoff, Charles B.: 257-58
Norman, William J.: See Lynch, William Joseph
Norris, Michael S.: 376
Norton, Francis Lay: 144-45
Norton, James: 25

O

O Ji Ja Tek Ka: 181
Oates, Tom: 371
O'Banion, Ansel E.: 191-91
Obregón, Alvaro: 202, 204
O'Brien, Michael: 115
O'Connor, John Henry: 157, 161
O'Donovan, Jeremiah: *See* Rossa, Jeremiah O'Donovan
Ogden, Peter: 8
O'Hara, Theodore: 57-58, 400
Older, Charles H.: 335
O'Mahony, John: 110
O'Neil, Roger: 158, 161
O'Neill, H.C.: 227-30
O'Neill, John: 112-16
O'Reilly, Edward S. "Tex": 195, 204-08
Orozco, Pascual: 202-08
Orr, Osborne John: 223
Osbon, B.S.: xvi, 48-50, 65-66
Osei, Godfrey: 381-82
O'Shaunssey, James: 42
Otis, H.G.: 211
Otis, Tom: See Oates, Tom
Overend, Edmund Fryer: 335

P

Pace, Giles: 393-94
Paine, Albert Bigelow: xvi, 50, 66
Pan-Yang "John" Wong: 281
Parker, Dorothy: 295
Parsons, Edwin C.: 258-60
Parsons, Mosby Monroe: 98
Parys, Edmund: 132
Pasha, Arabi: 142
Pasha, Ismail: 125
Pasha, Ratib: 127
Patriarca, Maresciallo Vincenzo: 288-91, 400
Pattison, Edward H.: 239, 242-43
Paulding, Hiram: 75
Pearson, James William: 223-24
Pedro II (emperor of Brazil): 107-08
Peixoto, Floriano: 142-43, 162
Perdue, Michael: 375-76
Pérez, Ignacio: 14-15
Perry, Matthew: 173
Peters, Herta: 234
Peterson, Chesley G. "Pete": 315, 320
Phelan, Joseph: 158
Pickett, John T.: 53, 57-58, 63
Pierce, Michael "Reb": 366

Pieri, Donald Mathew: 321
Píerola, Nicolas de: 147, 151
Pike, Frederick: 146, 149-50, 153
Pilsudski, Jozef: 265-67
Pineau, Cleo Francis: 224
Porter, David: 17-21, 132, 399-400
Porter, David Dixon: 19, 21, 132, 399
Porter, David Essex: 132, 399
Porter, David H.: 18-19, 21
Potemkin, Grigory Alexandovich (prince): 2-3
Powers, Ethel: 194
Prado, Ignacio: 102, 147, 151
Pragay, John: 63
Prescott, Robert W.: 335-36
Prevost, Theodosia: 10
Prichard, Robert W.: 376
Prince, Erik Dean: 395-98
Prince, Norman: 253-54, 259
Privensal, Arthur: 342
Prout, Henry G.: 132-33
Pryce, Carl ap Rhys Pryce: 212-16
Pulaski, Kazimierz: 267
Pulgar, Venancio: 139
Purdy, E. Sparrow: 133
Putnam, David Endicott: 263

Q
Quitman, John: 55

R
Randolph, Victor: 52
Rawlings, Jerry John: 381-82
Read, Charles William: 147-53
Redding, William: 58
Reed, Horatio B.: 133
Regenstriet, Solomon: See Gates, John
Reynolds, Alexander W.: 133, 400

Reynolds, Frank A.: 133
Reynolds, John Purdy: 35
Reynolds, Michael: xvi
Reynolds, Thomas: 98
Rhett, Thomas G.: 133
Rhodes, Cecil John: 167-71, 177-78,
Richardson, Tracy: 208
Rinehart, Howard Max: 197, 200
Roberts, Frederick S.: 170, 178-81
Robeson, Paul: 295
Robinson, Frank O.: 240
Robinson, John C.: 282-87, 400-01
Rockwell, Paul Ayres: 250, 275
Rockwell, Kriffin Y.: 254, 256, 259
Rodney, Thomas: 9
Rogers, Bogart: 219, 224
Rogers, Robert: 133
Rohrabacher, Dana: 397
Romero, Matías: 92
Rommel, Erwin Eugen "the Desert Fox": 323-25
Roosevelt, Archibald: 237
Roosevelt, Belle: 234-35
Roosevelt, Franklin D.: 232-33, 235, 328, 251, 372
Roosevelt, Kenneth Kermit: 231-37, 399
Roosevelt, Jr., Kenneth Kermit "Kim": 236
Roosevelt, Theodore: 5, 171, 192, 229, 231-33, 235
Root, George Wells: 243
Rosbert, Camile Joseph: 336
Rosbert, Joe R.: 342
Rose, James Madison: 36
Rose, Oren J.: 224, 270-71
Rossa, Jeremiah O'Donovan: xv-xvi, 154-58, 160-61
Rossi, John Richard "Dick": 336
Rugova, Ibrahim: 389
Rutherford, John: 112, 117
Ryan, Isaac: 36

Ryan, William (a.k.a. George Washington Ryan): 121, 124

S

Salmon, Norvell: 82
Salm-Salm, Felix: 93
Sambrook, Walter Laidlaw: 243
Sampson, Martin: 239
Sandell, Robert J. "Sandy": 336
Sanders, Charles: 372
Santa Anna, Antonio López de: 19, 27-37, 41, 78-79
Savage, Richard H.: 133, 400
Scaley, Eugene: 371
Scalon, Eugene: See Scaley, Eugene
Schikkerling, Roland: 180
Schlesinger, Louis: 61-62, 74
Schroeder, Mike J.: 342
Scoff, James: 342
Scott, Edward: 124
Scott, Winfield: 43-46, 59
Seeger, Alan: 250-52
Selassie, Haile: 282-84, 286-87
Selous, F.C.: 229-30
Sen, Moy: 140
Seymour, Lewis: 181-82
Shehu, Gani: 391, 394
Shelby, Joseph Orville: 96-99
Sheppherd, Francis: 124
Sheridan, Philip: 92
Sherman, William T.: 125-26
Shilling, Eriksen E. "Erik": 344, 346
Short, Robert McCawley: 280-81
Shui-Tin "Arthur" Chen: 280
Sibley, Henry Hopkins: 133
Sierra, Terencio: 186
Simmons, Cleveland Kinloch: 36
Simon, Walter Karl: 224
Sithole, Ndabaningi: 362

Smith, Edmund Kirby: 95
Smith, Ian: 361
Smith John H.: 148, 152
Smith, John William: 36
Smith, Paul "Silent": 215
Smith, Robert H. "Snuffy": 337
Smith, Robert Tharp: 337
Smith, Walker: 210
Smith, William "Hal": 342
Smyth, Thomas Alfred: 77
Sobieski, John: 92
Somoza, Anastasio "Tachito": 372-74
Somoza, Anastasio "Tacho": 372-74
Soong, T.V.: 280, 328
Spear, Samuel P.: 113, 116-17
Squier, George: 91
Stalin, Josef: 307-10
Stanley, William: See Williams, Stanley
Steck, Robert: 293, 298-99
Stephens, James: 113
Stevens, Walter Husted: 98
Stimson, Henry L.: 193
Stone, [fnu]: 215-16
Stone, Charles Pomeroy: 125-30, 134, 400
Stone, George Boynton: 120, 136-45, 163, 399
Sullivan, Stacy: 389, 392, 394
Sun Yat-sen: 87, 190, 192-94
Sun-Shui "Buffalo" Wong: 281
Swartwout, Sam: 8
Sweeney, Charles: 313
Sweeney, Frank A.: 366
Sweeny, Thomas: 111, 116

T

Tabler, Kramer Core: 243
Taulbee, James: 362, 366, 377, 397
Taylor, Edgar: 224
Taylor, William Henry: 243
Taylor, Zachery: 52, 60

Teel, Jim: 208
Terrell, Alexander Watkins: 99
Thaw, II, William: 253-56, 259-60
Thénault, Georges: 254
Thompson, George: 106
Thord-Gray, Ivor: 207
Thorwaldson, Albert Olafur: 342
Tiffin, Edward: 9
Tilley, Reade F.: 321
Ting Ju Chang: 173
Tinker, Jr., Frank Glasgow: 302-06
Titus, H.T.: 75, 77
Tobin, Eugene Q. "Red": 319-21
Tod, George Donald: 224
Tooker, E.S.: 225
Trammel, Burke: 36
Travis, William Barret: 29-36, 400
Trujillo, Rafael: 354
Tucker, John Randolph: 100-05
Tucker, Philip Thomas: 31, 37
Turnbull, Archibald: 20-21
Turner, Ben: 208
Turner, Timothy: 203, 207-08
Turner, William H.: 340
Tutein, Chester Robinson: 243
Tweed, William "Boss": 114
Tyler, Robert: 77
Tzu-Hsi (empress of China): 189

U

Unger, Kenneth Russell: 225
Urmy, John B.: 93
Urquiza, José: 64

V

Van Loon, Henrik Willem: 251
Vanderbilt, Cornelius: 71-72, 74-75
Vanderbilt, William K.: 254

Vega, Placido: 93
Victoria, Guadalupe: 15
Victoria (queen of England): 159, 181
Vilijoen, Ben: 208
Villa, Francisco "Pancho": 197-209, 258, 399
Von Hantleman, Georg: 263
Von Lettow-Vorbeck, Paul Emil: 227, 229
Von Rosen, Carl Gustaf: 287

W

Wade, Lance C.: 315, 321-22
Waldrop, William B.: 376
Walker, Asa: 36
Walker, James: 59
Walker, W. W.: 15
Walker, Waine: 366
Walker, William: 58-59, 63, 67-77, 79-85, 89, 186, 210, 212, 399-401
Wallace, Lewis "Lew": 92-93, 95
Walsh, Orin M.: 342
Wanamaker, Rodman: 304
Ward, Frederick Townsend: 84-90
Warman, Clive Wilson: 225
Warner, Goodwin: 243
Warren, Edward: 134
Warren, William D.: 342
Warren, Harris G.: 13, 15
Warren, T. Robinson: 48, 50, 68, 70
Warski, Heinrich: See Wharton, Henry Arthur "Hank"
Washington, George: 10-11, 267
Wassermann, Jeffery: 366
Wassermann, Margaret: 366
Watts, John: 46
Weaver, III, Claude "Weavy": 322
Webster, R.C.: 74
Weissberg, Benjamin: 378
Wharton, Henry A. "Hank": 356-60

Wheat, Chatham Roberdeau: 55, 58-60, 73, 77
Wheeler, David E.: 251
White, Harold Albert "Wilber": 225
White, Paul: 229
Whitehead, Alfred George: See Murphy, John Cadogan
Whyte, William Jewell: 243
Wilkinson, James: 7-9, 11, 13, 15
Willard, Belle Wyatt: See Roosevelt, Belle
Willauer, Whiting: 343-44
Williams, [fnu]: 138
Williams, Stanley: 212, 215
Wilson, Henry Hayward: See Clarke, Thomas J.
Winant, John: 324
Winkler, Darryl [also cited as Darrell]: 366
Winston, Robert A.: 310, 400
Wirz, Henry: 92, 95
Wise, [fnu]: 18
Wolff, Milton: 299
Wood, Sam: 216
Woods, Hugh "Woodie": 338
Woodward, Henry H. Houston: 263
Worden, John Hector: 200
Worth, William: 51
Wright, Al: 342
Wright, Jack Morris: 243

X

Xianfeng (Chinese emperor): 85

Z

Zapata, Emiliano: 202, 204-05
Zary, Henry Paul Michael: 322
Zedong, Mao: 87
Zemurray, Samuel: 187

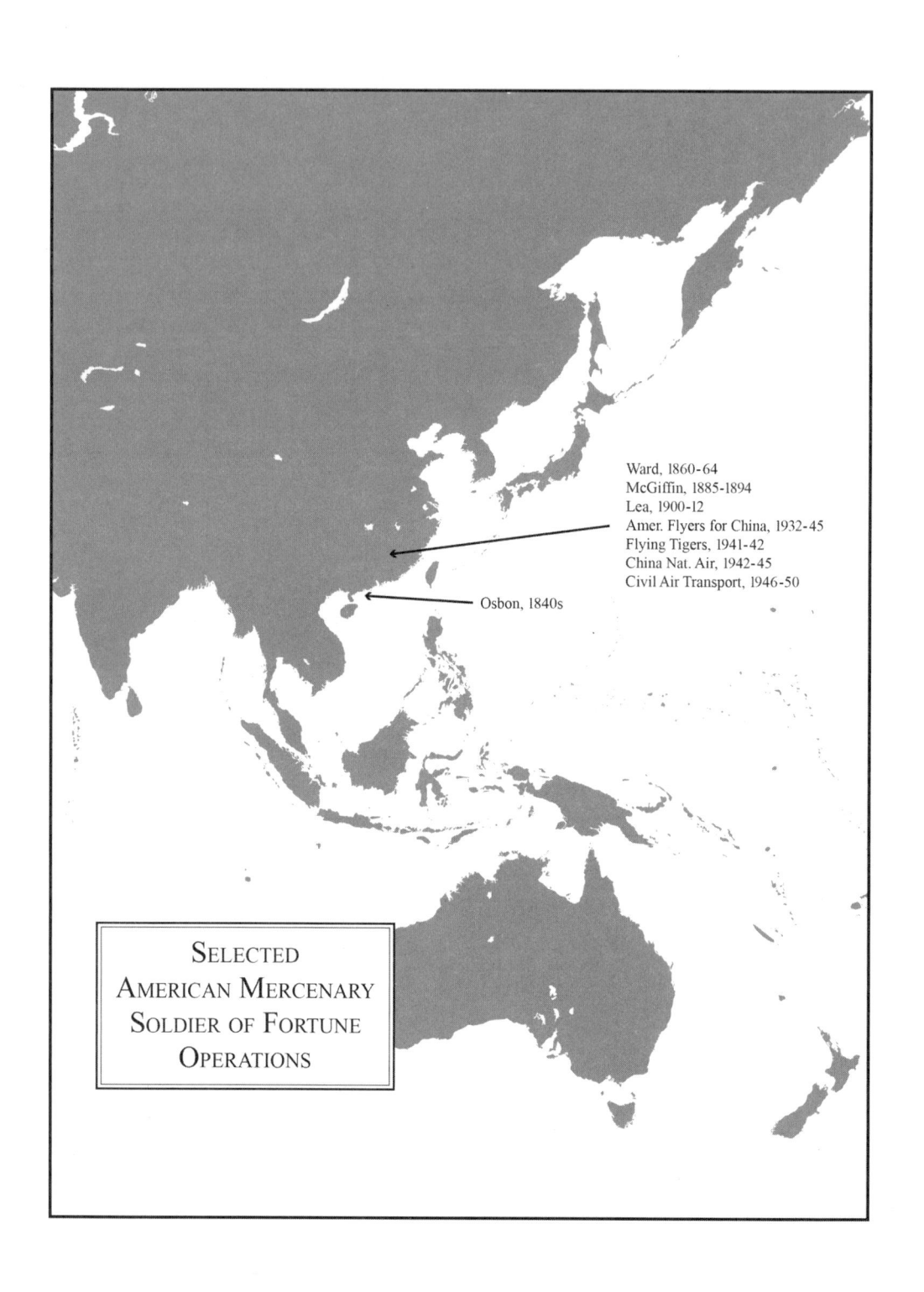

Ward, 1860-64
McGiffin, 1885-1894
Lea, 1900-12
Amer. Flyers for China, 1932-45
Flying Tigers, 1941-42
China Nat. Air, 1942-45
Civil Air Transport, 1946-50

Osbon, 1840s

SELECTED
AMERICAN MERCENARY
SOLDIER OF FORTUNE
OPERATIONS

To my beautiful children, I couldn't have done it without you!

Special thanks to:

Gloria Esau

Bella the Butterfly

Barbie Shannon
© October 2013
Published in the USA

Bella the Butterfly:

By: Barbie Shannon

All rights reserved. No part of this publication may be reproduced or transmitted in any form or by any means electronic, photocopied, mechanical, recording or otherwise without prior written consent of the author.

Bella the Butterfly

By: Barbie Shannon

Bella was a beautiful butterfly, sweet as one can be...

Always helping others, wanting them to see...

She gave all she had to give, some days more than most...

Only out of kindness, she was never one to boast.

Bella refused to overlook, those who were in despair...

She wanted them ALL to know, there WAS someone that cared!

Her wings would flap a mile, for anyone in need...

Offering all she could, never take in greed.

Bella loved to praise others victories, no matter how great or small...

To her they were all worth it, even the smallest of them all.

Some liked to take advantage, helping others they did not believe...

Secretly not caring, they were only anxious to deceive.

Bella had seen this many times, shaking her head in dismay...

Without a whispered word of warning, she would have to turn and fly away.

Feeling disappointed, those times made her sad…

Why couldn't they see that it was wrong...making others feel bad!

Bella didn't understand, she always tried to please...

How could they not care at all, and do so with such ease?

She was always reaching out, to help a willing mind...

Encourage them all to expand, any knowledge that they find.

Drying up her eyes, standing straight and tall...

While some might not like it, HER faith would not fall!

She believes deep down inside, what kindness can do...

Being gentle with others, they will be forgiving of you.

Bella doesn't believe, the outer appearance can compare...

To the soul someone has inside... that completely makes you rare!

Dear Parents,

   Thank you for purchasing and reading my book to your child. It is my wish that you will find many enjoyable hours with "Bella the Butterfly". Bella teaches us about caring for others; so vital to our children's lives.

Printed in Great Britain
by Amazon.co.uk, Ltd.,
Marston Gate.